Implementing Education Policies

Developing Schools as Learning Organisations in Wales

OECD

BETTER POLICIES FOR BETTER LIVES

This work is published under the responsibility of the Secretary-General of the OECD. The opinions expressed and arguments employed herein do not necessarily reflect the official views of OECD member countries.

This document, as well as any data and any map included herein, are without prejudice to the status of or sovereignty over any territory, to the delimitation of international frontiers and boundaries and to the name of any territory, city or area.

Please cite this publication as:
OECD (2018), *Developing Schools as Learning Organisations in Wales*, Implementing Education Policies, OECD Publishing, Paris.
https://doi.org/10.1787/9789264307193-en

ISBN 978-92-64-30718-6 (print)
ISBN 978-92-64-30719-3 (pdf)

Series: Implementing Education Policies
ISSN 2617-6572 (print)
ISSN 2617-6580 (online)

The statistical data for Israel are supplied by and under the responsibility of the relevant Israeli authorities. The use of such data by the OECD is without prejudice to the status of the Golan Heights, East Jerusalem and Israeli settlements in the West Bank under the terms of international law.

Photo credits: © Denisfilm / iStock
© optimarc / Shutterstock
© koya979 / Shutterstock

Foreword

This study is part of the OECDs efforts to support countries in the design and effective implementation of their education policies, grounding these efforts on evidence, and multidisciplinary tools and approaches.

Wales is committed to providing high-quality and inclusive education for all its citizens. It in 2011 embarked on a large-scale school improvement reform that has become increasingly comprehensive and focused on the ongoing development and implementation of a new, 21st century school curriculum. Wales considers the development of schools as learning organisations a key means for empowering them to bring the new curriculum to life. It recognises this will require concerted effort and in many cases it will mean that teachers, support staff, school leaders and many others involved will need to expand their skills. As such, the development of a thriving learning culture in schools and other parts of the education system is expected to play a pivotal role in putting the curriculum into practice in schools throughout Wales.

This report aims to support Wales in realising this objective. It assesses the extent to which schools in Wales have developed as learning organisations, and identifies areas for further improvement – at both school and system levels.

Following an introduction to this report and a description of Wales' school system (Part I, Chapter 1) the report is organised the following:

- Part II, the *Schools as Learning Organisations Assessment*, describes and analyses the extent to which the key characteristics of a learning organisation already exist in schools. It uses Wales' schools as learning organisations model as point of reference to identify strengths and areas of improvement. Both a general assessment (Chapter 2) and a more detailed analysis are provided (Chapter 3). It concludes by proposing some "points of reflection and action for schools" to consider as they embark on the journey to develop as learning organisations.

- Part III, *System Assessment of the Conditions for Developing Schools as Learning Organisations*, analyses the system-level conditions that can enable or hinder schools developing into learning organisations. It explores the question of what system-level policies are enabling or hindering schools to develop as learning organisations, and offers a number of concrete recommendations for strengthening policies, enhancing policy coherence and further policy action (Chapter 4).

It continues by exploring the question of how Wales can ensure the effective implementation, or "realisation" as it is often referred to in Wales, of its schools as learning organisations policy (Chapter 5). It concludes with a number of recommendations for consideration by the Welsh Government and other stakeholders at various levels of the system.

I hope this report will support Wales in its reform efforts and help realise its ambitions for its children and young people by bringing its new, 21st century curriculum to life in schools across the country. The OECD is there to help Wales in this effort.

Andreas Schleicher

Director for Education and Skills and Special Advisor
on Education Policy to the Secretary-General
OECD

Acknowledgements

This report has been developed as part of OECD's work on implementing education policies, conducted by the Policy Advice and Implementation Division of OECD's Directorate for Education and Skills. It is the result of an assessment of the development of schools as learning organisations in Wales, informed by international experience and best practices from OECD countries. The assessment made use of a mixed-methods study design, including a Schools as Learning Organisations Survey and many exchanges and consultations with different experts and stakeholders in Wales.

The OECD team (see Annex A) is indebted to the Welsh Government Education Directorate for supporting this innovative pilot initiative. We thank Kirsty Williams, the Cabinet Secretary for Education, for commissioning this assessment and her support throughout the process resulting in this report, including the launching of Wales' schools as learning organisations model. Furthermore, we would like to acknowledge the support of the Steve Davies, the Director of Education, who has been a driving force behind this assessment. We are also particularly grateful to Lisa Clarke, Professional Learning Programme Lead, and Joanne Davies, Professional Learning Policy Lead, for co-ordinating the whole assessment process.

We would like to also thank the members of the Schools as Learning Organisations (SLO) Pilot Group (see Annex B) who (among others) contributed to the development and implementation of the SLO survey, and provided in-depth feedback and advice on earlier drafts of this report.

Furthermore, we want to convey our appreciation to all those school leaders, teachers and learning support workers that found the time in their busy schedules to complete the SLO survey. Their views and comments have proven invaluable to this assessment.

Various policy missions were also conducted during 2017 and 2018 during which the OECD team was able to interview and consult a wide range of experts and stakeholders from various levels of the education system. Special thanks go to Graham Donaldson for his guidance and support throughout the whole process of conducting this assessment. We want to convey our sincere appreciation to all these people for providing us with a wealth of insights by sharing their views, experience and knowledge.

In addition, the courtesy and hospitality extended to us throughout our stays in Wales made our task as enjoyable as it was stimulating and challenging.

The OECD team was composed of Marco Kools, who also led the assessment, Beatriz Pont, Pierre Gouëdard and Thiffanie Rodriguez. The external experts on the team were Louise Stoll, University College London Institute of Education and Bert George, Erasmus University Rotterdam. The OECD team acknowledges the support from Andreas Schleicher, Director for Education and Skills; Paulo Santiago, Head of the Policy Advice and Implementation Division; and Kristina Sonmark, Javier Suarez-Alvarez, Nóra Revai, Hannah von Ahlefeld, David Liebowitz, and Eva Feron from the OECD Secretariat, who provided in-depth feedback and advice at critical stages of the development of the report.

Particular thanks go to Kristina Sonmark and Javier Suarez-Alvarez for their technical advice and support provided at various stages during the development of the SLO survey. Marta Rilling prepared the report for publication and provided administrative support, Sally Hinchcliffe edited the report, and Henri Pearson organised the publication process.

Table of contents

Tables

Figures

Boxes

Acronyms and abbreviations

ALN	Additional learning needs
ARG	Action research groups
ASCL	Association of School and College Leaders
CIEREI	Collaborative Institute for Education Research, Evidence and Impact
CSC	Central South Consortium (Central South Wales regional consortium)
DCF	Digital Competence Framework
EAS	Education Achievement Service (South East Wales regional consortium)
ERW	Ein Rhanbarth ar Waith (South West and Mid Wales regional consortium)
EWC	Education Workforce Council
FSM	Free school meals
GCSE	General Certificate of Secondary Education
GDP	Gross domestic product
GVA	Gross value added
GwE	Gwasanaeth Effeithiolrwydd (North Wales regional consortium)
ITE	Initial teacher education
LATOG	Learning and Teaching Observation Group
LPPA	Leading Parent Partnership Award
NPQH	National Professional Qualification for Headship
PGCE	Post-Graduate Certificate in Education
PISA	Programme for International Student Assessment
QTS	Qualified Teacher Status
SIG	School Improvement Group
SLO	Schools as learning organisations

Executive summary

Wales is committed to providing high-quality and inclusive education for all its citizens. It in 2011 embarked on a large-scale school improvement reform that has become increasingly comprehensive and focused on the ongoing development and implementation of a new, 21st century school curriculum. Wales considers the development of schools as learning organisations (SLOs) a key means for empowering them to bring the new curriculum to life.

This report supports Wales in realising this objective. It assesses the extent to which schools in Wales have developed as learning organisations, and identifies areas for further improvement – at both school and system levels. The study is part of OECD's efforts to support countries in the design and effective implementation of their education policies, grounding these efforts on evidence, and multidisciplinary tools and approaches.

Schools as learning organisations in Wales

A school as a learning organisation has the capacity to change and adapt routinely to new environments and circumstances as its members, individually and together, learn their way to realising their vision. Wales has set out to develop all schools as learning organisations in support of the ongoing curriculum reform.

This assessment has shown that:

- The majority of schools in Wales seem well on their way towards developing as learning organisations ...

- ... however, a considerable proportion of schools are still far removed from realising this objective.

- Schools are engaging unequally with the seven dimensions that make up Wales' SLO model.

  o Schools appear to be progressing well on the SLO dimensions "promoting team learning and collaboration among all staff" and "embedding systems for collecting and exchanging knowledge and learning".

  o Two dimensions are less well developed: "developing a shared vision centred on the learning of all students" and "establishing a culture of enquiry, innovation and exploration". Many schools could also do more to "learn with and from the external environment and larger system".

- Secondary schools are finding it more challenging to develop as learning organisations.

- More critical reflections are needed for deep learning and sustained progress to take place. High-stakes assessment, evaluation and accountability arrangements may have been a factor influencing people's willingness to critically reflect on their own behaviour, that of their peers and the school organisation at large.

Although schools need to be adequately supported to develop as learning organisations, many actions are within their control. There are school examples that show how budget pressures do not necessarily lead to a reduction in ambitions.

School leaders play a vital role in creating a trusting and respectful climate that allows for open discussions about problems, successful and less successful practices, and the sharing of knowledge. This is also essential for narrowing the gaps in perceptions between staff. The ongoing review of assessment, evaluation and accountability arrangements in Wales should be used to encourage people to do things differently and engage in critical reflections.

Teachers and learning support workers also need to do their part to work and learn with colleagues beyond their department, subject area or school. Engaging in professional dialogue with colleagues, learning with and from staff in other schools – including between primary and secondary schools – and drawing from the support provided by regional consortia (i.e. school improvement services) are some of the means that staff have at their disposal.

System-level policies enabling schools to develop into learning organisations

- Promoting a shared and future-focused vision centred on the learning of all students calls for reviewing the school funding model and developing a national definition of student well-being and ways of monitoring it.

- The development of professional capital and a learning culture in schools argues for: 1) basing selection into initial teacher education on a mix of criteria and methods; 2) promoting collaborations between schools and teacher education institutions; 3) prioritising professional learning in enquiry-based approaches to teaching and learning, strengthening inductions and promoting mentoring and coaching, observations and peer review; 4) a coherent leadership strategy promoting learning organisations across the system; and 5) greater support for secondary school leaders.

- Assessment, evaluation and accountability should promote SLOs through: 1) national criteria guiding school self-evaluations and Estyn (i.e. the education inspectorate) evaluations; 2) a participatory self-evaluation process; 3) Estyn evaluations safeguarding school quality, while focusing more on the rigour of self-evaluation processes; 4) clarifying the transition to a new system of school evaluations; 5) aligning performance measures to the ambitions of the new curriculum, and 6) system monitoring through sample-based student assessments, Estyn reports and research.

Realising schools as learning organisations

To support the effective implementation or "realisation" of Wales' SLO policy we looked at the four determinants that can facilitate or hinder this process, resulting in the following recommendations:

- Develop an easy-to-understand narrative that explains how Wales' SLO model forms an integrated part of the curriculum reform

- Continue strengthening the capacity of regional consortia to support schools developing as learning organisations

- Estyn to monitor the progress of consortia in enhancing and streamlining their services to schools

- Enhance the collaboration and alignment between the development of assessment, evaluation and accountability arrangements, and the curriculum

- Continue the SLO Implementation Group to support the realisation of Wales' SLO policy, while striving for greater policy coherence

- Expand the public dialogue generated by PISA results to align it to the ambitions of the new curriculum.

Wales has started developing an SLO implementation plan. This should form an integrated part of larger reform effort. This report has identified several issues that call for further action for which recommendations are provided. These aim to inform the development of the implementation plan.

Furthermore, attention should be paid to:

- The setting of objectives and the monitoring of progress should not become a high-stakes exercise for schools.

- Task allocation. Regional consortia play a pivotal role in supporting schools in their change and innovation journeys. Higher education institutions and other parties could complement the system infrastructure.

- The timing and sequencing of actions. One urgent action is to clarify the transition period to the new approaches to school self-evaluations and Estyn evaluations.

- A communication and engagement strategy with education stakeholders.

Assessment and recommendations

Introduction

Wales is committed to providing high-quality and inclusive education for all its citizens. However, the 2009 Programme for International Student Assessment (PISA) results showed it was a long way from realising this commitment, sparking a national debate on the quality and future of education in Wales. In response, in 2011 Wales embarked on a large-scale school improvement reform and introduced a range of policies to improve the quality and equity of its school system. Since then, education reform has become increasingly comprehensive and is focused on the ongoing development and implementation of the new school curriculum.

Wales considers the development of schools as learning organisations (SLO) a means for realising the new curriculum (see Box 1). A school as a learning organisation has the capacity to change and adapt routinely to new environments and circumstances as its members, individually and together, learn their way to realising their vision (Kools and Stoll, 2016[1]). Accomplishing this will require concerted efforts and means that teachers, teaching support staff, school leaders and many other people involved in bringing the new curriculum to life will need to expand their skills and learn new ones. The development of a thriving learning culture in schools across Wales is considered essential for making this happen.

This report, *Developing Schools as Learning Organisations in Wales*, aims to support Wales in realising this objective (Welsh Government, 2017[2]). It assesses the extent to which schools in Wales have developed as learning organisations, giving an indication of schools' "readiness for change", and identifies areas for further improvement at both school and system levels. The assessment has been guided by three questions:

- To what extent do the key characteristics of a learning organisation already exist in schools in Wales? (Chapters 2 and 3)

- Are Wales' system-level policies enabling (or hindering) schools to develop as learning organisations? (Chapter 4)

- How can Wales ensure the effective implementation or "realisation" of its schools as learning organisations policy? (Chapter 5)

These last two questions stem from the knowledge that, although many of the actions proposed by Wales' SLO model are within the control of schools, local authorities, parents and communities, some warrant policy action and a conducive context to enable and empower them to make this transformation.

Box 1. The schools as learning organisations model for Wales

The SLO model for Wales focuses the efforts of school leaders, teachers, support staff, parents, (local) policy makers and all others involved into realising seven dimensions in its schools. These seven action-oriented dimensions and their underlying elements highlight both what a school should aspire to and the processes it goes through as it transforms itself into a learning organisation. All seven dimensions need to be implemented for this transformation to be complete and sustainable.

Figure 1. The schools as learning organisations model for Wales

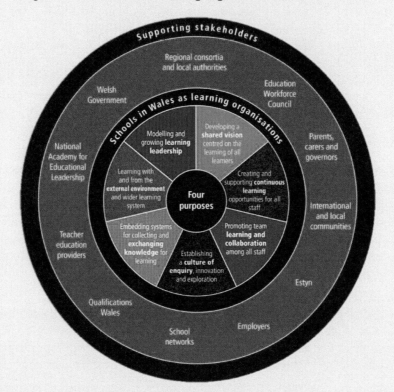

The realisation of the "four purposes" of the new school curriculum is placed at the heart of the model. These refer to developing children and young people into "ambitious capable and lifelong learners, enterprising and creative, informed citizens and healthy and confident individuals".

Wales' SLO model was designed through a process of co-construction. It was developed by the School as a Learning Organisation Pilot Group, which is part of the Professional Development and Learning Pioneer Schools Network that is supporting the development and implementation of the new school curriculum (Annex B). The developmental work was shaped through a series of workshops and meetings that were facilitated by the OECD between November 2016 and July 2017. The result of this collective effort is Wales' SLO model that was released in November 2017.

Source: Welsh Government (2017[31]), "Schools in Wales as learning organisations", http://gov.wales/topics/educationandskills/schoolshome/curriculuminwales/curriculum-for-wales-curriculum-for-life/schools-in-wales-as-learning-organisations/?lang=en.

Schools as learning organisations assessment

Following an introduction to Wales and its school system, this assessment report explored the extent to which the key characteristics of a learning organisation exist in schools in Wales. Using Wales' SLO model as a point of reference, a mixed-methods study design was used to identify strengths and areas for further development. The main findings of this assessment are presented below.

Key findings: Overview

The majority of schools in Wales seem well on their way towards developing as learning organisations …

According to the views of school leaders, teachers and learning support workers (i.e. Higher Level Teaching Assistants, Teaching Assistants, Foreign language assistants, Special needs support staff) the majority of schools in Wales are well on their way in putting the schools as learning organisations model into practice. The Schools as Learning Organisations (SLO) survey data (when aggregated to the school level) suggests that just under six out of ten schools (58%) in our sample had put five to seven dimensions of the learning organisation into practice. Out of these about one-third (30%) had put all seven dimensions into practice (Figure 2).

Figure 2. Progress by schools Wales in developing into learning organisations

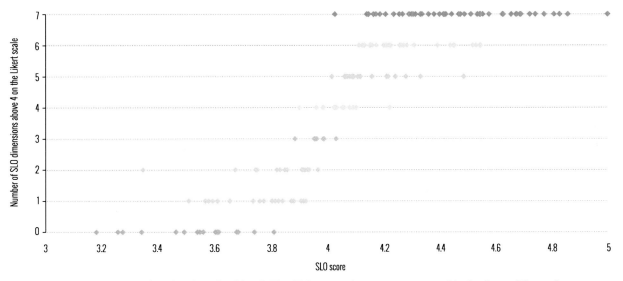

Note: Data were analysed at the school level. The SLO survey items were generated in the form of five-point Likert scale: 1) strongly disagree; 2) disagree; 3) neutral 4) agree; and 5) strongly agree. N: 174 schools. Four schools of the 178 were not taken into consideration as their staff had not completed the survey for all seven dimensions. An average school score of 4 or more across the survey items that make up one dimension was defined as the threshold for when a school is considered to have put the dimension into practice. Each point represents a school.
Source: OECD Schools as Learning Organisations Survey, 2017.

StatLink ᴍ℠ᴘ http://dx.doi.org/10.1787/888933837226

The data however also suggest that a considerable proportion of schools are still far removed from realising this objective; 12% of schools had put three or four dimensions in practice, while 30% of schools has realised only two or fewer. Some 10% of schools in our sample seem to have made insufficient progress in developing any of the seven dimensions.

... these however are optimistic estimates. More critical reflections are needed for deep learning and sustained progress to take place

These findings should be interpreted with some caution. First, they are based on one source of self-reported data and, although satisfactory, the response rate to the SLO survey was lower than hoped for. Additional data and interviews with stakeholders by the OECD team on some occasions found discrepancies with the SLO survey data and supported the conclusion that school staff need to be more critical about their own performance and that of their schools if deep learning and sustained progress are to take place. Several of those interviewed noted that the high-stakes assessment, evaluation and accountability arrangements are likely to have negatively influenced people's willingness, and in some cases even their ability, to critically reflect on their own behaviour, that of their peers and the school organisation at large.

Key findings for the seven schools as learning organisations dimensions

The assessment of the seven dimensions that make up Wales' SLO model shows schools are engaging in these to different degrees (see Figure 3). A general conclusion is that schools appear to be progressing well on the dimensions "promoting team learning and collaboration among all staff" and "embedding systems for collecting and exchanging knowledge and learning", while two dimensions are considerably less well developed: "developing a shared vision centred on the learning of all students (learners)" and "establishing a culture of enquiry, innovation and exploration". The text below elaborates on these and other findings.

Figure 3. Average score per SLO dimension, by school type

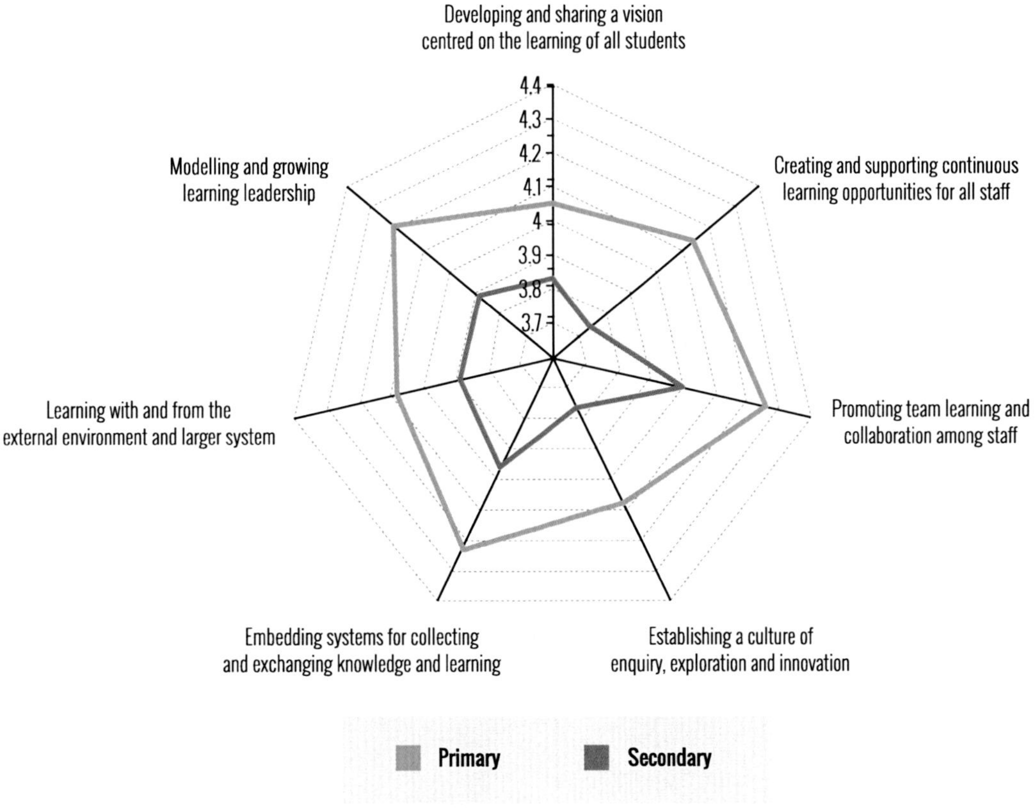

Note: Data are analysed at the school level. The survey items were generated in the form of five-point Likert scale: 1) strongly disagree; 2) disagree; 3) neutral; 4) agree; and 5) strongly agree. An average school score of 4 or more across the survey items that make up one dimension was defined as the threshold for when a school is considered to have put the dimension into practice. N is 151 for primary schools and 23 for secondary schools.
Source: OECD Schools as Learning Organisations Survey, 2017.

StatLink 🛝🖼 http://dx.doi.org/10.1787/888933837264

Developing and sharing a vision that is centred on the learning of all students

About 53% of schools in our sample had developed a shared vision centred on the learning of all students (an average school score of 4 or more on the Likert scale across the survey items that make up this dimension) – the lowest proportion of the seven SLO dimensions. While 56% of primary schools would seem to have developed such a vision, this was significantly lower among secondary schools (30%). Responses on the SLO survey items that make up this dimension also varied considerably.

Nine out of ten school staff (92%) reported that their school had a vision that focuses on students' cognitive and socio-emotional outcomes, including their well-being. A similar proportion (87%) reported that their school's vision emphasised preparing students for their future in a changing world. These are encouraging findings considering the ambitions set out in Wales' new school curriculum. However, further work will be needed to make such a vision into one that is truly shared among its staff and other key stakeholders. The involvement of staff, parents and external partners in the shaping of the vision are areas for improvement. For example 72% of respondents to the SLO survey indicated they were involved in the development of the school's vision, with significant differences by school type: 77% of primary school staff and 57% of secondary school staff.

Also, as is common in other countries, secondary schools in Wales seemingly find it more challenging to engage parents in the educational process and school organisation than primary schools (Borgonovi and Montt, 2012[4]; Byrne and Smyth, 2010[5]; Desforges and Abouchaar, 2003[6]). This issue is further discussed below.

Furthermore, various sources point to the conclusion that many schools in Wales are yet to put this shared vision that is centred on the learning of all students into practice. For example, PISA 2015 found that schools in Wales have relatively high levels of low performers and pointed to several areas of student well-being where further progress could be made, such as students' schoolwork-related anxiety and sense of belonging in school (OECD, 2017[7]; OECD, 2016[8]).

Creating and supporting continuous learning opportunities for all staff

The evidence suggests that many schools in Wales have, or are in the process of developing, a culture that promotes professional learning for their staff. Around 59% of schools in our sample would seem to have created and supported continuous learning opportunities for all staff. The SLO survey data revealed some significant differences between school types: almost two-thirds of primary schools (64%) would seem to have created and supported continuous learning opportunities for all staff (as reflected by an average score of 4 or more on this dimension). Among secondary schools this was around a quarter (26%).

Various sources of data and information also showed that induction and mentoring/coaching need to be strengthened in many schools across Wales. Some 35% of respondents to the SLO survey for example disagreed or were unsure whether there were mentors or coaches available in their school to help staff develop their practice (Table 1).

Table 1. Induction and mentoring and coaching support

	Strongly disagree	Disagree	Neutral	Agree	Strongly agree
All new staff receive sufficient support to help them in their new role	2.3%	7.8%	19.6%	44.5%	25.8%
Mentors/coaches are available to help staff develop their practice	2.5%	10.8%	22.1%	42.7%	22.0%

Note: Data are analysed at the individual level. N: 1 633 and 1 634 individuals respectively for the presented SLO survey statements.
Source: OECD Schools as Learning Organisations Survey, 2017.

As Wales has embarked on a curriculum reform, teachers and learning support workers will need to expand their pedagogical and assessment skills. This will make mentoring, coaching and other forms of continuous learning even more important.

Promoting team learning and collaboration among all staff

The evidence suggests that about seven out of ten schools in our sample (71%) are promoting team learning and collaboration among all its staff. Primary schools are faring better on this dimension; 75% of primary schools in our sample appear to promote team learning and collaboration among all staff, compared to 48% of secondary schools. Schools could still do more to ensure that staff learn to work together as a team, more regularly observe each other and tackle problems together. For example, some 25% of staff disagreed or were unsure whether staff in their schools observed each other other's practice and collaborate in developing it. Similarly, about 20% of staff were unsure or did not agree that staff thought through and tackled problems together. In both cases, teachers were most likely to respond critically.

This assessment pointed to further differences in perceptions across different staff categories on several of the elements that make up this dimension. For example, PISA 2015 found that 92% of head teachers in secondary schools in Wales reported that teacher peer review was used to monitor teachers, compared to an OECD average of 78% (OECD, 2016[8]). We have to interpret this data with some caution, as the evidence from our assessment suggests that teachers and learning support workers in Wales do not always share the views of their head teachers. For example, while 92% of secondary head teachers positively responded to the SLO survey statement "staff observe each other's practice and collaborate in developing it" in their schools, only 67% of teachers responded in a similar vein. While there are bound to be some differences in perceptions between staff categories, as some staff may simply be better informed due to the nature of their work, the sometimes sizable differences reported on this dimension (and others) suggest the need for more professional dialogue and sharing of information. This is again particularly an area for improvement in secondary schools.

Establishing a culture of enquiry, innovation and exploration

The OECD team were struck by a change in attitudes compared to the OECD 2014 review. That review found an education profession that seemed less open and willing to change and innovate their practice, with some school staff reporting signs of reform fatigue (OECD, 2014[9]). The many interviews by the OECD team with school staff, policy makers and other stakeholders suggest this situation to have changed considerably. However, the OECD team found that this general change in mindset is yet to materialise in a culture of enquiry, innovation and exploration in four out of ten schools in Wales (41%).

These findings may partially be explained by the high-stakes assessment, evaluation and accountability arrangements that are believed to have tempered people's willingness and confidence to do things differently and innovate their practice. This would seem particularly the case for secondary schools – the SLO survey data found just 26% of secondary schools in our sample had established a culture of enquiry, exploration and innovation, compared to 63% of primary schools (see Figure 4). Other data sources corroborate this pattern.

Despite recent steps to move towards a new assessment, evaluation and accountability framework, school staff expressed uncertainties about what this framework will actually look like. Greater clarity is thus urgently needed to give all schools the confidence to engage in enquiry, innovation and exploration of the new curriculum

Exploring the individual level responses to the SLO survey data revealed some significant differences across the four regions of Wales for several of the statements that make up this dimension, but also across the staff categories and levels of education (see Chapter 3). For example, while 96% of head teachers indicated that in their school staff were encouraged to experiment and innovate their practice, this proportion dropped to 82% among learning support workers. Interestingly this is one of the few SLO survey items on which learning support workers reported the lowest score from the different staff categories.

Figure 4. Average school scores on establishing a culture of enquiry, exploration and innovation, by school type

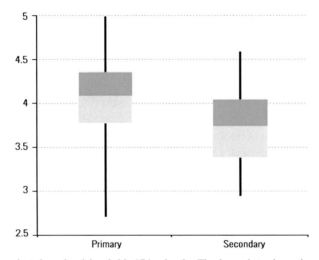

Note: Data are analysed at the school level. N: 174 schools. The box plots show the average school scores sorted into four equal sized groups, so 25% of all scores are placed in each group. The median (middle quartile) marks the mid-point of the data and is shown by the line that divides the box into two parts, in green and yellow. The middle "box", in green and yellow, represents the middle 50% of scores for the group.
Source: OECD Schools as Learning Organisations Survey, 2017.

StatLink ᐧᑎᔆ▄ http://dx.doi.org/10.1787/888933837359

Embedding systems for collecting and exchanging knowledge and learning

The interviews with stakeholders and findings from an earlier OECD assessment (2017[10]) suggest that systems for measuring progress seem well established in schools. The SLO survey data suggest that 70% of schools in our sample had put this dimension into practice, with embedded systems for collecting and exchanging knowledge and learning. Again, there were significant differences between primary and secondary schools: 76% of primary schools and 30% of secondary schools would seem to have embedded such systems for collecting and exchanging knowledge and learning. However, while the evidence suggests that the use of data is common in many schools across Wales, considerably fewer schools seem to be using research evidence to inform practice (see Figure 5).

Figure 5. Staff use of data and research evidence to improve their practice

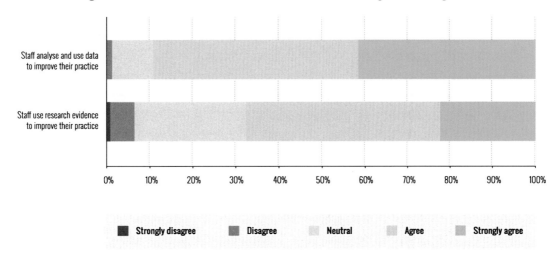

Note: Data analysed at the individual level. N: 1 604 and 1 595 individuals respectively for the presented SLO survey statements.
Source: OECD Schools as Learning Organisations Survey, 2017.

StatLink ᐧᐧᐧ http://dx.doi.org/10.1787/888933837397

Interviews and a review of policy documents and reports revealed that another area for improvement is the quality of school self-evaluations and development planning. Schools – as well as other parts of the system – spend considerable time and effort on analysing and upward reporting on a wide variety of mostly quantitative data, with far less attention being paid to qualitative sources, like classroom observations or peer review, for learning. The assessment, evaluation and accountability arrangements, which have focused attention on quantitative performance measures, are believed to have contributed to this practice. Part of the challenge also lies in the lack of a common understanding of what good school self-evaluation and development planning entails in Wales.

Learning with and from the external environment and larger system

Learning with and from the external environment and larger learning system is common practice in just over the majority of schools in our sample (55%). Differences between primary and secondary schools were relatively small for this dimension (the smallest among all dimensions) – with 57% of primary and 39% of secondary schools having an average score of at least 4.

One area for improvement is the engagement of parents and guardians in the educational process and organisation of the school (Figure 6). This is a particular challenge for secondary schools: only 57% of secondary school staff agreed that parents or guardians were partners in their schools' organisational and educational processes, compared to 71% of staff in primary schools.

Figure 6. Collaboration with external partners

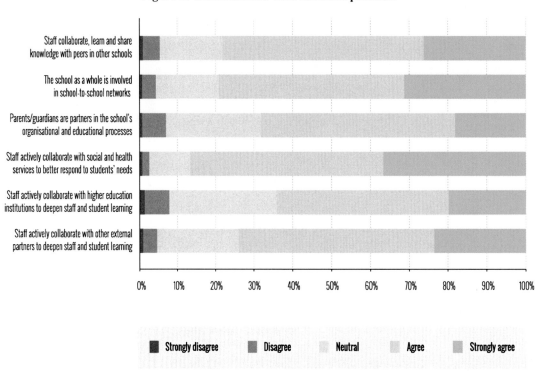

Note: Data analysed at the individual level. N: 1 593, 1 597, 1 592, 1 589, 1 593 and 1 592 individuals respectively for the presented SLO survey statements.
Source: OECD Schools as Learning Organisations Survey, 2017.

StatLink ᘓᔛ▄ http://dx.doi.org/10.1787/888933837416

There are also differences in responses between staff categories, with teachers consistently being the most critical. PISA 2015 found that secondary head teachers in Wales in 2015 almost unanimously reported that their school created a welcoming atmosphere for parents to get involved (99%) and provided families with information and ideas for families about how to help students at home with homework and other curriculum-related activities, decisions, and planning (98%) (OECD, 2017[7]). A further eight out of ten (79%) secondary head teachers reported that their school included parents in decision making (OECD average 78%). The SLO survey data and interviews provide a more critical perspective on the engagement of parents in the school's organisational and educational processes. The OECD team recognise it may be more challenging to engage parents of secondary students in the school organisation and education process, than at the primary level. However, as examples in this report show, it is possible to increase parental engagement, even at secondary level (see Chapter 3, Box 3.5).

Another area for improvement is collaboration with higher education institutions. The interviews revealed that stakeholders across the system are well aware of this challenge and are taking measures to improve the situation.

The SLO survey found that close to nine out of ten respondents (87%) reported that staff in their school actively collaborated with social and health services to better respond to students' needs. However, other data sources suggest Wales' school funding and governance model affects schools' ability to respond to the additional learning needs of all students.

Modelling and growing learning leadership

The SLO survey data suggest that about two-thirds (67%) of schools in our sample have leaders that are modelling and growing learning leadership. Primary schools also appear to be doing better for this: 70% of primary schools seem to have leaders that are modelling and growing learning leadership, compared with 39% of secondary schools.

One area for development is coaching by leaders of those they lead and the creation of settings in which trust can develop over time so that colleagues are more likely to engage in mutual learning. For example, 38% of teachers were unsure or did not agree that in their schools, leaders coached those they led.

Similarly, 13% of primary school staff and 16% of secondary school staff did not agree that leaders in their ensured that all actions were consistent with the school's vision, rising to 19% of primary teachers and 27% of secondary teachers. PISA 2015 also found that Wales was below the OECD average for ensuring that teachers work according to the school's educational goals (OECD, 2016[8]). This suggests that secondary head teachers in Wales could place a greater emphasis on ensuring their schools' actions reflect its vision and goals, and communicating these efforts better with their staff.

The generally high scores on this dimension were also contrasted by other data sources such as OECD team interviews and Estyn reports. The analysis of other SLO dimensions also points to several areas for further improvement. School leaders play a vital role in the promotion and strengthening of induction programmes, mentoring/coaching, peer review and creating a culture of enquiry, innovation and exploration in their schools. The establishment of these and other conditions for a learning culture to develop across the whole school organisation is particularly an area of improvement for leaders in secondary schools.

Points of reflection and action for schools

The evidence suggests that the majority of schools in Wales are well on their way in developing as learning organisations. Two dimensions however are considerably less well developed and deserve particular attention: "developing a shared vision centred on the learning of all students" and "establishing a culture of enquiry, innovation and exploration".

Although schools need to be adequately supported and enabled to develop into learning organisations, many actions are within the control of schools themselves. School leaders play a vital role in creating the conditions for a learning organisation to develop. They need to be supported in taking on this responsibility.

Teachers and learning support workers however need to also do their part to work and learn with colleagues beyond their department, subject area or school. Engaging in professional dialogue with colleagues, learning with and from staff in other schools – including between primary and secondary schools – and external partners, and drawing from the support provided by regional consortia are some of the means that staff have at their disposal.

Staff also need to more critically reflect on their own and their school's performance if deep learning and sustained progress to take place – and they need to be empowered to do this. School leaders play a pivotal role in creating a trusting and respectful climate that allows for open discussions about problems, successful and less successful practices, and the sharing of knowledge. This will also be essential to narrow the gaps in perceptions between staff about their own and schools' performance. The ongoing review of assessment, evaluation and accountability arrangements should be used to encourage and give people the confidence to do things differently and engage in critical reflections.

Secondary schools also clearly face more challenges in developing as learning organisations. Their more compartmentalised structure, which makes it harder to collaborate across departments and the organisation as a whole, is believed to be a factor in this. Also some leaders in secondary schools do not do enough to encourage a learning culture across the whole school organisation. This while the success of the curriculum reform will (among other things) depend on staff engaging in collective and cross-curricular learning and working, within and across schools.

However, this assessment also identified several examples of secondary schools that exhibit the dimensions of a learning organisation, demonstrating that it is possible.

Finally, although policy action will be required to reduce the variability in school funding between schools in similar circumstances, schools have the ability to take measures to ensure staff have the time and resources to engage in collaborative working and learning. The examples presented in this report show how budget pressures do not need to lead to a reduction in ambitions. Such examples should be systematically collected and shared widely to inspire and inform other schools in their change and innovation efforts. System assessment for developing schools as learning organisations

System assessment of the conditions for developing schools as learning organisations

System-level policies enabling schools to develop as learning organisations

Building on the qualitative and quantitative analysis (including the SLO survey), OECD team visits to Wales and stakeholder events, this report explored the question of whether Wales' system-level policies are enabling (or hindering) schools to develop as learning organisations. The following policy recommendations are aimed at empowering school staff, local partners and middle-tier agencies to develop their schools as learning organisations.

Policy issue 1: Promoting a shared vision centred on the learning and well-being of all students

The development of an inclusive and shared vision that promotes the learning and well-being of all students is central to the first dimension of Wales' SLO model. The realisation of the "four purposes" of the new school curriculum is also at the heart of the model. These refer to developing children and young people into "ambitious capable and lifelong learners, enterprising and creative, informed citizens and healthy and confident individuals" (Welsh Government, 2017[11]; Donaldson, 2015[12]).

The evidence suggests that this vision is widely shared throughout the school system. This is a strength of the curriculum reform effort. How well the four purposes are really understood by the education profession in terms of what they will actually mean for their daily practice is hard to judge. Putting them into practice will challenge practitioners' understanding and skills. This should be taken into consideration by policies supporting the development of professional capital and a thriving learning culture.

Furthermore, Wales' school system is based on equity guidelines. It has expressed a strong commitment to equity in education and student well-being (Welsh Government, 2017[2]) and has implemented various policies such as the Pupil Deprivation Grant and free school meals to target equity challenges in the school system. However, two issues call for urgent policy attention: the school funding model and the lack of a common understanding of what student well-being entails.

Policy issue 1.1: Wales' school funding model challenges equity

The evidence suggests that differences in local funding models are causing concerns about unequal treatment of schools in similar circumstances. The Welsh Government should therefore consider reviewing its school funding model if it is to realise its ambitions for equity in education and student well-being.

Recognising that a large overhaul of the funding model may not be feasible in the short or medium term, a concrete short-term action could be to conduct an in-depth analysis of school funding in Wales to explore a funding model that promotes greater equity and efficiency. For this it could look to countries and economies like the Flemish Community of Belgium, Latvia, Lithuania and the Netherlands that have established funding formulas to promote equity while increasing efficiency (OECD, 2017[13]; OECD, 2016[14]). For example, Lithuania defined the maximum proportion of funding municipalities can reallocate. This was adjusted several times to ensure sufficient funding was allocated to schools.

Policy issue 1.2: Student well-being needs to be defined and measured

Another challenge to realising Wales' commitment to equity and student well-being is the lack of a common understanding of and way(s) of monitoring the well-being of children and adolescents in Wales. The lack of clarity on and measurement of the concept has been recognised in Wales' new strategic education plan. The plan states the intention of the Welsh Government to work with partners, in Wales and beyond, to develop effective measurements of student well-being (Welsh Government, 2017[2]).

The first step will be to reach a common understanding of the concept, considering the equity and student well-being challenges in Wales. Schools will need guidance and support to respond to these challenges. The pilot of a national school self-evaluation and development planning toolkit that is scheduled to start in autumn 2018 provides a further reason to speed up this work.

Box 2. Recommendations promoting a shared vision centred on the learning of all students

Policy issue 1.1: Wales' school funding model challenges equity

Recommendation 1.1.1: Review the school funding model to realise Wales' commitment to equity and student well-being. The Welsh Government should consider conducting an in-depth analysis of school funding in Wales to explore a funding model that promotes greater equity and efficiency.

One option to explore is limiting the funding that local authorities are allowed to reallocate, excluding school transport costs to take into account the differences in population density. It should carefully monitor any such change in policy and adjust this threshold as needed to ensure sufficient funding is allocated to schools.

Policy issue 1.2: Student well-being needs to be defined and measured

Recommendation 1.2.1: Develop a national definition of student well-being and provide guidance and instrument(s) for monitoring it. This work should be fast-tracked so that the definition and supporting measurement instruments and guidance could be field tested as part of the piloting of the national school self-evaluation and development planning toolkit that is likely to start in autumn 2018 (see below). The field testing should allow for any necessary revisions to be made and the guidance and measurement instrument(s) to be shared with schools by September 2019 (i.e. the start of the academic year 2019/20).

Policy issue 2: Promoting the development of professional capital and a thriving learning culture

Schools as learning organisations reflect a central focus on professional learning of all staff, aimed at creating a sustainable learning culture in the organisation and other parts of the (learning) system. Wales has made good progress in several areas here, including the promotion of school-to-school collaborations and the clarification of professional expectations through its teaching and leadership standards.

Several issues deserve further policy attention, however, including the finding that high-quality inductions, coaching and mentoring, peer review, and enquiry-based teaching and learning are not yet well established across schools in Wales. Collaboration with higher education institutions also leaves scope for improvement. There also seem to be capacity challenges for school leaders, in particular among secondary school leaders, and those in leadership positions at other levels of the system.

Policy issue 2.1: Establishing stronger collaborations between schools and teacher education institutions

Many OECD countries have in recent years raised entry requirements for teacher education programmes (Schleicher, 2011[15]), and this includes Wales. However, this has been limited to raising entry grades. Teaching in the 21st century is a complex and challenging profession that calls on a mix of high-level cognitive and socio-emotional skills on a daily basis. Following the examples of systems like England, Finland and the Netherlands, Wales should consider making use of intake procedures and selection options that go beyond formal degree requirements. For example, Finland selects secondary graduates based on exam results, a written test on assigned books on pedagogy, observations in school situations and interviews (Sahlberg, 2010[16]).

Furthermore, partnerships between teacher education institutions and schools can benefit both partners but such collaborations are not common practice in Wales. One positive development is that the new accreditation requirements for higher education institutions offering initial teacher education programmes emphasise partnerships with schools. Schools should also play their part in establishing such potentially fruitful collaborations, however. The school self-evaluation process should recognise the contribution of schools to teacher education institutions more publicly. Furthermore, schools, higher education institutions, regional consortia and the Welsh Government should continue to invest in specific projects that promote such collaborations (see Chapter 3, Box 3.17).

Box 3. Recommendations promoting professional capital and a thriving learning culture

Policy issue 2.1: Establishing stronger collaborations between schools and teacher education institutions

Recommendation 2.1.1: Base selection into initial teacher education on a mix of criteria and methods. In line with the teaching and leadership standards, teacher education institutions should expand and pilot more elaborate, well-rounded selection criteria and intake procedures that cover a mix of cognitive and socio-emotional skills, values, and attitudes. Attention should be paid to assessing aspiring teachers' aptitude for teaching the new curriculum and engaging in continuous professional learning.

Recommendation 2.1.2: Promote strong collaborations between schools and teacher education institutions. In addition to the new teacher education programmes' accreditation process, the ongoing reviews of school evaluation (i.e. of self-evaluations and Estyn evaluations) should be used to encourage schools to establish sustainable partnerships with teacher education institutions. Schools, higher education institutions, regional consortia and the Welsh Government should continue investing in specific projects to help realise and grow such innovations, for example for strengthening induction programmes and/or promoting enquiry-based teaching and learning.

Policy issue 2.2: Promoting learning throughout the professional lifecycle

This assessment identified three priority areas for professional learning where further policy action would seem warranted. First, is the development of the skills and mindset for engaging in enquiry, exploration and innovation. This is believed to be of great importance for putting in practice the new curriculum that is being shaped around "big ideas" (Sinnema, 2017[17]) or, as it is often referred to in Wales, "what matters". This is particularly a challenge for secondary schools. The high-stakes assessment, evaluation and accountability arrangements are believed to have tempered people's willingness and confidence to do things differently and innovate and engage in enquiry-based practices. The implications for the ongoing review of assessment, evaluation and accountability arrangements are discussed below.

Recognising that enquiry-based approaches are challenging to implement and that there are concerns about teachers' abilities to conduct quality assessments, Wales needs to make a concerted effort to develop practitioners' skills in enquiry-based teaching and learning to ensure all schools in Wales are able to develop into learning organisations and to put the curriculum into practice. The national approach to professional learning that is under development to support the curriculum reform should therefore also focus on developing practitioners' skills in enquiry-based approaches. Higher education institutions are well placed to contribute to this effort. Wales could look to the example of British Columbia, Canada where school-to-school networks promote enquiry-based approaches on a large scale, while investing in the development of leadership capacity (see Chapter 4, Box 4.4).

Second, the evidence suggests there are challenges in terms of the number and quality of induction programmes in Wales, again, particularly in secondary schools. Wales has a mandatory one-year induction period for all newly qualified teachers – although not for learning support workers, who make up a large proportion of the school workforce. The Welsh Government and the regional consortia should explore ways to strengthen induction programmes to safeguard and enhance the quality of Wales' future education workforce. They could look to the example of the Netherlands which has piloted providing starting secondary teachers with a three-year induction programme that has been shaped in a collaboration between teacher education institutions and schools (see Chapter 4, Box 4.3) – a partnership of benefit to both partners.

Third, the evidence suggests that coaching/mentoring, classroom observations and peer review are not yet well established in schools throughout Wales. Once again the evidence points to more challenges in secondary schools. School leaders play a pivotal role in establishing the conditions for such collaborative practice to thrive and should be held to account for doing so. The OECD team learned this does not always happen in some local authorities. School leaders will need the necessary support and capacity development to take on this role. Part of the challenge is that school evaluations have insufficiently promoted coaching and mentoring, classroom observations, peer review and other forms of collaborative practice. The ongoing review of school evaluation processes should take these findings into consideration. The integration of Wales' SLO model into the national school self-evaluation and development planning toolkit will be important for promoting such collaborative practices.

Box 4. Recommendations promoting professional capital and a thriving learning culture

Policy issue 2.2: Promoting learning throughout the professional lifecycle

Recommendation 2.2.1: Prioritise the following areas for professional learning:

- Investing in the skills and mindset for enquiry, exploration and innovation to thrive and putting the new curriculum into practice. The national approach to professional learning that is being developed to support schools in putting the curriculum into practice should include developing teachers' and learning support workers' skills in enquiry-based approaches. Higher education/teacher education institutions are well placed to contribute to these efforts. The new assessment, evaluation and accountability arrangements (see below) should also encourage schools to explore new ways of doing things, engage in enquiry and innovate their practice.

- **Strengthening induction programmes.** The Welsh Government and the regional consortia should explore ways to strengthen induction programmes. Partnerships between teacher education institutions and schools should be promoted because of the benefits to both partners. Learning support workers should not be overlooked.

- **Promoting mentoring and coaching, observations and peer review.** School leaders play a pivotal role in promoting such collaborative practices and should be held accountable for this. However, they also need to be adequately supported in taking on this responsibility. Regional consortia should review their support services in light of these findings and prioritise support for secondary schools. The integration of Wales' SLO model into the national school self-evaluation and development planning toolkit will be important for promoting such collaborative practice.

Policy issue 2.3: Developing learning leadership in schools and other parts of the system

The need to invest in present and future school leaders and leaders at other levels of the system is well recognised in Wales. Wales has taken several steps recently to support their capacity development, some of which relate directly to the development of SLOs. These include the launch of the National Academy for Educational Leadership, the decision to integrate Wales' SLO model into all leadership development programmes (e.g. through the Academy for Educational Leadership endorsement process) and the commitments made by the Welsh Government's Education Directorate (and possibly other directorates) and several middle-tier organisations to themselves develop into learning organisations.

However, one finding that deserves policy attention is that many secondary schools are clearly finding it more challenging to develop into a learning organisation than primary schools. The recently established National Academy for Educational Leadership, which oversees the roll-out of support and development of education leaders in Wales, should pay particular attention to secondary school leaders. The regional consortia need to focus their efforts more strongly on the secondary sector and review their support services accordingly, and promote school-to-school collaboration not only between secondary schools but also with primary schools. The latter would seem relevant as significantly more primary schools appear to have developed as learning organisations, and it may also facilitate the transition of students between one level of education to the next.

Many governors are not doing enough to effectively fulfil their role as critical friend and often do not exert sufficient influence on school self-evaluation and development planning. The ongoing review of school self-evaluation and development planning provides an opportunity to revisit governors' roles and identify their development needs. In addition, many local authorities have undergone high levels of staff turnover in leadership positions. The evidence points to the need for further investments in the capacity of middle leaders and challenge advisors in the regional consortia.

These findings support earlier OECD findings that a concerted effort is needed to develop the leadership capacity across all levels of the system and to make leadership a driver of the reform effort (OECD, 2017[10]). Although some progress has been made recently, leadership development is yet to become the driving force behind the curriculum reform in Wales. The National Academy for Educational Leadership and other stakeholders may therefore look to education systems like Ontario, British Columbia in Canada, and Scotland, that have made significant investments in developing the capacity of school and system-level leaders, including those of middle-tier agencies.

Box 5. Recommendations promoting professional capital and a thriving learning culture

Policy issue 2.3: Developing learning leadership in schools and other parts of the system

Recommendation 2.3.1: Develop and implement a coherent leadership strategy that promotes the establishment of learning organisations across the system. Under the leadership of the National Academy for Educational Leadership, Wales should consolidate and speed up efforts to strengthen leadership capacity at all levels in the system. It should develop and implement a leadership strategy that promotes school leaders and other system leaders to develop their organisations into learning organisations.

Recommendation 2.3.2: Provide greater support to secondary school leaders and ensure they have the capacity to develop their schools as learning organisations. The National Academy for Educational Leadership should pay particular attention to the capacity development of secondary school leaders, making sure to include middle-level leaders. The regional consortia should also focus on supporting secondary school leaders. Collaborations between primary and secondary school leaders could be promoted. Future reviews of the (teaching and) leadership standards should place greater emphasis on school leaders' role in self-evaluations and development planning.

Policy issue 3: Assessment, evaluation and accountability should promote schools developing into learning organisations

Major improvements can be achieved when schools and school systems increase their collective capacity to engage in ongoing "assessment for learning", and regularly evaluate their interventions. However, if accountability demands dominate the ability to use the evaluation of data and information for the purpose of learning, sharing knowledge to support change and innovation, and taking collective responsibility for enhancing students' learning and well-being schools are unlikely to develop into learning organisations. Assessment, evaluation and accountability arrangements therefore play a pivotal role in empowering educators to do things differently and innovate their practice.

Wales' assessment, evaluation and accountability arrangements are currently undergoing review. This review is essential, as the existing arrangements lack coherence and are driven by accountability demands, rather than serving the purpose of learning and improvement.

Accountability plays an important role in safeguarding the quality of schools and the system at large, so the new assessment, evaluation and accountabilities should be implemented in a careful way to prevent unintended effects and encourage schools to engage in enquiry, innovation and exploration – a particular area for improvement for many schools in Wales.

Policy issue 3.1: Student assessments should put student learning at the centre

The work of the Pioneer Schools and other measures proposed in the action plan to strengthen teachers' assessment skills are important considering long-standing concerns about the capacity of teachers to conduct quality assessment. One promising step forward is the ongoing development of adaptive online personalised assessments that will replace paper-based reading and numeracy tests and that are scheduled to be extended to other areas of the new curriculum in the coming years. Another step forward is the planned review of qualifications which will be essential for aligning assessments and evaluations to the new curriculum.

Furthermore, the Welsh Government has indicated its plans to measure student well-being. This should start with defining the concept and developing guidelines and instruments for schools to use – see Recommendation 1.2.1.

Policy issue 3.2: School evaluations should serve the primary purpose of learning and improvement

The national school categorisation system is widely considered to be an improvement on its predecessor, but is still perceived by many as a high-stakes exercise due to the public colour coding of schools. According to those interviewed by the OECD team, this has led to "gaming" and stigmatisation of schools. The categorisation system and Estyn's inspection framework are also not well aligned and many see school self-evaluation as something done "for Estyn". In addition, there are a variety of self-evaluation and development guidelines and tools. The result is that schools do not have a clear picture of what is expected of them in terms of self-evaluation and development planning. This is believed to have contributed to the variable quality of these activities.

The ongoing development of a national school self-evaluation and development toolkit is an important policy response to these challenges. A working group has been charged with its development and could follow the example of many OECD countries and use the question "what is a good school?" to inform the establishment of common criteria for school self-evaluations and Estyn evaluations. For example, Scotland developed the publication *How Good is Our School?* (Education Scotland, 2015[18]) which has inspired school evaluations in several OECD countries (OECD, 2013[19]) could serve as a source of inspiration. Aspects to consider when developing criteria or quality indicators should include:

- **Focusing attention on student learning and well-being across the full breadth of the curriculum.** The new curriculum won't be available until January 2020 so this transition period will have to be carefully managed. For the immediate future, the Welsh Government has proposed retaining national performance indicators for the key subjects of English/Welsh, mathematics and science, but it should go beyond these. An additional action could be to require schools to have processes in place to monitor and support students' well-being. Such an indicator would give an important signal to schools that the new assessment, evaluation and accountability framework aims to cover the whole of the new curriculum.

- **Wales' SLO model and its underlying dimensions**: this will be vital for promoting a learning culture in schools across Wales.

- **Staff professional learning and well-being**: the development of SLOs, the ongoing curriculum reform and reported staff workload challenges all suggest attention should be paid to the professional learning and well-being of staff.

- **Student and parental engagement**: the findings of this assessment support the establishment of criteria that focus attention on facilitating student and parental engagement in the organisation and educational processes of schools, although this might be best as a cross-cutting measure.

Wales' SLO model also calls for school development plans to be based on learning from continuous self-evaluation that uses multiple sources of data for feedback. Contrary to common practice in many schools in Wales, self-evaluations should not just engage staff and students, but also the broader school community including school governors, parents, other schools, and possibly others to identify strengths, challenges and priorities for improvement. Following the examples of countries like Finland, Ireland and the Netherlands (OECD, 2013[19]), peer reviews among schools should complement this process. The variable quality of school self-evaluations and the proposed changes argue for investing in the capacity of all those involved in the process.

The regional consortia commonly review school self-evaluations and development planning as part of the national categorisation system and this should be continued. As many stakeholders the OECD team met have suggested, discontinuing the colour coding of schools would seem key to giving schools the confidence to do things differently and innovate their practice – as long as sufficient checks and balances are built into new assessment, evaluation and accountability arrangements to monitor progress and identify those schools that are not faring well and/or are in need of additional support.

Furthermore, Estyn has a key role to play in promoting SLOs through its external evaluation arrangements. It should encourage schools to develop their own capacity for self-evaluation (i.e. be about learning) and focus on identifying strengths and priorities for improvement. The proposed criteria for school self-evaluations and Estyn's external evaluations will be an important means for this and could allow Estyn to focus on monitoring the rigour of the process of school self-evaluations and development planning, as is done in countries like Ireland, Scotland and New Zealand. There will still need to be sufficient checks and balances in place to safeguard the quality of schools.

In addition, the grading of schools into four categories (i.e. excellent, good, adequate and needs improvement, and unsatisfactory and needs urgent improvement) by Estyn has driven many schools to focus on gathering evidence to meet the requirements of the inspection framework, rather than using self-evaluation for the purpose of learning. The proposed common criteria for school self-evaluations and Estyn evaluations will be an important response to this challenge. As recently proposed by Graham Donaldson (2018[20]), Estyn may need to temporarily reconsider this grading system to give school staff the confidence to change and innovate their practice. These changes call for sustained investments in developing the skills and attitudes of Estyn inspectors.

The Welsh Government is considering a transition period to introduce the changes to the assessment, evaluation and accountability framework and is engaging schools and other stakeholders in defining it. The OECD team agree schools should be provided with clarity on the transition as soon as possible to unleash the energy and willingness of people to engage in enquiry, exploration and innovation.

Box 6. Recommendations on assessment, evaluation and accountability promoting schools as learning organisations

Policy issue 3.2: School evaluations should serve the primary purpose of learning and improvement

Recommendation 3.2.1: Develop national criteria for school quality to guide self-evaluations and Estyn evaluations. These criteria or quality indicators should promote Wales' SLO model, monitor student learning and well-being across the full breadth of the curriculum, recognise staff learning needs and their well-being in staff development plans that in turn inform school development plans, and give students and parents a voice in organisational and educational matters. These and potentially other criteria or quality indicators should encourage schools to give an account of their own strengths and priorities for improvement – and as such should be about learning and improvement, rather than primarily serving the purpose of accountability.

Recommendation 3.2.2: School self-evaluations should be shaped through a participatory process involving the wider school community. Self-evaluations should involve staff, students, school governors, parents, other schools, higher education institutions and possibly others to identify priorities. Peer reviews among schools should complement this process. Regional consortia should furthermore continue to review school self-evaluations and development planning but this process should no longer result in the public colour coding of schools. A condition for doing so is that sufficient checks and balances are built into new assessment, evaluation and accountability arrangements.

These changes also call for substantial investment in the capacity of all those involved in self-evaluations and development planning. The pilot of the school self-evaluation and development planning toolkit should be used to identify the professional learning needs of all parties involved. Guidelines and tools should be part of the toolkit.

Recommendation 3.2.3: Estyn evaluations should safeguard the quality of schools, while focusing on the rigour of schools' self-evaluation processes and development planning. Estyn should promote schools' development of their own capacity for self-evaluation (i.e. be about learning) and focus on identifying strengths and priorities for improvement. It could focus more on monitoring the rigour of the process of self-evaluations and development planning in those schools that have shown to have the capacity for conducting quality self-evaluations. Sufficient checks and balances – as proposed in this report – would need to be in place, however, to monitor progress and identify those schools that are not faring well and/or are in need of additional support. These changes call for sustained investment in developing the skills and attitudes of Estyn inspectors.

Recommendation 3.2.4: Provide clarity to schools and other stakeholders on the transition to the new system of school self-evaluation and Estyn evaluations. Schools should be provided with clarity on the transition period as soon as possible to unleash the energy and willingness of people to engage in enquiry, exploration and innovation.

Policy issue 3.3: System-level monitoring and evaluation should promote learning – at all levels of the system

During the course of this assessment the Welsh Government's Education Directorate revealed its initial ideas for system-level evaluation through a number of "quality indicators" – rather than through the current range of mostly quantitative indicators. This is a positive development but the initial proposals do not seem to align sufficiently with the ambitions of Wales' SLO model and the new curriculum. For example, while the suggestion was made to give schools the freedom to determine key performance indicators based on local needs, national indicators for the key subjects of English/Welsh, mathematics and science would remain. These indicators are likely to continue to drive behaviour if no further actions are proposed. One option would be to consider indicators on student and staff well-being. This would underline the message that the intent is to move towards a new assessment, evaluation and accountability framework that responds to the full breadth of the curriculum, while recognising the importance of staff well-being.

Furthermore, teacher assessments of student performance at the end of Key Stages 2 and 3 are currently also used to monitor progress of schools and the system. This double purpose has made them high stakes and has challenged their reliability. Therefore, referring back to the recommendations of the *Successful Futures* report (Donaldson, 2015[12]) and following the examples of countries and economies like the Flemish Community of Belgium, Finland and New Zealand (OECD, 2013[19]), national monitoring of student learning and well-being should be informed by sample-based assessments instead.

In addition, Estyn could play a prominent role in the system-level monitoring of progress towards meeting the four purposes of the curriculum. Estyn's annual and thematic reports lend themselves well for this. These should draw on a wider range of evidence rather than on school evaluations alone, including PISA, the sample-based assessments proposed above and relevant research. It may look to the example of the Dutch Education Inspectorate whose annual report, *The State of Education in The Netherlands*, draws from various sources, including school inspections, results from national and international student assessments and research evidence (Inspectorate of Education of the Netherlands, 2017[21]).

Box 7. Recommendations on assessment, evaluation and accountability promoting schools as learning organisations

Policy issue 3.3: System-level monitoring and evaluation should promote learning – at all levels of the system

Recommendation 3.3.1: Performance measures should go beyond the key subjects of English/Welsh, mathematics and science – also in the transition period. The Welsh Government should consider performance measures (indicators) on student well-being and staff well-being – initially in the form of a process indicator until measurement instruments have been developed. This will be essential to align assessment, evaluation and accountability with the ambitions of the new curriculum and Wales' SLO model.

Recommendation 3.3.2: National monitoring of student learning and well-being should be informed by a rolling programme of sample-based assessments and Estyn reports, as well as research. These assessments should replace the use of teacher assessments of student performance at the end of Key Stages 2 and 3. There could be a timetable over a period of years with a single topic of the curriculum being assessed each year. Furthermore, Estyn's annual and thematic reports should be used to monitor progress in realising the four purposes of the curriculum. These reports should draw on a wider range of evidence, including the proposed sample based assessments, PISA and relevant research.

Realising schools as learning organisations

The strategic education action plan, *Education in Wales: Our National Mission* calls for all schools in Wales to develop as learning organisations (Welsh Government, 2017[2]). This policy was made more concrete through the launch of Wales' SLO model (see Box 1) that was developed through a series of stakeholder workshops and meetings facilitated by OECD. To support the effective implementation – or, as it is often referred to in Wales, its "realisation" – we looked at the four determinants that can facilitate or hinder this process: smart policy design, stakeholder engagement, a conducive context and an effective implementation strategy (Viennet and Pont, 2017[22]).

Implementation issue 1: Policy design: Enhance the policy justification, its logic and its feasibility

To enhance a policy's implementation potential – in this case the policy to develop all schools in Wales as learning organisations – it is important for it to be well justified, that is to be built on evidence and respond clearly to a need; to complement other policies; and to be feasible (Viennet and Pont, 2017[22]). The evidence suggests Wales' SLO policy has been well received by the education profession. Its justification and logic and its place in the larger curriculum reform effort is starting to be understood by parts of the education profession and other stakeholders in Wales, although there is clearly more work to be done here. Progress has also been made in recent years to strengthen the system infrastructure that is to support schools in developing as learning organisations.

Three issues call for further attention to ensure all schools are able to develop as learning organisations: better communication on the "why" and "how" of the SLO model, careful monitoring of the education budget and a review of the school funding model to ensure adequate funding for schools to develop as learning organisations, and the system infrastructure for developing schools as learning organisations.

Implementation issue 1.1: Improving the communication of the justification and logic of Wales' SLO policy and how it forms an integrated part of the curriculum reform and relates to other policies

For several years, the Welsh Government has been striving for policy coherence. It has been increasingly successful, but has not always been that successful in communicating its achievements in this area. It needs to do more to explain to schools and others at different levels about why this model was developed, how it can guide schools in their development and how it forms an integrated part of the curriculum reform effort and relates to other policies such as the new teaching and leadership standards. An accessible narrative that explains all this should form a key component of the communication strategy of a national SLO implementation plan and the curriculum reform more generally.

Implementation issue 1.2: Ensuring the education budget and school funding model support schools developing as learning organisations and putting the curriculum into practice

In terms of the feasibility of developing schools as learning organisations in Wales, the findings of this assessment suggest that although the majority of schools are making good progress towards developing as learning organisations, a considerable proportion are still far removed from achieving this objective and would need substantial support to make this transformation. However, only 40% of schools were invited to participate in the SLO survey as part of this study. A wider roll-out scheduled during the autumn term 2018 will significantly increase national engagement. It is obvious that some of our findings and recommendations have resource implications. Future resource requirements will have to be carefully estimated to inform the development of the proposed SLO implementation plan (see below).

The Welsh Government's fiscal situation – a decrease in the education budget compared to previous years, a trend that is expected to continue in the future – places further impetus on looking for ways to increase efficiency in public spending in education. It also calls for exploring creative and innovative ways of establishing a learning culture in and across schools with the resources available to them. Welsh Government should, as mentioned, consider reviewing its school funding model and using the proposed in-depth analysis of school funding in Wales to respond to concerns about unequal treatment of schools in similar circumstances as a result of different local funding models – see Recommendation 1.1.1.

Implementation issue 1.3: Continuing to strengthen the system infrastructure for supporting schools in their change and innovation efforts

A positive development is the progress made in recent years in providing resources and developing the system infrastructure, especially the school improvement services provided by regional consortia, to support schools in changing and innovating their practices in line with Wales' SLO model. Several challenges and areas for further improvement remain however.

- Realising the curriculum reform and developing SLOs are both likely to increase demand for support by schools, meaning the regional consortia will all need to be well organised and managed to respond to these demands.

- The regional consortia, to varying degrees, still emphasise challenging schools (by challenge advisors) rather than providing them with support and promoting a learning culture although they have recently started changing their operations to shift the balance. The regional consortia should continue investing in their staff, especially their challenge advisors who are the first points of contact for schools, to enhance their ability to develop schools into learning organisations and support schools in putting the new curriculum into practice.

- While there are examples of good collaboration between the consortia, for example on the development of Wales' SLO model, in other areas there is scope for deepening their collaboration and co-ordination – and lessening the competition between them. The senior management of the regional consortia have a vital role to play in this.

- Furthermore, more progress could be made on the monitoring and evaluation of the effectiveness of the regional consortia's school improvement services. Estyn should continue to monitor the progress consortia are making and ensure they collectively look for ways to enhance their services to schools. The same applies to the continued monitoring of local authorities.

Higher education institutions have also increasingly engaged with the school system, thereby expanding Wales' system infrastructure. This development however is still in its infancy. Several recommendations have been made in this report to promote such "win-win" collaborations.

Box 8. Recommendations for realising schools as learning organisations

Implementation issue 1.1: Improving the communication of the justification and logic of Wales' SLO policy and how it forms an integrated part of the curriculum reform and relates to other policies

Recommendation 1.1.1: Develop an easy-to-understand narrative that explains how Wales' SLO model can guide schools in their development, forms an integrated part of the curriculum reform and relates to other policies like the teaching and leadership standards, and contributes to realising the objective of a self-improving school system. This narrative should be shared widely through various means, including policy documents, blogs and presentations by policy makers.

Implementation issue 1.3: Continuing to strengthen the system infrastructure for supporting schools in their change and innovation efforts

Recommendation 1.3.1: Continue strengthening the capacity of the regional consortia to support schools developing as learning organisations. The Regional consortia should:

- **Continue their efforts to provide greater support to schools and promote a learning culture,** with less emphasis on challenging schools and greater attention to the secondary sector. Regional consortia should optimise their structures and services to be able to meet the demands for support by schools that are likely to grow because of the curriculum reform. Consortia should pay particular attention to enhancing challenge advisors' skills to support schools in establishing a learning culture and putting the new curriculum into practice.

- **Continue expanding and deepening collaborations and co-ordination between consortia.** The senior management of the consortia have a vital role to play in this, including by encouraging and facilitating their staff to work together on projects and activities, and explore ways to reduce duplications and streamline services.

- **Continue improving the monitoring and evaluating the effectiveness of their services provided to schools.**

Recommendation 1.3.2: Estyn should continue to monitor the progress the consortia are making in enhancing and streamlining of their services to schools. Local authorities should continue to also be monitored by Estyn.

Implementation issue 2: Continuing the process of co-construction for the realisation of SLOs across Wales, while supporting greater policy coherence

Whether and how key stakeholders are recognised and included in the design and implementation process is crucial to the success of any policy (Spillane, Reiser and Reimer, 2002[23]; Viennet and Pont, 2017[22]). The process of co-construction which characterises the reform approach in Wales has played a pivotal role in ensuring a strong ownership of policies and has helped bring about greater policy coherence (OECD, 2017[10]).

Despite the progress made, the OECD team identified several examples where there is scope for greater policy coherence. One such example is the ongoing development of the assessment, evaluation and accountability framework which does not seem to be sufficiently connected to the work on the development of the curriculum by the Pioneer Schools. There is also a need to better co-ordinate the ongoing work on the development of system-level key performance indicators with the development of the school self-evaluation and development planning toolkit. Failing to co-ordinate and align these strands of work may result in a lack of coherence between the curriculum and the assessment, evaluation and accountability arrangements (OECD, 2013[19]) which in turn puts the whole curriculum reform effort at risk.

Wales' SLO policy was also initially not directly linked to related policy areas, as it had not been fully integrated into the current reform narrative. However, the Welsh Government and other stakeholders have recognised the need for greater coherence with other policies and have taken steps to bring it about, such as integrating the SLO model into leadership development programmes.

Furthermore, the OECD team found significant differences in the extent and ways in which regional consortia have engaged with schools in their regions to disseminate the model and support them in putting it in practice. Continuing the work of the SLO Implementation Group may help ensure co-ordination and collaboration between the regional consortia and other stakeholders, to collectively look for the best ways to support schools in developing as learning organisations. Although room needs to be left for regional variance, one important step forward will be the intended joint formulation of a national SLO implementation plan that is partially made up of regional action plans.

However, the implementation group should have a clearer role in supporting the Welsh Government's efforts for greater policy coherence, aimed at realising the curriculum in schools throughout Wales. This includes co-ordinating and collaborating with those working on the establishment of a national professional learning model, the development of a school self-evaluation and development planning toolkit, and other related working groups. Additional stakeholders may also be engaged in the process. For example, the Education Workforce Council could be invited to join this working group given its mandate as the national regulator and promoter of professionalism and high standards within the education workforce.

Box 9. Recommendation for realising schools as learning organisations

Implementation issue 2: Continuing the process of co-construction for the realisation of SLOs across Wales, while supporting greater policy coherence

Recommendation 2.1: Enhance the collaboration and alignment between the various work strands on the development of assessment, evaluation and the curriculum. The ongoing development of the assessment, evaluation and accountability arrangements and the work by the Pioneer Schools on the curriculum and assessment arrangements call for better co-ordination. Similarly, is there a need to better co-ordinate and align the ongoing work on the system-level key performance indicators and the school self-evaluation and development planning toolkit. Failing to co-ordinate and align these work strands may lead to a lack of coherence and put the whole curriculum reform at risk.

Recommendation 2.2: The SLO Implementation Group should continue to support the realisation of Wales' SLO policy, while striving for greater policy coherence. The group should lead the development of an SLO implementation plan (see below), monitor progress in realising Wales' SLO policy and ensure further action is taken when necessary. The group should continue to support greater policy coherence, including through collective working and learning about how best to support schools in their innovation journeys. It should furthermore co-ordinate with and collaborate with other working groups, most immediately in the areas of professional learning and school self-evaluation and development planning, and agencies such as the Education Workforce Council.

Implementation issue 3: Continue shaping, monitoring and responding to the changing institutional, policy and societal context

The successful implementation, or realisation, of a policy is more likely when it takes into account the institutional, policy and societal context in which the policy is to be put into practice (Viennet and Pont, 2017[22]). In Wales, the institutional, policy and societal context has been conducive to large-scale education reform, and a wide range of stakeholders from all levels of the system have been fully engaged in shaping the process (OECD, 2017[10]).

The involvement of schools and other stakeholders in the development of Wales' SLO model has supported its ownership by the education profession. Furthermore, increasing alignment with and integration into other policies, like the leadership development programmes or the development of school self-evaluation and development planning toolkit, have helped place the SLO on the agenda of regional consortia and Education Directorate governance bodies like the Change Board.

This current fertile ground for reform is also contributing to schools' willingness to engage with Wales' SLO model. There are some contextual issues, however, that should be monitored and responded to in order to realise the SLO policy. There is a need to expand the public dialogue generated by PISA results to align it to the ambitions of the new curriculum. Wales should also ensure its governance arrangements enable all schools in Wales to develop as learning organisations and as such respond to the learning and other needs of all its students.

Implementation issue 3.1: The need to broaden the public dialogue generated by PISA results

The broad support for education reform in Wales was initially triggered by the disappointing 2009 PISA results. These served as a catalyst for public discussion on the future of education in Wales and resulted in a broad conviction in Welsh society that things needed to change. The resulting education reform has evolved into the current curriculum reform, of which Wales' SLO policy is a part. This reform is ongoing and it will surely take time for its results to transpire.

There were concerns expressed to the OECD team that if the PISA 2018 results did not show sufficient improvement in student performance, some may use this as evidence against the curriculum reform. However, it would be too soon to draw such conclusions as the whole curriculum will only be made available in April 2019, so the PISA 2018 results would not yet reflect any change.

Furthermore, attention should be paid to broadening the public dialogue on student performance to align it to the ambitions of the new curriculum. International comparisons of literacy, numeracy and science could be complemented with more in-depth analysis of the data in areas such as factors influencing student performance, collaborative problem-solving skills, and student motivation for learning and well-being. These are at the heart of Wales' ambitions for the new curriculum but are often overlooked in the public debate when PISA results are released in Wales. A more explicit recognition of such skills in the system-level monitoring of PISA results by the Welsh Government and Estyn may support broader discussions on the learning and well-being of students in Wales.

Implementation issue 3.2: The need to optimise governance arrangements to enable all schools in Wales to develop as learning organisations

The deployment of the SLO model in Wales has been designed with the current institutional arrangements in place. Representatives from various institutions of the three tiers of the education system (see Chapter 1) have been engaged in its development and will play a key role in helping schools make this transformation and shaping how Wales' SLO model is used in the future to support the wider curriculum reform effort.

This assessment has identified that one barrier to enabling all schools in Wales to develop as learning organisations is the current school governance model, which (among other issues) hampers the provision of services for students with additional learning needs (ALN). Evidence suggests that several of the 22 local authorities, especially the smaller ones, lack the capacity – both human and financial – to respond to the growing need for support for this group of students. Interviews and other sources of data suggest this situation has contributed to inequalities in schools' abilities to respond to the learning needs of all students – which is central to the first dimension of Wales' SLO model (Welsh Government, 2017[3]).

A new system for ALN is intended to respond to this challenge. Wales has developed an ALN Transformation Programme to support its realisation. This includes the establishment of five new positions, the "ALN transformation leads". Four of these are operating at the regional level and are responsible for supporting local authorities, schools, early years settings and local health boards as they prepare for and implement the new system (Welsh Government, 2018[24]). The Welsh Government should – as it intends to do – carefully monitor the progress made in developing the cross-sector collaboration and multi-agency work practices that are fundamental to the success of the new ALN system. If progress is lacking further action should be taken. This may require further optimisation of the governance structure.

A second potential barrier to the curriculum reform effort could be the possible reform of public services that is currently being considered in Wales. If this decision is indeed made to reduce the number of local authorities and restructure public services accordingly, the Welsh Government may want to consider delaying any immediate action on it, to help ensure all efforts remain focused on bringing the new curriculum to life in schools across Wales.

Box 10. Recommendation for realising schools as learning organisations

Implementation issue 3: Continue shaping, monitoring and responding to the changing institutional, policy and societal context

Recommendation 3.1: Expand the public dialogue generated by PISA results to align it to the ambitions of the new curriculum. Skills such as collaborative problem solving, and student motivation for learning and their well-being are central to the four purposes of the new curriculum but are often overlooked in public discussions about PISA in Wales. More explicit recognition of such skills in the system-level monitoring of PISA results by the Welsh Government and Estyn could help support a constructive and broader discussion about how PISA can inform the learning and well-being of students in Wales.

Recommendation 3.2: Continue monitoring the effectiveness of recent and possible further changes to governance structures to ensure all schools in Wales are able to developing as learning organisations and realise the ambitions of the new curriculum for all students.

Implementation issue 4: The need for a coherent implementation plan

While this report was being finalised, work had started on the development of an SLO implementation plan intended to form an integrated part of larger reform effort. Several activities have been taken already, are planned or ongoing that should be part of this plan. These include:

- the establishment of the SLO Pilot Group (see Box 1) (September 2016)
- the inclusion of the objective to develop all schools and other parts of the system into learning organisations in the education strategic action plan *Education in Wales: Our National Mission* (September 2017)
- the co-construction and release of Wales' SLO model (November 2017)
- the integration of the SLO model into leadership development programmes (autumn 2018)
- the ongoing development of the school self-evaluation and development planning toolkit in which the model is likely to be integrated (started in May 2018)
- ongoing development of an animation aimed at children and young people that explains Wales' schools as learning organisation model and its relation to the curriculum reform

- scheduled workshops for the regional consortia's challenge advisors (July 2018)

- ongoing development of an online SLO self-assessment survey that can be freely used by school staff (scheduled to be launched November 2018)

- ongoing efforts by the Welsh Government and several middle-tier organisations to develop into learning organisations.

The OECD team agree these are all important activities to support schools in their development efforts. However, this assessment has identified several other issues and policy areas (see above) that call for further action by the Welsh Government, regional consortia, local authorities, Estyn and other stakeholders at various levels of the system and as such should inform the development of the implementation plan.

Furthermore, there is a need for caution in defining objectives and the monitoring of progress. The development of SLOs should not become a high-stakes exercise for schools; this would stand at odds with the ambition of developing all schools in Wales into learning organisations and empowering the people working in them to realise a learning culture in their hearts and minds.

Box 11. Realising schools as learning organisations

Implementation issue 4: The need for a coherent implementation plan

Recommendation 4.1: Develop and put in practice a national SLO implementation plan to empower schools across Wales in developing as learning organisations. The SLO Implementation Group should lead the development of an SLO implementation plan, monitor progress in realising Wales' SLO policy, and ensure further action is taken when necessary.

The findings and recommendations of this report aim to inform the development of the implementation plan, not as a separate action plan but rather as an integrated part of the larger curriculum reform effort. The national action plan – to be partially made up of four regional action plans – should ensure *all* schools have the opportunity to develop as learning organisations and ultimately put the new curriculum into practice. Particular attention should be paid to bringing on board and supporting those schools that for various reasons are less likely to seek support, participate in school-to-school collaboration and other forms of collaborative learning and working, while needing it most. Furthermore, attention should be paid to:

- **The setting of objectives and the monitoring of progress should not become a high-stakes exercise for schools.** One option could be to regularly mine the anonymised data that will be collected through the online SLO survey. Qualitative research could complement the analysis, aimed at exploring progress, including identifying good practices that should be widely shared, challenges and areas for further improvement.

- **Task allocation**. The regional consortia play a pivotal role in supporting schools in their change and innovation journeys. However as highlighted through this report, higher education institutions and other parties could do their part and complement the system infrastructure.

- **The timing and sequencing of actions will require prioritisation.** Phasing in actions allows efforts to be focused, bearing in mind schools' capacity to develop as learning organisations and bring the new curriculum to life. One action that requires immediate attention is the need to clarify the transition period to the new approaches to school self-evaluations and Estyn evaluations.

- **Communication and engagement strategy with education stakeholders.** An important first step will be, as recommended above, to develop and widely share an easily understood narrative that explains how Wales' SLO model can guide schools in their development, forms an integrated part of the curriculum reform and relates to other policies. The systematic collection and sharing of good practice is another area to consider.

References

Borgonovi, F. and G. Montt (2012), "Parental involvement in selected PISA countries and economies", *OECD Education Working Papers*, No. 73, OECD Publishing, Paris, http://dx.doi.org/10.1787/5k990rk0jsjj-en. [4]

Byrne, D. and E. Smyth (2010), *Behind the Scenes? A Study of Parental Involvement in Post-Primary Education*, Liffey Press, Dublin. [5]

Desforges, C. and A. Abouchaar (2003), "The impact of parental involvement, parental support and family education on pupil achievements and adjustment: A literature review", *Research Report*, No. No. 433, Department for Education and Skills Publications, Nottingham. [6]

Donaldson, G. (2018), *A Learning Inspectorate*, http://dx.doi.org/ttps://www.estyn.gov.wales/sites/default/files/documents/A%20Learning%20Inspectorate%20-%20en%20-%20June%202018.pdf. [20]

Donaldson, G. (2015), *Successful Futures: Independent Review of Curriculum and Assessment Arrangements in Wales*, Welsh Government, http://gov.wales/docs/dcells/publications/150225-successful-futures-en.pdf. [12]

Education Scotland (2015), *How Good is our School?*, Education Scotland, https://education.gov.scot/improvement/Documents/Frameworks_SelfEvaluation/FRWK2_NIHeditHGIOS/FRWK2_HGIOS4.pdf. [18]

Inspectorate of Education of the Netherlands (2017), *The State of Education in The Netherlands 2015/2016 [De Staat van het Onderwijs in Nederland 2015/16]*, Inspectorate of Education of The Netherlands, Utrecht, https://english.onderwijsinspectie.nl/binaries/onderwijsinspectie_eng/documents/annual-reports/2017/04/12/the-state-of-education-in-the-netherlands-2015-2016/state+of+education+2015+2016+web.pdf. [21]

Kools, M. and L. Stoll (2016), "What makes a school a learning organisation?", *OECD Education Working Papers*, No. 137, OECD Publishing, Paris, http://dx.doi.org/10.1787/5jlwm62b3bvh-en. [1]

OECD (2017), *PISA 2015 Results (Volume III): Students' Well-Being*, PISA, OECD Publishing, Paris, http://dx.doi.org/10.1787/9789264273856-en. [7]

OECD (2017), *The Funding of School Education: Connecting Resources and Learning*, OECD Reviews of School Resources, OECD Publishing, Paris, http://dx.doi.org/10.1787/9789264276147-en. [13]

OECD (2017), *The Welsh Education Reform Journey: A Rapid Policy Assessment*, OECD, Paris, http://www.oecd.org/edu/The-Welsh-Education-Reform-Journey-FINAL.pdf. [10]

OECD (2016), *Education in Latvia*, Reviews of National Policies for Education, OECD Publishing, Paris, http://dx.doi.org/10.1787/9789264250628-en. [14]

OECD (2016), *PISA 2015 Results (Volume II): Policies and Practices for Successful Schools*, PISA, OECD Publishing, Paris, http://dx.doi.org/10.1787/9789264267510-en.   [8]

OECD (2014), *Improving Schools in Wales: An OECD Perspective*, OECD, Paris, http://www.oecd.org/edu/Improving-schools-in-Wales.pdf.   [9]

OECD (2013), *Synergies for Better Learning: An International Perspective on Evaluation and Assessment*, OECD Reviews of Evaluation and Assessment in Education, OECD Publishing, Paris, http://dx.doi.org/10.1787/9789264190658-en.   [19]

Sahlberg, P. (2010), "Educational change in Finland", in *Second International Handbook of Educational Change*, Springer Netherlands, Dordrecht, http://dx.doi.org/10.1007/978-90-481-2660-6_19.   [16]

Schleicher, A. (2011), *Building a High-Quality Teaching Profession: Lessons from around the World*, International Summit on the Teaching Profession, OECD Publishing, Paris, http://dx.doi.org/10.1787/9789264113046-en.   [15]

Sinnema, C. (2017), *Designing a National Curriculum with Enactment in Mind: A Discussion Paper*.   [17]

Spillane, J., B. Reiser and T. Reimer (2002), "Policy implementation and cognition: Reframing and refocusing implementation research", *Review of Educational Research*, Vol. 72/3, pp. 387-431, http://dx.doi.org/10.3102/00346543072003387.   [23]

Viennet, R. and B. Pont (2017), "Education policy implementation: A literature review and proposed framework", *OECD Education Working Papers*, No. 162, OECD Publishing, Paris, http://dx.doi.org/10.1787/fc467a64-en.   [22]

Welsh Government (2018), *Additional Learning Needs Transformation Leads*, Welsh Government website, https://gov.wales/topics/educationandskills/schoolshome/additional-learning-special-educational-needs/transformation-programme/implementation-transition-support/aln-transformation-leads/?lang=en.   [24]

Welsh Government (2017), *Education in Wales: Our National Mission. Action Plan 2017-21*, Welsh Government, Cardiff, http://gov.wales/docs/dcells/publications/170926-education-in-wales-en.pdf.   [2]

Welsh Government (2017), "Schools in Wales as learning organisations", *Welsh Government website*, http://gov.wales/topics/educationandskills/schoolshome/curriculuminwales/curriculum-for-wales-curriculum-for-life/schools-in-wales-as-learning-organisations/?lang=en (accessed on 30 November 2017).   [11]

Welsh Government (2017), *Schools in Wales as learning organisations*, Welsh Government website, http://gov.wales/topics/educationandskills/schoolshome/curriculuminwales/curriculum-for-wales-curriculum-for-life/schools-in-wales-as-learning-organisations/?lang=en (accessed on 30 November 2017).   [3]

Part I. Introduction

Chapter 1. Wales and its school system

This chapter starts with an introduction and background to the report. It then provides a description of Wales' school system and the context in which it operates. Wales is a small, bilingual country in English and Welsh that is part of the United Kingdom. It in 2011 embarked on a large-scale reform to improve the quality and equity of its school system. This has become increasingly focused on the reform of the school curriculum in recent years, aiming for all children and young people to develop into "ambitious capable and lifelong learners, enterprising and creative, informed citizens and healthy and confident individuals".

To support schools in this effort, Wales aims to develop them into learning organisations. This study supports Wales in this effort by gauging the extent to which schools have put into practice the characteristics of learning organisations and identifying areas for further development.

The statistical data for Israel are supplied by and under the responsibility of the relevant Israeli authorities. The use of such data by the OECD is without prejudice to the status of the Golan Heights, East Jerusalem and Israeli settlements in the West Bank under the terms of international law.

Introduction and background to the report

An education system in which all learners have an equal opportunity to reach their full potential can strengthen individuals' and societies' capacity to contribute to economic growth and social cohesion. In 2011 Wales embarked on a large-scale school improvement reform. It introduced a range of policies to improve the quality and equity of its school system. Education reform has since been a national priority in Wales and actors at all levels are committed to achieving system-wide improvement.

In support of these reform efforts, the Welsh Government invited the OECD to conduct a review of its school system. The resulting report, *Improving Schools in Wales: An OECD Perspective* (OECD, 2014[1]) analysed the strengths and challenges of the Welsh school system, and provided a number of policy recommendations to further strengthen it. The OECD recommended that Wales develop a long-term and sustainable school improvement strategy by investing in the teaching and school leadership profession, ensuring that schools and their staff can respond to the learning needs of all students, and establishing a coherent evaluation and assessment framework to underpin the school system.

Building on the OECD review and other research reports (Hill, 2013[2]; Estyn, 2013[3]), in 2014 the Welsh Government released *Qualified for Life: An Education Improvement Plan for 3 to 19 Year Olds in Wales.* The plan outlined the actions it would take over the next five years to improve educational attainment for all learners (Welsh Government, 2014[4]).

In September 2016, the Welsh Government invited the OECD back to Wales to undertake an "education rapid policy assessment" to take stock of the reforms initiated in recent years. The resulting report, *The Welsh Education Reform Journey: A Rapid Policy Assessment* (OECD, 2017) provided an analysis of the most prominent reforms, provided feedback on progress made since the policy advice provided by the OECD in 2014 and offered recommendations to inform the next steps.

After taking stock of the progress made with *Qualified for Life* (Welsh Government, 2014[4]) and responding to the findings and recommendation of a review of the curriculum and assessment arrangements in Wales (Donaldson, 2015[5]), and those provided by the OECD's rapid policy assessment, in September 2017 the Welsh Government released *Education in Wales: Our National Mission* (Welsh Government, 2017[6]). This action plan for 2017-21 presented the national vision for education and calls for all children and young people to access a curriculum that supports them in becoming:

- ambitious, capable learners who are ready to learn throughout their lives
- enterprising, creative contributors who are ready to play a full part in life and work
- ethical, informed citizens who are ready to be citizens of Wales and the world
- healthy, confident individuals who are ready to lead fulfilling lives as valued members of society.

To be able to deliver on these "four purposes" of the curriculum, the action plan proposes the following four key enabling objectives: 1) developing a high-quality education profession; 2) inspirational leaders working collaboratively to raise standards; 3) strong and inclusive schools committed to excellence, equity and well-being; and 4) robust assessment, evaluation and accountability arrangements supporting a self-improving system.

In support of these four objectives, and ultimately the realisation of the new curriculum, the plan calls for all schools and other parts of the system to develop into learning organisations. This is because schools that are learning organisations have the capacity to adapt more quickly to changes as well as explore and try out new approaches so that they can improve learning and outcomes for all their students (Welsh Government, 2017[7]).

The Welsh Government, regional consortia and other stakeholders have started supporting schools in developing into learning organisations with support from OECD, and developed a schools as learning organisations (SLO) model for Wales that was released in November 2017 (Welsh Government, 2017[7]).

This study aims to support Wales in this effort, gauging the extent to which schools have put into practice the characteristics of learning organisations and identifying areas for further development. It also examines the system-level conditions that can enable or hinder schools in Wales in developing as learning organisations.

The study is part of the OECD's efforts to support countries in the design and effective implementation of education policy, grounding these efforts on evidence, and multidisciplinary tools and approaches (Gurría, 2015[8]). It uses various quantitative and qualitative data sources:

- A desk study: a review of policy documents, studies and reports together with international and national data.

- An online Schools as Learning Organisations Survey: this was shared with school leaders, teachers and learning support workers (i.e. higher level teaching assistants, teaching assistants, foreign language assistants, special needs support staff) from a random sample of 571 schools, resulting in over 1 700 responses from 178 schools. Annex 2.A2 provides further details on the use of the SLO survey.

- School visits: the OECD team visited eight schools throughout Wales in June and July 2017. Over 80 school leaders, teachers and learning support workers were interviewed. The team complemented and triangulated the findings from the interviews with: 1) the schools' results in the SLO survey; 2) a desk study of the available data and information about the schools (e.g. school evaluation reports by Estyn, the Inspectorate for Education and Training in Wales); and 3) a short self-assessment questionnaire completed by the school leaders to showcase "good practices".

In addition, the OECD team (Annex A) conducted various policy missions during 2017 and early 2018 during which they interviewed and consulted a wide range of experts and stakeholders from various levels of the education system. These missions were part of the broader OECD Education Policy Implementation Support provided to the Welsh Government since September 2016. It consists of: 1) a rapid policy assessment; 2) strategic policy advice during policy meetings, conferences and other events; and 3) tailored implementation support for developing schools as learning organisations. This broader collaboration between the OECD and Wales has resulted in a rich exchange of views, experience and knowledge which have enriched the analysis of this report.

The preliminary findings of this assessment were furthermore discussed with a large number of stakeholders during several meetings, allowing their validation and further refinement where it was found necessary.

Outline of the report

This report is structured into three parts. Following the introduction (Part I), Part II, *The Schools as Learning Organisations Assessment*, describes and analyses the school as a learning organisation in Wales in context and Part III, *System Assessment of the Conditions for Developing Schools as Learning Organisations*, analyses the system-level conditions that can enable or hinder schools developing into learning organisations.

The report starts with Chapter 1 that provides a short overview of Wales and its school system. It describes some of the key features of its population, governance system and economy before turning to a description of the school system and performance of its students.

In Part II, Chapter 2 draws from multiple data sources to explore the question of to what extent schools in Wales have put in practice the country's SLO model (Welsh Government, 2017[7]).

Chapter 3 continues the assessment by exploring in greater depth to what extent schools in Wales have put in practice the seven action-oriented dimensions and underlying elements of Wales' SLO model. The chapter presents examples of good practice to exemplify the findings and provide practical guidance to those wanting to develop their schools into learning organisations in Wales and beyond. The chapter concludes by presenting the key findings of the assessment, offering points of reflection and action for schools.

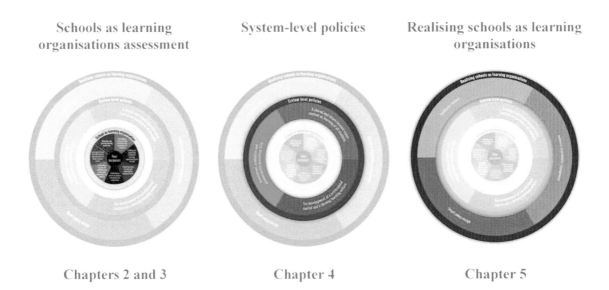

Schools as learning organisations assessment	System-level policies	Realising schools as learning organisations
Chapters 2 and 3	Chapter 4	Chapter 5

Part III of this report consists of two chapters. Chapter 4 sets out to answer the question of what system-level policies are enabling or hindering schools to develop as learning organisations, and offers a number of concrete recommendations for strengthening policies, enhancing policy coherence and further policy action.

Chapter 5 explores the question of how Wales can ensure the effective implementation, or "realisation" as it is often referred to in Wales, of its SLO policy (Viennet and Pont, 2017[9]). It concludes with a number of recommendations for consideration by the Welsh Government and other stakeholders at various levels of the system.

The Welsh context

Wales is a small country that is part of the United Kingdom (UK) and the island of Great Britain. It is bordered by England to its east and the Atlantic Ocean and Irish Sea to its west. The country has about 3.1 million inhabitants, about 5% of the United Kingdom population (Office for National Statistics, 2016[10]). The country is officially bilingual in English and Welsh. In 2017 around 19% of the population spoke Welsh – which represents half a million people – and 11% reported they use Welsh every day (Welsh Government, 2017[11]).

Wales has a form of self-government similar to Scotland and Northern Ireland. The Government of Wales Act (1998) created the National Assembly, following a referendum the year before. The Welsh political body is made up of the 60 elected Assembly Members and the Welsh Government, which consists of the First Minister and his or her cabinet. Although in the beginning the Assembly had no powers to initiate primary legislation, in 2006 it gained law-making powers over 20 areas such as economic development, local government, health, social welfare, and education and training. These law-making powers were expanded in 2011 but some policy areas are not included in the devolution process, including policing and criminal justice; foreign affairs, defence and security issues; and welfare, benefits and social security. These are matters on which the UK Parliament legislates.

Further devolution of powers is being considered, for example in the area of teachers' salaries. In June 2016, the Welsh Government established the Ministerial Supply Model Taskforce to consider issues around supply teachers, which reported to the Cabinet Secretary for Education (Jones, 2017[12]). Following this report, a cross-party amendment was introduced in the committee stages of the Wales Bill which sees teachers' pay and conditions devolved to Wales at some stage in the coming years (Parliament of the United Kingdom, 2017[13]).

Local governments have significant responsibility for public service delivery in Wales. The 22 local authorities are politically accountable through elections held every 4 years. Local authorities have locally elected councils that are responsible for a range of services such as trading standards, education, housing, leisure and social services. The structure of the local authorities is currently being reviewed, with a proposal to reduce their number to nine by 2021 (WLGA, 2015[14]).

The main urban areas are located in the local authorities of Cardiff, Swansea and Newport; almost 24% of the population is concentrated in these areas (StatsWales, 2017[15]). In 2016, the Welsh population had increased by almost 1.5% since 2011. Similar to many OECD countries, population growth is limited, partly due to the ageing population. Wales' fertility rate also remains below the replacement level, at 1.77 in 2015 (OECD, 2018[16]).[1]

The population of Wales is projected to increase from 3.1 million in 2016 to 3.21 million by 2026 and 3.26 million by 2041. The number of children aged under 16 is projected to increase to 568 000 by 2026. Overall, the number of children is projected to decrease by 1.5% between 2016 and 2041. The number of people aged 16-64 is projected to decrease by 81 000 (4.2%) between 2016 and 2041 while the number of people aged 65 and over is projected to increase by 232 000 (36.6%) between 2016 and 2041 (Office for National Statistics, 2017[17]).

Since the 1970s the Welsh economy has undergone major restructuring and has managed to transform itself from a predominantly industrial to a post-industrial economy. The country's traditional extractive and heavy industries are either gone or are in decline and have been replaced by new ones in light and service industries, the public sector, manufacturing, and tourism. While there was a need for low-skilled workers in Wales in the past, the changes in the Welsh economic profile are likely to demand highly skilled and service-oriented workers (OECD, 2014[1]).

While the economic crisis had a negative effect on the Welsh economy and on the lives of many of its people, it steadily recovered and officially came out of the crisis in 2011-12 (Figure 1.1) (Eurostat, 2018[18]). Figure 1.1 however shows a decrease in gross domestic product (GDP) in 2016 which can be partially attributed to the insecurity caused by the (at the time) potential decision of the UK to withdraw from the European Union, often referred to as "Brexit".

Figure 1.1. Gross domestic product at current market prices in Euro per inhabitant as a percentage of the EU-28 average

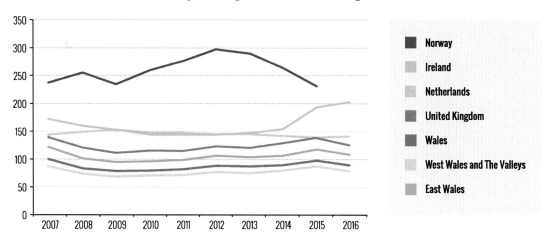

Note: EU-28 = 100. West Wales and The Valleys consists of the local authorities Isle of Anglesey, Gwynedd, Conwy and Denbighshire, South West Wales, Central Valleys, Gwent Valleys, Bridgend and Neath Port Talbot, and Swansea. East Wales consists of Monmouthshire and Newport, Cardiff and Vale of Glamorgan, Flintshire and Wrexham, and Powys.
Source: Eurostat (2018[18]), *Gross Domestic Product (GDP) at Current Market Prices by NUTS 2 Regions*, http://appsso.eurostat.ec.europa.eu/nui/show.do?dataset=nama_10r_2gdp&lang=en.

StatLink ⫯⫮⫯ http://dx.doi.org/10.1787/888933837150

GDP in Wales is below that of the other regions of the UK and other OECD countries like Ireland, the Netherlands and Norway, but is above that of countries like Poland, Portugal and Spain (not shown in Figure 1.1). The differences in socio-economic opportunities across Wales are also extensive. In West Wales and The Valleys for example GDP per capita was EUR 23 100 in 2016, while it was EUR 31 500 in East Wales (Eurostat, 2018[18]).

For the three months to May 2017, the unemployment rate was 4.6%, which is close to the UK average (4.5%) and below the OECD average (6%) (Figure 1.2) (OECD, 2017[19]; Welsh Government, 2017[20]). This is a significant decrease in the unemployment rate compared to five years before, when 8.6% of the labour force was unemployed (Welsh Government, 2017[20]).

Figure 1.2. Unemployment rates in Wales, the European Union and the United Kingdom (2005-15)

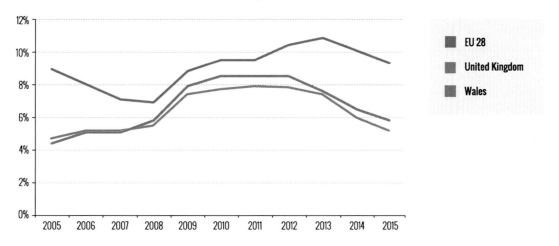

Note: Rate of economically active people aged 16 and over unemployed for less than 12 months.
Source: Welsh Government (2016[21]), "European Union harmonised unemployment rates by gender, area and year", https://statswales.gov.wales/Catalogue/Business-Economy-and-Labour-Market/People-and-Work/Unemployment/ILO-Unemployment/ilo-unemployment-europeanunionharmonisedunemploymentrates-by-gender-area-year.

StatLink ⧉ http://dx.doi.org/10.1787/888933837169

Close to a quarter (24%) of all people in Wales were living in relative income poverty[2] between 2014/15 and 2016/17 (i.e. the financial years ending March 2015 and March 2017). This is up from 23% between 2013/14 and 2015/16, the rate it had stood at for the last five time periods.

Children are the group most likely to be in relative income poverty in Wales and this has remained unchanged for some time: 28% of children in Wales were living in relative income poverty between 2014/15 and 2016/17. However, the rate has fallen from 30% between 2013/14 and 2015/16. A possible reason for children consistently being the age group most likely to be in relative income poverty is that adults with children are more likely to be out of work or in low-paid work due to childcare responsibilities (Welsh Government, 2018[22]).

School education in Wales: A brief overview

The Welsh school system is relatively small. In January 2017 there were approximately 467 000 school and pre-school students in Wales, in 11 nurseries, 1 287 primary schools, 10 middle schools (which include both primary and secondary education), 200 secondary schools and 39 special schools. There were 1 547 "maintained" – i.e. public – schools and 70 private (independent) schools in Wales that year (Welsh Government, 2017[23]).

In January 2017, there were 151 fewer public schools than there had been in 2012, while the student population remained stable (Welsh Government, 2012[24]; Welsh Government, 2017[23]). This resulted from the closing and consolidation of mostly (very) small schools by local councils. During the same period Wales also witnessed a small increase in the number of independent schools, from 66 to 70. In response to the closures of small schools, the Welsh Government created a small and rural school grant to encourage innovation and school-to-school work. Also, closures can now only be pursued if all viable alternatives have been explored (Welsh Government, 2016[25]).

Education is compulsory in Wales from the age of 5 to 16, but 98% of children begin their education as 4-year-olds and 80% continue beyond 16 (Eurydice, 2016[26]). The period of compulsory education is divided into four stages: Foundation Phase, Key Stage 2, Key Stage 3 and Key Stage 4 (see Table 1.1). Vocational education is available for students in post-compulsory education, and students may take a combination of academic and vocational courses.

Table 1.1. Overview of education phases, ages and International Standard Classification of Education (ISCED) levels

Educational phase	Stage	Ages	ISCED 2011 level
Early years/primary	Foundation Phase	3-7	ISCED 0 and 1
Primary	Key Stage 2	7-11	ISCED 1
Secondary	Key Stage 3	11-14	ISCED 2
Secondary	Key Stage 4	14-16	ISCED 3

Source: Eurypedia (2016[26]), "Overview: United Kingdom (Wales)", https://webgate.ec.europa.eu/fpfis/mwikis/eurydice/index.php/United-Kingdom-Wales:Overview.

The Foundation Phase, introduced in 2010, combines early years education with the first two years of compulsory education (formerly known as Key Stage 1) and aims to produce a more developmental, experiential and play-based approach to teaching and learning (Welsh Government, 2015[27]). The Foundation Phase included all 3-7 year-olds for the first time in 2011/12 and initial evaluations have found that children are more likely to have higher levels of well-being and involvement in learning when they attend schools that make greater use of Foundation Phase pedagogies (Welsh Government, 2015[28]).

Students with some form of special education needs[3] make up approximately 23% of all students in Welsh public schools; however, only about 12% of these have official statements of special education needs. A major challenge is that statements are often interpreted differently across local authorities; there are no nationally defined, clear criteria for giving statements (OECD, 2017[29]). The Welsh Government is in the process of transforming the existing special education system into a more unified one with the aim to better support learners with "additional learning needs" – the preferred term in Wales nowadays – from age 0 to 25.

Wales has a distinct cultural identity and is officially a bilingual nation. Education is delivered in Welsh-medium, English-medium and/or bilingual settings. Regardless of the medium of instruction, all children in Wales are required to learn Welsh throughout the compulsory schooling period (Eurydice, 2016[26]). As of January 2016, about 33% of public primary schools and 24% of public secondary schools were Welsh-medium schools.

Welsh-medium pre-school education is also available, and some further and higher education courses are also taught in Welsh (Eurydice, 2016[26]). In addition, in 2006 the Welsh Baccalaureate was made available to secondary students at all levels: foundation, intermediate or advanced, in academic or vocational qualifications. Since 2005, the Welsh Government has also offered an intensive Welsh language sabbatical for teachers, lecturers, instructors and classroom assistants who want to raise their standard of Welsh and gain confidence in using the language in their teaching practice (Duggan, Thomas and Lewis, 2014[30]).

Towards a new school curriculum

Welsh schools follow the National Curriculum for Wales for 3-19 year-olds (Welsh Government, 2016[31]), which specifies the compulsory subjects and programmes of study (Eurydice, 2016[26]). The curriculum is now being revised following an independent review of curriculum and assessment arrangements by Graham Donaldson in 2015. The review has provided the background for developing a 21st century curriculum in Wales from the Foundation Phase to Key Stage 4 (ages 3 to 16). In his review Donaldson took note of a wide number of independent reports, visited around 60 schools and met various other key stakeholders, including students, parents and representatives of the further education sector, resulting in the *Successful Futures* report (Donaldson, 2015[5]).

The recommendations of the report were accepted in full by the Welsh Government in June 2015 and have provided Wales with the foundations for developing a 21st century curriculum. The report that followed, *A Curriculum for Wales – A Curriculum for Life*, set out, in broad terms, the steps that Wales will take to achieve the *Successful Futures* report (Welsh Government, 2015[32]) (see Box 1.1).

One of the first steps the government took was to establish the Pioneer Schools Network. In autumn 2015 schools were invited to become "Pioneer Schools" to work with local authorities, regional consortia, the Welsh Government, Estyn (Her Majesty's Inspectorate for Education and Training), and a range of experts on the design and implementation of a new curriculum for Wales (see Box 1.2). The work of the network of almost 200 Pioneer Schools is given shape through three strands of work:

- designing and developing the Digital Competence Framework (DCF)
- designing and developing the curriculum and assessment arrangements
- supporting the professional development and learning of the workforce.

Box 1.1. A new curriculum for Wales

A Curriculum for Wales – A Curriculum for Life (Welsh Government, 2015[32]) calls for all children and young people in Wales to develop as:

- ambitious, capable learners, ready to learn throughout their lives

- enterprising, creative contributors, ready to play a full part in life and work

- ethical, informed citizens of Wales and the world

- healthy, confident individuals, ready to lead fulfilling lives as valued members of society (Donaldson, 2015[5]).

These "four purposes" of the new curriculum will be operationalised in six Areas of Learning and Experiences and include cross-curriculum responsibilities: 1) expressive arts; 2) health and well-being; 3) humanities; 4) literacy, languages and communication; 5) mathematics and numeracy; and 6) science and technology.

The new curriculum consists of a cross-curricular framework rather than a subject-based framework. Digital competencies will be given the same priority as literacy and numeracy as part of the three cross-curriculum responsibilities. The Digital Competence Framework (DCF) was the first element of the new curriculum to be developed and was launched in September 2016. The framework encourages the integration of digital skills across the full range of lessons and has four strands: citizenship, interacting and collaborating, producing, and data and computational thinking.

Source: Donaldson, G. (2015[5]), *Successful Futures: Independent Review of Curriculum and Assessment Arrangements in Wales,* http://gov.wales/docs/dcells/publications/150225-successful-futures-en.pdf.

Each of the three strands of work has been responsible for specific policy initiatives to achieve its objectives. For example, the Pioneer Schools working on the professional development and learning of the workforce have been contributing to the development of a new framework of professional standards for teachers and formal leaders, *the Professional Standards for Teaching and Leadership* (see below) (Welsh Government, 2017[33]). A sub-group of this network of schools also took the lead in the development of Wales' SLO model.

While writing this report the development of the new curriculum was starting to take shape as were the initial parameters of new assessment, evaluation and accountability arrangements being clarified. In addition, a large scale reform of initial teacher education was ongoing to ensure the quality of Wales' present and future work force. These are some of the major policy initiatives that are part of Welsh Government's strategy to support schools in putting the new curriculum into practice in all schools across Wales. (Welsh Government, 2017[6]). As will be explained in Chapter 2, schools developing as learning organisations is considered an essential means for realising this objective.

Box 1.2. Objectives of the Pioneer Schools Network

The Pioneer Schools Network consists of three subgroups working on the following objectives (Welsh Government, 2017[34]):

Digital Pioneer Schools (13 schools)

- Design and develop the DCF and make it available from September 2016.

- Refine the DCF, based on feedback from the sector (December 2016 and ongoing).

- Support the integration of the DCF into the emerging curriculum.

- Develop the professional support required so that practitioners are confident and capable in applying the framework (by September 2017).

Curriculum and Assessment Pioneer Schools (94 schools)

- Design the high-level framework for the new curriculum based on clear design principles and taking account of key cross-cutting themes:

  o enrichment and experiences

  o Welsh dimension, international perspective and wider skills

  o cross-curriculum responsibilities (see Box 1.1)

  o assessment and progression

- Develop the Areas of Learning and Experience with the aim of making the new curriculum and assessment arrangements available for feedback from April 2019.

- Make the final curriculum and assessment arrangements available by January 2020. In September 2022 all public schools should be using the new curriculum and assessment arrangements.

Professional Development and Learning Pioneer Schools (83 schools)

- Shape the professional learning offer to support practitioners and leaders to acquire the skills they need now and for the curriculum of the future.

- Have a leading role in developing and exemplifying the characteristics and behaviour that all schools in Wales need to show to be successful learning organisations.

- Work with the regional consortia to build capacity so that all schools and settings in Wales are able to develop the characteristics and behaviours needed to be effective learning organisations.

- Work with the regional consortia (see below) to develop a wide range of high-quality professional learning opportunities that is nationally consistent and accessible to all practitioners.

Source: Welsh Government (2017[34]), "Announcement of further Pioneer Schools focussing on curriculum design and development", http://gov.wales/about/cabinet/cabinetstatements/2017/pioneerschools/?lang=en.

The education profession

Teachers

In January 2017 the school system of Wales had 22 531 qualified teachers in service. The number of qualified teachers in public schools in each local authority ranged from 3 103 in Cardiff to 470 in Merthyr Tydfil. The average student-teacher ratio was 22:1 at the primary level and 16:1 at the secondary level, compared to the OECD averages of 15:1 and 13:1 respectively (Welsh Government, 2016[35]; OECD, 2016[36])

To qualify as a teacher in Wales requires a bachelor's degree and Qualified Teacher Status (QTS). Individuals can take a university-based route or through employment-based training that offers a way to qualify while working in a public school. For the former, individuals can either study at undergraduate level and achieve QTS at the same time as undertaking their degree, or pursue a post-graduate course of study (PGCE) after they obtained their bachelor's degree.

For the employment-based route, individuals with a bachelor's degree can undertake the Graduate Teacher Programme to gain QTS while they work as an unqualified teacher in a school. They can work as an unqualified teacher until they successfully complete the programme or cease the programme (Welsh Government, 2013[37]). They can also enter Teach First Cymru that offers a two-year programme during which they teach in the most deprived schools. The evidence shows however that many of the Teach First Cymru participants leave the country after completing the programme to teach outside Wales (Estyn, 2016[38]).

During recent years a range of policies have been implemented to improve the quality of the teaching workforce in Wales. For example, in 2014 the requirements to enter initial teacher education were raised. Since then aspiring teachers must have at least a General Certificate of Secondary Education (GCSE) grade B in English and mathematics. In addition, aspiring primary teachers need at least a GCSE grade C in science to enter teacher education.

Furthermore, the Welsh Government recently established the mentioned new framework of professional standards for teachers and formal leaders (Welsh Government, 2017[33]). Among other things, these new standards aim to set clear expectations about effective practice throughout a practitioner's career and to allow them to reflect on their practice, individually and collectively. Newly qualified teachers must complete an induction period of three school terms or the equivalent. Those who started induction after September 2017 were required to work to the new standards. All practising teachers and formal leaders are expected to use them by September 2018.

Wales has also developed a number of tools to support teachers in their professional learning. For example, it introduced the Professional Learning Passport in 2015. This digital tool aims to help teachers plan and record their professional learning (Education Workforce Council, 2017[39]) in line with the new professional standards.

Various actors such as the regional consortia, local authorities and private companies offer professional learning opportunities for teachers and other school staff in the form of workshops, courses and programmes. In recent years, however, school-to-school collaboration and engagement in networks have gained in prominence as a means of facilitating professional learning in and across schools. Wales is moving away from a model of delivering professional learning within the school setting, towards a more collaborative, practitioner-led experience which is embedded in classroom practice. The professional learning model for Wales currently under development is aimed at reflecting and further promoting this development.

School leaders

In January 2017 Wales had 3 641 school leaders working in public schools. This number consisted of 1 577 head teachers, 1 170 deputy head teachers and 894 assistant head teachers.

Head teachers in Wales must hold a National Professional Qualification for Headship (NPQH) qualification, have QTS and be registered with the Education Workforce Council. The NPQH is a professional learning programme aimed at practitioners who aspire to become head teachers. The programme lasts between 6 and 18 months (depending on the speed of study and the credentials of candidates). Candidates must complete three mandatory modules: 1) leading and improving teaching; 2) leading an effective school; and 3) succeeding in headship, as well as two modules of choice. They are also required to spend at least nine days in a school from a different context to their own and undertake a final assessment which is made up of two interviews and a case study exercise (Welsh Governement, 2016[40]).

In recent years, several reports have raised concerns about the quality of leadership and management in a significant number of schools in Wales (Estyn, 2016[41]; Hill, 2013[2]; OECD, 2014[1]; OECD, 2017[29]). These reports have highlighted the lack of attractiveness of the profession, mostly due to administrative burdens and the lack of succession planning, as well as the very few professional learning opportunities for senior and middle-level leaders and teachers.

In its 2016/17 annual report Estyn concluded that the overall quality of leadership has been good or better in around three-quarters of primary schools and around a half of secondary schools. These proportions have changed little during recent years (Estyn, 2018[42]). It also found that in a quarter of primary schools and two-fifths of secondary schools, leadership requires improvement. In these schools, there is a lack of strategic direction that focuses on improving outcomes for students. Their leaders have not established a culture of professional learning where staff have open and honest discussions about their own practice and its impact on student learning and outcomes. As a result of these and other shortcomings, leaders are not well prepared for their role in supporting teachers to improve their practice (Estyn, 2018[42]).

In recent years, the Welsh Government has shown a clear intention to develop leadership capacity across the education system, but many national-level efforts to foster leadership seem to have either stalled or are still in the planning and design phase (OECD, 2017[29]). An important step forward has been the recent establishment of the National Academy for Educational Leadership (in June 2018). The academy has the mandate to promote leadership across education, including senior and middle-level leaders in schools, local authority education staff, and Welsh Government education officials. The academy will also consider the structure of qualifications of head teachers, including the NPQH, and develop career routes for aspiring head teachers.

Support staff

The proportion of support staff in Wales is high compared to other OECD countries (OECD, 2014[1]). In January 2017 there were 23 559 full-time equivalent support staff in public schools; comparing this with the number of full-time equivalent qualified teachers and school leaders means support staff make up more than half (54%) of the total staff in schools in Wales (Welsh Government, 2017[23]).

Wales does not currently require its support staff to have specific qualifications, including those deployed in the classroom to support teachers and work directly with students (i.e. higher level teaching assistants, teaching assistants, foreign language assistants, special needs support staff). This group of support staff make up the majority of support staff and in Wales are often referred to as "learning support workers".

In 2007, the Higher Level Teaching Assistants policy was introduced to determine and recognise teaching assistants who meet the teaching assistant standards, but this is not mandatory. Since April 2016, however, support staff are required to register with the Education Workforce Council, which regulates teachers and support staff in Wales (see below). This is intended to help build a more detailed picture of Wales' support staff, what they do and what qualifications they have. It is also aimed at offering essential assurances to students, parents and the public about the credentials, conduct and performance of support staff (Education Workforce Council, 2017[39]). The government's action plan, *Education in Wales: Our National Mission*, also states plans to develop professional standards for support staff working directly with students, i.e. learning support workers, to enable them to improve their skills, commit to professional learning and facilitate clearer pathways to the role of Higher Level Teaching Assistant (Welsh Government, 2017[6]).

Appraisal and performance management of school staff

Teachers' and school leaders' appraisals are expected to be conducted on a yearly basis within schools as part of their performance management. Teachers are normally reviewed by their direct line managers, which might include members of the school leadership team, while school leaders are appraised by a panel comprising members of the school governing board and local authority representatives. For both school leaders and teachers, objectives are set and reviewed during performance management discussions, which can help address their professional learning needs. All practising teachers and formal leaders are as mentioned expected to use the new teaching and leadership standards by 1 September 2018.

Support staff are currently not required to go through appraisals. It appears however that many schools do ensure they are appraised and these form an integrated part of the school's performance management. Despite these mechanisms, appraisals remain underdeveloped in Wales (Education Workforce Council, 2017[39]; OECD, 2014[1]).

Governance of the school system

Since the devolution settlement in 1999, Wales, like Scotland and Northern Ireland, has had responsibility for nearly all areas of education policy, except for teachers' pay and working conditions. However, as mentioned above, a new amendment was included in the Wales Act 2017 to devolve teachers' pay and conditions to the National Assembly and the Welsh Government in the coming years (Parliament of the United Kingdom, 2017[13]).

The Welsh Government's Education Directorate is the highest-level planner and policy maker (Tier 1 in Figure 1.3) and is responsible for administering all levels of education, except for further and higher education. Although the overall responsibility for the school system lies in the hands of the Directorate, the 22 local authorities in Wales are responsible for direct allocations of funding to publicly funded schools (see Chapters 4 and 5) and for supporting vulnerable students. The local authorities work closely with the governing bodies of education institutions and the four regional consortia, collectively considered to be the second tier of governance.

Figure 1.3. The education system three-tier model

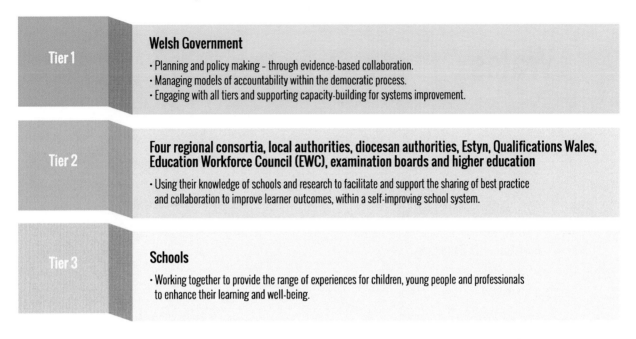

Source: Welsh Government (2017[6]), *Education in Wales: Our National Mission*, http://gov.wales/docs/dcells/publications/170926-education-in-wales-en.pdf.

Wales established the regional consortia in 2012 to help local authorities streamline their school improvement services and to reshape local school improvement functions. Their profiles vary (see Figure 1.4 and Table 1.2). In 2014 the Welsh Government established its National Model for Regional Working that further clarified the consortia's core responsibilities and services (Welsh Government, 2016[43]). These include challenge and support strategies to improve the teaching and learning in classrooms, collating data from local authorities and schools on school and student performance and progress, using that data for improvements, and delivery of the national system for categorising schools. The model has helped promote improvements in the quality of services the regional consortia provide to schools and signalled a deeper commitment to regional working. It emphasised a model of school improvement based on mutual support that was largely new across most of Wales.

Figure 1.4. Map of regional consortia and local authorities in Wales

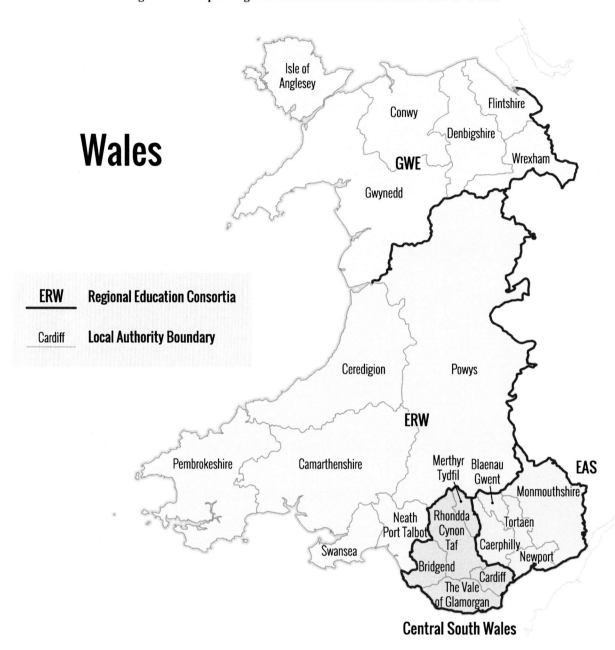

Note: Wales has four regional school improvement services. Gwasanaeth Effeithiolrwydd (GwE) in North Wales; Ein Rhanbarth ar Waith (ERW) in South West and Mid Wales; Education Achievement Service (EAS) in South East Wales; and Central South Consortium (CSC) in Central South Wales.
Source: Crown Copyright and database right 2014, Ordnance Survey 100021874, Cartographics, Welsh Government, January 2014.

Table 1.2. Profiles of the four regional consortia in Wales

Regional profile indicators	Gwasanaeth Effeithiolrwydd (GwE), North Wales	Ein Rhanbarth ar Waith (ERW), South West and Mid Wales	Education Achievement Service (EAS), South East Wales	Central South Consortium (CSC), Central South Wales
Percentage of students in Wales	22	28	19	31
Number of public schools	439 public schools; 28% of all public schools	513 public schools; 32% of all public schools	245 public schools; 15% of all public schools	398 public schools; 25% of all public schools
Percentage of self-reported Welsh speakers aged 3+ (Welsh average 19%)	31	24	10	11
Percentage of students eligible for free school meals (Welsh average 19%)	16	17.5	20.8	20.7
Percentage of population belonging to an ethnic minority	2	4	4	7
Percentage of looked-after children in Wales	18	27	19	36

Note: Children in care are children who are "looked after" by a local authority under the Children Act 1989 and Social Services and Well-being Act 2014.

Source: Estyn (2016[41]), *A Report on the Quality of the School Improvement Services Provided by the ERW Consortium,* www.estyn.gov.wales/sites/default/files/documents/ERW%20Eng.pdf; Estyn (2017[44]), *A Report on the Quality of the School Improvement Services Provided by the EAS Consortium,* www.estyn.gov.wales/sites/default/files/documents/EAS%20Consortium.pdf; Estyn (2017[45]), *A Report on the Quality of the School Improvement Services Provided by the Central South Consortium,* www.estyn.gov.wales/sites/default/files/documents/Central%20South%20Consortium_0.pdf; Estyn (2017[46]), *A Report on the Quality of the School Improvement Services Provided by the North Wales Consortium,* www.estyn.gov.wales/sites/default/files/documents/GwE_1.pdf.

Schools, networks of schools and school communities (Tier 3) have an evolving role in the co-construction of education policy. These local-level stakeholders are increasingly considered a primary resource for designing and putting in practice sustainable and innovative policies and practices. The development of the new school curriculum through the Pioneer Schools Network is a case in point.

Estyn, Her Majesty's Inspectorate for Education and Training in Wales, is responsible for inspecting the education system. This includes pre-school education, public and private schools, initial teacher education, further educational institutions, local authorities, and the regional consortia. To assess these various actors and levels of the education system, Estyn uses different components of the Common Inspection Framework (Estyn, 2017[47]). From September 2017, Estyn applied a new inspection framework that focused on five aspects: 1) standards; 2) well-being and attitudes to learning; 3) teaching and learning experiences; 4) care, support and guidance; and 5) leadership and management. Schools are judged using a 4 point scale:

- Excellent – Very strong, sustained performance and practice

- Good – Strong features, although minor aspects may require improvement

- Adequate and needs improvement – Strengths outweigh weaknesses, but important aspects require improvement

- Unsatisfactory and needs urgent improvement – Important weaknesses outweigh strengths.

Schools receive 15 working days' written notice of an inspection. Inspection reports are aimed to be shorter than before and focus more on actions to be taken to support improvement, with a follow-up by the inspection and support by the providers and the local authority. The new inspection period lasts seven years so the aim is for all schools to be inspected at least once during this period.

While writing this report however an independent review into the role of Estyn in supporting education reform in Wales was ongoing (Donaldson, 2018[48]). The review report was released in June 2018 and contained 34 recommendations. Welsh Government and Her Majesty's Chief Inspector of Education and Training had not responded to the report's recommendations at the time of finalising this report. It is expected however that the review report will result in changes to the inspection framework (see Chapter 4).

The Education Workforce Council (EWC) was established in 2014. The EWC acts as an independent regulatory body for teachers in public schools and further education institutions and is responsible for safeguarding the interests of learners, parents and the public; and maintaining trust and confidence in the education workforce (Eurydice, 2016[26]). It also plays a role in improving teaching and professional learning through several reform initiatives, such as the development of the Professional Learning Passport mentioned above. The Education Workforce Council has fourteen members. Seven members are directly appointed through the Welsh Government public appointments system and seven members are appointed following nomination from a range of stakeholders. Council members are appointed for a period of four years. The Council sets the strategic direction for the EWC, and is responsible for its governance.

Qualifications Wales was established in 2015 as the independent regulator of qualifications in Wales. It aims to ensure that the qualifications system effectively meets the needs of learners and the economy while promoting public confidence in Welsh qualifications. Currently, Qualifications Wales does not have awarding functions, but regulates non-degree qualifications, general qualifications such GCSEs and Advanced Levels (A Levels),[4] and vocational qualifications. It has already introduced new GCSEs that aim to emphasise students' understanding of concepts and the ability to function in various types of situations – similar to how skills are assessed in OECDs Programme for International Student Assessment (PISA) (Welsh Government, 2014[49]). It furthermore revised the Welsh Baccalaureate and A Level qualifications in 2015 (Qualifications Wales, 2015[50]).

Student performance

The PISA 2015 results showed that students in Wales performed below the OECD average in the mathematics, reading and science tests (see Figure 1.5). Although the data suggests student performance had improved compared to PISA 2012, their performance in science was worse than in previous PISA cycles (OECD, 2016[51]). The mean performance in PISA 2015 in Wales was:

- 478 score points in mathematics, 10 points higher than the score in 2012 but still below the OECD average (490 score points). Wales performed below England (493), Northern Ireland (493) and Scotland (491), but above the United States and similar to Lithuania, Malta and Hungary.

- 477 score points in reading, significantly below the OECD average (493 score points), England (500), Northern Ireland (497) and Scotland (493) and similar to Luxembourg, Lithuania and Iceland.

- 485 score points in science, below the OECD average (493 score points), England (512), Northern Ireland (500) and Scotland (497), but similar to Latvia, Russia, Luxembourg and Italy.

Figure 1.5. PISA results for Wales (2006-15)

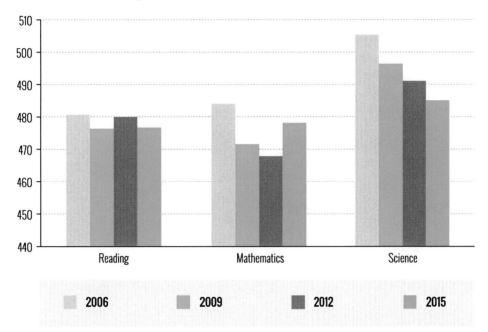

Note: In 2015 changes were made to the test design, administration, and scaling of PISA. These changes add statistical uncertainty to trend comparisons that should be taken into account when comparing 2015 results to those from prior years. Please see the Reader's Guide and Annex A5 of *PISA 2015 Results (Volume I): Excellence and Equity in Education* (OECD, 2016[51]) for a detailed discussion of these changes.
Source: OECD (2016[51]), *PISA 2015 Results (Volume I): Excellence and Equity in Education*, http://dx.doi.org/10.1787/9789264266490-en; OECD (2014[52]), *PISA 2012 Results: What Students Know and Can Do (Volume I, Revised edition, February 2014): Student Performance in Mathematics, Reading and Science*, http://dx.doi.org/10.1787/9789264208780-en; OECD (2010[53]) *PISA 2009 Results: What Students Know and Can Do: Student Performance in Reading, Mathematics and Science (Volume I)*, http://dx.doi.org/10.1787/9789264091450-en; OECD (OECD, 2007[54]), *PISA 2006: Science Competencies for Tomorrow's World: Volume 1: Analysis*, http://dx.doi.org/10.1787/9789264040014-en.

StatLink ⫘⫘ http://dx.doi.org/10.1787/888933837188

National student performance data show that results are slightly improving, although there are some comparability issues as several changes have been made in the way student performance is measured at Key Stage 4. These changes are a result of a 2011 review of qualifications for 14-19 year-olds (Welsh Government, 2012[55]). Reporting on school performance is based on the assessment results of students enrolled in Year 11 (aged 15). Overall performance figures now include data on children who are educated other than at school and no longer include results for independent schools (Welsh Government, 2016[56]). This creates year-to-year comparability issues but the figures suggest that examination results are slightly on the rise. In 2016/17, close to 55% of students in Year 11 achieved the Level 2 threshold in each of the core subjects,[5] meaning that these students achieved GCSE at grades A*-C in English or Welsh language and mathematics; under the former system this translates to roughly 1.8 percentage points higher than the previous year (Welsh Government, 2016[56]).

Wales has a relatively equitable education system according to the PISA results. PISA 2015 suggests that students' socio-economic background in Wales has less impact on their performance than for students in other parts of the United Kingdom. Less than 6% of the variation in student performance in science is associated with students' socio-economic status in Wales, which is significantly lower than the OECD average (13%) and other UK countries (see Figure 1.6). The difference in science scores between the most disadvantaged students and the most advantaged is also only 52 points, whereas in England, Northern Ireland and Scotland this difference is at least 80 points (OECD, 2016[51]).

Figure 1.6. Science performance and equity (PISA 2015)

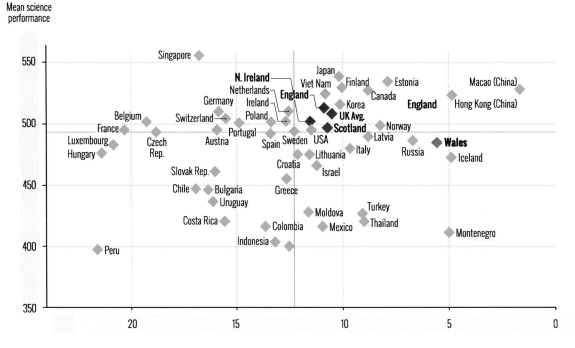

Source: OECD (2016[51]), *PISA 2015 Results (Volume I): Excellence and Equity in Education,* http://dx.doi.org/10.1787/9789264266490-en.

StatLink ⟨msl⟩ http://dx.doi.org/10.1787/888933837207

However, Wales still faces a number of equity challenges, including large performance variability within schools. In addition, many students are low performers and there are few high performers. For the 2015 PISA mathematics assessment, for example, 23% of students did not achieve the Level 2 threshold – similar to the OECD average, which is considered the baseline level of proficiency needed to fully participate in society.

Furthermore, although the gap between students who receive free school meals (FSMs), a proxy measure of students living in poverty, and those that don't (i.e. non-FSM students) has steadily decreased across the years, their performance is still lower at all levels of education (Welsh Government, 2016[57]).

School performance

In addition to school self-evaluations, school performance is externally evaluated in Wales through Estyn inspections and the national school categorisation system; two different approaches that are considered by many to be not well aligned (OECD, 2017[29]).

Starting with the first of these, over the period 2010-17 Estyn carried out some 2 700 inspections. All education and training providers in Wales were inspected at least once during this six year inspection cycle. Inspections were guided by a common inspection framework aimed to bring greater consistency and transparency to the inspection of all education functions across the system in Wales, including schools, other education providers and local authorities through its Common Inspection Framework (OECD, 2014[1]). An Estyn inspection results in an inspection report that highlights recommendations for improvement and results in a grading of schools into four categories: "excellent", "good", "adequate and needs improvement", and "unsatisfactory and needs urgent improvement". The introduction of inspection follow-ups is believed to have helped make inspection more proportionate, as well as focusing attention onto the schools that need it most (OECD, 2014[1]).

Estyn's annual report 2016-17 shows that almost eight out of ten of primary schools had good or excellent provision (Estyn, 2018[42]). This judgement is based on an assessment of students' learning experiences, teaching, support and the learning environment. Outcomes were more polarised at the secondary level: the share of excellent schools rose to 16%, higher than any year since 2010, but the share of unsatisfactory schools also increased (Estyn, 2015[58]; Estyn, 2016[59]).

Overall, Estyn's 2016-17 annual report reveals that half (50%) of the secondary schools it inspected have good or excellent outcomes. The share of secondary schools judged to be good or excellent for their provision decreased from 72% in 2013-14 to 58% in 2016-17 (Estyn, 2015[58]; Estyn, 2018[42]) although this trend needs to be interpreted with some caution because of the small sample sizes. Estyn notes inconsistency in the quality of teaching or assessments as one of the main factors influencing the performance of secondary schools.

In September 2017 Estyn as mentioned revised its inspection framework. As part of this new framework, Estyn plans to move away from overall judgements in favour of paragraphs summarising findings that focus on actions to support improvement – a positive development that fits well with the directions set out for the new curriculum. The cycle of Estyn inspections is also extended to seven years to allow schools enough time to implement changes, while following up with low-performing schools to monitor improvements more closely. Further changes to Estyn inspections are envisaged in response to the independent review into the role of Estyn in supporting education reform in Wales as will be elaborated in Chapter 4.

Since 2014 a national school categorisation system has been in place; a system that combines school self-evaluation with external evaluation or review by challenge advisors of the regional consortia. Developed collectively by the regional consortia and the Welsh Government, this system identifies schools most in need of support over a three-year period, using a three-step colour coding strategy. Step 1 assesses publicly available school performance data and Step 2 the school's own self-evaluation in respect to leadership, learning and teaching. Challenge advisors examine how the school's self-evaluation corresponds to the performance data under Step 1. This is intended to ensure the process is robust. Under Step 3, judgements reached in the first two steps lead to an overall judgement and a corresponding categorisation of each school into one of four colours: green, yellow, amber and red. Categorisation then triggers a tailored programme of support, challenge and intervention agreed by the local authority and the regional consortia (Welsh Government, 2016[43]).

Although national school categorisation in general is considered an improvement on the system it replaced ("school banding"), it is still perceived by some as a high-stakes exercise and may stigmatise professionals and schools working in the most challenging communities (OECD, 2017[29]). The lack of synergies between Estyn inspections and the national categorisation system has been recognised as an area for improvement. Chapter 4 will elaborate on this issue.

Conclusion

Wales finds itself in the middle of an ambitious curriculum reform, aimed at the successful implementation, or as it is often referred to in Wales the "realisation" of the new curriculum in all schools across Wales by September 2022. The reform approach taken by the Welsh Government can be characterised by a drive for greater policy coherence and a process of construction of policies with stakeholders across the three "tiers" of Wales' education system. This chapter has highlighted some of the changes and new policy initiatives taken in recent years to enable schools to make the transition to the new curriculum.

The Welsh Government and other stakeholders however recognise it will take sustained effort to achieve this objective. In many cases teachers, learning support workers, school leaders and many others involved will need to expand their skills (Donaldson, 2015[5]; Welsh Government, 2017[6]). As such, the Welsh Government considers the development of schools as learning organisations essential for putting the curriculum into practice in schools throughout Wales (Welsh Government, 2017[7]).

This report (*Developing Schools as Learning Organisations in Wales*) aims to support Wales in realising this objective. It assesses the extent to which schools in Wales have developed as learning organisations and as such gives an indication of schools' "readiness for change". It identifies areas for further improvement at both school- and system levels. The assessment has been guided by three questions:

1. To what extent do the key characteristics of a learning organisation already exist in schools in Wales? (see Chapters 2 and 3).

2. Are the system-level policies enabling (or hindering) schools to develop in learning organisations? (see Chapter 4).

3. How to ensure the effective implementation or "realisation" of Wales' schools as learning organisations policy? (see Chapter 5).

These last two questions stem from the knowledge that although many actions proposed by Wales' schools as learning organisation model (Welsh Government, 2017[7]) are within the control of schools, local authorities, parents and communities, some warrant policy action and a conducive context to enable and empower them to make this transformation.

The analysis has allowed the formulation of several points for reflection and action for schools, as well as a number of concrete policy recommendations that are aimed at empowering schools and local partners to develop their schools as learning organisations.

Notes

[1] The total fertility rate in a specific year is defined as the total number of children that would be born to each woman if she were to live to the end of her child-bearing years and give birth to children in alignment with the prevailing age-specific fertility rates. It is calculated by totalling the age-specific fertility rates as defined over five-year intervals (OECD, 2018[16]).

[2] Living in relative income poverty is defined as when a person is living in a household where the total household income from all sources is less than 60% of the average UK household income (as given by the median) (Welsh Government, 2018[22]).

[3] The Special Educational Needs Code of Practice for Wales (Welsh Assembly Government, 2004[61]) defines that children have special educational needs if they have a learning difficulty which calls for special educational provision to be made for them. Children have a learning difficulty if they: (a) have a significantly greater difficulty in learning than the majority of children of the same age; or (b) have a disability which prevents or hinders them from making use of educational facilities of a kind generally provided for children of the same age in schools within the area of the local education authority and (c) are under compulsory school age and fall within the definition at (a) or (b) above or would so do if special educational provision was not made for them.

[4] General Certificates of Secondary Education (GCSEs) are the main Level 1 and Level 2 general qualifications for 14-19 year-olds in Wales. They are available in a wide range of subjects and are compulsory. A-Levels are the main general qualifications for Level 3 and are usually taken at age 16-19. They can be used as a basis for higher level study or training, or direct entry into employment (Qualifications Wales, 2015[50]).

[5] For students in Key Stage 4, learning outcomes and objectives are contained within subject criteria for General Certificate of Secondary Education (GCSE) examinations. GCSEs are examinations in single subjects taken at the end of Key Stage 4. The pass grades, from highest to lowest, are: A* ("A-star"), A, B, C, D, E, F and G. Grade U (ungraded/unclassified) is issued when students have not achieved the minimum standard to achieve a pass grade; the subject is then not included on their final certificate. A GCSE at grades D–G is a Level 1 qualification, while a GCSE at grades A*–C is a Level 2 qualification. GCSEs at A*-C (Level 2) are much more valued by employers and educational institutions. Level 1 qualifications are required to advance to Level 2 qualifications. Likewise, Level 2 qualifications are required to advance to Level 3 qualifications (Eurydice, 2012[60]).

References

Donaldson, G. (2018), *A Learning Inspectorate*, https://www.estyn.gov.wales/sites/default/files/documents/A%20Learning%20Inspectorate%20-%20en%20-%20June%202018.pdf. [48]

Donaldson, G. (2015), *Successful Futures: Independent Review of Curriculum and Assessment Arrangements in Wales*, Welsh Government, http://gov.wales/docs/dcells/publications/150225-successful-futures-en.pdf. [5]

Duggan, B., H. Thomas and S. Lewis (2014), "Evaluation of the Welsh-medium education strategy: Review of the Welsh-language sabbatical scheme for educational practitioners: Participant experiences 2011-2012", *Social Research* 04/2014. [30]

Education Workforce Council (2017), *National Education Workforce Survey, Research Report, April 2017*, Education Workforce Council, Cardiff. [39]

Estyn (2018), *The Annual Report of Her Majesty's Chief Inspector of Education and Training in Wales 2016-2017*, Estyn, Cardiff, https://www.estyn.gov.wales/document/annual-report-2016-2017. [42]

Estyn (2017), *Changes to inspection arrangements from September 2017*, Estyn, http://www.estyn.gov.wales/changes-inspection-arrangements-september-2017 (accessed on 29 August 2017). [47]

Estyn (2017), *Report Following the Monitoring of GwE Consortium*, Estyn, Cardiff. [46]

Estyn (2017), *Report Following the Monitoring Visit to the Central South Consortium*, Estyn, Cardiff. [45]

Estyn (2017), *Report Following the Monitoring Visit to the EAS Consortium*, Estyn, Cardiff. [44]

Estyn (2016), *A Report on the Quality of the School Improvement Services Provided by the ERW Consortium*, Estyn , Cardiff, http://www.estyn.gov.wales/sites/default/files/documents/ERW%20Eng.pdf. [41]

Estyn (2016), *The Annual Report of Her Majesty's Chief Inspector of Education and Training in Wales 2014-2015*, Estyn, Cardiff, http://www.estyn.gov.wales/sites/default/files/documents/ESTYN_Annual%20Report%202016%20FINAL_ENGLISH_Accessible_WEB.pdf. [59]

Estyn (2016), *The Impact of the Additional Training Graduate Programme (Teach First)*, https://www.estyn.gov.wales/sites/default/files/documents/Thematic%20survey%20report%20teach%20first.pdf. [38]

Estyn (2015), *The Annual Report of Her Majesty's Chief Inspector of Education and Training in Wales 2013-2014*, Estyn, Cardiff, http://www.estyn.gov.wales/sites/default/files/documents/The_Annual_Report_of_Her_Majestys_Chief_Inspector_of_Education_and_Training_in_Wales_2013-2014.pdf. [58]

Estyn (2013), *The Annual Report of Her Majesty's Chief Inspector of Education and Training in Wales 2011-12*, Estyn, Cardiff. [3]

Eurostat (2018), *Gross Domestic Product (GDP) at Current Market Prices by NUTS 2 Regions*, Eurostat, http://appsso.eurostat.ec.europa.eu/nui/show.do (accessed on 17 August 2017). [18]

Eurydice (2016), *Overview: United Kingdom (Wales)*, Eurydice, https://webgate.ec.europa.eu/fpfis/mwikis/eurydice/index.php/United-Kingdom-Wales:Overview. [26]

Eurydice (2012), *Key Competences in the Curriculum – Wales, Eurydice in NFER Unit for England, Wales and Northern Ireland*, Eurydice, https://www.nfer.ac.uk/pdf/KeyCompetencesWales.pdf. [60]

Gurría, A. (2015), "21 for 21: A proposal for consolidation and further transformation of the OECD", OECD, Paris, https://www.oecd.org/about/secretary-general/21-for-21-A-Proposal-for-Consolidation-and-Further-Transformation-of-the-OECD.pdf. [8]

Hill, R. (2013), *The Future Delivery of Education Services in Wales*, Department for Education and Skills, Welsh Government, http://gov.wales/docs/dcells/consultation/130621-delivery-of-education-report-en.pdf. [2]

Jones, S. (2017), *Ministerial Supply Model Taskforce: Report to the Cabinet Secretary for Education*, Department for Education and Skills, Welsh Government, http://learning.gov.wales/docs/learningwales/publications/170201-supply-model-taskforce-en.pdf. [12]

OECD (2018), *Fertility rates* (indicator), http://dx.doi.org/10.1787/8272fb01-en (accessed on 14 March 2018). [16]

OECD (2017), *The Welsh Education Reform Journey: A Rapid Policy Assessment*, OECD, Paris, http://www.oecd.org/edu/The-Welsh-Education-Reform-Journey-FINAL.pdf. [29]

OECD (2017), *Unemployment rate* (indicator), http://dx.doi.org/10.1787/997c8750-en (accessed on 20 September 2017). [19]

OECD (2016), *Education at a Glance 2016: OECD Indicators*, OECD Publishing, Paris, http://dx.doi.org/10.1787/eag-2016-en. [36]

OECD (2016), *PISA 2015 Results (Volume I): Excellence and Equity in Education*, OECD Publishing, Paris, http://dx.doi.org/10.1787/9789264266490-en. [51]

OECD (2014), *Improving Schools in Wales: An OECD Perspective*, OECD Publishing, Paris, http://www.oecd.org/edu/Improving-schools-in-Wales.pdf. [1]

OECD (2014), *PISA 2012 Results: What Students Know and Can Do (Volume I, Revised edition, February 2014): Student Performance in Mathematics, Reading and Science*, OECD Publishing, Paris, http://dx.doi.org/10.1787/9789264208780-en. [52]

OECD (2010), *PISA 2009 Results: What Students Know and Can Do: Student Performance in Reading, Mathematics and Science (Volume I)*, OECD Publishing, Paris, http://dx.doi.org/10.1787/9789264091450-en. [53]

OECD (2007), *PISA 2006: Science Competencies for Tomorrow's World: Volume 1: Analysis*, OECD Publishing, Paris, http://dx.doi.org/10.1787/9789264040014-en. [54]

Office for National Statistics (2017), *National Population Projections*, Office for National Statistics, https://gov.wales/statistics-and-research/national-population-projections/?lang=en. [17]

Office for National Statistics (2016), *Population Estimates for UK, England and Wales, Scotland and Northern Ireland: Mid-2016*, Office for National Statistics, https://www.ons.gov.uk/peoplepopulationandcommunity/populationandmigration/populatione stimates/bulletins/annualmidyearpopulationestimates/mid2016 (accessed on 24 August 2017). [10]

Parliament of the United Kingdom (2017), *Wales Act 2017*, Parliament of the United Kingdom. [13]

Qualifications Wales (2015), *What's changed since September 2015*, Qualifications Wales website, http://qualificationswales.org/schools-and-colleges/changes-for-sept-2015/?lang=en. [50]

StatsWales (2017), *Mid-year Population Estimates (1991 Onwards), by Welsh Local Authorities, English Regions and UK Countries, for Single Year of Age and Gender*, https://statswales.gov.wales/Catalogue/Population-and-Migration/Population/Estimates/nationallevelpopulationestimates-by-year-age-ukcountry. [15]

StatsWales (2016), *European Union harmonised unemployment rates by gender, area and year*, Welsh Government, https://statswales.gov.wales/Catalogue/Business-Economy-and-Labour-Market/People-and-Work/Unemployment/ILO-Unemployment/ilo-unemployment-europeanunionharmonisedunemploymentrates-by-gender-area-year. [21]

Viennet, R. and B. Pont (2017), "Education policy implementation: A literature review and proposed framework", *OECD Education Working Papers*, No. 162, OECD Publishing, Paris, http://dx.doi.org/10.1787/fc467a64-en. [9]

Welsh Assembly Government (2004), *The Special Educational Needs Code of Practice for Wales*, Welsh Assembly Government, http://learning.gov.wales/docs/learningwales/publications/131016-sen-code-of-practice-for-wales-en.pdf. [61]

Welsh Governement (2016), *National Professional Qualification for Headship - Assessment process*, http://learning.gov.wales/yourcareer/leadershipdevelopment/leadership-programmes/national-professional-qualification-for-headship/assessment-process/?lang=en (accessed on 02 October 2017). [40]

Welsh Government (2018), *Poverty statistics (formerly known as Households below average income)*, https://gov.wales/statistics-and-research/households-below-average-income/?lang=en (accessed on 25 August 2017). [22]

Welsh Government (2017), *Announcement of further Pioneer Schools focussing on curriculum design and development*, Ministerial statement, Welsh Government, http://gov.wales/about/cabinet/cabinetstatements/2017/pioneerschools/?lang=en. [34]

Welsh Government (2017), *Education in Wales: Our National Mission. Action plan 2017-21*, Welsh Government, Cardiff, http://gov.wales/docs/dcells/publications/170926-education-in-wales-en.pdf. [6]

Welsh Government (2017), "Key economic statistics - July 2017", *Statistical Bulletin*, Vol. 33, http://gov.wales/docs/statistics/2017/170718-key-economic-statistics-july-2017-en.pdf. [20]

Welsh Government (2017), *Professional Standards for Teaching and Leadership*, Welsh Government, Cardiff, http://learning.gov.wales/docs/learningwales/publications/170901-professional-standards-for-teaching-and-leadership-en.pdf. [33]

Welsh Government (2017), "School Census Results, 2017", *Statistical First Release* 77/2017, http://gov.wales/docs/statistics/2017/170726-school-census-results-2017-en.pdf. [23]

Welsh Government (2017), "Schools in Wales as learning organisations", *Welsh Government website*, http://gov.wales/topics/educationandskills/schoolshome/curriculuminwales/curriculum-for-wales-curriculum-for-life/schools-in-wales-as-learning-organisations/?lang=en (accessed on 30 November 2017). [7]

Welsh Government (2017), "Welsh Language (Cymraeg)", *Wales website*, http://www.wales.com/language (accessed on 17 August 2017). [11]

Welsh Government (2016), "Achievement and entitlement to free school meals", *Welsh Government website*, http://gov.wales/statistics-and-research/academic-achievement-free-school-meals/?lang=en (accessed on 17 August 2017). [57]

Welsh Government (2016), "Current Curriculum", *Learning Wales website*, http://learning.gov.wales/resources/improvementareas/curriculum/?lang=en (accessed on 02 October 2017). [31]

Welsh Government (2016), "Examination results in Wales, 2015/2016 (Provisonal)", *Statistical First Release*, Vol. 136, http://gov.wales/docs/statistics/2016/161012-examination-results-2015-16-provisional-en.pdf. [56]

Welsh Government (2016), *National School Categorisation System Guidance Document for Schools, Local Authorities and Regional Consortia, Guidance*, Welsh Government, Cardiff, http://gov.wales/docs/dcells/publications/150121-guidance-en-v3.pdf. [43]

Welsh Government (2016), *New rules to support rural schools in Wales unveiled – Kirsty Williams*, http://gov.wales/newsroom/educationandskills/2016/new-rules-to-support-rural-schools-in-wales-unveiled--kirsty-williams/?lang=en (accessed on 24 August 2017). [25]

Welsh Government (2016), "School Census Results, 2016", *Statistical First Release* 87/2016, http://gov.wales/docs/statistics/2016/160727-school-census-results-2016-en.pdf. [35]

Welsh Government (2015), *Curriculum for Wales: Foundation Phase Framework*, Department for Education and Skills, Welsh Government, http://gov.wales/docs/dcells/publications/150803-fp-framework-en.pdf. [28]

Welsh Government (2015), "Evaluating the Foundation Phase: Final report", *Social Research*, Vol. 25, http://gov.wales/docs/caecd/research/2015/150514-foundation-phase-final-en.pdf. [27]

Welsh Government (2015), *Qualified for Life: A Curriculum for Wales – A Curriculum for Life*, Welsh Government, Cardiff, http://gov.wales/docs/dcells/publications/151021-a-curriculum-for-wales-a-curriculum-for-life-en.pdf. [32]

Welsh Government (2014), *Qualified for Life: An Education Improvement Plan for 3 to 19-year-olds in Wales*, Welsh Government, Cardiff, http://gov.wales/topics/educationandskills/allsectorpolicies/qualified-for-life-an-educational-improvement-plan/?lang=en. [4]

Welsh Government (2014), *Qualified for Life: How Qualifications in Wales are Changing*, Welsh Government, Cardiff, http://learning.gov.wales/docs/learningwales/publications/140616-qualified-for-life-how-qualifications-in-wales-are-changing-en.pdf. [49]

Welsh Government (2013), *Teaching and Teaching Qualifications*, Welsh Government, Cardiff, https://gov.wales/docs/dcells/publications/240513-teaching-and-teachers-qualifications-en.pdf#page=5. [37]

Welsh Government (2012), *Review of Qualifications for 14 to 19-Year-Olds in Wales*, Welsh Government, Cardiff, http://gov.wales/docs/dcells/publications/121127reviewofqualificationsen.pdf. [55]

Welsh Government (2012), "School Census Results, 2012", *Statistical First Release* 108/2012, http://gov.wales/docs/statistics/2012/120711sdr1082012en.pdf. [24]

WLGA (2015), *Localism 2016-21: A Plan for Public Services in Wales*, Welsh Local Government Association, http://www.local.gov.uk/sites/default/files/documents/2-c81.pdf. [14]

Part II. The schools as learning organisations assessment

Chapter 2. Schools as learning organisations in Wales: A general assessment

This chapter explores the question of to what extent the key characteristics of learning organisations already exist in schools in Wales. It uses Wales' schools as learning organisations (SLO) model as point of reference for this. The chapter starts with a description of the model and its place in the curriculum reform. This is followed by an overall assessment of the extent to which schools in Wales have put into practice the dimensions of a learning organisation, identifying strengths and areas for further development.

This Schools as Learning Organisations Assessment suggests that the majority of schools in Wales are well on their way towards developing as SLOs. A considerable proportion of schools is however still far removed from realising this objective. Secondary schools clearly face more challenges in this, compared to primary schools. More critical reflections seem to be needed for deep learning and sustained progress to take place.

Introduction

Wales has formulated the ambition that all schools should develop as learning organisations, as they have the capacity to adapt more quickly and explore new approaches to improve learning and outcomes for all their students (Welsh Government, 2017[1]). The development of schools as learning organisations (SLOs) aims to support schools in putting the new curriculum into practice.

This study aims to support Wales in this effort. Drawing from multiple data sources, this chapter explores the question of to what extent the key characteristics of learning organisations already exist in schools in Wales. It uses Wales' schools as learning organisations model as point of reference for this (Welsh Government, 2017[2]).

The chapter starts with a description of the SLO model and its place in the education reform effort the country has embarked on. It follows with an overall assessment of the extent to which schools in Wales have put in practice the dimensions of the model, looking at strengths and challenges and areas for further development.

The school as learning organisation: A key component of education reform in Wales

The strategic education plan, *Education in Wales: Our National Mission* (2017–2021) (Welsh Government, 2017[1]) presents Wales' national vision for education and outlines how it aims to realise this in the years to come. Informed by an extensive review of the school curriculum and assessment and evaluation arrangements (Donaldson, 2015[3]), the vision calls for all children and young people to have access to a new, 21st century curriculum.

To be able to realise the curriculum's "four purposes" (see Chapter 1, Box 1.1), the vision suggests that children and young people in Wales will need to be highly literate and numerate, be increasingly bilingual, and be confident users of digital technology that will deepen their learning in all fields. The successful realisation of the new curriculum – the primary objective of the education strategy – requires a focus on four key enabling objectives:

1. developing a high-quality education profession

2. inspirational leaders working collaboratively to raise standards

3. strong and inclusive schools committed to excellence, equity and well-being

4. robust assessment, evaluation and accountability arrangements supporting a self-improving system (see).

Figure 2.1. Four key enabling objectives for delivering the new curriculum

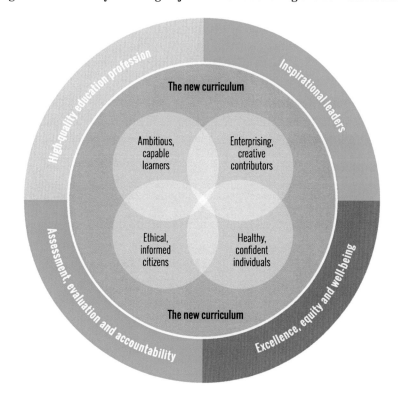

Source: Welsh Government (2017[1]), *Education in Wales: Our National Mission*, http://gov.wales/docs/dcells/publications/170926-education-in-wales-en.pdf.

Why develop schools in Wales into learning organisations?

The Welsh Government considers the development of SLOs (see Box 2.1) as vital for realising these four enabling objectives and supporting schools to put the new curriculum into practice. A growing body of research evidence shows that schools that operate as learning organisations can react more quickly to changing external environments and embrace changes and innovations in their internal organisation (Senge et al., 2012[4]; Silins, Zarins and Mulford, 2002[5]; Watkins and Marsick, 1999[6]).

The evidence furthermore shows a positive relationship between the development of a school as a learning organisation and a range of staff outcomes like job satisfaction, self-efficacy, readiness for change and experimentation (Schechter, 2008[7]; Silins, Mulford and Zarins, 2002[8]; Schechter and Qadach, 2012[9]; Erdem, İlğan and Uçar, 2014[10]; Razali, Amira and Shobri, 2013[11]).

Although this is an area for further research, some studies also show the SLO is positively associated with student outcomes (Caprara et al., 2006[12]; Klassen and Chiu, 2010[13]; Silins and Mulford, 2004[14]). More elaborate is the research evidence on the underlying dimensions that make up a SLO and their relationship with student outcomes. For example, there is a growing body of evidence that shows that teachers' and school leaders' professional learning (which are central to a SLO) can have a positive impact on student performance and their practice (Timperley et al., 2007[15]). Other studies have found evidence of a positive relationship between student outcomes and the development of a shared vision and directing teaching and learning in a school in line with this vision

(Leithwood and Day, 2007[16]; Silins and Mulford, 2004[14]), while other studies have shown how school leaders that focus on the development of the school culture can positively influence student outcomes (Leithwood and Day, 2007[16]; Robinson, 2007[17]). Kools and Stoll (2016[18]) drew heavily from these and other (school effectiveness) studies when proposing their SLO model – that in turn informed the development of Wales' SLO model.

Wales recognises it will require concerted effort to put the new curriculum into practice and in many cases the teachers, learning support workers (i.e. higher level teaching assistants, teaching assistants, foreign language assistants, special needs support staff), school leaders and many others involved will need to expand their skills (Donaldson, 2015[3]; Welsh Government, 2017[1]).

Previous OECD reviews and other reports have pointed to several challenges in this regard, including those relating to the capacity of teaching staff to conduct quality assessments and differentiated teaching approaches, as well as challenges in terms of the quality of some school leaders and leaders at other parts of the system (OECD, 2014[19]; OECD, 2017[20]; Estyn, 2018[21]). As such, the development of a thriving learning culture in schools and other parts of the education system is expected to play a pivotal role in putting the curriculum into practice in schools throughout Wales. To this end, Wales has developed an SLO model for Wales (Box 2.1).

Co-constructing the schools as learning organisations model in Wales

The Welsh Government aims for all reforms and policies in education – from the classroom to the system level – to be geared towards supporting the realisation of the curriculum. "Policy coherence" and "co-construction" of policies are key phrases characterising the national approach to reform (Welsh Government, 2017[1]). For example, guided by the four purposes of the new curriculum, the new teaching and leadership standards were developed by the education profession and other key stakeholders. The standards are aligned with Wales' ambitions for the new school curriculum.

Box 2.1. The schools as learning organisations model for Wales

The SLO model for Wales focuses the efforts of school leaders, teachers, support staff, parents, (local) policy makers and all others involved into realising seven dimensions in its schools (see Figure 2.2). These seven action-oriented dimensions and their underlying elements highlight both what a school should aspire to and the processes it goes through as it transforms itself into a learning organisation. All seven dimensions need to be implemented for this transformation to be complete and sustainable.

Figure 2.2. The schools as learning organisations model for Wales

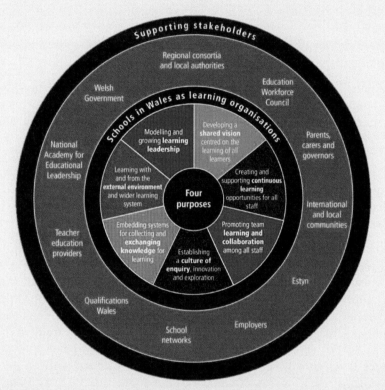

The realisation of the "four purposes" of the new school curriculum is placed at the heart of the model. These refer to developing children and young people into "ambitious capable and lifelong learners, enterprising and creative, informed citizens and healthy and confident individuals".

Source: Welsh Government (2017[21]), "Schools in Wales as learning organisations", https://beta.gov.wales/schools-learning-organisations.

Wales' SLO model has been designed through a similar process of co-construction and deliberate efforts to ensure policy coherence, with particular reference to the new teacher and leadership standards. The model has been developed by a specifically established Schools as Learning Organisations Pilot Group, which is part of the Professional Development and Learning Pioneer Schools Network (see Chapter 1, Box 1.2) that is supporting the development and implementation of the new school curriculum. Pilot group members consisted of representatives of 24 Pioneer Schools, the regional consortia, Estyn, the National Academy for Educational Leadership, the Education Directorate of the Welsh Government and the OECD. Informed by the OECD Education Working Paper "What makes a school a learning organisation?" (Kools and Stoll, 2016[18]), the developmental work was shaped through a series of workshops and meetings that were facilitated by the OECD between November 2016 and July 2017.

The result of this collective effort is the SLO model for Wales; a model intended to stimulate thinking and offer practical guidance on how school staff can individually and collectively learn together to transform their schools into a learning organisation (Welsh Government, 2017[2]). The model offers an approach where schools can self-evaluate against seven dimensions as an integrated part of their self-evaluations and use the results to inform school development planning (see Chapter 4).

Schools as learning organisations in Wales: Overall assessment

To what extent do the characteristics of learning organisations already exist in schools in Wales?

The starting point for getting an insight into the answer to this question was the SLO survey data – which were enriched and triangulated with multiple sources of data and information (see Box 2.2). The SLO survey data were analysed at both the individual level and school level (see Annex 2.A), with particular reference to the latter in this chapter. This is because the SLO is an organisational concept and ideally should be analysed to get an insight into the extent to which a school – in the eyes of its staff – has already put in practice the SLO dimensions. Annex 2.A explains how the responses by school leaders, teachers and learning support staff were aggregated and weighted to define an average school score for each of the SLO dimensions.

Following discussions with the SLO Pilot Group in Wales (see above), no threshold for the minimal number of dimensions was defined to be put in practice for a school to be considered a learning organisation. For the purpose of discussing the SLO survey data and getting an insight into the question raised above, however, the OECD team found it necessary to define a threshold for when a school could be considered to have put a SLO dimension into practice. The discussions with the SLO Pilot Group resulted in a threshold of an average school score of 4 or more across the survey items that make up the dimension (see Box 2.2 and Annex 2.B). In other words, school staff on average had to "agree" or "strongly agree" that their school has put in practice the SLO dimension.

Whether school-level or individual-level data are used is explained in the text and the notes below the figures also make this explicit.

Box 2.2. How was the Schools as Learning Organisation Assessment conducted?

To examine the question to what extent schools in Wales have realised the key characteristics of learning organisations, the team used various quantitative and qualitative data sources, allowing the analysis to be deepened and to triangulate the findings (see Figure 2.3).

Figure 2.3. Main sources of data and information

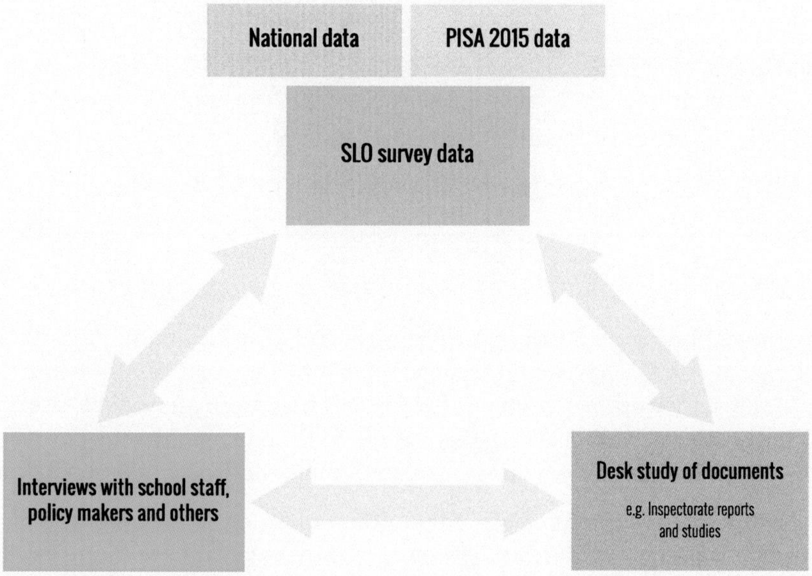

Eight schools across Wales were visited by the OECD team in June and July 2017. More than 80 school leaders, teachers and learning support workers were interviewed through semi-structured interviews, and the OECD team were able to speak to a large number of students. Two schools were visited in each of the four regions of Wales; one primary school and one secondary school in each. Other selection criteria concerned the variance in school performance, meaning a range of "stronger" and "weaker" performing schools according to Estyn inspections or the national school categorisation system (see Chapter 1).

In addition, the Schools as Learning Organisations Survey (see Annex 2.B) was used to collect the views of school leaders, teachers and teaching support staff on a number of statements that correspond to Wales' SLO model. The SLO survey items were phrased as statements, and asked school staff to reflect on the situation in their school in the 12 months prior to the survey, using a five-point Likert scale: 1 = strongly disagree, 2 = disagree, 3 = neutral, 4 = agree, 5 = strongly agree. In addition, an open question gave respondents the option to highlight anything they considered important for the OECD team to know.

Staff from a random sample of 571 schools (38% of primary, middle and secondary schools in Wales in 2017) were asked to complete the online SLO survey. A total of 1 703 school staff – 194 head teachers, 87 deputy head teachers, 55 assistant head teachers, 811 teachers and 382 learning support workers – from 178 different schools throughout Wales did so, thereby providing valuable insights on the extent to which their schools have put the dimensions of a learning organisation into practice, and the challenges and opportunities they faced in this.

Furthermore, the team linked administrative data available on the My Local School website (http://mylocalschool.wales.gov.uk/?lang=cy) to the SLO survey data to deepen and extend the analysis, including by exploring some of the factors believed to influence schools developing as learning organisations (e.g. school size and school type).

In addition, the analysis was enriched with interviews with school staff, policy makers and other stakeholders the OECD team spoke to during several visits to Wales, a desk research of documents and data, such as Estyn reports and studies, and data from OECD's Programme for International Student Assessment (PISA) 2015, which allowed for triangulation of research findings.

The preliminary findings of the Schools as Learning Organisations Assessment (Chapters 2 to 3) were also discussed with a large number of stakeholders during two meetings in Wales, allowing for their validation and further refinement where needed.

Overview of progress of schools developing into learning organisations

The data presented in Figure 2.4 suggest that three out of every ten schools in the sample (30%) had put all of the seven dimensions of a learning organisation into practice – according to the staff working in them. The data furthermore show that three out of ten schools in the sample (28%) had put five or six SLO dimensions into practice – which suggests they are well on their way towards developing into learning organisations.

Figure 2.4 however also shows that more than four out of ten schools in the sample (42%) seem to need to make greater efforts if they are to develop into learning organisations; 12% of schools had put three or four dimensions in practice, while 30% of schools had realised only two or fewer. Some 10% of schools in the sample seem to have made insufficient progress in developing any of the seven dimensions.

The next section considers how schools in Wales match up against each of the seven SLO dimensions. The SLO survey is used as a starting point of the analysis and as such is based on self-perceptions which can bias the analysis. Acknowledging this risk we made use of multiple sources of data and information to deepen and triangulate the analysis. The analysis aims to help identify relative strengths of schools and areas for improvement.

Figure 2.4. Schools in Wales developing as learning organisations, 2017

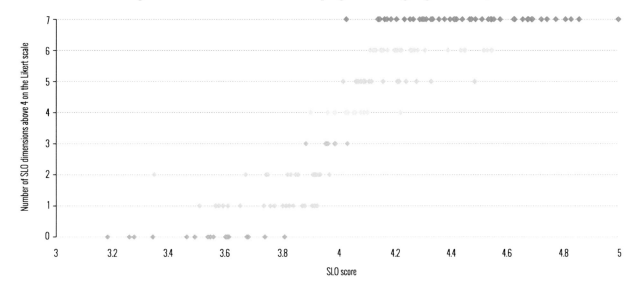

Note: Data are analysed at the school level. The SLO survey items were generated in the form of five-point Likert scale: 1) strongly disagree; 2) disagree; 3) neutral 4) agree; and 5) strongly agree. An average school score of 4 or more across the survey items that make up one dimension was defined as the threshold for when a school is considered to have put the dimension into practice. N: 174 schools. Four schools of the 178 were not taken into consideration as their staff had not completed the survey for all seven dimensions. Each point represents a school.
Source: OECD Schools as Learning Organisations Survey, 2017.

StatLink ᔇᴸᔕᴘ http://dx.doi.org/10.1787/888933837226

An assessment against each of the SLO dimensions

The data from the sample of schools presented in Figure 2.5 suggest that on average, schools scored well on all dimensions, with average scores above 4 (see Box 2.2). When analysed at the school level, the data suggest that two SLO dimensions were less developed: "developing and sharing a vision centred on the learning of all students" (average score of 4.02) and "establishing a culture of enquiry, innovation and exploration" (average score of 4.04). The data suggest that many schools could also do more to "learn with and from the external environment and larger system" (average score of 4.06).

The strongest dimensions were "promoting team learning and collaboration among staff" (4.23) and "embedding systems for collecting and exchanging knowledge and learning" (4.20) in schools in Wales on average.

While the average scores on the SLO dimensions were arguably quite high – something that will be discussed further in the report – there was significant variance between and within the SLO dimensions. For example, for the dimension "modelling and growing learning leadership" there was a significant difference between the highest scoring school (5.00) and lowest (1.75) (standard deviation of 0.47).

Figure 2.5. Average score per SLO dimension

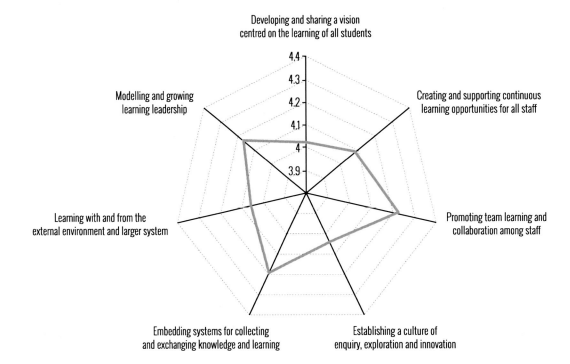

Note: Data are analysed at the school level. The SLO survey items were generated in the form of a five-point Likert scale: 1) strongly disagree; 2) disagree; 3) neutral; 4) agree; and 5) strongly agree. An average school score of 4 or more across the survey items that make up one dimension was defined as the threshold for when a school is considered to have put the dimension into practice. N: 174 schools.
Source: OECD Schools as Learning Organisations Survey, 2017.

StatLink 🖳 http://dx.doi.org/10.1787/888933837245

There were also clear differences between primary and secondary schools, shown in Figure 2.6. While these were relatively small for the dimension "learning with and from the external environment and larger system", they were more substantial for the dimensions "promoting and supporting continuous professional learning for all staff" and "establishing a culture of enquiry, exploration and innovation". These differences are examined in detail in the following section.

A more detailed analysis of the SLO survey data, in combination with other sources of data and information collected as part of this assessment (see also Chapter 3), confirms these findings and points to the conclusion that on average primary schools are faring better than secondary schools in the extent they have put in practice the dimensions that make a school into a learning organisation in Wales (Welsh Government, 2017[2]).

Figure 2.6. Average score per SLO dimension, by school type

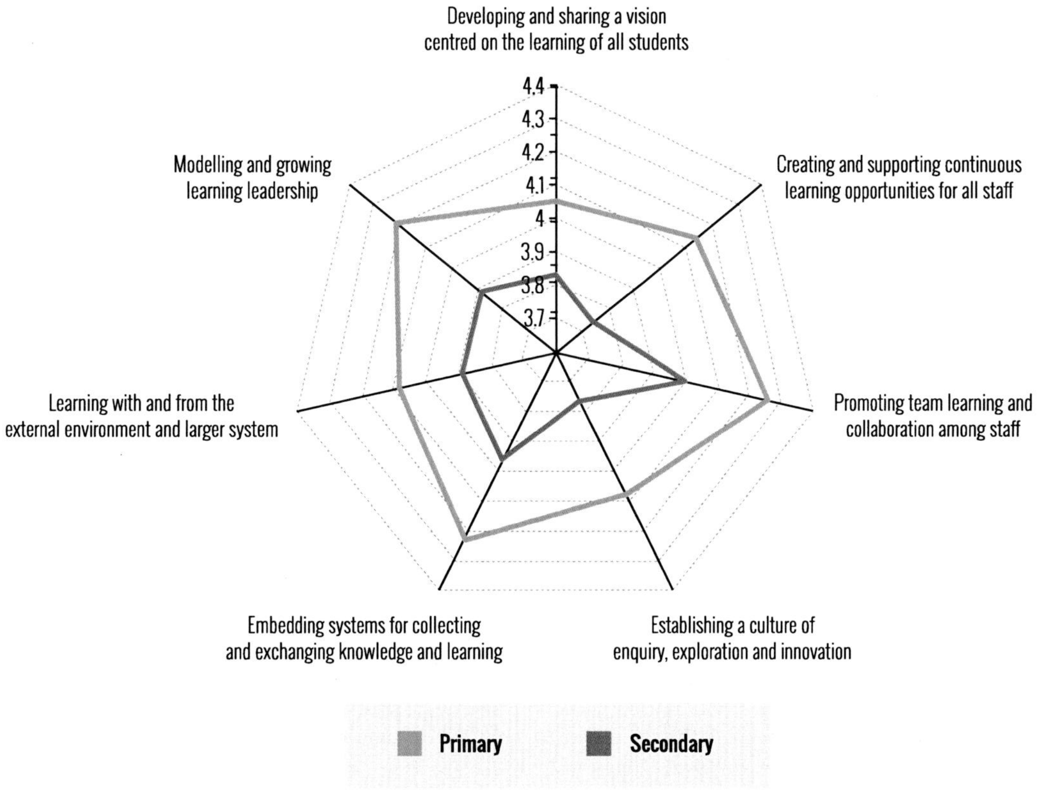

Note: Data are analysed at the school level. The SLO survey items were generated in the form of a five-point Likert scale: 1) strongly disagree; 2) disagree; 3) neutral; 4) agree; and 5) strongly agree. An average school score of 4 or more across the survey items that make up one dimension was defined as the threshold for when a school is considered to have put the dimension into practice. N is 151 for primary schools and 23 for secondary schools so 15% of schools in the sample are secondary schools. This is slightly above the national share (13%).
Source: OECD Schools as Learning Organisations Survey, 2017.

StatLink ᔕᓯᔕ▀ http://dx.doi.org/10.1787/888933837264

Developing and sharing a vision centred on the learning of all students

According to the literature, a school that is a learning organisation has a shared and inclusive vision that gives it a sense of direction and serves as a motivating force for sustained action to achieve student and school goals (Schlechty, 2009[22]; Silins, Zarins and Mulford, 2002[5]). The evidence collected through the SLO survey, school visits and other sources suggests that the majority of schools in Wales have developed an inclusive and shared vision. This is evident from the average school score of 4.02 on this dimension (see Figure 2.7). Over half the schools in the sample (53%) had an average score of 4 or more on this dimension. In other words, the staff in these schools, on average, agreed or strongly agreed that their school had developed and shared a vision centred on the learning of all students.

Figure 2.7. Average school scores on developing and sharing a vision centred on the learning of all students

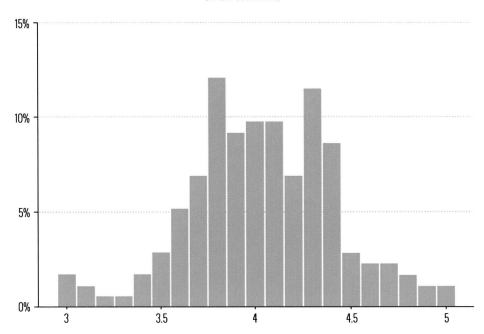

Note: Data are analysed at the school level. The SLO survey items were generated in the form of a five-point Likert scale: 1) strongly disagree; 2) disagree; 3) neutral; 4) agree; and 5) strongly agree. N: 174 schools. An average school score of 4 or more across the survey items that make up one dimension was defined as the threshold for when a school is considered to have put the dimension into practice. The y-axis shows the percentage of schools in the sample that had an average score on the five-point scale. For example, 9% of schools in the sample had an average school between ≥ 4.0 and < 4.1 on this dimension.
Source: OECD Schools as Learning Organisations Survey, 2017.

StatLink ᵃˢˡ http://dx.doi.org/10.1787/888933837283

Nonetheless, the evidence suggests that for a sizable proportion of schools in Wales this dimension offers scope for further action. For example, 29% of the sample of schools (i.e. 50 schools) had an average score of below 3.8. About 9% of schools (15 schools) scored below 3.5 and two even had an average score below 3, indicating this is a particular area for further development for these schools.

The evidence points to significant differences on this dimension between the levels of education. While 56% of primary schools in the sample would seem to have developed a shared vision centred on the learning of all students (average score of 4 or higher on this dimension), only 30% of secondary schools had.

A closer look at the elements that make up this dimension through an exploration of the individual SLO survey items (see also Chapter 3) revealed that nine out of ten school staff (92%) reported that their school has a vision that focuses on students' cognitive and socio-emotional outcomes, including their well-being. Also, almost as many school staff (89%) responded that the school's vision emphasises preparing students for their future in a changing world. These are encouraging findings, considering that the direction set out in the new curriculum reflects a holistic understanding of what learning in the 21st century entails (Donaldson, 2015[3]).

Nonetheless the evidence suggests that many schools in Wales have yet to put this vision into practice when considering the equity challenges they face. Schools in Wales are faced with relatively high levels of child poverty and a high proportion of low performers in PISA 2015 (OECD, 2016[23]). The PISA 2015 results also pointed to some areas of student well-being where further progress could be made, for example concerning students' schoolwork-related anxiety and sense of belonging in school (OECD, 2017[24]). Chapters 3 and 4 elaborate on this important issue.

Figure 2.8. Involvement in shaping the school's vision

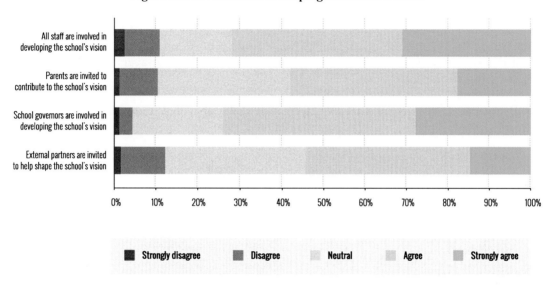

Note: Data are analysed at the individual level. N: 1 699, 1 697, 1 692 and 1 692 individuals respectively for the presented survey statements. School governors are elected members of a school governing board that has a central role in decisions about budgets and recruitment of the school. Members consist of teaching staff, parents, councillors and community representatives.
Source: OECD Schools as Learning Organisations Survey, 2017.

StatLink 🖼️ http://dx.doi.org/10.1787/888933837302

Further work would also seem needed to make the school's vision into one that is shared among its staff and other key stakeholders. The involvement of staff, parents and external partners in the shaping of the vision are areas for improvement (see Figure 2.8), in particular for secondary schools. For example, while 77% of primary school staff indicated they were involved in the development of the school's vision, among secondary school staff this was 57%.

Also, as is common in other countries, secondary schools in Wales seemingly find it more challenging to engage parents in the educational process and school organisation than primary schools (Borgonovi and Montt, 2012[25]; Byrne and Smyth, 2010[26]; Desforges and Abouchaar, 2003[27]). This issue is discussed further below.

Creating and supporting continuous learning opportunities for all staff

The kind of education needed today requires teachers who constantly advance their own professional knowledge and that of their profession. Scholars, educators and policy makers around the world increasingly support the notion of investing in quality, career-long opportunities for professional development and ensuring ongoing, active practice-based professional learning (Schleicher, 2018[28]; Timperley et al., 2007[15]). For it to be effective it should incorporate most if not all of the following elements: it has to be content focused, incorporate active learning, support collaboration, use models of effective practice, coaching and expert support, feedback and reflection, and has to be of sustained duration (Darling-Hammond, Hyler and Gardner, 2017[29]).

A school which is a learning organisation therefore creates continuous learning opportunities for teachers but also all other staff to enhance their professional learning and growth (Welsh Government, 2017[2]; Thompson et al., 2004[30]).

The evidence suggests that many schools in Wales have, or are in the process of developing, a culture that promotes professional learning for their staff (see Figure 2.9). Six out of ten schools in the sample (59%) would seem to have created and supported continuous learning opportunities for all staff (as reflected by an average score of 4 or more on this dimension).

Figure 2.9. Average school scores on creating and supporting continuous learning opportunities for all staff

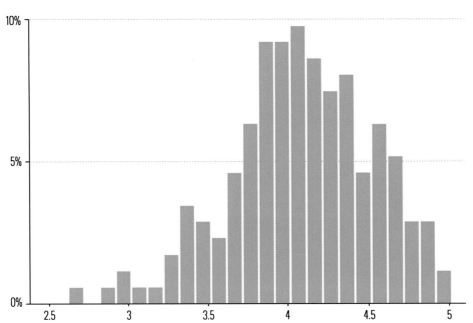

Note: Data are analysed at the school level. The SLO survey items were generated in the form of a five-point Likert scale: 1) strongly disagree; 2) disagree; 3) neutral; 4) agree; and 5) strongly agree. N: 174 schools. An average school score of 4 or more across the survey items that make up one dimension was defined as the threshold for when a school is considered to have put the dimension into practice. The y-axis shows the percentage of schools in the sample that had an average score on the five-point scale. For example, 9% of schools in the sample had an average school between ≥ 4.0 and < 4.1 on this dimension.
Source: OECD Schools as Learning Organisations Survey, 2017.

StatLink http://dx.doi.org/10.1787/888933837321

The school-level data however revealed significant differences between the levels of education. From the sample almost two-thirds of primary schools (64%) had an average score of 4 or more. Among secondary schools this was around a quarter (26%). Furthermore, 23% of schools in the sample (i.e. 40 schools) had an average below 3.8.

Various sources of data and information show that induction and mentoring/coaching need to be strengthened in many schools across Wales. For example, 35% of respondents to the SLO survey disagreed or were unsure whether there were mentors or coaches available in their school to help staff develop their practice (see Table 2.1).The evidence again points to more challenges at4 the secondary level; 18% of secondary school staff indicated that mentoring and coaching support was not available for all staff, compared to 12% in primary schools. The OECD team's interviews with various stakeholders corroborated these findings. As Wales has embarked on a curriculum reform, teachers and learning support workers will need to expand their pedagogical and assessment skills. This puts greater emphasis on mentoring, coaching and other forms of continuous learning.

Table 2.1. Induction and mentoring and coaching support

	Strongly disagree	Disagree	Neutral	Agree	Strongly agree
All new staff receive sufficient support to help them in their new role	2.3%	7.8%	19.6%	44.5%	25.8%
Mentors/coaches are available to help staff develop their practice	2.5%	10.8%	22.1%	42.7%	22.0%

Note: Data are analysed at the individual level. N: 1 633 and 1 634 individuals respectively for the presented survey statements.
Source: OECD Schools as Learning Organisations Survey, 2017.

The SLO survey data revealed significant differences between staff depending on their position (i.e. staff category), and between primary and secondary schools (see Chapter 3). For example, about 81% of respondents in primary schools positively responded to the statement that "professional learning of staff is considered a high priority" in their school. This was 10% lower in secondary schools.

Promoting team learning and collaboration among all staff

Team learning and collaboration are central to a school that is a learning organisation and to the development of its staff (Silins, Zarins and Mulford, 2002[5]; Schlechty, 2009[22]; Senge et al., 2012[4]). In order to ensure that teachers and other school staff feel comfortable in turning to each other for advice and engaging in team learning and working, schools need to create an enabling environment that is characterised by mutual trust and respect (Cerna, 2014[31]).

The evidence suggests that the majority of schools are promoting team learning and collaboration among all their staff. The SLO survey data suggest that some 71% of schools in the sample were promoting team learning and collaboration among all their staff (i.e. a score of at least 4), while in only a small proportion of schools was such practice less developed; 25 schools (14%) had an average score below 3.8, with one having an average score of 3.1. At the other side of the spectrum, more than half the schools (52%) had an average score of 4.2 or more.

The data suggest primary schools are also faring better in relation to this dimension; about 75% of primary schools appeared to promote team learning and collaboration among all staff (average score of 4 or more), compared with 48% of secondary schools.

This assessment points to specific areas for further improvement that apply to both primary and secondary schools (although in varying degrees). Schools could do more to ensure that staff learn to work together as a team, more regularly observe each other and tackle problems together. For example, 25% of staff disagreed or responded neutrally to the SLO survey statement "staff observe each other other's practice and collaborate in developing it". Similarly, 20% of staff were neutral or disagreed with the statement "staff think through and tackle problems together" (Figure 2.10). Such practices will be essential given the ongoing curriculum reform, which, as mentioned, will partially depend on staff engaging in trial and error learning and tacking problems together if it is to succeed. For both statements, teachers were the most critical in their responses.

Figure 2.10. Collaborative learning and working

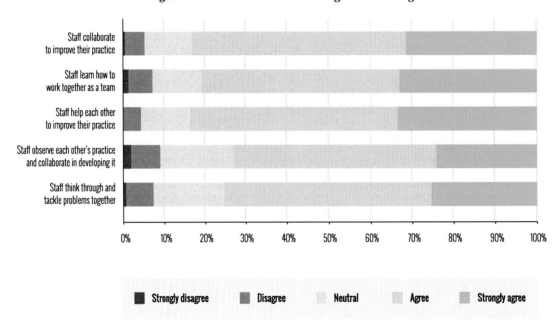

Note: Data analysed at the individual level. N: 1 627, 1 625, 1 621, 1 624 and 1 625 individuals respectively for the presented survey statements.
Source: OECD Schools as Learning Organisations Survey, 2017.

StatLink 🔗 http://dx.doi.org/10.1787/888933837340

There were differences in perceptions across staff categories on several of the elements that make up this dimension. For example, in PISA 2015 about 92% of head teachers in secondary schools in Wales reported that teacher peer review (of lesson plans, assessment instruments, lessons) was used to monitor the practice of teachers, compared to an OECD average of 78% (OECD, 2016[32]). This data needs to be interpreted with some caution, as the evidence from the assessment suggests that teachers and learning support workers in Wales do not always share the views of their head teachers. For example, while 92% of secondary head teachers positively responded to the SLO survey statement "staff observe each other's practice and collaborate in developing it" in their schools, only 67% of teachers responded in a similar vein.

Although there are bound to be some differences in perceptions between staff categories, as some staff may simply be better informed due to the nature of their work, the sometimes sizable differences reported on this dimension (and others) suggest the need for more professional dialogue and sharing of information. This was found again particularly an area for improvement in secondary schools.

Furthermore, in both this and the previous SLO dimension ("creating and supporting continuous learning opportunities for all staff"), this assessment's evidence suggests schools in Wales do not have equal access to time and resources to support their staff in their professional learning. Several interviewees raised the issue of differences in local funding models causing inequalities for both students and school staff across the 22 local authorities. This issue will be further discussed in Chapter 4, as policy action would seem needed.

It is however important to note that many of the steps needed to ensure staff have the time and resources to engage in continuous learning and collaborative working and team learning are within the control of schools. Chapter 3 presents several examples from Wales and internationally which provide testament to this.

Establishing a culture of enquiry, exploration and innovation

One of the marks of any professional is his or her ability to reflect critically on both their profession and their daily work, to be continuously engaged in self-improvement. To be able to do this within an organisation requires a pervasive spirit of enquiry, initiative and willingness to experiment with new ideas and practices (Watkins and Marsick, 1996[33]). This mindset is critical if schools are to develop as learning organisations.

The OECD team were struck by a general change in attitudes since the OECD 2014 review. At that time, the team found an education profession that seemed less open and willing to change and innovate their practice, with some school staff reporting signs of reform fatigue (OECD, 2014[19]). The many interviews by the OECD team with school staff, policy makers and other stakeholders suggest this situation has changed considerably. However, the OECD team found that this general change in mindset is yet to have resulted in a culture of enquiry, innovation and exploration in a significant proportion of schools in Wales. Four out of ten schools from the sample (41%) do not seem to have established such a culture yet (i.e. an average score of 4 or higher on this dimension). Some 31% of schools in the sample had an average score of below 3.8 on this dimension, with one school scoring as low as 2.71.

These findings may partially be explained by the high-stakes assessment, evaluation and accountability arrangements that are believed to have tempered people's willingness and confidence to do things differently and innovate their practice. This would seem particularly the case for secondary schools – the SLO survey data found about 26% of secondary schools in the sample had established a culture of enquiry, exploration and innovation, compared to 63% of primary schools (see Figure 2.11). Other data sources corroborate this pattern.

Despite recent steps to move towards a new assessment, evaluation and accountability framework, school staff expressed uncertainties about what this framework will actually look like. As discussed in Chapter 4, greater clarity is thus urgently needed to give all schools the confidence to engage in enquiry, innovation and exploration of the new curriculum.

Exploring the individual-level responses to the SLO survey data revealed some significant differences across the four regions of Wales for several of the statements that make up this dimension, but also across the staff categories and levels of education (see Chapter 3). For example, while 96% of head teachers indicated that in their school staff were encouraged to experiment and innovate their practice, this proportion dropped to 82% among learning support workers. Interestingly this is one of the few SLO survey items for which learning support workers reported the lowest score of the different staff categories.

Figure 2.11. Average school scores on establishing a culture of enquiry, exploration and innovation, by school type

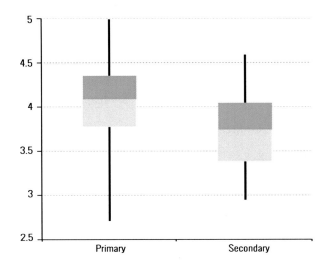

Note: The SLO survey items were generated in the form of five-point Likert scale: 1) strongly disagree; 2) disagree; 3) neutral 4) agree; and 5) strongly agree. An average school score of 4 or more across the survey items that make up one dimension was defined as the threshold for when a school is considered to have put the dimension into practice. The box plots show the average school scores sorted into four equal sized groups, so 25% of all scores are placed in each group. The middle "box", in green and yellow, represents the middle 50% of scores for the group. The median marks the mid-point of the data and is shown by the line that divides the box into two parts, in green and yellow.
Source: OECD Schools as Learning Organisations Survey, 2017.

StatLink ᠍᠍᠍᠍ http://dx.doi.org/10.1787/888933837359

Embedding systems for collecting and exchanging knowledge and learning

SLOs develop processes, strategies and structures that allow them to learn and react effectively in uncertain and dynamic environments. They institutionalise learning mechanisms in order to revise existing knowledge. Without these a learning organisation cannot thrive (Watkins and Marsick, 1996[33]; Schechter and Qadach, 2012[9]). Effective use of data by teachers, school leaders and support staff has become central to school improvement in countries around the globe (OECD, 2013[34]), and this includes Wales.

The evidence suggests that schools throughout Wales and the system at large are "data-rich". The interviews with stakeholders and findings from an earlier OECD assessment (2017[20]) suggest that schools seem to have well-established systems for measuring progress. These findings were corroborated by the SLO survey data which showed that about 70% of schools had embedded systems for collecting and exchanging knowledge and learning (i.e. a score of at least 4). About 12% of schools in the sample had an average score below 3.8 (Figure 2.12).

Again, there were significant differences between primary and secondary schools (the largest among all dimensions): 76% of primary schools and 30% of secondary schools in the sample seemed to have embedded such systems for collecting and exchanging knowledge and learning.

Figure 2.12. Average school scores on embedding systems for collecting and exchanging knowledge and learning

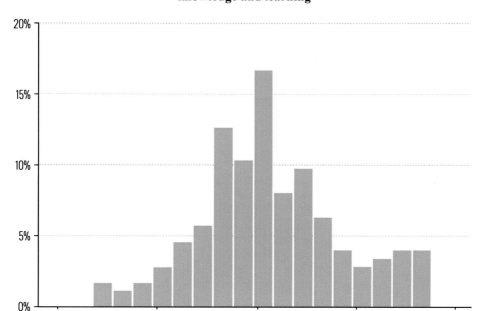

Note: Data are analysed at the school level. The SLO survey items were generated in the form of a five-point Likert scale: 1) strongly disagree; 2) disagree; 3) neutral; 4) agree; and 5) strongly agree. N: 174 schools. An average school score of 4 or more across the survey items that make up one dimension was defined as the threshold for when a school is considered to have put the dimension into practice. The y-axis shows the percentage of schools in the sample that had an average score on the five-point scale. For example, 9% of schools in the sample had an average school between ≥ 4.0 and < 4.1 on this dimension.
Source: OECD Schools as Learning Organisations Survey, 2017.

StatLink ᐧᒣᔕᐧ http://dx.doi.org/10.1787/888933837378

In addition, a closer look at the data from the individual SLO survey items that make up this dimensions points towards an issue in the use of research by school staff. While the use of data was common in many schools across Wales, the proportion of schools using research evidence to inform their practice was considerably lower (see Figure 2.13). The school staff and other education stakeholders the OECD team interviewed recognised this as an area for improvement. The OECD team identified several recent measures taken at various levels of the system in response to this finding (see Chapters 3 and 4).

Figure 2.13. Staff use of data and research evidence to improve their practice

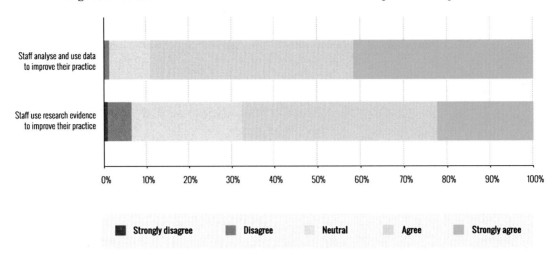

Note: Data analysed at the individual level. N: 1 604 and 1 595 individuals respectively for the presented survey statements.
Source: OECD Schools as Learning Organisations Survey, 2017.

StatLink ⟪ms⟫ http://dx.doi.org/10.1787/888933837397

Furthermore, although the vast majority of school staff agreed that development planning in their schools was informed by learning from continuous self-assessments (91%), the interviews by the OECD team found that the quality of school self-evaluations and development planning is an area for improvement for many schools in Wales. This finding was corroborated by Estyn's 2016/17 annual report (2018[21]) that noted that in one-third of primary schools and half of secondary schools, leaders did not make sure that self-evaluation and school improvement planning were ongoing processes, focused on improving teaching and learning. The report highlighted an over-reliance on data analyses at the expense of gathering first-hand evidence by listening to learners and scrutinising their work.

These findings resonated with the perception of the OECD team that schools in Wales – as well as other parts of the system – generally spend considerable time and effort on analysing and reporting upward on a wide variety of mostly quantitative data, which seems to negatively affect the desired focus on maintaining a rhythm of continuous improvement in schools. Part of the challenge seems to lie in the fact that there is no common understanding of what good self-evaluation and development planning actually entails for schools in Wales. This issue will be further discussed in Chapter 4.

Learning with and from the external environment and larger learning system

Schools do not operate in a vacuum; they are "open systems" that are sensitive to their external environment, including social, political and economic conditions. They forge partnerships with networks of students, teachers, parents and members of their local communities to complement and enrich their own capacity (OECD, 2013[35]; Kools and Stoll, 2016[18]).

As the previous OECD assessment (2017[20]) also found, learning with and from other schools and external partners has become common practice in many schools in Wales.

The SLO survey data showed that over half of schools in the sample (55%) were learning with and from their external environment and larger learning system (i.e. had an average score of at least 4 or more on this dimension). About one-third (35%) had an average score of 4.2 or more. At the other end of the spectrum, 22% of schools scored below 3.8, with one having an average score of 2.80.

Differences between primary and secondary schools were relatively small for this dimension (the smallest among all dimensions) – with 57% of primary and 39% of secondary schools having an average score of at least 4.

A closer look at the data reveals some areas of improvement for this dimension, such as engaging parents and guardians in the educational process and organisation of the school (see Figure 2.14). This is a particular challenge for secondary schools: 57% of secondary school staff responded positively to the SLO survey statement "parents/guardians are partners in the school's organisational and educational processes", compared to 71% of staff in primary schools (see Chapter 3).

Figure 2.14. Collaboration with external partners

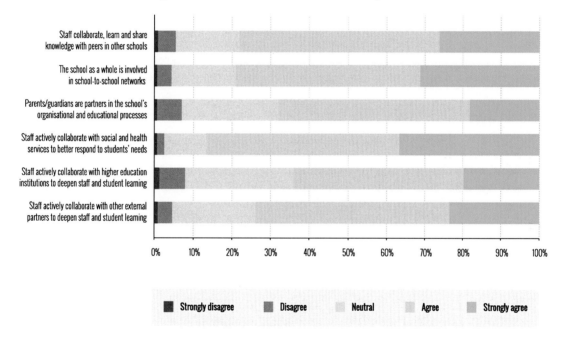

Note: Data analysed at the individual level. N: 1 593, 1 597, 1 592, 1 589, 1 593 and 1 592 individuals respectively for the presented survey statements.
Source: OECD Schools as Learning Organisations Survey, 2017.

StatLink ᑔᑐ http://dx.doi.org/10.1787/888933837416

There were also differences in responses between staff categories, with teachers consistently being the most critical. PISA 2015 provides further information on this issue (OECD, 2017[24]). It found that secondary head teachers in Wales in 2015 almost unanimously reported that their school created a welcoming atmosphere for parents to get involved (99%) and provided information and ideas for families about how to help students at home with homework and other curriculum-related activities, decisions, and planning (98.1%). A further eight out of ten (79.3%) secondary head teachers reported that their school included parents in decision making (OECD average: 78.4%). The SLO survey data and interviews provide a more critical perspective on the engagement of parents in schools' organisational and educational processes. The OECD team recognise it may be more challenging to engage parents of secondary students in the school organisation and education process, than at the primary level – a finding that is also commonly reported in other countries. However, examples from Wales presented in this report and internationally show that it is possible to increase parental engagement in the school and the learning of their children – even at secondary level (see Chapter 3).

Furthermore, the fact that about one-third of school staff responded neutrally or did not agree with the statement that in their school "staff actively collaborate with higher education institutions to deepen staff and student learning" suggests this is another area for improvement for many schools – as well as higher education institutions – in Wales. The interviews revealed that stakeholders across the system were aware of this challenge and were taking measures to improve the situation. This issue will be further discussed in Chapter 4.

The SLO survey data furthermore showed that close to nine out of ten respondents (87%) indicated that in their school "staff actively collaborate with social and health services to better respond to students' needs" – 88% in primary schools and 80% in secondary schools. Interviews with various stakeholders however suggest Wales' school funding and governance model provides challenges to schools' ability to respond to the additional learning needs of all students. This issue will also be further explored in Chapters 4 and 5.

Modelling and growing learning leadership

Leadership is the essential ingredient that binds all the separate parts of the learning organisation together. Leadership should set the direction, take responsibility for putting learning at the centre and keeping it there, and use it strategically so that the school's actions are consistent with its vision, goals and values (OECD, 2013[34]; Fullan, 2014[36]; Marsick and Watkins, 1999[37]; Schleicher, 2018[28]).

The SLO survey data suggested that two-thirds of schools in the sample (67%) had leaders that were modelling and growing learning leadership. Less than one-fifth of schools (18%) in the sample had an average score below 3.8. At the other end of the spectrum, almost half the schools in the sample (47%) had an average score of 4.2 or more.

Figure 2.15 shows that primary schools also appeared to be doing better on this dimension. The SLO survey data point to several other areas for improvement. These include the need for leaders to enhance their coaching of those they lead and the creation of settings in which trust can develop over time so that colleagues are more likely to engage in mutual learning. For example, 38% of teachers were unsure or did not share the view that in their schools "leaders coach those they lead" (see Figure 2.16). Indeed, across all the items that make up this dimension, school leaders had a significantly more positive view than other staff of their learning leadership, with the difference between the more positive leadership group and teachers rising to as much as 20-25% in some cases.

Figure 2.15. School scores on modelling and growing learning leadership, by school type

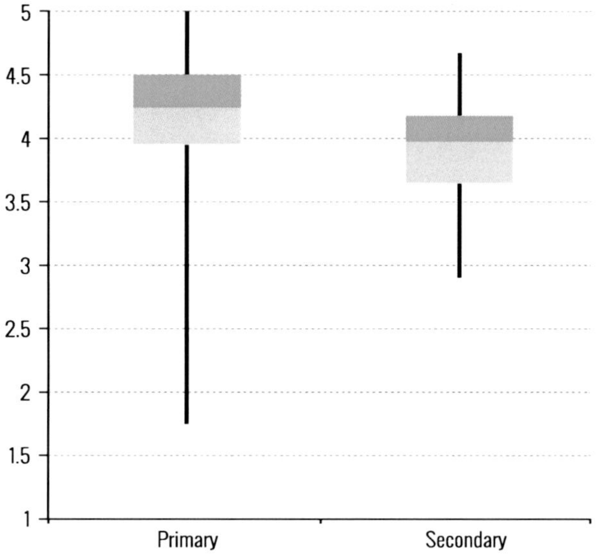

Note: The SLO survey items were generated in the form of five-point Likert scale: 1) strongly disagree; 2) disagree; 3) neutral 4) agree; and 5) strongly agree. The box plots show the average school scores sorted into four equal sized groups, so 25% of all scores are placed in each group. The middle "box", in green and yellow, represents the middle 50% of scores for the group. The median marks the mid-point of the data and is shown by the line that divides the box into two parts, in green and yellow.
Source: OECD Schools as Learning Organisations Survey, 2017.

StatLink ⇒ http://dx.doi.org/10.1787/888933837435

Furthermore, for the SLO survey statement "leaders ensure that all actions are consistent with the school's vision, goals and values", 13% of primary school staff and 16% of secondary school staff responded negatively or neutrally which may suggest they don't know for sure. For both levels of education teachers were the most critical with 19% of primary teachers and 27% of secondary teachers responding in a similar vein. PISA 2015 offers an international perspective on this issue. It found that 39% of secondary school head teachers in Wales reported they ensured that teachers work according to the school's educational goals more than once a month, compared to an OECD average of 53% (OECD, 2016[32]). This suggests that secondary head teachers in Wales could place greater emphasis on ensuring their schools' actions respond to their vision and goals, and communicating these efforts better with their staff.

Figure 2.16. Coaching by leaders, by staff category

Responses to the statement "Leaders coach those they lead"

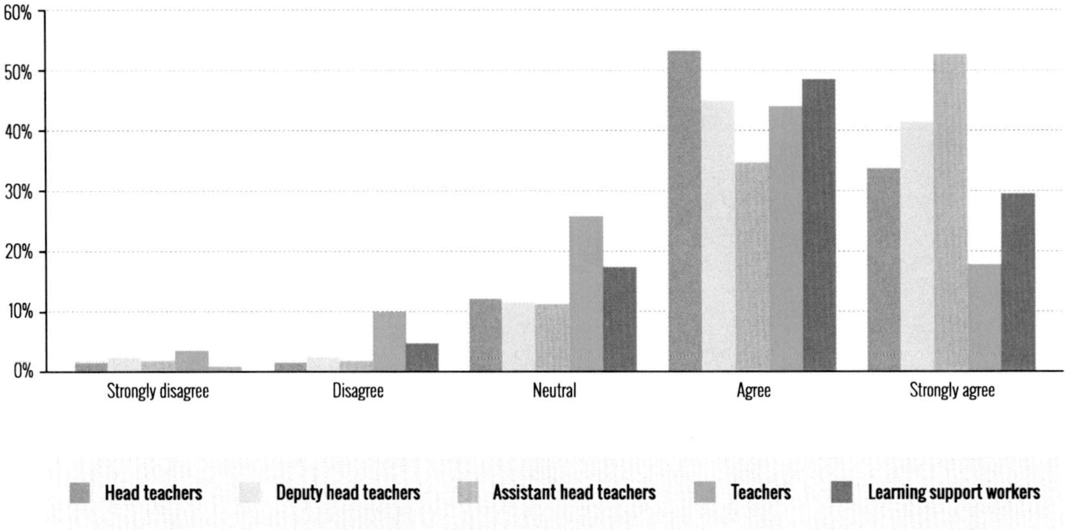

Note: Data analysed at the individual level. N: 1 570 individuals.
Source: OECD Schools as Learning Organisations Survey, 2017.

StatLink 🔢 http://dx.doi.org/10.1787/888933837454

Furthermore, school leaders should not underestimate the pivotal role they will need to play in leading and supporting teachers and learning support workers in putting the curriculum into practice. This is bound to stretch people's skills sets and take them out of their comfort zones – and this includes school leaders themselves. These changes may encounter resistance if this process isn't carefully managed and facilitated.

The generally high scores on this dimension are contrasted by other data sources such as OECD team interviews and Estyn reports that pointed to several areas for further improvement. School leaders play a vital role in the promotion and strengthening of induction programmes, mentoring/coaching, peer review and creating a culture of enquiry, innovation and exploration in their schools. The establishment of these and other conditions for a learning culture to develop across the whole school organisation is particularly an area of improvement for leaders in secondary schools. These findings suggest that school leaders, but also teachers and learning support workers, need to reflect more critically on their own performance and that of their colleagues for deep learning to take place and sustained progress to be made.

Annex 2.A. Information on the analysis of the SLO survey data

As discussed, this study used various quantitative and qualitative data sources to examine the question to what extent the key characteristics of learning organisations exist in schools in Wales. The mixed-methods design of the first part of this report, the Schools as Learning Organisations Assessment, includes the SLO survey data, analysed at two levels: individual level and school level. While Chapter 3 only analyses the SLO survey data at the individual level, to get an insight into the extent to which school staff in Wales perceive their school to have put the dimensions and underlying elements of a learning organisation into practice, Chapter 2 also explores the data at the school level. This is because the SLO is an organisational-level concept and ideally should be analysed as such. The benefit of using both approaches is that it allows the analysis to be deepened. Each method has its benefits and drawbacks that are important to be aware of when reading this report.

Analysis of data at the individual level

Research suggests that a people's positions in the hierarchy of an organisation is one of the factors influencing their perceptions of it (Enticott, Boyne and Walker, 2008[38]; George and Desmidt, 2018[39]). The analysis of the SLO survey data also shows that the perceptions of staff about their school vary across the staff categories, sometime considerably. The data revealed a clear pattern where those in leadership positions held more positive views about their school than other staff. Teachers were the most critical category of staff, except for a few items where learning support workers were more critical. Although the differences between teachers and learning support workers were relatively minor on several of the survey items, their answers differed significantly from those provided by school leaders.

Annex Table 2.A.1shows the response rates of staff by the position they hold in their schools. It shows how response rates vary from the national average school composition, with school leaders and, to a lesser extent, teachers being over-represented at the expense of learning support workers. The reader should be aware of this when interpreting reported average results. This finding was addressed by analysing the data for each of the survey items across the different staff positions, reporting relevant findings.

Annex Table 2.A.1. Overview of SLO survey responses by staff position

Position	Total number of staff in schools in Wales by position	Percentage of total staff in schools in Wales by position	Number of responses to the SLO survey by position	Percentage of responses to the SLO survey by position
School leaders	3 641	7.6%	336	22.0%
Teachers	22 531	47.2%	811	53.0%
Learning support workers*	21 583	45.2%	382	25.0%
Total	47 755		1 529	

Note: * "Learning support workers" is a term regularly used in Wales to indicate a sub-group of support staff in schools, consisting of higher level teaching assistants (HLTA), teaching assistants, foreign language assistants and special needs support staff. N: 1 703 individuals, consisting of 194 head teachers, 87 deputy head teachers, 55 assistant head teachers, 811 teachers, 382 learning support workers and 174 respondents who did not indicate their position. The latter group was not taken into account when specifically reporting on staff perceptions across the different staff categories. For all other situations this group was included in the analysis.

Source: Welsh Government (2018[40]), "School staff", https://statswales.gov.wales/Catalogue/Education-and-Skills/Schools-and-Teachers/teachers-and-support-staff/School-Staff; OECD Schools as Learning Organisations Survey, 2017.

Analysis of data at the school level

As mentioned earlier the SLO is an organisational concept and ideally should also be examined as such. The SLO survey was distributed among school leaders (i.e. head teachers, deputy head teachers and assistant head teachers), teachers and learning support workers so it was therefore needed to carefully consider how to aggregate the data into one overall score per school.

Recognising that people's positions in the hierarchy of an organisation influence their perceptions of it, it was important to carefully consider these differences in views and ensure a fair and accurate estimate of the views of all school staff. The OECD team considered the ideal method of calculating the average school score would take into consideration a school's actual staff composition across the three staff categories as a basis for weighting the average response rates for each of categories. So for example, if a school's staff consisted of 10% school leaders, 50% teachers and 40% learning support workers, these proportions would be used to weigh the average responses for each of these three staff categories. For this method to work, the team needed to have accurate data on the staff composition for each school in the sample. However, the administrative data shared by the Welsh Government revealed some inconsistencies, causing the OECD team to explore an alternative method.

The OECD team opted for the alternative of using the national composition of school staff to weigh the average response rates for each of three staff categories in a school (see Annex Table 2.D.1). So the average score of the school leaders of a school in the sample would be weighted by a factor of 7.6; that of teachers by a factor of 47.2; and that of learning support workers by a factor of 45.2.

The team did not define a minimum threshold for the number of responses per school (or staff category), knowing that many schools in Wales are (very) small in size, especially primary schools. This was also the case in the sample of schools. The administrative data provided by the Welsh Government suggested that about a quarter of schools (24%) in the sample had fewer than 15 staff across the three staff categories; 12% had fewer than 10 staff. Defining a threshold for each of the staff categories or the school at large would have resulted in disqualifying a considerable proportion of smaller schools from the school-level analysis.

One consequence of applying national weights to the answers from different staff categories, was to downgrade the school-level average for items where there were no answers from one or more of the staff categories for a given school. Since it was considered that each school should contribute equally to the survey, a correcting formula[1] was used to restore the information contribution of these schools while respecting the relative weights between staff categories.

This method resulted in sample of 178 schools (31% of the randomly selected schools) used to conduct the school-level analysis. The OECD team recognise the limitations of this aggregation method, and also the relatively small size of the sample of schools, so advise interpreting the school-level analysis with some caution.

However, as discussed above, these school-level data were analysed as part of a mixed-methods design (see Box 2.2) that allowed for deepening and triangulating the findings – with explicit mention of any variations in the evidence from the different data sources in the report. This gives confidence in using the school-level data, as one of the data sources used, to get an indication of the extent to which schools in Wales have put in practice the dimensions of a learning organisation, their strengths and areas for further improvement.

Analysis of information collected through the open question

The SLO survey contained one open question (i.e. "Do you have any comments on …?") which gave respondents the opportunity to comment on anything they found relevant. A total of 118 of the 1 703 respondents (about 7%) made use of this opportunity. The information was analysed by first clustering the comments around certain themes or issues. Apart from the many respondents using the opportunity to express their positive views on their school and work (31 comments), two clusters of comments stood out. The first related to challenges in terms of workload, time and financial resources (27 comments). Budget pressures were raised several times as part of these (11 comments).

The second cluster pointed to staff concerns about the capacity of school leaders (12 comments) with several of them referring to the negative influence of the current assessment, evaluation and accountability arrangements in driving school leaders and other staff to focus on providing evidence in response by accountability demands, rather than focusing on teaching and learning.

The general trends that came out of these open comments corroborated the findings from other data sources used in this assessment. These and other findings were used to enrich other data sources, with occasional mentions of these anecdotal data in the report.

Annex 2.B. Data and information collected as part of the school visits

The mixed-methods design of the first part of this study, the Schools as Learning Organisations Assessment, used various quantitative and qualitative data sources (see Box 2.2). An important part of the latter were the interviews that were conducted in eight schools across Wales that were visited by the OECD team in June and July 2017.

More than 80 school leaders, teachers and learning support workers were interviewed, and the OECD team were also able to speak to a large number of students. Two schools were visited in each of the four regions of Wales; one primary school and one secondary school in each. Another selection criterion concerned the variance in school performance, meaning a range of "stronger" and "weaker" performing schools according to Estyn inspections or the national school categorisation system.

The interviews were semi-structured, with one set of questions for school leaders, teachers and learning support workers concerning 1) their understanding of the school as learning organisation concept; 2) their views on the curriculum reform (of which Wales' SLO model is a part); and 3) their reflections on their own school against the seven dimensions of Wales' SLO model.

The OECD team complemented and triangulated these interview findings with:

1. the schools' results on the SLO survey (see Annex 2.C)

2. a desk study of the available data and information about the schools (e.g. school evaluation reports by Estyn)

3. a short self-assessment questionnaire completed by the school leaders to showcase "good practices" against an earlier shared template. Recognising a school can be good or excellent in many different ways the questionnaire asked school leaders to showcase their school against three different "profiles": 1) The school as a learning organisation; 2) excellence, innovation, equity and well-being in the curriculum; 3) excellence, equity and innovation in your educational approach/process

The examples of good practices collected as part of the school visits were later complemented by those collected by the SLO Pilot Group. Several of these have been used to exemplify the findings and offer ideas and practical guidance to those wanting to develop their schools into learning organisations in Wales and beyond (see Chapter 3).

At the end of the day of conducting school visits the OECD team members met to collectively process and consolidate the collected data and information. Among other things this resulted in a strengths, weaknesses, opportunities and threats (SWOT) analysis for each of the eight schools that were visited. Two levels of analysis were differentiated: at the school level and the system level, thereby informing the two related parts of this report.

The use of these various data sources provided the OECD team with a wealth of data and information on the policies and practices in schools in Wales, their strengths and challenges, and the opportunities they face in developing as learning organisations and ultimately realising the new curriculum.

Annex 2.C. Schools as Learning Organisations Survey, 2017

Questionnaire for school leaders, teachers and teaching support staff

Guidance for completing the questionnaire: *(to be further tailored to local context)*

- This questionnaire is to be completed by school leaders, teachers and learning support workers.

- There are no right or wrong answers to the questions – your answers should reflect your honest and critical opinion on the current situation in your school.

- The questionnaire starts with a question on your position, followed by a set of questions for each of the seven dimensions of the school as learning organisation (background questions are not included).

- Please answer all questions in relation to the time frame of the last 12 months.

- Select one answer per question.

- The questionnaire should take approximately 10 minutes to complete.

QUESTIONS

A. Developing a shared vision centred on the learning of *all* students

"In my school, …."	Strongly disagree	Disagree	Neutral	Agree	Strongly agree
A1. The school's vision is aimed at enhancing student's cognitive and social-emotional outcomes, including their well-being	O	O	O	O	O
A2. The school's vision emphasises preparing students for their future in a changing world	O	O	O	O	O
A3. The school's vision embraces all students	O	O	O	O	O
A4. Learning activities and teaching are designed with the school's vision in mind	O	O	O	O	O
A5. The school's vision is understood and shared by all staff working in the school	O	O	O	O	O
A6. Staff are inspired and motivated to bring the school's vision to life	O	O	O	O	O
A7. All staff are involved in developing the school's vision	O	O	O	O	O
A8. School governors are involved in developing the school's vision	O	O	O	O	O
A9. Students are invited to contribute to the school's vision	O	O	O	O	O
A10. Parents are invited to contribute to the school's vision	O	O	O	O	O
A11. External partners are invited to help shape the school's vision	O	O	O	O	O

B. Promoting and supporting continuous professional learning for all staff

"In my school, …"	Strongly disagree	Disagree	Neutral	Agree	Strongly agree
B1. Professional learning of staff is considered a high priority	O	O	O	O	O
B2. Staff engage in professional learning to ensure their practice is critically informed and up to date	O	O	O	O	O
B3. Staff are involved in identifying the objectives for their professional learning	O	O	O	O	O
B4. Professional learning is focused on students' needs	O	O	O	O	O
B5. Professional learning is aligned to the school's vision	O	O	O	O	O
B6. Mentors/coaches are available to help staff develop their practice	O	O	O	O	O
B7. All new staff receive sufficient support to help them in their new role	O	O	O	O	O
B8. Staff receive regular feedback to support reflection and improvement	O	O	O	O	O
B9. Students are encouraged to give feedback to teachers and support staff *	O	O	O	O	O
B10. Staff have opportunities to experiment with and practise new skills	O	O	O	O	O
B11. Beliefs, mindsets and practices are challenged by professional learning	O	O	O	O	O

C. Fostering team learning and collaboration among staff

"In my school, …"	Strongly disagree	Disagree	Neutral	Agree	Strongly agree
C1. Staff collaborate to improve their practice	O	O	O	O	O
C2. Staff learn how to work together as a team	O	O	O	O	O
C3. Staff help each other to improve their practice	O	O	O	O	O
C4. Staff observe each other's practice and collaborate in developing it *	O	O	O	O	O
C5. Staff give honest feedback to each other	O	O	O	O	O
C6. Staff listen to each other's ideas and opinions	O	O	O	O	O
C7. Staff feel comfortable turning to others for advice	O	O	O	O	O
C8. Staff treat each other with respect	O	O	O	O	O
C9. Staff spend time building trust with each other	O	O	O	O	O
C10. Staff think through and tackle problems together	O	O	O	O	O
C11. Staff reflect together on how to learn and improve their practice	O	O	O	O	O

D. Establishing a culture of enquiry, exploration and innovation

"In my school, …"	Strongly disagree	Disagree	Neutral	Agree	Strongly agree
D1. Staff are encouraged to experiment and innovate their practice	O	O	O	O	O
D2. Staff are encouraged to take initiative	O	O	O	O	O

	Strongly disagree	Disagree	Neutral	Agree	Strongly agree
D3. Staff are supported when taking calculated risks	O	O	O	O	O
D4. Staff spend time exploring a problem before taking action	O	O	O	O	O
D5. Staff engage in enquiry (i.e. pose questions, gather and use evidence to decide how to change their practice, and evaluate its impact)	O	O	O	O	O
D6. Staff are open to thinking and doing things differently	O	O	O	O	O
D7. Staff are open to others questioning their beliefs, opinions and ideas	O	O	O	O	O
D8. Staff openly discuss failures in order to learn from them	O	O	O	O	O
D9. Problems are seen as opportunities for learning	O	O	O	O	O

E. Embedding systems for collecting and exchanging knowledge and learning

"In my school, . . . "	Strongly disagree	Disagree	Neutral	Agree	Strongly agree
E1.The school's development plan is based on learning from continuous self-assessment and updated at least once every year	O	O	O	O	O
E2. Structures are in place for regular dialogue and knowledge sharing among staff	O	O	O	O	O
E3. Evidence is collected to measure progress and identify gaps in the school's performance	O	O	O	O	O
E4. Staff analyse and use data to improve their practice	O	O	O	O	O
E5. Staff use research evidence to improve their practice	O	O	O	O	O
E6. Staff analyse examples of good/great practices and failed practices to learn from them	O	O	O	O	O
E7. Staff learn how to analyse and use data to inform their practice	O	O	O	O	O
E8. Staff regularly discuss and evaluate whether actions had the desired impact and change course if necessary	O	O	O	O	O

F. Learning with and from the external environment and larger system

"In my school, …"	Strongly disagree	Disagree	Neutral	Agree	Strongly agree
F1. Opportunities and threats outside the school are monitored continuously to improve our practice *	O	O	O	O	O
F2. Parents/guardians are partners in the school's organisational and educational processes *	O	O	O	O	O
F3. Staff actively collaborate with social and health services to better respond to students' needs	O	O	O	O	O
F4. Staff actively collaborate with higher education institutions to deepen staff and student learning	O	O	O	O	O
F5. Staff actively collaborate with other external partners to deepen staff and student learning	O	O	O	O	O
F6. Staff collaborate, learn and share knowledge with peers in other schools	O	O	O	O	O
F7. The school as a whole is involved in school-to-school networks or collaborations	O	O	O	O	O

G. Modelling and growing learning leadership

"In my school…"	Strongly disagree	Disagree	Neutral	Agree	Strongly agree
G1. Leaders participate in professional learning to develop their practice	O	O	O	O	O
G2. Leaders facilitate individual and group learning	O	O	O	O	O
G3. Leaders coach those they lead	O	O	O	O	O
G4. Leaders develop the potential of others to become future leaders	O	O	O	O	O
G5. Leaders provide opportunities for staff to participate in decision making	O	O	O	O	O
G6. Leaders provide opportunities for students to participate in decision making	O	O	O	O	O
G7. Leaders give staff responsibility to lead activities and projects	O	O	O	O	O
G8. Leaders spend time building trust with staff	O	O	O	O	O
G9. Leaders put a strong focus on improving learning and teaching	O	O	O	O	O
G10. Leaders ensure that all actions are consistent with the school's vision, goals and values	O	O	O	O	O
G11. Leaders anticipate opportunities and threats	O	O	O	O	O
G12. Leaders model effective collaborations with external partners	O	O	O	O	O

Note: * Indicates the survey items that the principal component analysis and reliability analysis found not to fit the SLO concept i.e. Wales' SLO model. These items were excluded from the list of items used to calculate the average scores for each of the SLO dimensions and as such were also not included in the average SLO score reported on in Chapter 2.

Annex 2.D. Development and application of the Schools as Learning Organisations Survey, 2017

Overview of the Schools as Learning Organisations Survey design process

The OECD commenced the work on the Schools as Learning Organisations (SLO) Survey in May 2016, following the completion of the OECD Education Working Paper "What Makes a School a Learning Organisation?" by Kools and Stoll (2016[18]) who proposed an integrated SLO model. This exercise should be viewed as a first endeavour at developing a scale that allows for the holistic measurement of the SLO.

For each of the seven dimensions and underlying elements of the model, items were generated in the form of five-point Likert scale with the options "strongly disagree", "disagree", "neutral", "agree" and "strongly agree". This type of self-reported scale is commonly used in public administration to measure core public management and governance concepts (McNabb, 2015[41]; George and Pandey, 2017[42]). Several background items were also generated concerning staff members' position, employment status, years of experience, etc. In addition, the survey included an open question to give respondents the option to highlight anything they considered important.

An early draft of the survey instrument was trialled at a workshop at the UCL Institute of Education in England in June 2016 where 30 school and system leaders who were asked to review and provide feedback on it. A revised survey instrument was discussed during an expert meeting organised by the OECD on 1 July 2016 in Paris. The panel was made up of 14 international experts whose expertise included (but was not limited to) survey design and statistical analysis, the (school as) learning organisation, innovative learning environments, and school improvement more broadly.

The survey was then tailored to the Welsh context by the SLO Pilot Group, which had been established to develop a SLO model for Wales. These strands of work were conducted in parallel and shaped through a series of workshops that were organised in Cardiff between November 2016 and April 2017. The developmental work included a field trial of the survey in 32 schools.

These efforts resulted in a scale that was aligned to Wales' SLO model and consisted of 69 items across the seven SLO dimensions that was ready for use as part this OECD study in Wales.

Application of the Schools as Learning Organisations Survey

Sample and response rate

The OECD and the Welsh Government's Education Directorate agreed on the drawing of a random sample of 40% of schools in Wales whose staff would be invited to complete the online survey. The Welsh Government was responsible for drawing the random sample of schools and presenting OECD with the list of sampled schools. The Welsh

Government excluded a number of schools from the initial list for several reasons, including some scheduled closures or mergers of schools which are changing the structure of Wales' school system. By 2017, the number of schools in Wales had fallen by 109 from 1 656 schools in 2013, a drop of close to 7% (Giles and Hargreaves, 2006[43]). The final sample consisted of 571 schools (i.e. 38% of primary, middle and secondary schools in Wales in 2017) whose staff were asked to complete the online SLO survey.

A total of 1 703 school staff from 178 different schools throughout Wales responded to the survey. This was lower than the OECD team had hoped for. Welsh Government Education Directorate staff however noted the response rate was in fact quite high compared with other surveys conducted in Wales in recent years. Part of the explanation for the (low) response rate may lie in the fact that schools in Wales were in the middle of an ambitious curriculum reform so completion of the survey may not have received equal attention in schools.

Although the responses from the 178 schools only represented 31% of the target sample schools, we controlled for the representativeness of the final sample of schools and found this to match the overall school population in Wales. The representatives of the sample of schools were controlled for by comparing the SLO survey data with the data from the latest school census (Welsh Government, 2017[44]). First the proportion of primary and secondary schools was compared in the sample with that of the overall school population. On January 2017 there were 1 287 primary schools and 200 secondary schools in Wales, so 86.6% of these schools were primary schools and 13.4% were secondary schools. The sample showed a very similar proportion of 85.8% primary schools and 14.2% secondary schools.

Satisfied with this finding, the next step was to control the sample of schools against several of the characteristics of the school system by looking at the values of a number of available variables at the country and regional levels (Annex Table 2.D.1).

Annex Table 2.D.1. Comparison of the sample of schools against several characteristics of Wales' school system

	North Wales			South West and Mid Wales			South East Wales			South Wales			Total
	P	S	t	P	S	t	P	S	t	P	S	t	
Percentage of schools (public)	26	26		32	27		16	15		25	32		100 100
School size	255	289	0.9	286	280	-0.2	408	363	-0.9	391	364	-0.7	
Consortium percentage of students eligible for free school meals	17	16	-0.6	17	17	0.1	19	22	1	21	22	0.4	

Note: P, S and t stand for Population, Sample and t-stat. A * indicates that the sample is significantly different from the population at the 5% level.

The statistical test employed is a one-sample, two-tailed test of equality of means.[2] By definition, the t statistic cannot be calculated for a variable that does not vary within a region, such as the percentage of public schools. Conversely, the total number of students and the share of students eligible for free school meals are not constant between schools, which allowed for the computation of standard deviations and the comparison with the total population. The results showed no systematic differences at the 5% significance level between the sample and the total population, because the null hypothesis of equality of means in each of the four regions cannot be rejected. In other words, no significant differences were found between the specified populations.

These results gave us confidence that the schools drawn during the random sampling exercise closely match the overall school population in Wales.

Principal component analysis and reliability analysis

For the development of the SLO scale a construct validity exercise that consisted of a principal component analysis and reliability analysis was conducted. It showed that Wales' SLO model held up well. A relatively small number of the survey items, i.e. four items of the original questionnaire were found not to fit SLO model according to the views of respondents (see Annex 2.C). The data however revealed an eight-component/dimension model, instead of the theorised seven-dimension model that was proposed by Kools and Stoll (2016[18]). The data suggested the SLO dimension "developing a shared vision centred on the learning of all students" in fact consists of two dimensions. The two dimensions that split the theorised SLO dimension "developing a shared vision centred on the learning of all students" were labelled as "shared vision centred on the learning of all students" and "partners invited to contribute to the school's vision" (Kools et al., 2018[45]),.

Presentation of the analysis against the seven dimensions of Wales' SLO model

Following a discussion with the Welsh Government Education Directorate and other members of the SLO Pilot Group, the decision was made to present the analysis of this report based on the seven dimensions of Wales' SLO model as this would make the analysis more recognisable to schools and other stakeholders, who are now familiar with the seven-dimension SLO model for Wales (Welsh Government, 2017[2]). The scores for these dimensions were therefore averaged to define one score for the SLO dimension "developing and sharing a vision centred on the learning of all students".

Furthermore, the four survey items that the principal component analysis and reliability analysis found not to fit the SLO concept, i.e. Wales' SLO model, were excluded from the list of items that were used to calculate the average score for each of the SLO dimensions and as such were also not included in the average SLO scores reported on in Chapter 2. However, appreciating that many school staff across Wales had given their time to report on these four items, the OECD team choose to include them in the presentation of the individual level analysis of the data that is primarily reported on in Chapter 3.

For further information on the development of the in this report used SLO scale please have a look at Kools et al. (2018[45]), "The School as a Learning Organisation in Wales and its Measurement, OECD Publishing, Paris.

Notes

[1] The correcting formula is of the form $\frac{\sum_{i=1}^{3} a_i x_i}{\sum_{i=1}^{3} a_{i_{x_i \neq 0}}}$, where a_i is the staff category and x_i the item response.

[2] The calculated t statistic follows a Student's law and is computed as: $= \frac{\bar{x} - \mu}{s / \sqrt{n}}$, with $\bar{x}$ the average in the sample and μ the population average, s represents the sample standard deviation and n the sample size.

References

Borgonovi, F. and G. Montt (2012), "Parental involvement in selected PISA countries and economies", *OECD Education Working Papers*, No. 73, OECD Publishing, Paris, http://dx.doi.org/10.1787/5k990rk0jsjj-en. [25]

Byrne, D. and E. Smyth (2010), *Behind the Scenes? A Study of Parental Involvement in Post-Primary Education*, Liffey Press, Dublin. [26]

Caprara, G. et al. (2006), "Teachers' self-efficacy beliefs as determinants of job satisfaction and students' academic achievement: A study at the school level", *Journal of School Psychology*, Vol. 44/6, pp. 473-490. [12]

Cerna, L. (2014), "Trust: What it is and why it matters for governance and education", *OECD Education Working Papers*, No. 108, OECD Publishing, Paris, http://dx.doi.org/10.1787/5jxswcg0t6wl-en. [31]

Darling-Hammond, L., M. Hyler and M. Gardner (2017), *Effective Teacher Professional Development*, Learning Policy Institute, Palo Alto.. [29]

Desforges, C. and A. Abouchaar (2003), "The impact of parental involvement, parental support and family education on pupil achievements and adjustment: A literature review", *Research Report*, No. No. 433, Department for Education and Skills Publications, Nottingham. [27]

Donaldson, G. (2015), *Successful Futures: Independent Review of Curriculum and Assessment Arrangements in Wales*, Welsh Government, http://gov.wales/docs/dcells/publications/150225-successful-futures-en.pdf. [3]

Enticott, G., G. Boyne and R. Walker (2008), "The use of multiple informants in public administration research: Data aggregation using organizational echelons", *Journal of Public Administration Research and Theory*, Vol. 19/2, pp. 229-253. [38]

Erdem, M., A. İlğan and H. Uçar (2014), "Relationship between learning organization and job satisfaction of primary school teachers", *International Online Journal of Educational Sciences*, Vol. 6/1, pp. 8-20, http://dx.doi.org/10.15345/iojes.2014.01.002. [10]

Estyn (2018), *The Annual Report of Her Majesty's Chief Inspector of Education and Training in Wales 2016-2017*, Estyn, Cardiff, https://www.estyn.gov.wales/document/annual-report-2016-2017. [21]

Fullan, M. (2014), *The Principal: Three Keys to Maximizing Impact*, Jossey-Bass and Ontario Principal's Council, Toronto. [36]

George, B. and S. Desmidt (2018), "Strategic-decision quality in public organizations: An information processing perspective", *Administration & Society*, Vol. 50/1, pp. 131-156, http://dx.doi.org/10.1177/0095399716647153. [39]

George, B. and S. Pandey (2017), "We know the yin—but where is the yang? Toward a balanced approach on common source bias in public administration scholarship", *Review of* [42]

Public Personnel Administration, Vol. 37/2, pp. 245-270.

Giles, C. and A. Hargreaves (2006), "The sustainability of innovative schools as learning organizations and professional learning communities during standardized reform", *Educational Administration Quarterly*, Vol. 42/1, pp. 124-156. [43]

Klassen, R. and M. Chiu (2010), "Effect on teachers' self-efficacy and job satisfaction: Teacher gender, years of experience, and job stress", *Journal of Educational Psychology*, Vol. 102/3, pp. 741-756. [13]

Kools, M. and L. Stoll (2016), "What makes a school a learning organisation?", *OECD Education Working Papers*, No. 137, OECD Publishing, Paris, http://dx.doi.org/10.1787/5jlwm62b3bvh-en. [18]

Kools, M. et al. (2018), *The School as a Learning Organisation and its Measurement*, OECD Publishing, Paris. [45]

Day, C. and K. Leithwood (eds.) (2007), *Starting with What We Know*, Springer, Dordrecht. [16]

Marsick, V. and K. Watkins (1999), *Facilitating Learning Organizations: Making Learning Count*, Gower Publishing Limited, Aldershot. [37]

McNabb, D. (2015), *Research Methods in Public Administration and Nonprofit Management (second edition)*, Routledge, New York. [41]

OECD (2017), *PISA 2015 Results (Volume III): Students' Well-Being*, PISA, OECD Publishing, Paris, http://dx.doi.org/10.1787/9789264273856-en. [24]

OECD (2017), *The Welsh education reform journey: A rapid policy assessment*, OECD, Paris, http://www.oecd.org/edu/The-Welsh-Education-Reform-Journey-FINAL.pdf. [20]

OECD (2016), *PISA 2015 Results (Volume I): Excellence and Equity in Education*, PISA, OECD Publishing, Paris, http://dx.doi.org/10.1787/9789264266490-en. [23]

OECD (2016), *PISA 2015 Results (Volume II): Policies and Practices for Successful Schools*, PISA, OECD Publishing, https://doi.org/10.1787/9789264267510-en (accessed on 06 November 2017). [32]

OECD (2014), *Improving Schools in Wales: An OECD Perspective*, OECD Publishing, Paris, http://www.oecd.org/edu/Improving-schools-in-Wales.pdf. [19]

OECD (2013), *Innovative Learning Environments*, Educational Research and Innovation, OECD Publishing, Paris, http://dx.doi.org/10.1787/9789264203488-en. [35]

OECD (2013), *Synergies for Better Learning: An International Perspective on Evaluation and Assessment*, OECD Reviews of Evaluation and Assessment in Education, OECD Publishing, Paris, http://dx.doi.org/10.1787/9789264190658-en. [34]

Razali, M., N. Amira and N. Shobri (2013), "Learning organization practices and job satisfaction among academicians at public niversity", *International Journal of Social* [11]

Science and Humanity, Vol. 3/6, pp. 518-521, http://dx.doi.org/10.7763/IJSSH.2013.V3.295.

Robinson, V. (2007), *The Impact of Leadership on Student Outcomes: Making Sense of the Evidence*, http://research.acer.edu.au/research_conference_2007/5/. [17]

Schechter, C. (2008), "Organizational learning mechanisms: The meaning, measure, and implications for school improvement", *Educational Administration Quarterly*, Vol. 44/2, pp. 155-186. [7]

Schechter, C. and M. Qadach (2012), "Toward an organizational model of change in elementary schools: The contribution of organizational learning mechanisms", *Educational Administration Quarterly*, Vol. 48/1, pp. 116-153, http://dx.doi.org/10.1177/0013161X11419653. [9]

Schlechty, P. (2009), *Leading for Learning: How to Transform Schools into Learning Organizations*, John Wiley & Sons. [22]

Schleicher, A. (2018), *World Class: How to Build a 21st-Century School System*, OECD Publishing, Paris, http://dx.doi.org/10.1787/4789264300002-en. [28]

Senge, P. et al. (2012), *Schools That Learn (Updated and Revised): A Fifth Discipline Fieldbook for Educators, Parents, and Everyone Who Cares about Education*, Crown Business. [4]

Silins, H. and B. Mulford (2004), "Schools as learning organizations: Effects on teacher leadership and student outcomes", *School Effectiveness and School Improvement*, Vol. 15, pp. 443-466, https://doi.org/10.1080/09243450512331383272. [14]

Silins, H., B. Mulford and S. Zarins (2002), "Organizational learning and school change", *Educational Administration Quarterly*, Vol. 38/5, pp. 613-642. [8]

Silins, H., S. Zarins and B. Mulford (2002), "What characteristics and processes define a school as a learning organisation? Is it a useful concept to apply to schools?", *International Education Journal*, Vol. 3/1, pp. 24-32. [5]

Thompson, M. et al. (2004), "Study of the impact of the California Formative Assessment and Support System for Teachers, Report 1: Beginning teachers' engagement with BTSA/CFASST", *ETS Research Report Series*, No. RR-04-30, Educational Testing Service. [30]

Timperley, H. et al. (2007), *Teacher Professional Learning and Development: Best Evidence Synthesis Iteration*, Ministry of Education New Zealand, Wellington. [15]

Watkins, K. and V. Marsick (1999), "Sculpting the learning community: New forms of working and organizing", *NASSP Bulletin*, Vol. 83/604, pp. 78-87, https://doi.org/10.1177/019263659908360410. [6]

Watkins, K. and V. Marsick (1996), *In Action: Creating the Learning Organization*, American Society for Training and Development, Alexandria. [33]

Welsh Government (2018), *School Staff*, StatsWales website, [40] https://statswales.gov.wales/Catalogue/Education-and-Skills/Schools-and-Teachers/teachers-and-support-staff/School-Staff.

Welsh Government (2017), *Education in Wales: Our National Mission: Action Plan 2017-21*, Education Wales, Welsh Government, http://gov.wales/docs/dcells/publications/170926-education-in-wales-en.pdf.   [1]

Welsh Government (2017), *School Census Results, 2017*, Statistics for Wales, https://gov.wales/docs/statistics/2017/170726-school-census-results-2017-en.pdf.   [44]

Welsh Government (2017), *Schools in Wales as Learning Organisations*, Welsh Government website, https://beta.gov.wales/schools-learning-organisations.   [2]

Chapter 3. Schools as learning organisations in Wales: A detailed analysis

This chapter continues the Schools as Learning Organisations Assessment by exploring in greater depth the extent schools have put in practice the seven dimensions and underlying elements of Wales' schools as learning organisations (SLO) model.

The analysis suggests schools are progressing well on the dimensions "promoting team learning and collaboration among all staff" and "embedding systems for collecting and exchanging knowledge and learning". Two dimensions are considerably less well developed: "developing a shared vision centred on the learning of all students (learners)" and "establishing a culture of enquiry, innovation and exploration". Many schools could also do more to "learn with and from the external environment and larger system".

The presented examples show how challenges such as budget pressures do not need to lead to a reduction in ambitions. Such examples should be systematically collected and shared widely to inspire and inform other schools in their change and innovation efforts.

Introduction

This chapter continues the *Schools as Learning Organisations Assessment* that was started in Chapter 2 by exploring in greater depth to what extent schools in Wales have put in practice the seven action-oriented dimensions and underlying "elements" of Wales' schools as learning organisations (SLO) model. The chapter uses various sources of data and information (see Chapter 2, Box 2.2) and showcases some good practices that were identified through the OECD team's school visits and by representatives of the Schools as Learning Organisations Pilot Group (see Chapter 2), as well as from other OECD projects. These are used to exemplify the findings and offer ideas and practical guidance to those wanting to develop their schools as learning organisations in Wales and beyond. The chapter concludes by summarising the key findings of the Schools as Learning Organisations Assessment presented in Chapters 2 and 3, and offers some points of reflection and action for schools.

An assessment of schools as learning organisations by dimension and underlying elements

Developing and sharing a vision centred on the learning of all students

General overview

A school that is a learning organisation (SLO) has a shared and inclusive vision that gives it a sense of direction and serves as a motivating force for sustained action to achieve student and school goals (Schlechty, 2009[1]; Senge et al., 2012[2]). The evidence collected through the SLO survey (see Box 3.1), school visits and other sources suggests that on average the majority of schools in Wales had developed such an inclusive and shared vision.

Similarly, almost all school staff indicated that their school's vision embraced all students. These are encouraging findings considering that the new school curriculum promotes a broad range of learning outcomes and Wales' commitment to equity and student well-being (Welsh Government, 2017[3]).

Nonetheless, the answers for three of the survey statements that make up this dimension were significantly less positive; the involvement of staff, parents and external partners in the shaping of the vision were areas for improvement.

Furthermore, the data revealed some variation across different staff categories and school types (i.e. primary or secondary). These and other findings will be discussed further in the text below.

Box 3.1. Survey items for the SLO dimension "developing and sharing a vision centred on the learning of all students"

- The school's vision is aimed at enhancing student's cognitive and social-emotional outcomes, including their well-being.

- The school's vision emphasises preparing students for their future in a changing world.

- The school's vision embraces all students.

- Learning activities and teaching are designed with the school's vision in mind.

- The school's vision is understood and shared by all staff working in the school.

- Staff are inspired and motivated to bring the school's vision to life.

- All staff are involved in developing the school's vision.

- School governors[1] are involved in developing the school's vision.

- Students are invited to contribute to the school's vision.

- Parents are invited to contribute to the school's vision.

- External partners are invited to help shape the school's vision.

The school's vision emphasises preparing students for the future and enhancing their cognitive and social-emotional outcomes, including their well-being

For a school's vision to be perceived as truly relevant it needs to include a moral purpose (Hiatt-Michael, 2001[4]; Fullan, 1999[5]). This moral purpose should focus on the future and appeal to the common good of the community and become the core force that binds individuals together – it is the "cultural glue" between all parties. In line with the aspirations of the new school curriculum, Wales' SLO model includes a moral purpose by calling for the realisation of "the four purposes" of the new curriculum that emphasises on equipping young people for the future by focusing on cognitive and social-emotional outcomes, including well-being (see Chapter 1, Box 1.1).

Figure 3.1 shows that most respondents agreed or strongly agreed that their school had such a moral purpose in their school's vision. It shows that more than nine out of ten school staff (92%) reported that their school had a vision that focuses on students' cognitive and socio-emotional outcomes, including their well-being. Also, almost as many school staff (87%) responded that the school's vision emphasised preparing students for their future in a changing world. This is encouraging, although school leaders were significantly more positive than other categories of staff. For example, while 59% of head teachers strongly agreed with this, the same was true for a third of teachers (33%). And, as will be shown below, staff did not always feel inspired and motivated to bring the vision to life. This will be of critical importance to the success of the new curriculum.

Figure 3.1. Inclusion of moral purpose in schools' visions

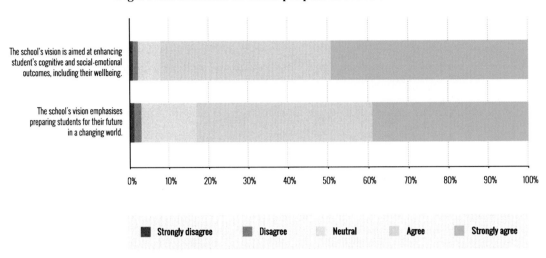

Note: N: 1 701 and 1 702 individuals for the presented SLO survey statements.
Source: OECD Schools as Learning Organisations Survey, 2017.

StatLink ᵃˢᵖ http://dx.doi.org/10.1787/888933837473

The information collected from school staff during the school visits also supports these findings and provides an insight into how some schools are bringing their vision to life (see Box 3.2).

Several of the schools the OECD team visited also systematically collected information about their students' well-being to identify those students who may need additional support.

For example, **Craigfelen Primary School** in the local authority of Swansea aimed to enhance all students' cognitive and social-emotional outcomes, including their well-being through various measures which is a challenge considering the level of student deprivation. These measures include using the "Boxall Profile" (https://boxallprofile.org/) which is an online resource for the assessment of children and young people's social, emotional and behavioural development. The two-part checklist, which is completed by staff who know the child and young person best, is quick – and, very importantly, identifies the levels of skills the children and young people possess to access learning. The information is used by teachers and management to respond to students' needs and has contributed to setting up the "Blue Room". Curtained off, this area is a safe space in the school where children can go to when they are angry, have had a breakdown or are facing other issues, to talk about their feelings with a pastoral assistant. In this quiet and cosy room, the pastoral assistant draws on a range of resources to help vulnerable children to open up.

Other examples are provided by **Dwr-y-Felin Comprehensive School** in the local authority of Neath Port Talbot, where students complete the "Respect and How Safe Do You Feel" online survey every term, and **Sully Primary School** in the local authority of Vale of Glamorgan which uses the "Social and Emotional Learning for Improvement Elsewhere" (SELFIE) survey to identify student well-being issues, improve these and use it to promote good relationships between students.

Box 3.2. An example of using team learning and collaboration to develop pedagogy to bring the new curriculum to life – Connah's Quay High School

Connah's Quay High School is a secondary school (958 students in 2017) in the local authority of Flintshire, North Wales. Like many schools throughout Wales the school recognises the benefits of a collaborative learning culture for putting in practice the new curriculum. The school promotes collaborative working and learning through various means including through the use of professional learning communities that invite practitioners to improve specific areas of their teaching through a collaborative process of enquiry (Welsh Government, 2016[6]).

As part of this model, a group of teaching staff (teachers and learning support workers) choose a pedagogical principle outlined in the *Successful Futures* report (Donaldson, 2015[7]). Examples include "building on prior learning and engagement", "learning autonomy" (learning to learn) or "blended teaching". The group engage in pedagogical research to deepen their understanding of the subject. Group members discuss new teaching strategies and experiment with them in their classrooms. Staff feed back to the group on what worked and what didn't. Conversations often lead to a "refining" stage, to further enhance the teaching strategies used. Outcomes and lessons learned are shared to other colleagues via a whole-school "sharing event" but also through the school's Learning and Teaching Newsletter.

Source: Information collected by the OECD team as part of the school visits; Estyn (2017[8]), "Effective distribution of staff responsibilities to promote professional learning and shared responsibility", www.estyn.gov.wales/effective-practice/effective-distribution-staff-responsibilities-promote-professional-learning-and.

The systematic monitoring of student well-being is important in any country, but would seem particularly important to Wales considering the equity challenges it faces. As mentioned in Chapter 1, although PISA 2015 suggests that students' socio-economic background in Wales has less impact on their performance than for students in other parts of the United Kingdom, it faces relatively high levels of child poverty and a high proportion of low performers in PISA 2015 (OECD, 2017[9]). The data from PISA 2015 also allow for an internationally comparable measurement of the well-being of 15-year-old students (see Box 3.3). The PISA 2015 results found that Wales performed well for some elements of student well-being, while in others areas it has room for further improvement. On the positive side, 15-year-olds in Wales performed relatively well when compared internationally in the "motivation to achieve" and "parents and the home environment" measures (OECD, 2017[9]).

Box 3.3. Student well-being in PISA 2015

PISA 2015 for the first time analysed students' motivation to perform well in school, their relationships with peers and teachers, their home life, and how they spend their time outside of school. Students' well-being as defined in *PISA 2015 Results: Students' Well-Being* refers to the psychological, cognitive, social and physical functioning and capabilities that students need to live a happy and fulfilling life. Well-being is thus first and foremost defined by the quality of life of students as 15-year-old individuals.

PISA 2015 offers a first-of-its-kind set of well-being indicators for adolescents that covers both negative outcomes (e.g. anxiety) and the positive impulses that promote healthy development (e.g. interest, motivation to achieve). Most of the PISA data on well-being are based on students' self-reports, and thus give adolescents the opportunity to express how they feel, what they think of their lives, and what aspirations they have for their future. PISA also allows those well-being indicators to be related to students' academic achievement across a large number of economies.

While it is extremely important to invest in future outcomes for children and adolescents, policy makers and educators need to pay attention to students' well-being now, while they are students. Well-being is also conceptualised in this report as a dynamic state: without sufficient investment to develop their capacities in the present, students are unlikely to enjoy well-being as adults.

Source: OECD (2017[9]) *PISA 2015 Results (Volume III): Students' Well-Being,* http://dx.doi.org/10.1787/9789264273856-en.

On the other hand, schoolwork-related anxiety and sense of belonging in school were two areas that appeared deserving of further attention. For example, 55% of 15-year-olds in Wales reported getting very tense when they study, which was significantly above the OECD average of 37% (OECD, 2017[9]). The Welsh Government is well aware of these findings, which support the attention given to equity and student well-being in Wales' strategic education plan, *Education in Wales: Our National Mission* (Welsh Government, 2017[3]) and the direction set out for the development of the new curriculum, promoting students' holistic development. The curriculum aims for children and young people to become ambitious and capable as well as healthy and confident (see Chapter 1, Box 1.1).

As will be further discussed in Chapter 4, the lack of a common definition and common understanding of student well-being in Wales is an issue which deserves urgent policy attention to ensure Wales' ambitions for its children and young people are put into practice.

A shared and inclusive vision that aims to enhance the learning experiences and outcomes of all students

Research evidence shows that one of the biggest challenges facing communities around the world is integrating those on the margins of society whose difficulties in learning undermine their self-confidence (Kools and Stoll, 2016[10]) – and Wales unfortunately is no exception to this. Schools throughout the country face challenges arising from poverty and other barriers to student learning (Estyn, 2017[11]; Welsh Government, 2017[3]). A SLO in Wales should therefore encourage inclusion, including through defining a vision centred on the learning of all students (Welsh Government, 2017[12]).

It is encouraging that nine out of ten (91%) respondents to the SLO survey indicated that their school's vision embraced all students. Very few respondents answered negatively (3%). However, an SLO does not just adopt a moral purpose within its vision but puts that vision into practice by aligning its activities and operations to it. This process is known as vertical alignment (Andrews et al., 2011[13]) and implies that learning activities and teaching are designed with the school's vision in mind. The SLO survey also found that nine out of ten school staff (89%) agreed that in their school, learning activities and teaching were designed with the school's vision in mind. Only 3% responded negatively.

This finding was exemplified by several of the schools the OECD team visited. For example, **Cathays High School** offers a 12-week induction programme to new arrivals to the country who enter Year 10 (in Key Stage 3) but do not speak English. These students are offered six weeks of intensive English classes, followed by a further six weeks when students are gradually integrated into mainstream lessons on a part-time basis. After this period, most students are able to follow the regular programme. Furthermore, for students who arrive at the end of Year 10 and Year 11, a tailored programme is offered including a progressive entry to Level 2 classes. The induction programme is one of the various measures Cathays High School has taken to realise the school's motto "opportunities for all" (see Box 3.4).

Although the vast majority of staff responding to the SLO survey shared the view that teaching and learning in their schools were geared towards the realisation of an inclusive vision centred on the teaching and learning of all students, other evidence shows that many schools are yet to realise this ambition. For example, Estyn (i.e. the inspectorate for education and training in Wales) has found that secondary schools in general display more excellence, but also more unsatisfactory practice, than primary schools (Estyn, 2017[11]; Estyn, 2018[14]). There is also a performance gap between girls and boys, and between students eligible for free school meals and other students. This gap widens as students progress from primary to secondary schooling. This suggests that secondary schools, which are often larger and more compartmentalised than primary schools, find it more challenging to respond to the learning and other needs of all their students (as well the needs of their staff, as the evidence presented in Chapter 2 and below suggests).

Box 3.4. Examples of ensuring equity in learning opportunities

The motto at **Cathays High School** (782 students in 2017) in Cardiff is "opportunities for all". With over 63 different languages spoken as a first language and more than three-quarters of its students from an ethnic background other than White British, this reflects the strong commitment of the school to support vulnerable students in their learning. Cathays High School developed a set of strategies to increase attendance and improve basic literacy skills for minority groups. For example, students from the Czech and Slovak Roma community generally had low attendance rates in their home countries. In order to engage them, the school established an Inclusion and Well-being team composed of Higher Level Teaching Assistants and the assistant head teacher to assist parents in educating their children. A volunteer from the Czech and Slovak Roma community was assigned to improve the communication between the school, the parents and the children. Witnessing the success of this position, the school's leadership established the team to further assist parents in their children's education. The team is in charge of translating documents, meeting with parents before the beginning of the term and facilitating the involvement of students and their families in extra-curricular activities such as reading sessions or sports. Thanks to these initiatives, student attendance at Cathays High School increased from 88% in 2011 to 94.1% in 2017.

In 2014, **Van Ostade Primary School** (425 students in 2017) in the city of The Hague in the Netherlands was awarded the prestigious "Excellent School" award for the third consecutive year. The primary school is located in the Schilderswijk, one of the most disadvantaged neighbourhoods of The Hague. All of its students are from immigrant and low socio-economic backgrounds. In response the school has placed "upbringing", "education" and "the environment" (of the child) at the heart of the organisation of the school, and with good results. At the end of their primary education, students in the school obtain much better results than would be normally expected given their socio-economic background. This is evident from their relatively high scores in the end of primary exams. The school sets high standards and wants to bring the results of all the students at the level of the national average. The success of Van Ostade school can be attributed to how it has managed to establish a collaborative learning culture within the school, but also beyond the school boundaries. The school has established strong collaborations with a wide range of partners in order to also bring the quality of education in neighbouring schools to a higher level by working together.

Teachers also regularly meet with parents, sometimes at their homes or during information evenings at school. The school offers courses on child upbringing and care, organises festivities, and involves parents in the setting of school policy. These and other measures are at the heart of the school as a learning organisation and through them the school has managed to create a learning culture that is characterised by a professional learning mindset among its staff and strong engagement with parents, the community and other partners, and its students, who are learning to be self-confident and have an inquisitive attitude towards their own learning.

Source: Information of Cathays High School in Wales was collected by the OECD team as part of the school visits; Information on Van Ostade Primary School in the Netherlands was collected as part of the school visits of a review of the Dutch education system, see OECD (2016[151]), *Netherlands 2016: Foundations for the Future*, http://dx.doi.org/10.1787/9789264257658-en.

The school's vision is the outcome of a process involving all staff

An SLO does not take a top-down approach to developing its vision and putting it into practice. Rather it involves all staff in shaping and realising the school's vision (Fullan, 2006[16]). Research evidence clearly shows that this participation process is a condition for success (Pont and Viennet, 2017[17]). Table 3.1 presents the responses to three statements from the SLO survey that measure internal participation in the development of a school's vision. While the majority of school staff tended to respond positively, the data also showed sizable proportions of staff responded negatively or neutrally which may suggest they were in doubt or simply did not know. Almost one-quarter of school staff responded negatively or neutrally to the statement "staff are inspired and motivated to bring the school's vision to life", with teachers in particular less positive: 30% of teachers responded neutrally or negatively, compared with 8% of head teachers. This is a worrying finding. It should be noted here that if a school was truly a learning organisation one would expect only a few people – ideally hardly any – to respond neutrally or negatively.

Table 3.1. Staff involvement in the development of the school vision

Statement	Strongly disagree	Disagree	Neutral	Agree	Strongly agree
The school's vision is understood and shared by all staff working in the school	1.2%	6.0%	13.3%	46.9%	32.6%
Staff are inspired and motivated to bring the school's vision to life	1.6%	5.7%	17.3%	46.7%	28.6%
All staff are involved in developing the school's vision	2.3%	8.7%	17.1%	41.1%	30.7%

Note: N: 1 692, 1 697 and 1 699 individuals for the presented SLO survey statements.
Source: OECD Schools as Learning Organisations Survey, 2017.

The data also showed that staff in different categories had significantly different perceptions of how much staff in their school were involved in the shaping of the school's vision. For example, 14% of teachers and 10% of learning support workers responded negatively and a further 20% of teachers and 18% of learning support workers neutrally to the statement that "all staff are involved in developing the school's vision", compared with 3% and 6% respectively among head teachers (see Figure 3.2).

The responses also revealed significant differences by school type: 77% of primary school staff indicated they were involved in vision development, while in secondary schools this proportion drops to 57%. Close to one in five respondents in secondary schools (18%) stated they were not involved in shaping the school's vision, while at the primary level this was significantly lower, close to one in twelve (8%).

Figure 3.2. Staff involvement in developing the school's vision, by staff category

Responses to the statement "All staff are involved in developing the school's vision"

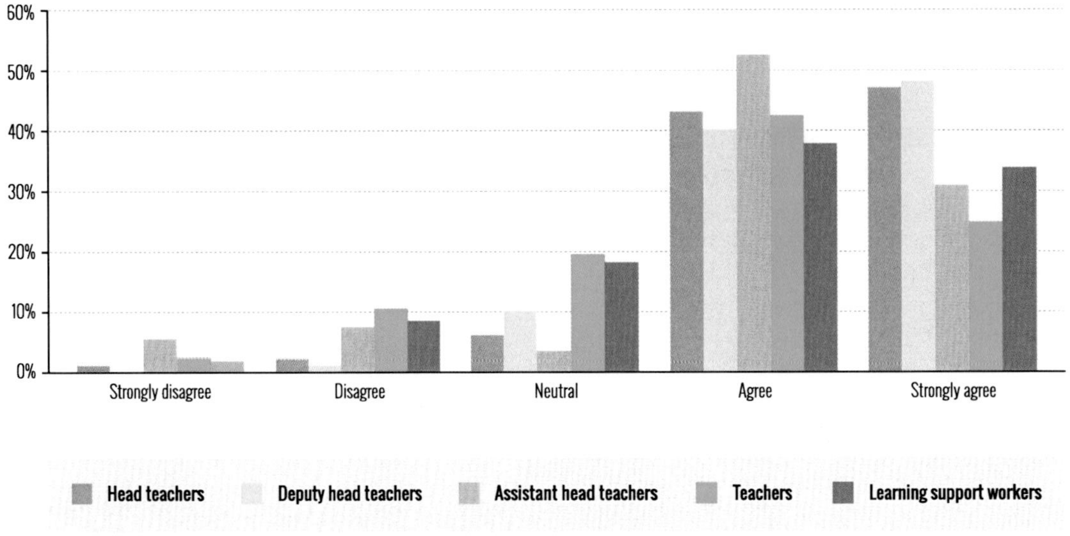

Note: N: 1 527 individuals.
Source: OECD Schools as Learning Organisations Survey, 2017.

StatLink ⧉ http://dx.doi.org/10.1787/888933837492

Student involvement in shaping the school's vision

"Student voice" is a key component of the SLO that runs through its organisational and educational processes. Involving students is key to increasing their engagement in the organisation of the school and the extent to which they feel a sense of agency over their own learning (OECD, 2013[18]). As Senge et al. (2000[19]) note: "Students can be some of the most effective instigators for organizational learning" (p. 25). For a school to be a learning organisation in Wales, giving students a meaningful voice should include having them contribute to shaping the school's vision (Welsh Government, 2017[12]).

The SLO survey found eight out of ten (79%) respondents agreed with the statement that in their school "students are invited to contribute to the school's vision". Only about 5% responded negatively to this statement, with little differences between staff categories.

Craigfelen Primary School in the local authority of Swansea provides an example of how students can be an important part of the development of the school's vision and goals and how schools can recognise their pre-eminence in decision making throughout Wales. Its students elect fellow classmates to represent them in the School Council. The School Council works closely with the governing board to inform the school's development plan. For example, to see how teaching and learning could be improved, council members launched a survey among students to collect data on teaching and the curriculum. The research process, entirely led by students, included interviews with students, questionnaires and photographs. After a year, students were asked again about their learning and one of the students acted as a "progress tracker" to compare the results with previous data. Students presented their findings to the school governing board who took them into account in their review of the school development plan.

The issue of student voice in organisational and educational processes will be discussed later as there are clear indications that this practice is less established than the responses to the SLO survey data may suggest.

Parents, the community and other external partners are invited to contribute to the school's vision

To be relevant for students and society, the development of a school's vision should include other stakeholders such as parents, the community, other educational institutions and businesses. They have a common stake in each other's future and the future of their community. Successful realisation of any school's vision increasingly depends on such partnerships as a means to grow social and professional capital (Hargreaves and Fullan, 2012[20]), and to sustain innovative change (OECD, 2013[18]; Harris and van Tassell, 2005[21]; George, Desmidt and De Moyer, 2016[22]).

Figure 3.3 provides an overview of the responses to the three SLO survey statements that captured this involvement of external partners in the shaping of the school's vision. It shows that school governors were far more involved than parents and external partners. While 74% of school staff reported that school governors were involved in shaping the school's vision, only 58% reported that for parents. External partners were seemingly least involved: 12% of respondents indicated that external partners were not invited to contribute to the school's vision.

Figure 3.3. Involvement in shaping the school's vision

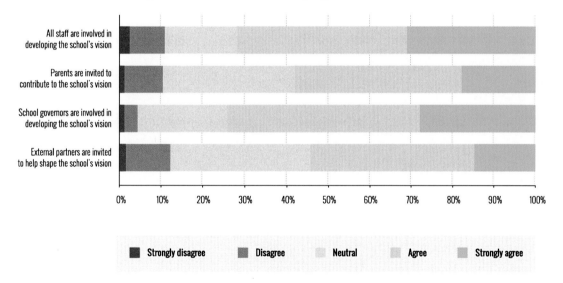

Note: N: 1 692, 1 697 and 1 692 individuals for the presented SLO survey statements.
Source: OECD Schools as Learning Organisations Survey, 2017.

StatLink 🔗 http://dx.doi.org/10.1787/888933837511

The data highlight significant differences between school types. For example, while 61% of respondents from primary schools reported that parents were invited to contribute to the school's vision, this dropped to 50% in secondary schools. This issue was also raised as a challenge by several of the staff of the secondary schools the OECD team visited. As is common in other countries, secondary schools in Wales appear to find it more challenging to engage parents in the educational process and school organisation than primary schools (Borgonovi and Montt, 2012[23]; Byrne and Smyth, 2010[24]; Desforges and Abouchaar, 2003[25]; Williams, Williams and Ullman, 2002[26]). The examples of **Van Ostade Primary School** presented above (Box 3.4) and that of **Ysgol Emrys ap Iwan** in the local authority of Conwy in Wales (Box 3.5) show that it is entirely possible to increase the engagement of parents in their school's organisation and educational process. Inviting parents to contribute to the school's vision is an important first step towards realising this aim.

Box 3.5. An example of parental engagement – Ysgol Emrys ap Iwan secondary school

Ysgol Emrys ap Iwan secondary school (987 students in 2017) in the local authority of Conwy has been recognised for its efforts to engage parents in the school's operations and educational process. In 2017, the school was awarded the Leading Parent Partnership Award (LPPA) 2017-2020, a national award that recognises the school's work with parents. The assessment by the LPPA team highlighted that "the school has a strong commitment to parent partnership which is supported by the head teacher, senior leadership team, staff and governors. The school has created a welcoming, friendly environment for parents through its open-door policy and senior leaders and staff who welcome discussions with parents and listen to their views." The LPPA provides a framework for action to help schools identify strengths and areas of improvement. This award was won after two years of dedication and collaboration among staff, governors and leadership team to meet LPPA standards. For example, the school has organised a month-long "Parent Learner Cooking" class in Years 7, 8 and 9. Parents and students cooked lasagne, shepherd's pie and chicken curry from scratch together, alongside sweet treats, including fairy cakes, biscuits and syrup sponges.

Source: Information collected by the OECD team as part of the school visits.

Creating and supporting continuous learning opportunities for all staff

General overview

The kind of education needed today requires teachers who constantly advance their own professional knowledge and that of their profession. A growing body of evidence shows that teachers' professional development can have a positive impact on student performance and teachers' practice. An SLO therefore creates continuous learning opportunities for teachers but also all other staff to enhance their professional learning and growth (Timperley et al., 2007[27]; Senge et al., 2012[2]).

The evidence suggests that many schools in Wales have, or are in the process of developing, a culture that promotes professional learning for their staff. For many of the 11 SLO survey statements used to measure this dimension (see Box 3.6) over three-quarters of respondents either agreed or strongly agreed with them, which suggests that overall professional learning is high on the agenda of schools in Wales.

Box 3.6. Survey items for the SLO dimension "creating and supporting continuous learning opportunities for all staff"

- Professional learning of staff is considered a high priority.

- Staff engage in professional learning to ensure their practice is critically informed and up to date.

- Staff are involved in identifying the objectives for their professional learning.

- Professional learning is focused on students' needs.

- Professional learning is aligned to the school's vision.

- Mentors/coaches are available to help staff develop their practice.

- All new staff receive sufficient support to help them in their new role.

- Staff receive regular feedback to support reflection and improvement.

- Students are encouraged to give feedback to teachers and support staff.

- Beliefs, mindsets and practices are challenged by professional learning.

There are however clear areas for improvement. Various sources of data and information show that induction and mentoring/coaching need to be strengthened in many schools across Wales. For example, only two-thirds of staff indicated that in their school there were mentors or coaches available to help staff develop their practice. Furthermore, the use of student feedback to teachers and support to enhance their teaching and professional learning was not yet common in schools throughout Wales and some staff seemed unsure as to whether professional learning was stimulating deep change to practices, beliefs and mindsets. The interviews with various stakeholders corroborated these findings.

The SLO survey data also revealed some significant differences between staff across school types, staff categories, staff ages and their highest level of formal education.

All staff engage in continuous professional learning to ensure their practice is critically informed and up to date

Scholars, educators and policy makers around the world increasingly support the notion of investing in quality, career-long opportunities for professional development and ensuring ongoing, active professional learning (Schleicher, 2018[28]). An SLO has a supportive culture, and invests time and other resources to ensure all staff engage in quality professional learning opportunities.

Although staff on average reported that engagement in professional learning was a high priority in schools across Wales, the data presented in Table 3.2 suggest there is scope for further improvement. For example, 30% responded negatively or neutrally to the statement that in their school "beliefs, mindsets and practices are challenged by professional learning". Also, one in five staff (21%) responded negatively or neutrally to the statement that "professional learning of staff is considered a high priority" in their school.

Table 3.2. Engagement in professional learning to ensure practice is up to date

	Strongly disagree	Disagree	Neutral	Agree	Strongly agree
Professional learning of staff is considered a high priority	1.8%	5.5%	13.7%	43.8%	35.1%
Staff engage in professional learning to ensure their practice is critically informed and up to date	1.1%	4.4%	14.2%	49.5%	30.8%
Beliefs, mindsets and practices are challenged by professional learning	0.8%	3.9%	24.0%	50.4%	21.0%
Staff have opportunities to experiment with and practise new skills	0.7%	6.1%	13.6%	50.5%	29.3%

Note: N: 1 632, 1 636, 1 635 and 1 651 individuals for the presented SLO survey statements.
Source: OECD Schools as Learning Organisations Survey, 2017.

The data also revealed some significant differences between staff categories. For example, while school leaders almost unanimously reported that professional learning was a high priority in their schools, 10% of teachers did not share their view and a further 16% responded neutrally. For learning support workers these proportions were 7% and 18% respectively. And while only 14% of all school leaders were neutral or disagreed that beliefs, mindsets and practices were challenged by professional learning, 28% of learning support workers and 30% of teachers shared this view. Again, we would not expect to find such large proportions of neutral responses in an SLO.

Furthermore, while 81% of respondents in primary schools responded positively to the statement that "professional learning of staff is a high priority" in their school, this was 10% lower in secondary schools.

New staff receive induction support and all staff have access to coaching and mentoring support

Research evidence shows that well-designed induction programmes increase teacher retention and satisfaction and improve teaching quality (Kessels, 2010[29]; Ingersoll and Strong, 2011[30]). Wales has had a mandatory one-year induction period for all newly qualified teachers for a long time. This is important, as well-structured and well-resourced induction programmes can support new teachers in their transition to full teaching responsibilities (Schleicher, 2012[31]).

The OECD team however learned that little is known about the quality of these induction programmes in Wales. The evidence from this assessment suggests challenges exist in terms of the quantity and quality of such programmes in some schools and parts of the country. For example, the SLO survey data showed that about 30% of respondents disagreed or responded neutrally to the statement that in their school "all new staff receive sufficient support to help them in their new role" (see Table 3.3).

Also, while 11% of staff under 30 years old responded negatively and 24% neutrally to this, among staff aged 60 years and older only 13% responded neutrally and none of them disagreed. This may mean that older staff are not fully aware of the support younger colleagues are receiving as they start their careers. Where these older staff are leaders – which frequently is the case – some may believe that support systems are in place when they are not seen as such by new staff.

The data also suggest that slightly fewer new staff in secondary schools benefit from sufficient induction support than their peers in primary schools: 13% of secondary school staff disagreed that new staff received sufficient support, while in primary schools this was slightly lower (9%). Several policy makers and other stakeholders the OECD team interviewed were pleasantly surprised by the relatively minor difference between the two school types.

Table 3.3. Induction and mentoring and coaching support

	Strongly disagree	Disagree	Neutral	Agree	Strongly agree
All new staff receive sufficient support to help them in their new role	2.3%	7.8%	19.6%	44.5%	25.8%
Mentors/coaches are available to help staff develop their practice	2.5%	10.8%	22.1%	42.7%	22.0%

Note: N: 1 633 and 1 634 individuals for the presented SLO survey statements.
Source: OECD Schools as Learning Organisations Survey, 2017.

Furthermore, although PISA 2015 found that virtually all secondary head teachers (98%) reported that teacher mentoring was used as a means of quality assurance in their school, compared to an OECD average of 78% (Jerrim and Shure, 2016[32]), the SLO survey data provide a less positive view of the situation. About 18% of secondary school respondents indicated that mentoring and coaching support was not available for all staff in their school, and 12% of those in primary schools. In addition, at both levels of education, teachers – and to a lesser extent learning support workers – were more critical about this issue than those in leadership positions (Figure 3.4).

Figure 3.4. Availability of mentoring or coaching support, by staff categories

Responses to the statement "mentors or coaches are available to help staff develop their practice"

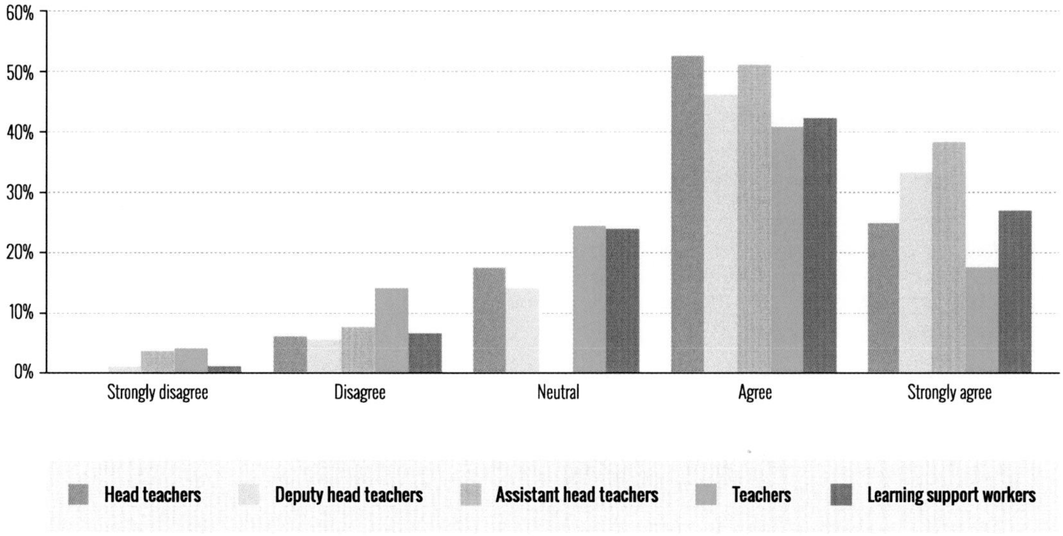

Note: N: 1 522 individuals.
Source: OECD Schools as Learning Organisations Survey, 2017.

StatLink ⓢ http://dx.doi.org/10.1787/888933837530

These are important findings considering that Wales is in the middle of a curriculum reform that is likely to require teachers and learning support workers to extend their skills and engage in trial and error learning. They would benefit from close relationships with colleagues who have had prior training and experience in the new curriculum (Thompson et al., 2004[33]). This is an issue which deserves further attention from school leaders – in particular those working in secondary schools – but also from Pioneer Schools, local authorities, regional consortia and the Welsh Government to ensure schools have the capacity and support to make high-quality induction and coaching and mentoring common practice in all schools in Wales.

Staff are fully engaged in identifying the priorities for their own professional learning – which is focused on student learning and school goals

In an SLO, staff are involved in identifying their professional learning needs, which also need to be aligned with students' needs and the school's goals (Kools and Stoll, 2016[10]). The SLO survey contains three statements related to this:

- Staff are involved in identifying the objectives for their professional learning.

- Professional learning is focused on students' needs.

- Professional learning is aligned to the school's vision.

On average about eight out ten school staff responded positively to these statements, with relatively little difference between the levels of education or across regions. There were some differences between staff categories though. For example, close to all head teachers, deputy head teachers and assistant head teachers (about 95%) responded positively to the first statement listed above, while for teachers and learning support workers this dropped significantly (81% for both).

The interviews with school staff and other stakeholders found that there was still a tendency among staff in some schools to focus professional learning on individuals' needs and interests rather than the strategic goals and learning needs of students. Also, according to Estyn (Estyn, 2018[14]) a quarter of primary schools and two-fifths of secondary schools have not established a culture of professional learning where staff have open and honest discussions about their own practice and its impact on student learning and outcomes.

Professional learning is based on assessment and feedback, including by students

Effective professional learning and growth depends on regular assessment and feedback. When shaped in a purposeful manner this can have a strong positive influence on teachers' professional development and their daily practice (Schleicher, 2015[34]; Hattie and Timperley, 2007[35]; Timperley et al., 2007[27]). Educators need feedback and other reflection approaches to challenge their thinking and assumptions about their practice. As such, reflection and challenge to thinking patterns, including by students, are central to Wales' SLO model (Welsh Government, 2017[12]).

Starting with the most important stakeholders, i.e. students, the SLO survey data showed that almost two out of three staff (64%) responded that in their school "students are encouraged to give feedback to teachers and support staff" to enhance their teaching and professional learning. This is an encouraging finding but at the same time points to the need for further improvement as 12% responded negatively to this statement – 11% of primary school staff and 17% of secondary staff.

Although almost three-quarters of school staff (72%) indicated that "staff receive regular feedback to support reflection and improvement" in their school, some 10% responded negatively to this statement (14% in secondary schools and 9% in primary schools) and a further 17% responded neutrally, which may suggest they were not sure or had mixed feelings.

The data also pointed to differences depending on the ages of staff and highest level of formal education. For example, while 74% of staff with a bachelor's degree agreed that staff received regular feedback, the figure was 7 percentage points lower among staff with A Levels or an equivalent qualification (67%). Several of the school staff, policy makers and other stakeholders the OECD team interviewed recognised this as area for further improvement for many schools in Wales – more than these data would suggest. The exchange of good practice and peer learning in the two schools showcased in Box 3.7 and other similar examples could contribute to such an improvement effort.

Box 3.7. Examples of professional learning based on assessment and feedback

Penygarn Community Primary School (471 students in 2017) in the local authority of Torfaen provides training for middle-level leaders to develop their role further according to the principles outlined in the *Excellence in Teaching* framework. This framework is a tool that is used by the school's teachers to review and receive feedback on their teaching and learning development. Among its various uses are recording and sharing data from observations, lesson planning, marking, and working with colleagues. For every element – i.e. subject knowledge, challenge and expectation, engagement and enthusiasm, resource and time, assessment, progress, and standards and behaviour for learning – teachers can range from unsatisfactory to excellent according to a set of characteristics.

Middle-level leaders also receive training responding to identified developmental needs and are taught how to write evaluation reports on their practice. They have adopted a "Focus-Analyse-Do-Evaluate" (FADE) approach to self-evaluation that facilitates a regular review of progress.

Olchfa School is a secondary school (1 693 students in 2017) in the local authority of Swansea. In 2006, the school established a Learning and Teaching Observation Group (LATOG), a peer teaching observation scheme to offer advice to teachers and share good practice across departments. Observations take place in a culture of trust and provide a starting point for dialogue about teaching and learning among staff. The school has a team of ten LATOG staff who are responsible for observing staff in various departments and promoting continuous professional learning. After being observed, teachers receive verbal and written feedback on their lessons. In order to keep the process efficient, oral commentaries are provided on the same day as the observation and the written feedback comes within seven days. The team is reviewed every year and any new observers are required to follow a training programme when they join the team.

The school is also piloting a new project involving a group of trained students who accompany LATOG staff during peer observations. The students are asked to give written feedback on selected areas. This use of feedback involving students gives them a greater voice and more participation in the school organisation.

Source: Information collected by the OECD team as part of the school visits; Estyn (2011[36]), "With a little help from my friends", www.estyn.gov.wales/effective-practice/little-help-my-friends.

Promoting team learning and collaboration among all staff

General overview

Schools offer great potential for collaborative working and learning. Where this does not occur, people are less likely to reap the benefits that team work and joint reflection can bring to enhancing their practice. Team learning and collaboration are central to the SLO and to the development of its staff (Senge et al., 2012[2]). To ensure that teachers and other school staff feel comfortable in turning to each other for advice and engaging in team learning and working, schools need to create an enabling environment characterised by mutual trust and respect (Cerna, 2014[37]). Box 3.8 lists the survey items related to this dimension.

Box 3.8. Survey items for the SLO dimension "promoting team learning and collaboration among all staff"

- Staff collaborate to improve their practice.
- Staff learn how to work together as a team.
- Staff help each other to improve their practice.
- Staff observe each other's practice and collaborate in developing it.
- Staff think through and tackle problems together.
- Staff reflect together on how to learn and improve their practice.
- Staff give honest feedback to each other.
- Staff listen to each other's ideas and opinions.
- Staff feel comfortable turning to others for advice.
- Staff treat each other with respect.
- Staff spend time building trust with each other.

The evidence suggests that on average collaborative working and learning are well embedded in schools throughout Wales. This assessment also points to some areas for further improvement for this SLO dimension, however. For example, schools could do more to ensure that "staff observe each other's practice and collaborate in improving it", that "staff think through and tackle problems together" and that "staff spend time building trust with each other". More than one-fifth of staff responded neutrally or disagreed with these SLO survey statements. For these statements, teachers were the most critical in their responses.

This assessment also suggests that some schools need more frequent and open discussions between school leaders, teachers and learning support workers to diminish the differences in their perceptions. Although there are bound to be some differences in perceptions between staff categories, as some staff may simply be better informed due to the nature of their work, the sizable differences reported in this section – and also other sections of this chapter – suggest the need for more professional dialogue and sharing of information. This is again particularly the case in secondary schools. This is all the more essential considering the ongoing curriculum reform, where success will partly depend on staff engaging in trial and error learning and tacking problems together.

Staff learn and work collectively to improve their practice

In an SLO, staff learn to work together and learn collectively – whether face-to-face or using technology – with peer networking playing an important role in enhancing the professionalism of teachers and school leaders. Wales aims to have a collaborative education profession, driven by a deep understanding of pedagogy and their subject matter, and with a shared understanding of key responsibilities across the entire system (Welsh Government, 2017[38]).

The data presented in Figure 3.5 suggest that on average collaborative working and learning are well embedded in schools throughout Wales. An earlier OECD assessment (OECD, 2017[39]) and the OECD team's interviews with school staff and other stakeholders corroborate this finding.

Figure 3.5. Collaborative learning and working

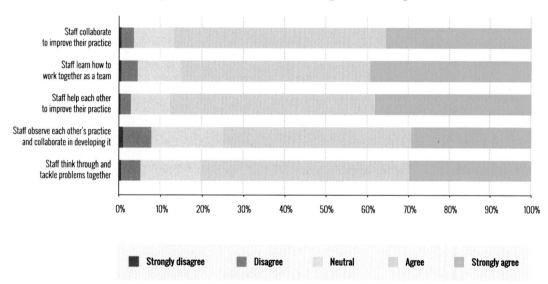

Strongly disagree ■ Disagree ■ Neutral ■ Agree ■ Strongly agree

Note: N: 1 627, 1 625, 1 621, 1 624 and 1 625 individuals for the presented SLO survey statements.
Source: OECD Schools as Learning Organisations Survey, 2017.

StatLink http://dx.doi.org/10.1787/888933837549

At the same time this assessment points to some areas for further improvement. For example, the SLO survey data suggest schools could do more to ensure that "staff observe each other's practice and collaborate in improving it" and that "staff think through and tackle problems together" (see Figure 3.5). More than one in five staff responded neutrally or indicated they disagreed with these statements. For both statements teachers were most critical.

Younger staff were also slightly more critical in their views about how far staff in their school observe each other's practice and collaborate in improving. For example, while 27% of staff under the age of 30 responded negatively or neutrally to this statement, this proportion fell to 22% among 50-59 year-olds and 5% among staff aged 60 and over. This difference is partially explained by the fact that those in leadership positions are on average older; the data show that staff in leadership positions were more likely to respond positively to this survey statement than other staff.

It is unclear whether younger staff thought that they themselves did not have the opportunity to observe others and collaborate, or whether they thought it was not true of their colleagues. Either way, in an SLO, it is generally expected that staff share their insights and findings on learning and teaching with colleagues (Kools and Stoll, 2016[10]). For some staff, this will come naturally but others may need encouragement and support to display and internalise such behaviour. It is important that the support provided to staff is not limited to those new to the school but should involve all staff in order to establish a thriving learning culture. In the SLO survey, some 15% of staff responded negatively or neutrally to the statement that in their school "staff learn how to work together as a team" – 21% in secondary schools and 11% in primary schools.

The assessment also found differences in perceptions across different staff categories in this area. For example, in PISA 2015, 92% of head teachers in secondary schools in Wales reported that teacher peer review (of lesson plans, assessment instruments and lessons) was used to monitor the practice of teachers, compared to an OECD average of 78.1% (OECD, 2016[40]). This figure may have to be interpreted with some caution, as the evidence from the assessment suggests that teachers and learning support workers in Wales do not always share the views of their head teachers. For example, while 92% of secondary head teachers responded positively to the SLO survey statement "staff observe each other's practice and collaborate in developing it" in their schools, only 67% of teachers responded in a similar vein.

These are significant differences that suggest the need for more professional dialogue and sharing of information among all staff. The assessment learned of several examples that may act as a source of ideas for schools wishing to strengthen their professional dialogue and information sharing (see Box 3.2, Box 3.7 (Olchfa School) and Box 3.9).

Box 3.9. An example of promoting team learning and collaboration among all staff – Ysgol Gymunedol Comins Coch, a primary school

Ysgol Gymunedol Comins Coch is a primary school (184 students in 2017) in the local authority of Ceredigion, Mid Wales. The school's leadership promotes collaborative learning through a whole-school approach that includes peer observation, staff mentoring and training. Teaching staff and teaching assistants identify good practice during regular peer observations and align them with school priorities. Staff share videos of good practice within the school. Open discussions about these videos, as well as whole-school book scrutiny sessions guarantee dialogue among all staff, a clear understanding of the school vision and co-operation.

Furthermore, all staff members and representatives from the school's governing body join together on school training days to reflect on and evaluate the current priorities. Through these and other means the school aims to engage all staff in a professional dialogue and collective learning throughout the year.

Source: Information collected by the OECD team as part of the school visits; Estyn (2017[8]), "Effective distribution of staff responsibilities to promote professional learning and shared responsibility", www.estyn.gov.wales/effective-practice/effective-distribution-staff-responsibilities-promote-professional-learning-and.

A school culture characterised by mutual trust and respect

In an SLO, staff have a positive attitude towards collaboration and team learning. Trust and mutual respect are core values. They form the glue that holds the school together and allows for co-operation between individuals and teams to thrive. When people trust and respect each other, other means of governance and control can be minimised (Cerna, 2014[37]; Bryk and Schneider, 2002[41]). Creating an organisational culture of trust and respect in which team learning and collaboration can thrive naturally involves most, if not all, members of the organisation.

Figure 3.6 suggests that in many schools throughout Wales trust and mutual respect are core values which are being worked on regularly. For example, about 85% of respondents to the SLO survey indicated that "staff listen to other's ideas and opinions" and "treat each other with respect". However, respondents were slightly more critical about the extent to which "staff give honest feedback to each other" and "spend time building trust with each other" – as can be seen from the proportions of staff who disagreed with these statements or responded neutrally.

Looking at differences between staff categories, it was again found that teachers in general held more critical views, followed by learning support workers – although they were considerably more positive (see for example Figure 3.7).

Although differences across the regions are relatively small in general for this SLO dimension, a common finding is that staff in secondary schools were less positive about the extent to which they engage in collaborative working and learning. This is clearly an issue for action especially for school leaders, including those in middle leadership positions, and the challenge advisors in the regional consortia and their professional learning offers.

Figure 3.6. Trust and mutual respect in learning and working together

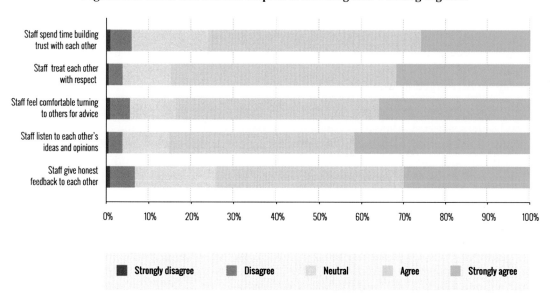

Note: N: 1 625, 1 626, 1 625, 1 626 and 1 620 individuals respectively.
Source: OECD Schools as Learning Organisations Survey, 2017.

StatLink ᴪᴪᴘ http://dx.doi.org/10.1787/888933837568

Figure 3.7. Building mutual trust, by staff categories

Responses to the statement "staff spend time building trust with each other"

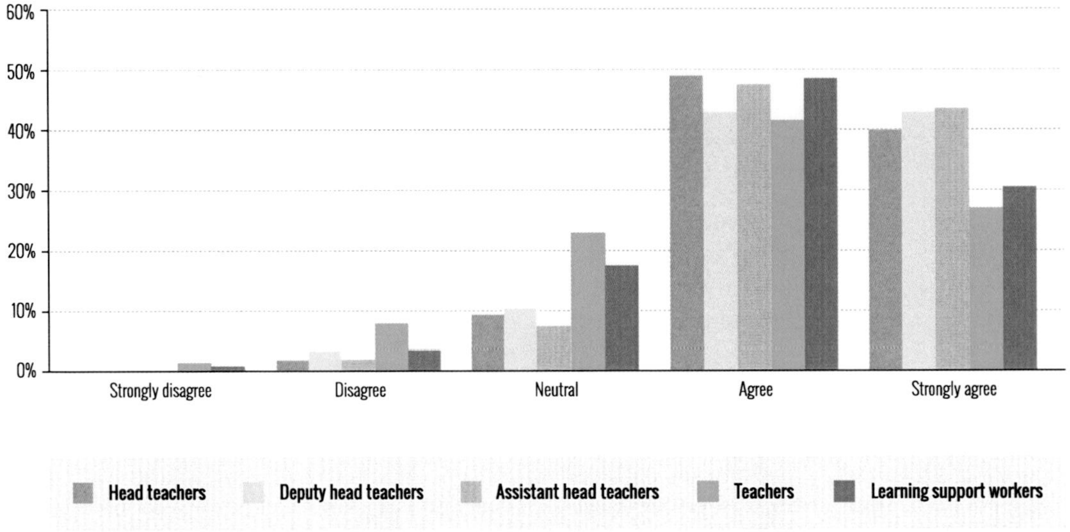

Head teachers   Deputy head teachers   Assistant head teachers   Teachers   Learning support workers

Note: N: 1 521 individuals.
Source: OECD Schools as Learning Organisations Survey, 2017.

StatLink ᵐˢᵖ http://dx.doi.org/10.1787/888933837587

Time and other resources are provided to support professional learning – both individual and collaborative

Research evidence shows that a key factor behind schools developing as learning organisations is the extent to which staff perceive that there are sufficient resources for learning to occur (Silins, Zarins and Mulford, 2002[42]). The importance placed on professional learning and collaborative working is reflected in the allocation of time and other resources, such as a weekly schedule of regular hours devoted to team meetings (Somech and Drach-Zahavy, 2007[43]), and time for colleagues to observe each other and engage in networked learning.

This evidence, as well as the OECD team's interviews with school staff and other stakeholders, suggest schools in Wales do not have equal access to time and resources to support them in their professional learning. Concerns about staff workloads were raised several times in the interviews with school staff, policy makers and other stakeholders. These findings were corroborated by those of the 2017 National Education Workforce Survey (Education Workforce Council, 2017[44]) which pointed to clear challenges in terms of the workload of teachers and learning support workers and the amount of administration they need to do as part of their daily duties.

Time is one of the four cross-cutting themes of an SLO (Kools and Stoll, 2016[10]). It seems to be a factor of influence that may pose a challenge to schools as they develop into learning organisations and, ultimately, put the new curriculum into practice. The issue of workload reduction is therefore high on the policy agenda in Wales. A guidance note for teachers and head teachers has been produced to help them reduce workload issues (Estyn, 2017[45]). However, schools are likely to need further guidance to realise the note's suggestions which in many cases will require breaking with old habits. The regional consortia's challenge advisors will have a pivotal role in helping school staff do this. The new assessment, evaluation and accountability arrangements should also support this by promoting more efficient ways of working (see Chapter 4).

The issue of financial resources is also directly related. An issue that was raised several times by interviewees was that differences in local funding models are causing inequalities for both students and school staff across the 22 local authorities. Also, out of the 118 open comments received through the SLO survey, 11 referred to challenges in terms of funding and another 16 to the directly related issue of time and workload challenges. These issues will be further discussed in Chapter 4 as policy action seems needed.

Although schools need to be adequately supported and enabled to develop as learning organisations, they do have the power to implement many actions to ensure staff have the time and resources to engage in collaborative working and learning to establish "a rhythm of continuous improvement". Several examples from Wales presented in this report provide testament to this, while Box 3.10 gives an international example.

Box 3.10. An example of allocating time and resources for collaborative working and learning – Arroyo Grande High School in the United States

Arroyo Grande High School in the Lucia Mar Unified school district, in California (United States) (2 206 students in 2017) was a participant in the pilot of the PISA-based Test for Schools (known in the United States as the OECD Test for Schools) in 2012. The school's results from the pilot showed a large proportion of its students to be low performers; 29% of its students performed below level 2 in reading, 39% in maths and 20% in science. These findings triggered the school to take a number of concrete measures including a revision of its formative assessments to provide a greater focus on developing students' literacy skills and helped teachers understand how to embed critical thinking skills into their teaching. Teachers have since then used a variety of tactics to embed critical thinking activities into the classroom, with particular attention paid to strategies promoted by Advancement Via Individual Determination (AVID). Opportunities for rich discussion among students, coupled with group engagement work like Philosophical Chairs and Socratic Seminars, where students discuss their views on a given topic, have increased critical thinking in the classroom. The school also put in place a school-wide focus on critical reading and writing, which included the use of rubrics by each department to help teachers assess and support students' progress.

To facilitate these and other changes, the school changed its schedule to allow for more professional learning time for its teachers. The new schedule includes Late Start Mondays every week for teachers, when teachers work in collaborative groups to analyse and reflect on student data, collaboratively plan lessons, and identify areas for remediation and acceleration as needed.

These efforts have certainly paid off. Between the 2012 pilot and the 2014-15 administration of the OECD Test for Schools, the percentage of students performing below level 2 decreased by 15% in reading, 9% in maths and 9% in science, while the proportion of students performing at the highest proficiency levels rose in all three subjects.

Source: Information collected by the OECD team of America Achieves (www.americaachievesednetworks.org/) as part of the school visits; PISA for Schools project documents.

Establishing a culture of enquiry, innovation and exploration

General overview

A mark of any professional is the ability to reflect critically on both their profession and their daily work, to be continuously engaged in self-improvement. For such behaviour to pervade throughout organisations, it is necessary to cultivate a learning habit in people and a culture where a spirit of enquiry, initiative and willingness to experiment with new ideas and practices predominates (Watkins and Marsick, 1996[46]; Kools and Stoll, 2016[10]; Earl and Timperley, 2015[47]). This mindset is critical if schools are to develop as learning organisations. Box 3.11 lists the survey items for this dimension.

As discussed in Chapter 2, the findings of this assessment suggest that on average staff in the majority of schools in Wales thought that staff were willing and dared to take the initiative, experiment and do things differently. The OECD team members were in fact struck by the difference in attitudes compared with the review the OECD undertook in 2013 (OECD, 2014[48]). Although on more than one occasion school staff expressed uncertainty about how far Estyn inspections and other parts of the new assessment, evaluation and accountability framework under development would support innovations, the OECD team clearly found a great deal of enthusiasm within the system to change and innovate teaching and learning which the SLO survey data corroborate. This is an important step forward for realising Wales' ambitious education reform agenda.

Box 3.11. Survey items for the SLO dimension "establishing a culture of enquiry, innovation and exploration"

- Staff are encouraged to experiment and innovate their practice.

- Staff are encouraged to take initiative.

- Staff are supported when taking calculated risks.

- Staff spend time exploring a problem before taking action.

- Staff engage in enquiry (i.e. pose questions, gather and use evidence to decide how to change their practice, and evaluate its impact).

- Staff are open to thinking and doing things differently.

- Staff are open to others questioning their beliefs, opinions and ideas.

- Staff openly discuss failures in order to learn from them.

- Problems are seen as opportunities for learning.

Despite progress in recent years, the evidence suggests that this is one of the least-developed SLO dimensions in schools in Wales on average. This may partially be the result of the high-stakes assessment, evaluation and accountability arrangements that have characterised the system for years (Donaldson, 2015[7]) (see also Chapter 4).

Furthermore, the data point to some significant differences between school types, staff categories and the four regions of Wales. For example, the SLO survey found different response patterns to the statement "staff openly discuss failures in order to learn from them" across the regions, with school staff in North Wales being most positive (78%

responded positively) and staff in schools in South Wales the least positive (67% responded positively).

Staff engage in enquiry and spend time exploring a problem before taking action

An SLO continually expands its capacity to create its future. This is not a linear or mechanistic process; rather it involves an iterative organisational learning process of reflection and "thinking in circles" through a series of decisions, actions and feedback loops (Earl and Katz, 2002[49]; Earl and Timperley, 2015[47]). Table 3.4 shows that 75% respondents agreed or strongly agreed that staff in their school engaged in enquiry to enhance their practice.

Table 3.4. Staff engaging in enquiry

	Strongly disagree	Disagree	Neutral	Agree	Strongly agree
Staff engage in enquiry (i.e. pose questions, gather and use evidence to decide how to change their practice, and evaluate its impact)	1.1%	5.8%	18.5%	50.6%	24.0%
Staff spend time exploring a problem before taking action	1.2%	6.5%	22.0%	50.8%	19.6%

Note: N: 1 662 and 1 657 individuals for the presented SLO survey statements.
Source: OECD Schools as Learning Organisations Survey, 2017.

However, true engagement in enquiry also depends on the ability to tolerate ambiguity and holding back from rushing to judgements. The SLO survey data found that around 70% of staff agreed that time was spent exploring a problem before taking action – 73% of staff in primary schools and 62% of staff in secondary schools. Again leaders were more positive, with 81% of all leaders agreeing that this happened in contrast with 65% of teachers.

The school supports and recognises the taking of initiative and risks

For a school to be a learning organisation, it is essential that people feel confident and dare to innovate in their daily practice and are supported and rewarded for taking initiatives and risks (Welsh Government, 2017[12]). Building on the core values of trust and mutual respect, people need to have an open mind about new ways of doing things. Staff are thus helped to overcome the uncertainties of such challenges as engaging with a new curriculum through collegial and open dialogue, exchanging ideas and sharing experiences, and experimenting.

Figure 3.8 shows the extent to which respondents to the SLO survey agreed that staff were encouraged to experiment and innovate their practice, take the initiative and do things differently. More than eight out of ten staff responded positively to these statements, with the exception of two items, regarding calculated risks and openness to questioning – although these still scored highly.

The data revealed only minor differences between primary and secondary schools, but significant differences between staff categories. For example, while 96% of head teachers and assistant head teachers, and 94% of deputy head teachers, indicated that in their school staff were encouraged to experiment and innovate their practice, this proportion fell to 82% among learning support workers. Interestingly this is one of the few SLO survey items on which learning support workers recorded the lowest score across the different staff categories.

Figure 3.8. Staff attitudes to experimentation, initiative and risk taking

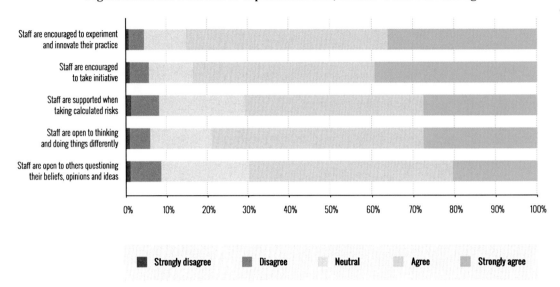

Note: N: 1 665, 1 660, 1 659, 1 661 and 1 661 individuals for the presented SLO survey statements.
Source: OECD Schools as Learning Organisations Survey, 2017.

StatLink ᘇᵔᔭ▱ http://dx.doi.org/10.1787/888933837606

Willingness and openness to take the initiative, experiment and do things differently were also apparent in the interviews the OECD team had with school staff and other stakeholders. One example is provided by **Ygsol San Sior** primary school in the city of Llandudno, showing how enquiry can serve creativity and create a stimulating and challenging learning environment for its students, as well as for the staff working in the school (see Box 3.12). For example, the evidence seemed to suggest that chickens will lay more eggs if music is being played to them. Putting this to the test, as part of their music lessons, students performed for the school's chickens to investigate whether this was indeed the case. At the time of the visit by the OECD team, the investigation was ongoing but regardless of the outcome this example shows how the staff of Ygsol San Sior use enquiry and creativity to stimulate and motivate students in their daily learning.

As mentioned in Chapter 2, the OECD team were struck by the difference in attitudes compared with the review the OECD undertook in 2013 when it found a more conservative attitude to changing and innovating practice and reform fatigue seemed to reign in schools throughout Wales. Despite the staff uncertainty mentioned above about whether Estyn inspections and new assessment, evaluation and accountability arrangements would support innovations, the OECD team noticed a positive change in mindset among school staff towards innovating their practice. This will be an asset for Wales when realising its curriculum reform and as such should be nurtured and further enhanced where possible.

This assessment may help with this as it points to several areas for improvement. Apart from once more finding that teachers were most critical in their responses to the survey statements, it was also found that staff in secondary schools were slightly more negative in their responses than those in primary schools. For example, while 74% of primary school staff responded positively to the statement that "staff are supported when taking calculated risks", the figure was 11 percentage points lower among secondary school staff (63%).

Figure 3.9 shows secondary school staff were less positive about the extent to which staff in their school are open to others questioning their beliefs, opinions and ideas. Around 28% of primary school staff responded negatively or neutrally to the statement that "staff are open to others questioning their beliefs, opinions and ideas", about 10 percentage points less than their peers in secondary schools.

Figure 3.9. Openness to questioning among staff, by school type

Responses to the statement "staff are open to others questioning their beliefs, opinions and ideas"

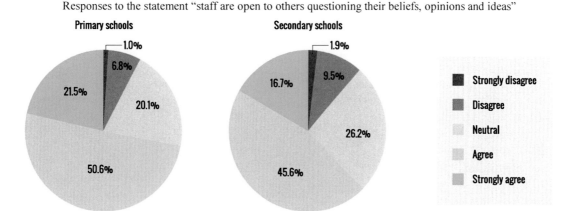

Note: N: 1 664 individuals.
Source: OECD Schools as Learning Organisations Survey, 2017.

StatLink ⫘⫘⪢ http://dx.doi.org/10.1787/888933837625

For both levels of education, teachers were most critical: 11% of teachers reported that in their school staff were not open to others questioning their beliefs, opinions and ideas, compared to 6% of learning support workers, deputy head teachers and assistant head teachers, and 3% of head teachers.

These findings suggest that further efforts should be made to help increase people's willingness to consider new ways of working, find ways to promote greater openness and move towards a learning culture built on trust in all schools in Wales. School leaders have an important role in creating these conditions (as will be further discussed below), and this particularly seems to be a challenge for leaders of secondary schools.

Box 3.12. An example of doing things differently – Ygsol San Sior, a farm school

Ygsol San Sior is a primary school (242 students in 2016) in the city of Llandudno in the local authority of Conwy, North Wales. The school exemplifies how doing things differently can help create a stimulating and challenging learning environment that explores the opportunities offered by the wider environment to enrich student learning.

The school is considered a "farm school" and is the only school in Wales allowed to sell eggs to retail establishments. Like many Welsh primary schools, Ygsol San Sior keeps chickens and animals in the school garden. In 2013, the school had seven chickens, essentially for pedagogical purposes. In 2017, the activity has grown; its 99 chickens produce over 20 000 eggs a year. These eggs are stamped by the Egg Marketing inspector and sold to parents and the local community.

In 2014, the school won the Welsh Government's Best Enterprise Award for the San Sior Enterprise. This award demonstrates the entrepreneurial skills acquired by the students through the links with retail outlets selling the eggs. Every student, from nursery to Year 6 is involved in the school business. Teachers adapt their lesson plans to include the enterprise in the students' learning, so they are not only collecting eggs, for example, but also driving standards in literacy and numeracy. Each week, teachers and support staff link their classes to an aspect of the school farm and the duties it generates. For example, students have to write creative stories about how to catch a chicken, learn accounting and calculate the profits from the egg sales, or write an egg cookbook. These cross-curricular activities – the result of joint lesson planning and intense collaboration between staff – have spillovers, since students improve their performance in literacy and numeracy while tending the chickens. Activities are also geared towards the community's well-being. Students are taught how to become active citizens: for example measuring the decibels of noise from the "nuisance cockerel" and how it affects the local community. The profit from the chicken enterprise is put into outdoor projects, such as the creation of a beehive, and is also used to buy better equipment for sports, according to School Council initiatives. The school also invested part of the profit in cameras to record the bees' activity and display it in the foyer.

In addition to chickens, bees and the school garden, the school foyer houses an exotic collection of hedgehogs, hamsters, reptiles and insects that are incorporated into lessons and cared for by students, thereby complementing the stimulating and challenging curriculum of this extraordinary school.

Source: Information collected by the OECD team during the school visit and from the school's website, www.sansior.co.uk/.

Failures and problems are discussed and seen as opportunities for learning

SLOs systematically learn from failure. This is important as some initiatives and experiments will fail, while others succeed – and both offer valuable lessons. Problems and mistakes are thus seen as opportunities for learning and are considered a natural, even essential part of making progress in a learning organisation (Watkins and Marsick, 1996[46]; Cannon and Edmondson, 2005[50]).

Although the majority of respondents shared the view that in their schools "staff openly discuss failures in order to learn from them" and "problems are seen as opportunities for learning" the survey also suggested that about one-third of them did not know for certain or disagreed with these statements (see Table 3.5). The data here also showed notable differences in reporting patterns between staff categories, school types and the four regions of Wales. For example, 15% of teachers did not share the view that staff in their schools openly discussed failures in order to learn from them, compared with 7% of learning support workers and 6% of head teachers and deputy head teachers. Assistant head teachers were interestingly more critical than their colleagues in formal leadership roles; some 11% did not agree with this statement. This finding is notable because assistant heads were generally extremely positive in their responses to the survey – frequently more so than head teachers and deputy head teachers. As many assistant head teachers have a role closely connected with leading learning and teaching or professional learning, their observations can shine a valuable light on the process of change in schools.

Table 3.5. Staff attitudes to failure and problems

	Strongly disagree	Disagree	Neutral	Agree	Strongly agree
Staff openly discuss failures in order to learn from them	1.9 %	9.6 %	20.7 %	47.2 %	20.6 %
Problems are seen as opportunities for learning	2.1 %	7.8 %	20.6 %	47.7 %	21.8 %

Note: N: 1 664 and 1 657 individuals for the presented SLO survey statements.
Source: OECD Schools as Learning Organisations Survey, 2017.

Figure 3.10 shows the differences in responses between staff in primary and secondary schools which, although relatively minor, confirm the common trend throughout this section that establishing a culture of enquiry, experimentation and innovation seems more challenging for secondary schools in Wales. Wales' high-stakes assessment, evaluation and accountability arrangements are believed to be a factor of influence in this. Chapter 4 will elaborate on this issue.

As mentioned above, the data in this dimension point to some differences across the regions. For example, just under two-thirds (65%) of staff of schools in South Wales responded positively to the statement that "problems are seen as opportunities for learning", compared with 73% for schools in South East Wales and 75% for schools in North Wales. In South West and Mid Wales, the share was 69% of school staff.

Figure 3.10. Staff attitudes to failure and problems, by school type

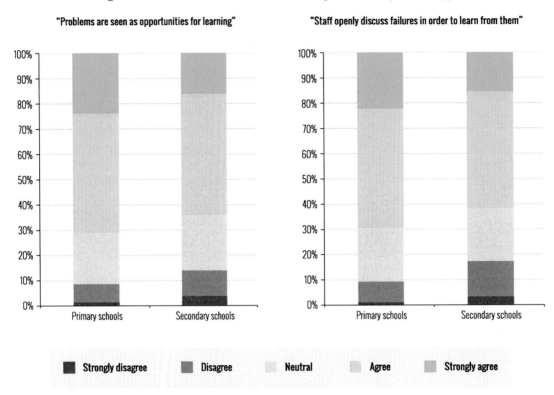

Strongly disagree   Disagree   Neutral   Agree   Strongly agree

Note: N: 1 657 and 1 664 individuals for the presented SLO survey statements.
Source: OECD Schools as Learning Organisations Survey, 2017.

StatLink 🔒🖙 http://dx.doi.org/10.1787/888933837644

There were also different response patterns for the statement "staff openly discuss failures in order to learn from them", with school staff in the South West and Mid Wales being most positive (78% responded positively) and staff in schools in South Wales the least positive (67% responded positively).

Embedding systems for collecting and exchanging knowledge and learning

General overview

SLOs develop processes, strategies and structures that allow them to learn and react effectively in uncertain and dynamic environments. They institutionalise learning mechanisms in order to revise existing knowledge. Without these, a learning organisation cannot thrive (Schechter and Qadach, 2012[51]). Effective use of data by teachers, school leaders and support staff has thus become central to school improvement in countries around the globe (OECD, 2013[52]), and this includes Wales.

The evidence suggests that schools throughout Wales and the system generally are "data-rich". Schools have well-established systems for measuring progress and the vast majority of staff agreed that in their school data were analysed and used to inform practice. The items for this dimension can be found in Box 3.13.

Box 3.13. Survey items for the SLO dimension "embedding systems for collecting and exchanging knowledge and learning"

- Evidence is collected to measure progress and identify gaps in the school's performance.

- Staff analyse and use data to improve their practice.

- Staff use research evidence to improve their practice.

- Staff analyse examples of good/great practices and failed practices to learn from them.

- Staff learn how to analyse and use data to inform their practice.

- Structures are in place for regular dialogue and knowledge sharing among staff.

- Staff regularly discuss and evaluate whether actions had the desired impact and change course if necessary.

- The school development plan is based on learning from continuous self-assessment and updated at least once every year.

While the vast majority of school staff indicated that structures were in place for regular dialogue and knowledge sharing among staff in their school, there were significant differences between the levels of education. The SLO survey data and OECD team's interviews also point to the need to improve the use of research evidence by staff to inform their practice.

Furthermore, although school development planning is informed by continuous self-assessments (self-evaluations) in the vast majority of schools, as Chapter 2 discusses, many schools in Wales could improve the quality of school self-evaluations and development planning. Part of the challenge lies in a lack of a common understanding of what good school self-evaluation and development planning entails in Wales. This issue is further discussed in Chapter 4.

Systems are in place to examine progress and gaps between current and expected impact

International evidence shows that embedding systems for capturing and sharing learning is essential for organisational learning and improvement to take place (Yang, Watkins and Marsick, 2004[53]). In line with their vision and goals, SLOs therefore create systems to measure progress and any gaps between current and expected impact.

An earlier OECD review (2014[48]) found that schools in Wales and the wider system were "data-rich". This is still the case today. The evidence from the SLO survey suggests that systems for measuring progress were well established in schools throughout Wales. For example, more than nine out of ten (92%) school staff responded positively to the statement that "evidence is collected to measure progress and identify gaps in the school's performance". Several of the schools the OECD team visited exemplified this.

Structures for regular dialogue and knowledge sharing

Having a large amount and range of data available does not guarantee that data will be used well. For example, a study on the use of education data in schools in five EU countries (Germany, Lithuania, the Netherlands, Poland and England) found that data and reports were still rarely used to take action to improve teaching and learning, despite the quantity of data sources available (Schildkamp, Karbautzki and Vanhoof, 2014[54]).

Being "data-rich" or, more appropriately, "knowledge-rich" is clearly not what matters; it takes social processing in the school context to bring information to life so that data can be used to make wise decisions about changes in practice. For this to happen, schools and other organisations need to create the structures for regular dialogue and knowledge sharing among staff, and ensuring their staff have the skills to analyse and use the data (Fullan, Cuttress and Kilcher, 2005[55]; Vincent-Lancrin and González-Sancho, 2015[56]).

It is encouraging to find that almost nine out of ten staff (89%) reported that staff in their school "analyse and use data to improve their practice". Furthermore, 85% of school staff responded positively to the SLO survey statement that, in their schools, "structures are in place for regular dialogue and knowledge sharing among staff". The data however also point to differences in response patterns between the levels of education. While 87% of primary school staff responded positively to this statement this fell to 77% among staff in secondary schools.

Having the skills to analyse and use data and information effectively

As mentioned above, an SLO ensures that staff have the capacity to analyse and use data. Again the vast majority of respondents to the SLO survey indicated they recognise such practice in their schools; close to 78% of staff responded positively to the statement "staff learn how to analyse and use data to inform their practice" with only 4% responding negatively.

Figure 3.11, however, shows the differences in response patterns across the staff categories. For example, while 90% of head teachers responded positively to this statement, positive responses among teachers and learning support workers were around 10-15% lower.

Figure 3.11. Building capacity to analyse and use data, by staff categories

Responses to the statement "staff learn how to analyse and use data to inform their practice"

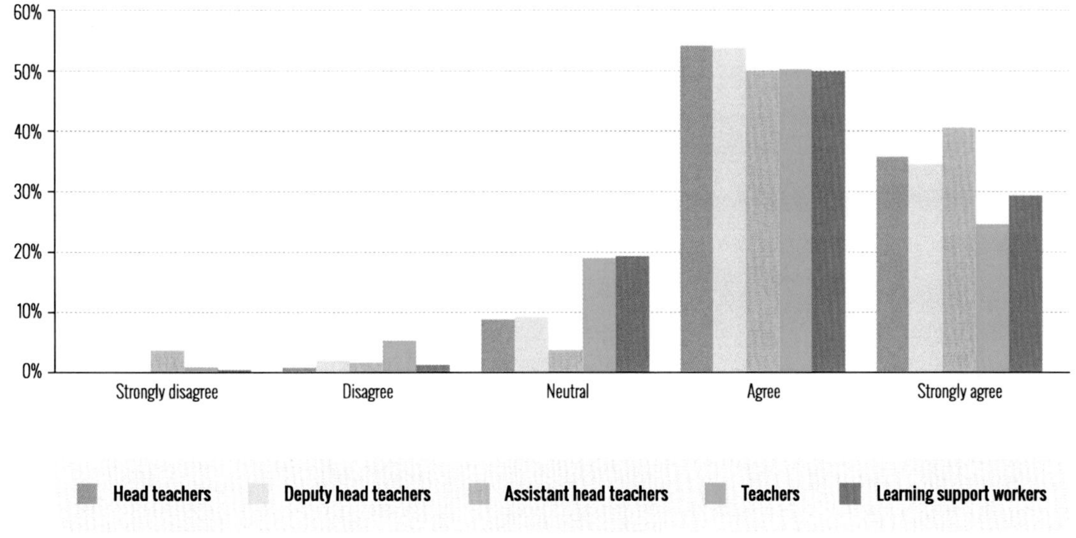

Note: N: 1 597 individuals.
Source: OECD Schools as Learning Organisations Survey, 2017.

StatLink 🔗 http://dx.doi.org/10.1787/888933837663

Staff use research evidence to improve their practice.

Many scholars argue that the use of research evidence is essential to improving practices (Kools and Stoll, 2016[10]; Brown, 2015[57]; Hattie, 2012[58]). Nevertheless, in many countries, teachers' involvement in research remains sparse, due to lack of motivation and limited time and resources. The evidence suggests this is also an area for improvement for Wales.

While the use of data appears to be common in many of schools across Wales, use of research evidence to inform practice is less so (see Figure 3.12). The SLO survey data revealed that just over two-thirds of respondents (68%) agreed or strongly agreed with the statement that "staff use research evidence to improve their practice" in their school. Here learning support staff were considerably more positive in their responses (78%) than teachers (62%).

There were also minor differences between the regions: at one end of the spectrum 67% of staff in schools in South Wales responded positively to this statement, while at the other end, the figure was 72% of staff in schools in North Wales.

PISA 2015 data complements these findings and places them in an international context. It found that 57% of secondary head teachers in Wales reported that they promoted teaching practices based on recent educational research at least once a month (OECD, 2016[40]). Although this was above the OECD average of 41% it was still significantly below the United Kingdom average (65%) or the average in countries like Australia (76%) or the United States (84%).

Figure 3.12. Staff use of data and research evidence to improve their practice

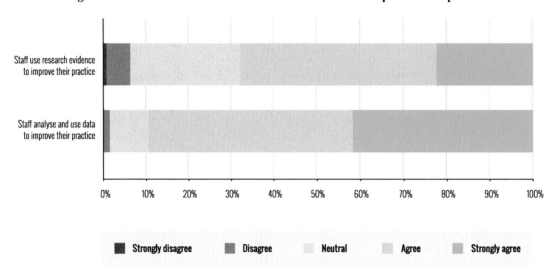

Note: N: 1 595 and 1 604 individuals for the presented SLO survey statements.
Source: OECD Schools as Learning Organisations Survey, 2017.

StatLink 🖳 http://dx.doi.org/10.1787/888933837682

Many of the stakeholders the OECD team interviewed saw this as a clear area needing attention in many schools in Wales. Several of the school visits the OECD team undertook, as well as the interviews with policy makers, showed that research, often in the form of "action research", was increasingly seen as a key component of school improvement strategies (e.g. Box 3.14, Box 3.16 and Box 3.17). The regional consortia are clearly playing a pivotal role in promoting the use of research in schools, with gradually increasing engagement of higher education institutions apparent in recent years.

Staff analyse examples of good and failed practices to learn from them

A school that is or strives to become a learning organisation makes lessons learned – whether good or bad – available to all staff in order to learn from these. Close to eight out of ten school staff (78%) responded positively to the statement that "staff analyse examples of good/great practices and failed practices to learn from them" in their school.

However, the data point to significant differences between the staff categories. Around 84% of head teachers and 86% of assistant head teachers indicated that sharing examples of good and failed practices to learn from them was common practice in their schools, while among teachers this was more than 10 percentage points lower (73%).

Several of the stakeholders the OECD team interviewed mentioned this issue as an area for development for many schools in Wales – possibly more than these data would suggest. They spoke of the high-stakes evaluation, assessment and accountability arrangements as a reason for people being cautious about sharing failed or less successful practices. These stakeholders also highlighted the need for greater clarity on the new assessment, evaluation and accountability framework currently under development, as this could positively influence people's willingness to innovate and also share their less successful practices. Still, even when greater clarity is provided to schools, it is likely to take time and concerted effort and encouragement for all staff in schools throughout Wales to feel confident enough to start sharing less successful practices; however, this will be essential for true learning to take place (Leithwood, Jantzi and Steinbach, 1998[59]).

Box 3.14. An example of developing action research groups – Ysgol Eirias secondary school

Ysgol Eirias secondary school (1 375 students in 2016) in the local authority of Conwy, North Wales, took part in the pilot of the SLO survey in April 2017. Every pilot school received an SLO "snapshot" that showed its strengths and weaknesses according to the views of the school staff. The staff critically reflected on the findings presented in the snapshot. In light of these and the new Teacher and Leadership Standards, they agreed that establishing a culture of enquiry, exploration and innovation, and exchanging knowledge and learning was an area for improvement for the school.

The school created action research groups (ARGs) building on the positive experiences with research-based approaches such as Lesson Study [1], and on steadily growing interest among some staff to engage in research to inform and innovate their practice. ARGs are composed of particular interest groups (e.g. assessment for learning (AfL), mentoring, additional learning needs (ALN), or literacy and numeracy) covering most of the pedagogical principles of the school (see Figure 3.13). Ysgol Eirias decided to partner with Bangor University to benefit and learn from their research expertise, starting with a presentation on how to conduct effective action research by two tutors from Bangor University at the start of the academic year.

Figure 3.13. Action research groups and pedagogical principles

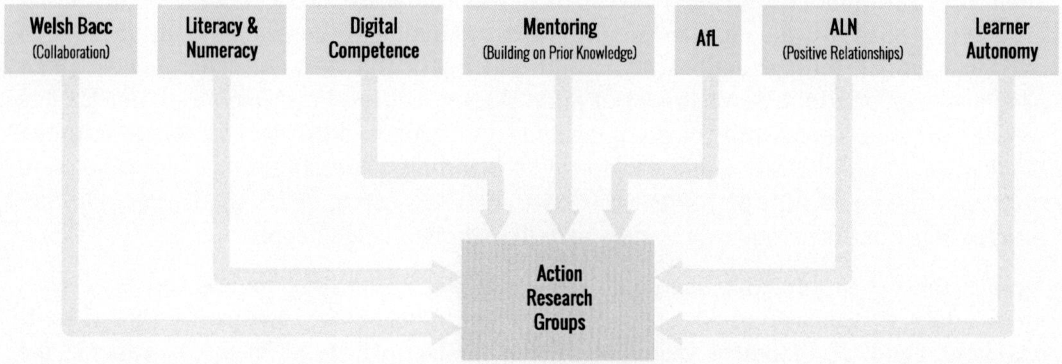

The decision was made that all groups would give feedback on the lessons learned to the whole school throughout the year, for example during training days or faculty meetings, depending on the nature of the research and findings. This decision was not only aimed at disseminating lessons learned, but also at gradually building the interest and willingness of other staff to engage in enquiry and experiment with new ideas and practices.

Note: 1. "Lesson Study" is a Japanese method of action research in which triads of teachers work together to target an identified area for development in their teaching and learning practices. Teachers use existing evidence and collaboratively research, plan, teach and observe a series of lessons.
Source: Information collected by the OECD team as part of the school visits.

Staff regularly discuss and evaluate whether actions had the desired impact and change course if necessary

In an SLO, staff evaluate the impact of their actions in order to learn from them and make adjustments where needed. This implies regular discussion about the expected outcomes of these actions as well as their evaluation and must involve the effective use of data and information (Earl and Timperley, 2015[47]; Schechter and Qadach, 2012[51]).

The SLO survey data showed that more than three-quarters (77%) of the respondents agreed or strongly agreed that "staff regularly discuss and evaluate whether actions had the desired impact and change course if necessary", with small differences between the levels of education and staff categories. Around 73% of secondary school staff responded positively to this statement, while the share was 5 percentage points higher among primary school staff (78%).

School leaders were most positive on this statement and teachers the most critical. For example, 85% of head teachers agreed with the statement, compared to 71% of teachers. In secondary schools these proportions fell to 80% for head teachers and 65% for teachers. The OECD team were surprised by these high numbers. The interviews and other sources of evidence, like Estyn's annual report (2018[14]), suggest this is an issue for further improvement for many schools in Wales.

School development planning is informed by continuous self-assessment

The vast majority of respondents to the SLO survey indicated that "the school development plan is based on learning from continuous self-assessment and updated at least once every year" (91%). These findings are not surprising given that much attention has been paid in Wales to promoting school self-evaluation and development planning. One such example is provided by **King Henry VIII Comprehensive School** in the local authority of Monmouthshire. In June 2016 it was found by Estyn to have made strong progress in its self-evaluation and improvement planning processes since its inspection two years earlier, through actions such as introducing peer reviews of departments, which have also supported the development of middle-level leaders. Furthermore, senior leaders were found to be successfully challenging and supporting middle-level leaders to improve the quality of self-evaluation and improvement planning, which in turn had contributed to improvements in student performance (Estyn, 2017[11]; Estyn, 2016[60]). These and other sources confirm the pivotal role leaders play in making change happen.

Despite these achievements, as mentioned in Chapter 2, the desk review and interviews by the OECD team revealed a need to further improve the quality of school self-evaluation and development planning (Estyn, 2018[14]; Estyn, 2017[11]). Part of the challenge seems to lie in a lack of a common understanding of what good school self-evaluation and development planning entails in Wales. At the time of writing, efforts are ongoing to develop a national school self-evaluation and development planning toolkit. This provides an important opportunity for realising a common understanding of good school self-evaluation and development planning in Wales (see Chapter 4).

Learning with and from the external environment and larger learning system

General overview

Schools do not operate in a vacuum; they are "open systems" that are sensitive to their external environment, including social, political and economic conditions. The SLO therefore enables its staff to learn collaboratively and continuously and put what they learn to use in response to social needs and the demands of their environment (Silins, Zarins and Mulford, 2002[42]; Kools and Stoll, 2016[10]). Such schools also forge partnerships with, and networks of, students, teachers, parents and members of the local communities to complement and enrich their own capacity. Box 3.15 lists the survey items used to measure this dimension.

The evidence suggests that Wales has made much progress in recent years in learning with and from the external environment and larger learning system. The regional consortia have played a vital role in this development. However, there remain clear areas of improvement. For example, there seems scope to engage further with parents and guardians in the educational process and organisation of the school, particularly for secondary schools.

Box 3.15. Survey items for the SLO dimension "learning with and from the external environment and the larger system"

- Opportunities and threats outside the school are monitored continuously to improve practice.

- Staff collaborate, learn and share knowledge with peers in other schools.

- The school as a whole is involved in school-to-school networks or collaborations.

- Parents/guardians are partners in the school's organisational and educational processes.

- Staff actively collaborate with social and health services to better respond to students' needs.

- Staff actively collaborate with higher education institutions to deepen staff and student learning.

- Staff actively collaborate with other external partners to deepen staff and student learning.

Furthermore, there are significant differences between primary and secondary school staff in the extent to which they engage in collaborative learning and working with their peers in other schools.

Although it was not apparent when looking only at the SLO survey data, the interviews the OECD team conducted, as well as an earlier OECD assessment (2017[39]), suggested that Wales' school governance model challenges schools' ability to collaborate with social and health services in order to respond to students with additional learning needs (i.e. special education needs). Several local authorities, especially smaller ones, are believed to lack the capacity to respond to the seeming growing need for support for this diverse group of students (see also Chapter 4). These and other issues will be elaborated further below.

The school as learning organisation is an open system

Schools in the 21st century are not sustained by working in isolation but instead have to be responsive to the changing demands of society. As such, the SLO is proactive in continuously scanning the environment to monitor and respond to external challenges and opportunities as appropriate (Silins, Zarins and Mulford, 2002[42]).

The vast majority of respondents to the SLO survey indicated that in their school opportunities and threats outside the school were monitored continuously to improve practice: 72% of staff responded positively to this statement, 25% neutrally (which may suggest they did not know) and 3% negatively.

Genuine partnerships

Schools' urgent drive to avoid isolation comes from the awareness that significant innovation cannot be achieved and sustained alone. As learning organisations, schools connect with their community and partners in their external environment to enrich their capacity to serve their students (Hargreaves and Fullan, 2012[20]; OECD, 2013[18]). This section discusses schools' partnerships with parents, other schools, higher education institutions, social services and other external partners.

Parents and guardians

Parents or guardians are key partners for schools in the organisation and educational process and thereby strengthen it (Epstein, 2001[61]; Domina, 2005[62]). Without co-operation between families and schools, it is unlikely that all students will meet the high expectations set by a demanding society. An SLO shares information with parents and considers them to be partners in the educational process and organisation of the school.

This, as mentioned, is an area for development for many schools in Wales and is a particular challenge for secondary schools: 57% of secondary school staff responded positively to the SLO survey statement "parents/guardians are partners in the school's organisational and educational processes", compared with 71% of staff in primary schools.

There are also differences in responses between staff categories, with teachers being the most critical. Just over half (53%) of secondary school teachers agreed that parents/guardians were partners in their schools' organisation and educational processes, compared with 62% of secondary head teachers. For primary schools, these proportions showed also differences but were significantly higher, 65% and 85% respectively.

The data also pointed to some differences across the four regions of Wales; 65% of school staff in South Wales responded positively to this statement, a proportion that increased to 69% in the North Wales, 70% in South East Wales, and 72% in South West and Mid Wales.

PISA 2015 provides further information on this issue (OECD, 2017[9]). It found that secondary head teachers in Wales in 2015 almost unanimously reported that their school created a welcoming atmosphere for parents to get involved (99%) and that it provided information and ideas for families about how to help students at home with homework and other curriculum-related activities, decisions, and planning (98%). A further eight out of ten (79%) secondary head teachers reported that their school included parents in decision making (OECD average: 78%). The OECD team recognise it may be more challenging to engage parents of secondary students in the school organisation and education process, than at the primary level – a finding that is also commonly reported in other countries (Borgonovi and Montt, 2012[23]; Byrne and Smyth, 2010[24]; Desforges and Abouchaar, 2003[25]; Williams, Williams and Ullman, 2002[26]). However, examples from Wales and internationally show that it is possible to increase parental engagement in the school and the learning of their children – even at the secondary level (e.g. Box 3.5).

Figure 3.14. Collaboration with external partners

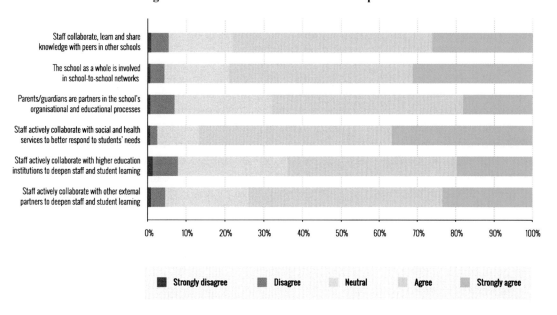

Strongly disagree   Disagree   Neutral   Agree   Strongly agree

Note: N: 1 593, 1 597, 1 589, 1 592, 1 592 and 1 593 individuals for the presented SLO survey statements.
Source: OECD Schools as Learning Organisations Survey, 2017.

StatLink ⟨⟨⟨⟩⟩ http://dx.doi.org/10.1787/888933837701

School-to-school collaborations

As the previous OECD assessment also found (2017[39]), learning with and from other schools and external partners has become common practice in many schools in Wales. The regional consortia have played an important role in this development (e.g. Box 3.16). The data from the SLO survey corroborated these findings (see Figure 3.14), and found only minimal differences across the regions of Wales. Primary school staff seem most likely to engage in collaborative learning and working with their peers in other schools: 80% of primary school staff responded positively to this item, compared with 73% of their peers in secondary schools. The interviews with regional consortia and Estyn representatives corroborated this finding.

There are significant differences between the staff categories. Close to nine out of ten head teachers (95%), deputy heads and assistant head teachers (90% and 93% respectively) reported that in their school "staff collaborate, learn and share knowledge with peers in other schools", whereas this ratio dropped to eight out of ten learning support workers (83%) and seven out of ten teachers (70%).

Box 3.16. An example of school-to-school collaboration – School Improvement Groups

Since 2014, the Central South Consortium and its five local authorities have been collaborating in order to find more effective ways of improving the quality of education for all of their children and young people. One of the outcomes of this effort are the School Improvement Groups (SIGs), a cross-local authority model where a head teacher in each group acts as a convenor and co-ordinates a group of school leaders collaborating on school improvement. The purpose of the SIG is for schools to work together to share best practices around common interests and priorities. Each of the 38 SIGs [1] is composed of schools from different local authorities, in different places on their development and with students from different socio-economic backgrounds.

The regional consortium finances the programme and each school is in charge of releasing staff to attend joint training and planning events. The consortium also leads an evaluation for each project. Schools are individually responsible for gathering data for specific projects and are expected to share information and lessons learned through newsletters to parents, websites and governors or other means. For example, one SIG in 2017 focused on developing the role of senior leaders in performance management and the monitoring of standards through the use of Continua, an online developmental self-evaluation tool for teachers and school development. Senior leaders attended Continua training and in turn conducted training for all staff in their schools.

Note: 1. 32 primary SIGs and 6 secondary.
Source: Information collected by the OECD team.

Higher education institutions

Partnerships with higher education institutions can offer schools clear advantages in drawing on these institutions' expertise and capacity, and bringing an external perspective (Ainscow, Booth and Dyson, 2006[63]; OECD, 2013[18]). The benefits can work both ways, as innovative ideas and practices can in turn influence the higher education/university level, and the teacher education and service missions of universities or teachers colleges may be very well served by such partnerships (OECD, 2013[52]).

About two-thirds of school staff (64%) responded positively to the statement that "staff actively collaborate with higher education institutions to deepen staff and student learning". A further 8% responded negatively and 28% neutrally which may suggest they are not certain.

The data pointed to differences between the regions, with 68% of school staff in North Wales responding positively to this survey statement, falling to 60% for staff in schools in South East Wales. In the South West and Mid Wales and South Wales the figures were 65% and 63% respectively.

Various stakeholders the OECD team interviewed highlighted this as an area for improvement for Wales' education system as a whole. The OECD team learned of positive developments in the accreditation of new teacher education programmes, which require higher education institutions to demonstrate they work in partnerships with schools. As will be discussed further in Chapter 4, one difficulty in encouraging schools to work in closer partnership with higher education institutions is that is voluntary, with no incentives to promote such partnerships. As a result, few schools are willing to make long-term commitments, often withdrawing, sometimes at the last minute, particularly if they are facing an Estyn inspection (Furlong, 2015[64]).

The OECD team however learned that such partnerships are gradually becoming more established across the school system of Wales. Further encouragement and incentives seem to be needed (see Chapter 4). Boxes 3.14 and 3.17 show how such partnerships can contribute to schools' capacity for using research evidence to inform their development planning.

Box 3.17. An example of partnership between higher education institutions and schools – the Collaborative Institute for Education Research, Evidence and Impact (CIEREI)

The Collaborative Institute for Education Research, Evidence and Impact (CIEREI) is a strategic collaboration between three equal partners: 1) university researchers (Bangor University); 2) schools at a regional level; and 3) GwE, the regional consortium for North Wales, but other bodies and institutions also contribute. Based on the ambitions set out in the *Successful Future* report (Donaldson, 2015[7]) its strategic aims are to:

- build a vibrant research community that will inform current educational practice, initial teacher education programmes and the ongoing professional development of teachers

- work collaboratively and strategically with existing groups and centres that undertake educational research

- develop and strengthen teachers' and school leaders' skills and knowledge in evidence-based educational practice

- create an educational environment that supports the innovation and evaluation of educational practice

- support the Welsh Governments' strategic education plan *Education in Wales: Our National Mission* and contribute to the existing "what works" guidelines

Bangor University works with GwE to evaluate the quality of their school improvement programmes in the consortium. For example, CIEREI has evaluated GwE's Headsprout Online Reading Programme that consisted of two online training programmes for teachers on early reading and comprehension. Phase 1 of the evaluation consisted of pilot studies in small schools to take measures of reading skills before and after the implementation of Headsprout programmes. Phase 2 consisted of larger-scale evaluation projects involving more than 60 primary schools on different topics (parents' involvement in the programme, early reading skills, etc.). During the process, researchers worked closely with schools to identify barriers to the implementation of the programme and ensure that schools were helped to overcome those limitations. Embracing national objectives, particular attention was paid to reducing the attainment gap between students. At the end of the process, CIEREI was able to deliver evaluation reports for each school and used the findings to support GwE in the development of its regional action plan.

Source: Bangor University (2017[65]), *Collaborative Institute for Education Research, Evidence and Impact*, http://cierei.bangor.ac.uk/about.php.en (accessed on 20 November 2017).

Social and health services

The SLO survey data showed that close to nine out of ten respondents (87%) indicated that in their school "staff actively collaborate with social and health services to better respond to students' needs" (Figure 3.14 above) – 88% in primary schools and 80% in secondary schools – with minimal differences between the regions. Teachers were again the most critical: for instance, 76% of secondary teachers agreed with this statement, compared to 96% of secondary head teachers. While all secondary deputy head teachers agreed with this statement, only 89% of secondary assistant head teachers did, with the other 11% responding neutrally.

The interviews with stakeholders, as well as the findings of an earlier OECD assessment (2017[39]), suggest that Wales' school funding and governance model provides challenges to schools' ability to respond to the additional learning needs of all students, however. Several local authorities, especially the smaller ones, are believed to lack the capacity, both human and financial, to respond to the seemingly growing need for support for the diverse group of students with additional learning needs (i.e. special education needs). An additional complication is the separation of responsibilities between local authorities, which manage the social and health services, and the regional consortia, which are responsible for school improvement services (OECD, 2017[39]). This issue is further discussed in Chapters 4 and 5.

Modelling and growing learning leadership

General overview

Leadership is the essential ingredient that binds all of the separate parts of the learning organisation together. Leadership should set the direction and take responsibility for putting learning at the centre and keeping it there, and using learning strategically so that the school's actions are consistent with its vision, goals and values (Fullan, 2014[66]; Schleicher, 2018[28]; OECD, 2013[67]).

As noted in an earlier OECD assessment (2017[39]) it is key that Wales continues its investments in the development of its school leadership – as well as leadership at other levels of the system – to ensure greater consistency throughout the system. These investments will be essential in the years to come, considering the areas for further improvement reported in this chapter to develop SLOs, and thus help ensure the readiness of staff to engage with the new curriculum and bring it to life.

Box 3.18 lists the survey items used to assess this dimension. The information collected during the school visits and their interviews with various stakeholders at other levels of the systems, point to the conclusion that investment in leadership development has received much attention in recent years, particularly at the regional and local levels.

Areas for further improvement include enhancing leaders' coaching of those they lead and the creation of settings in which trust can develop over time so that colleagues are more likely to engage in mutual learning. Leaders in secondary schools seem to find it more challenging to develop their schools into learning organisations. The more compartmentalised structures and leadership practices appear to be factors of influence here.

Box 3.18. Survey items for the SLO dimension "modelling and growing learning leadership"

- Leaders participate in professional learning to develop their practice.

- Leaders facilitate individual and group learning.

- Leaders coach those they lead.

- Leaders develop the potential of others to become future leaders.

- Leaders provide opportunities for staff to participate in decision making.

- Leaders provide opportunities for students to participate in decision making.

- Leaders give staff responsibility to lead activities and projects.

- Leaders spend time building trust with staff.

- Leaders put a strong focus on improving learning and teaching.

- Leaders ensure that all actions are consistent with the school's vision, goals and values.

- Leaders anticipate opportunities and threats.

- Leaders model effective collaborations with external partners.

As mentioned in Chapter 2, the generally high survey scores on this dimension were in contrast to other data sources like OECD team interviews and Estyn reports. The analysis of other SLO dimensions presented above also points to several areas for further improvement – several of which are under the direct control of school leaders. School leaders play a vital role in the promotion and strengthening of induction programmes, mentoring/coaching, peer review and creating a culture of enquiry, innovation and exploration in their schools. The establishment of these and other conditions for a learning culture to develop across the whole school organisation is particularly an area of improvement for leaders in secondary schools.

Leaders model and promote participation in professional learning

By engaging in appropriate professional learning as "lead learners" (Barth, 2001[68]), and creating the conditions for others to do the same, school leaders model and champion such professionalism throughout the school and beyond the school boundaries (Marsick and Watkins, 1999[69]; Kools and Stoll, 2016[10]). Participating in teachers' professional learning is also a key strategy for leaders to improve student learning (Robinson, 2011[70]). The vast majority of staff (86%) responded positively to the statement that "leaders participated in professional learning to develop their practice" with hardly any answering negatively (3%) (Figure 3.15).

A closer look at the data showed that all the respondents in leadership positions agreed that they participated in professional learning to develop their practice. Although less an issue for primary schools, the fact that 8% of teachers in secondary schools responded negatively to this statement and another 21% responded neutrally suggests that leaders in secondary schools could make their participation in professional learning more visible.

Figure 3.15. Modelling, coaching and promoting professional learning

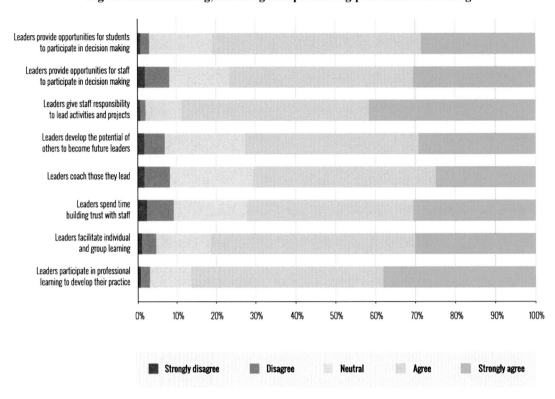

Note: N: 1 576, 1 575, 1 570, 1 575, 1 570, 1 574, 1 570 and 1 576 individuals for the presented SLO survey statements.
Source: OECD Schools as Learning Organisations Survey, 2017.

StatLink ᵃᵢˢᴾ http://dx.doi.org/10.1787/888933837720

School leaders are the nerve centre of school improvement and play a vital role in establishing a learning culture, and promoting and facilitating individual, group and ultimately organisational learning (Schlechty, 2009[1]; OECD, 2013[67]; Schleicher, 2018[28]). Figure 3.15 shows that close to eight out of ten respondents to the SLO survey (82%) responded positively to the statement that "leaders facilitate individual and group learning".

The OECD team also learned of several examples of schools where school leaders serve as creative change agents and have created the structures and conditions to facilitate individual and group learning (e.g. Box 3.19). The stakeholders the OECD team interviewed noted that it is important for Wales to continue to identify and "share and move knowledge and good practices around" while promoting peer learning between school leaders within and across schools. This issue is further discussed in Chapter 4.

Box 3.19. An example of creating the conditions for professional dialogue, peer learning and knowledge exchange – the Fern Federation

The Fern Federation consists of two primary schools: **Craig Yr Hesg Primary School** (146 students in 2017) and **All Saints Church in Wales School** (246 students in 2017) located in deprived areas of Central South Wales. The schools were federated after an improvement strategy showed unsatisfactory results. The appointed executive head teacher took a range of measures to create the conditions for professional dialogue, peer learning and knowledge exchange among staff within and between the schools – as well as with other schools.

Informed by consultations with staff and an evaluation of teaching in both schools, the head teacher launched a strategic development plan with a strong focus on professional learning aimed at improving teachers' competencies in both general and subject pedagogy. Structures set up as part of the development plan include:

- shared leadership with a large share of the teaching staff assuming some kind of leadership role (e.g. leader of data: tracking and monitoring individual student data, following up with teachers, leader of literacy improvement)

- "teaching and learning workshops" every two weeks focusing on a chosen area of practice to improve

- co-coaching sessions (leaders of teaching and learning coach teachers to provide pedagogical support)

- mentoring (for teachers failing to make progress, mentoring sessions are in place to ensure practice progress).

The development plan included investment in resources to facilitate systematic enquiry, reflection and peer learning. These included:

- a classroom with a one-way mirror that allows observers to watch the class and teaching staff in practice without disturbing or influencing children's behaviour

- video cameras

- a video library system with individual accounts for each teacher where they can upload their recordings, add reflection notes to them and share them with other users.

Teachers are ensured dedicated time to conduct individual or collaborative research projects, and to reflect on their impact on their own learning.

Source: OECD (2018[71]) TALIS initial teacher preparation study, www.oecd.org/education/school/talis-initial-teacher-preparation-study.htm; Révai, N. (2018[72]) "Teachers' knowledge dynamics and innovation in education – Part II", http://dx.doi.org/10.21549/NTNY.21.2018.1.1.

One area of improvement for school leaders would seem to be in creating settings in which trust can develop over time so that colleagues are more likely to engage in mutual learning (Figure 3.16). Around 9% of respondents disagreed that "leaders spend time building trust with staff" in their school, with a further 19% responding neutrally which may suggest they did not know for sure. Moreover, as Figure 3.16 illustrates, there were differences across staff categories with 14% of teachers disagreeing with this statement as opposed to none of the school leaders. The responses also suggest secondary schools faced slightly more challenges: 18% of secondary teachers did not share the view that leaders spent time building trust in their school, compared with 13% of primary teachers.

Figure 3.16. Building trust, by staff categories

Responses to the statement "Leaders spend time building trust with staff"

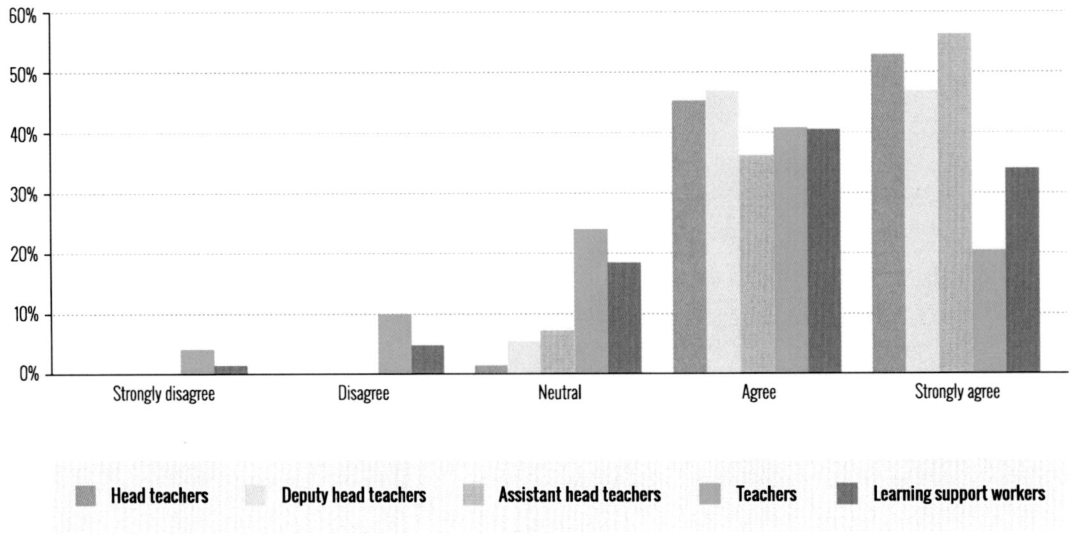

Note: N: 1 525 individuals.
Source: OECD Schools as Learning Organisations Survey, 2017.

StatLink ᵐˢᴾ http://dx.doi.org/10.1787/888933837739

Extending and growing leadership

The demands of leadership in the 21st century are far too extensive for any one person. Because head teachers' work has become so complex, some of these responsibilities need to be more broadly shared with others, both inside and outside the school (Schleicher, 2012[31]; Fullan, 2011[73]; Hallinger and Heck, 2010[74]). SLOs therefore have a culture of shared responsibility for school issues, and staff are encouraged to actively participate in decision making. Through mentoring and coaching, school leaders prepare those they lead to take on more senior-level responsibilities and ensure sustainable leadership through succession.

Just over seven out of every ten respondents to the SLO survey indicated that "leaders coach those they lead" (71%) and that "leaders develop the potential of others to become future leaders" (73%) – which is a positive finding. Indeed, there are examples throughout this chapter that exemplify this (e.g. Box 3.20).

Box 3.20. An example of extending and growing leadership – Dwr-y-Felin secondary school

Dwr-y-Felin is a secondary school (1 134 students in 2017) located in the city of Neath, in South West and Mid Wales. The school values each member of staff as a dynamic member in the school organisation. The head teacher mentors other senior leaders to develop through the School Challenge Cymru Programme. This programme for secondary schools gave the school additional resources for improvement. The school used these resources to develop its middle leaders and encouraged them to explore the work of senior leadership by offering them opportunities to shadow and work alongside leadership colleagues. This enabled them to develop a better understanding of the expectations, functions and accountability arrangements associated with school leadership.

In 2017, the school had 22 staff in middle leadership roles, all of whom had been coached by the senior leadership team. Many of them also take leadership courses at the University of Wales Trinity Saint David with support of the regional consortium (ERW) through its Leadership and Development Programme.

Source: Information collected by the OECD team as part of the school visits.

The SLO survey data found some differences in responses between staff categories, levels of education and the four regions. For example, the data showed that some 13% of teachers and 5% of learning support workers did not agree that in their schools, leaders coached those they led, while hardly any school leaders did so. Among secondary school staff, 65% agreed, compared to 72% in primary schools.

When looking across the regions of Wales over two-thirds (68%) of staff in schools in South Wales agreed that leaders coached those they led in their school. The proportion increased to over three quarters (76%) for staff in schools in the South West and Mid Wales (see Figure 3.17).

Figure 3.17. Coaching by leaders, by region

Responses to the statement "Leaders coach those they lead"

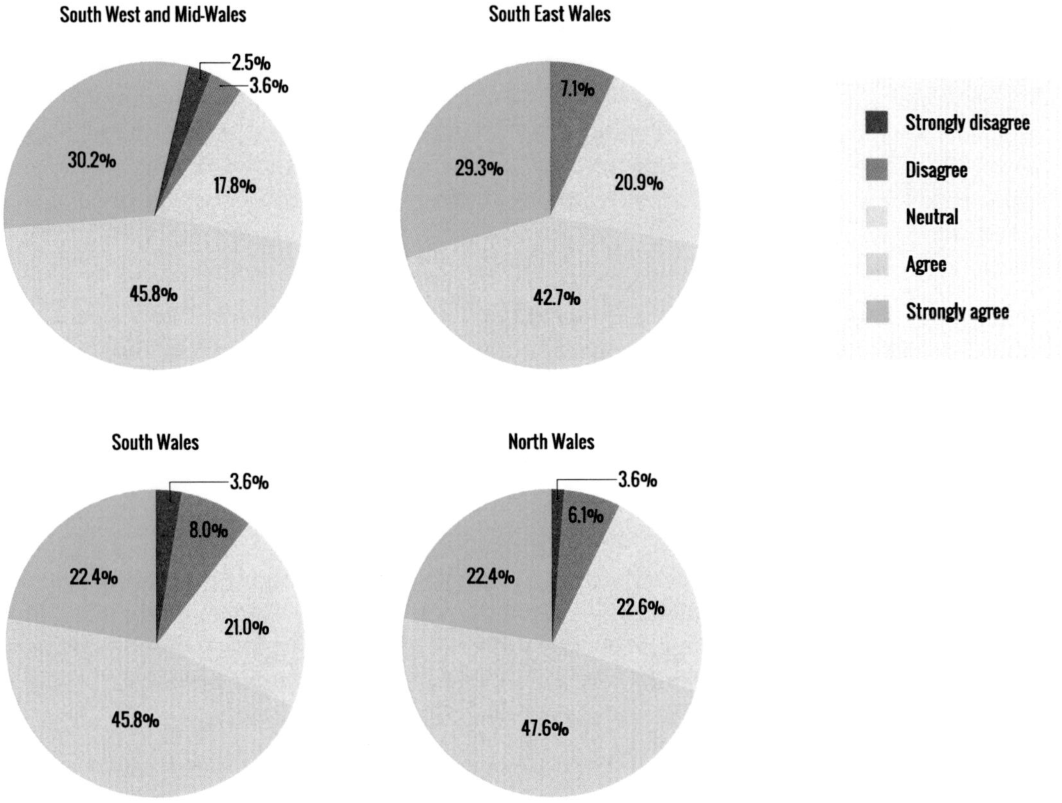

Note: N: 1 570 individuals.
Source: OECD Schools as Learning Organisations Survey, 2017.

StatLink ᵃᵢˢ᷋ http://dx.doi.org/10.1787/888933837758

Leaders providing opportunities to others to participate in decision making

Data from the SLO survey (see Figure 3.15 above) suggested that providing opportunities for others to participate in decision making was a strength of those in leadership positions in schools throughout Wales.

The SLO survey data suggest that distributed leadership practices were slightly better established in primary schools than in secondary schools. For example, 12% of staff in secondary schools disagreed with the statement "leaders provide opportunities for their staff to take part in decision making", compared with 7% in primary schools.

However, in terms of the recognition of the importance of "student voice" in the decision making of the school – in organisational and educational matters, the interviews with school staff and other stakeholders revealed a more critical view than the survey data. These suggested that students' input is often restricted to issues such as uniform or canteen provision, rather than concerning teaching and learning or the actual organisation of the school. The OECD team learned that students' role in school self-evaluations and development planning is also often minimal or even non-existent. This issue is further discussed in Chapter 4.

A focus on learning and teaching and ensuring actions respond to the school's vision, goals and values

The people the OECD team interviewed, whether they were working in schools or other parts of the system, strongly supported the view that school leaders in Wales are focused on improving the teaching and learning of their students. They also confirmed that the vast majority of school leaders work to ensure their actions respond to the school's vision, goals and values. The data from the SLO survey corroborated these findings (see Table 3.6) and, for both elements, showed relatively minor differences between the regions and school types.

Table 3.6. Focus of school leaders

	Strongly disagree	Disagree	Neutral	Agree	Strongly agree
Leaders put a strong focus on improving learning and teaching	0.4%	1.4%	7.6%	43.1%	47.5%
Leaders ensure that all actions are consistent with the school's vision, goals and values	1.1%	2.3%	12.0%	46.3%	38.3%

Note: N: 1 574 and 1 577 individuals for the presented SLO survey statements.
Source: OECD Schools as Learning Organisations Survey, 2017.

For example, as mentioned earlier in Chapter 2, for the statement "leaders ensure that all actions are consistent with the school's vision, goals and values" the data showed that 13% of primary school staff and 16% of secondary school staff responded negatively or neutrally which may suggest they did not know for sure. For both levels of education, teachers were the most critical with 19% of primary teachers and 27% of secondary teachers responding in a similar vein.

PISA 2015 data enriches and offers an international perspective on this issue. It found that 39% of secondary school head teachers in Wales reported they ensured that teachers work according to the school's educational goals more than once a month, compared with an OECD average of 53% (OECD, 2016[40]). This suggests that secondary head teachers in Wales could place a greater emphasis on ensuring their schools' actions respond to its vision and goals, communicating these efforts better with their staff, and engaging them in decision making.

Connecting strategically and systemically

In SLOs, school leaders are "system players" who promote the establishment of strong collaborations with other schools, parents, the community and higher education institutions (Fullan, 2014[66]; Dimmock, Kwek and Toh, 2013[75]).

The SLO survey data corroborated the OECD team's interview findings that school leaders in Wales on average were well aware of the opportunities and threats that lay in their schools' external environment. Close to three-quarters of school staff responded positively to the statement "leaders anticipate opportunities and threats" (77%), but with significant differences between levels of education: 79% of primary staff but 70% of secondary staff responded positively. At both levels of education, teachers were the least positive. Interviews with secondary school leaders and other stakeholders suggested that the former sometimes find it challenging to make all of their actions visible to all staff, with school size playing a role in this.

Three-quarters of respondents to the SLO survey (76%) agreed that leaders effectively modelled collaborations with external partners, with relatively minor differences between the regions. For example, in South East Wales 78% of school staff responded positively to this statement, compared with 73% of staff in schools in South Wales.

Key findings of the Schools as Learning Organisations Assessment and points of reflection and action for schools

Chapters 2 and 3 have explored the extent to which schools in Wales have already put in practice the key characteristics of a learning organisation. Using Wales' SLO model as a point of reference, a mixed-methods study design was used to identify strengths and areas for further development. The main findings of this assessment are presented below.

The majority of schools in Wales seem well on their way in developing as learning organisations …

According to the views of school leaders, teachers and learning support workers the majority of schools in Wales are well on their way in putting the SLO model into practice. The SLO survey data (when aggregated to the school level) suggested that close to six out of ten schools (58%) in the sample have put five or more of the seven dimensions of the learning organisation into practice.

The data however also suggested that a considerable proportion of schools are still far removed from realising this objective; 12% of schools had put three or four dimensions in practice, while 30% of schools had realised only two or fewer. Some 10% of schools in the sample seem to have made insufficient progress in developing any of the seven dimensions.

… these however are optimistic estimates. More critical reflections are needed for deep learning and sustained progress to take place

These findings need to be interpreted with some caution. First, they are based on one source of self-reported survey data and, although satisfactory, the response rate to the SLO survey was not optimal. Additional data and interviews with stakeholders by the OECD team on some occasions found discrepancies with the SLO survey data and supported the conclusion that school staff need to be more critical about their own performance and that of their schools for deep learning and sustained progress to take place.

Several of those interviewed noted that the high-stakes assessment, evaluation and accountability arrangements are likely to have negatively influenced people's willingness, and in some cases even their ability, to critically reflect on their own behaviour, that of their peers and the school organisation at large.

Key findings for the seven schools as learning organisations dimensions

The assessment of the seven dimensions that make up Wales' SLO model shows schools are engaging in these to different degrees. A general conclusion is that schools appear to be progressing well on the dimensions "promoting team learning and collaboration among all staff" and "embedding systems for collecting and exchanging knowledge and learning", although on the latter the differences between primary and secondary schools are particularly large, with primary schools faring better.

Two dimensions are considerably less well developed: "developing a shared vision centred on the learning of all students (learners)" and "establishing a culture of enquiry, innovation and exploration".

The data suggest that many schools in Wales could also do more to "learn with and from the external environment and larger system". The text below elaborates on these and other findings.

Many schools in Wales could do more to improve their development and realisation of a shared vision centred on the learning of all students

Some 53% of schools in the sample reported that their school had developed a vision centred on the learning of all students which was shared by staff – the lowest proportion of the seven SLO dimensions. Responses to the SLO survey items that make up this dimension varied considerably.

Nine out of ten school staff (92%) reported that their school has a vision that focuses on students' cognitive and socio-emotional outcomes, including their well-being. A similar proportion (87%) reported that their school's vision emphasises preparing students for their future in a changing world. These are encouraging findings considering the ambitions set out in Wales' new school curriculum. Various sources however point to the conclusion that many schools in Wales are yet to put this vision centred on the learning of all students into practice.

Further work is also needed to make such a vision into something that is truly shared among schools' staff and other key stakeholders. The involvement of staff, parents and external partners in the shaping of the vision are areas for improvement, in particular for secondary schools. For example, while 77% of primary school staff indicated they were involved in the development of the school's vision, among secondary school staff this was 57%.

High-quality inductions and mentoring/coaching support are not common practice

The evidence suggested that many schools in Wales have, or are in the process of developing, a culture that promotes professional learning for their staff. Around 59% of schools would seem to have created and supported continuous learning opportunities for all staff (i.e. put this dimension into practice). The data however revealed significant differences between the levels of education: 64% of primary schools and 26% of secondary schools seem to have put this dimension into practice.

Various sources of data and information also showed that induction and mentoring/coaching need to be strengthened in many schools across Wales. For example, some 35% of respondents to the SLO survey disagreed or were unsure whether their school had mentors or coaches available to help staff develop their practice. As Wales has embarked on a curriculum reform, teachers and learning support workers will need to expand their pedagogical and assessment skills. This will make mentoring, coaching and other forms of continuous learning – and collaborative learning and working – more important.

More needs to be done to promote team learning and peer review and encourage staff to tackle problems together

The evidence suggested that about seven out of ten schools in the sample (71%) are promoting team learning and collaboration among all its staff. Primary schools however fare better in this: 75% of primary schools in the sample appeared to promote team learning and collaboration among all staff, compared to 48% of secondary schools. Furthermore, schools could do more to ensure that staff learn to work together as a team, observe each other more regularly and tackle problems together.

For several of the elements that make up this dimension, there were also different perceptions depending on staff categories. For example, 92% of secondary head teachers in the SLO survey agreed that staff in their schools observed each other's practice and collaborated in developing it, compared with only 67% of teachers. Although there are bound to be some differences in perceptions between staff categories, as some staff may simply be better informed due to the nature of their work, the sometimes sizable differences reported in this dimension (and others) suggest the need for more professional dialogue and sharing of information. This is again particularly an area for improvement in secondary schools

A culture of enquiry, innovation and exploration is underdeveloped in many schools, particularly in secondary schools

The OECD team were struck by a change in attitudes compared to the OECD 2014 review. At that time, it found an education profession that seemed less open and willing to change and innovate their practice, with some school staff reporting signs of reform fatigue (OECD, 2014[48]). This situation appears to have changed considerably. However, the OECD team found that this general change in mindset is yet to result in a culture of enquiry, innovation and exploration in a significant proportion of schools in Wales. Four out of ten schools from the sample (41%) do not yet seem to have established such a culture.

These findings may partially be explained by the high-stakes assessment, evaluation and accountability arrangements that are believed to have tempered people's willingness and confidence to do things differently and innovate their practice. This would seem particularly the case for secondary schools – the SLO survey data found just 26% of secondary schools in the sample had established a culture of enquiry, exploration and innovation, compared to 63% of primary schools. Other data sources corroborated this finding.

Systems for collecting and exchanging knowledge are well established, but the quality of school self-evaluations and development planning is variable

Systems for measuring progress seem well established in schools across Wales. The SLO survey data suggested that 70% of schools in the sample had put this dimension into practice, with embedded systems for collecting and exchanging knowledge and learning. Again, there were significant differences between primary and secondary schools: 76% of primary schools and 30% of secondary schools would seem to have embedded such systems for collecting and exchanging knowledge and learning (the largest difference of all SLO dimensions).

The evidence also suggested that, while the use of data is common in many schools across Wales, considerably fewer schools seem to have staff that are using research evidence to inform their practice.

Interviews and a review of policy documents and reports revealed that another area for improvement is the quality of school self-evaluations and development planning. Schools – as well as other parts of the system – spend considerable time and effort on analysing and reporting upwards on a wide variety of mostly quantitative data, with far less attention being paid to qualitative sources, like classroom observations or peer review, for learning. Wales' assessment, evaluation and accountability arrangements, which have focused attention on quantitative performance measures, are believed to have contributed to this practice. Part of the challenge lies in the fact that there is no common understanding of what good school self-evaluation and development planning entails in Wales.

School-to-school collaborations are common practice, but collaborations with some external partners need to be strengthened

Learning with and from the external environment and larger learning system is common practice in just over the majority of schools in the sample (55%): 57% of primary schools and 39% of secondary schools in the sample of schools seemed to have put this dimension in practice (the smallest difference of all dimensions).

One area for improvement is the engagement of parents and guardians in the educational process and organisation of the school. This was found to be a particular challenge for secondary schools: only 57% of secondary school staff agreed that parents or guardians were partners in their schools' organisational and educational processes, compared to 71% of staff in primary schools. The OECD team recognise it may be more challenging to engage parents of secondary students in the school organisation and education process, than at the primary level. However, as examples in this report have shown, it is possible for schools to increase parental engagement, even at the secondary level.

Another area for improvement is the collaboration with higher education institutions. The interviews revealed that stakeholders across the system are well aware of this challenge and are taking measures to improve the situation.

Furthermore, the SLO survey found that close to nine out of ten respondents (87%) reported that staff in their school actively collaborated with social and health services to better respond to students' needs. However, interviews with various stakeholders and the figures on average student expenditure per school suggest that the school funding and governance model in Wales affects schools' ability to respond to the needs of all students.

The need for continued investment in the capacity of school leaders to model and grow learning leadership

The SLO survey data suggested that about two-thirds (67%) of schools in the sample have leaders that are modelling and growing learning leadership. Primary schools also appeared to be doing better for this dimension: 70% of primary schools seemed to have leaders that are modelling and growing learning leadership, compared with 39% of secondary schools.

Particular areas for development are the coaching by leaders of those they lead and the creation of settings in which trust can develop over time so that colleagues are more likely to engage in mutual learning. In addition, the evidence suggested that secondary head teachers in Wales could place a greater emphasis on ensuring their schools' actions reflect its vision and goals, and communicating these efforts better with their staff.

The generally high scores on this dimension however were in contrast to other data sources like OECD team interviews and Estyn reports. The analysis of other SLO dimensions also pointed to several areas for further improvement. School leaders play a vital role in the promotion and strengthening of induction programmes, mentoring/coaching, peer review and creating a culture of enquiry, innovation and exploration in their schools. The establishment of these and other conditions for a learning culture to develop across the whole school organisation is particularly an area of improvement for leaders in secondary schools.

Points of reflection and action for schools

The evidence suggested that the majority of schools in Wales are well on their way to developing as learning organisations. On the dimensions "promoting team learning and collaboration among all staff" and "embedding systems for collecting and exchanging knowledge and learning" schools appear to be progressing well. Although on the latter differences between primary and secondary schools are particularly large, with primary schools faring better, and also school self-evaluation and development planning stands out as an area for further attention.

Two dimensions were found to be considerably less well developed and deserve particular attention: "developing a shared vision centred on the learning of all students (learners)" and "establishing a culture of enquiry, innovation and exploration". The data also suggested that many schools in Wales could do more to "learn with and from the external environment and larger system".

Although schools need to be adequately supported and enabled to develop into learning organisations, many actions are within the control of schools themselves. School leaders play a vital role in creating the conditions for a learning organisation to develop. They need to be supported in taking on this responsibility. Teachers and learning support workers however need to also do their part to work and learn with colleagues beyond their department, subject area or school. Engaging in professional dialogue with colleagues, learning with and from staff in other schools – including between primary and secondary schools – and external partners, and drawing from the support provided by regional consortia are some of the means that staff have at their disposal.

Staff also need to more critically reflect on their own and their school's performance if deep learning and sustained progress to take place – and they need to be empowered to do this. School leaders play a pivotal role in creating a trusting and respectful climate that allows for open discussions about problems, successful and less successful practices, and the sharing of knowledge. This will also be essential to narrow the gaps in perceptions between staff about their own and schools' performance. The ongoing review of assessment, evaluation and accountability arrangements should be used to encourage and give people the confidence to do things differently and engage in critical reflections.

Secondary schools also clearly face more challenges in developing as learning organisations. Their more compartmentalised structure, which makes it harder to collaborate across departments and the organisation as a whole, is believed to be a factor in this. Also some leaders in secondary schools do not do enough to encourage a learning culture across the whole school organisation. This while the success of the curriculum reform will (among other things) depend on staff engaging in collective and cross-curricular learning and working, within and across schools. However, this assessment also identified several examples of secondary schools that exhibit the dimensions of a learning organisation, demonstrating that it is possible for them to develop as learning organisations.

Finally, although policy action will be required to reduce the variability in school funding between schools in similar circumstances, schools have the ability to take measures to ensure staff have the time and resources to engage in collaborative working and learning. The examples presented in this report show how budget pressures do not need to lead to a reduction in ambitions. Such examples should be systematically collected and shared widely to inspire and inform other schools in their change and innovation efforts.

Note

[1] School governors are elected members of a school governing board that has a central role in decisions about budgets and recruitment of the school. Members consist of teaching staff, parents, councillors and community representatives.

References

Ainscow, M., T. Booth and A. Dyson (2006), "Inclusion and the standards agenda: negotiating policy pressures in England", *International Journal of Inclusive Education*, Vol. 10/4, pp. 295-308, http://dx.doi.org/10.1080/13603110500430633. [63]

Andrews, R. et al. (2011), "Strategy implementation in public service performance", *Administration & Society*, Vol. 43, pp. 643–671. [13]

Bangor University (2017), *Collaborative Institute for Education Research, Evidence and Impact*, Bangor University, http://cierei.bangor.ac.uk/about.php.en (accessed on 27 November 2017). [65]

Barth, R. (2001), *Learning by Heart*, Jossey-Bass. [68]

Borgonovi, F. and G. Montt (2012), "Parental involvement in selected PISA countries and economies", *OECD Education Working Papers*, No. 73, OECD Publishing, Paris, http://dx.doi.org/10.1787/5k990rk0jsjj-en. [23]

Brown, C. (2015), *Leading the use of Research & Evidence in Schools*, Institute of Education Press, London. [57]

Bryk, A. and B. Schneider (2002), *Trust in Schools: A Core Resource for School Improvement*, Russell Sage, New York. [41]

Byrne, D. and E. Smyth (2010), *Behind the Scenes? A Study of Parental Involvement in Post-Primary Education*, Liffey Press, Dublin. [24]

Cannon, M. and A. Edmondson (2005), "Failing to learning and learning to fail (intelligently): How great organisations put failure to work to improve and innovate", *Long Range Planning*, Vol. 38, pp. 299-319. [50]

Cerna, L. (2014), "Trust: What it is and why it matters for governance and education", *OECD Education Working Papers*, No. 108, OECD Publishing, Paris, http://dx.doi.org/10.1787/5jxswcg0t6wl-en. [37]

Desforges, C. and A. Abouchaar (2003), "The impact of parental involvement, parental support and family education on pupil achievements and adjustment: A literature review", *Research Report*, No. 433, Department for Education and Skills Publications, Nottingham. [25]

Dimmock, C., D. Kwek and Y. Toh (2013), *Leadership for 21st Century Learning*, OECD Publishing, Paris, https://doi.org/10.1787/20769679. [75]

Domina, T. (2005), "Leveling the home advantage: Assessing the effectiveness of parental involvement in elementary school", *Sociology of Education*, Vol. 78/3, pp. 239-249, https://doi.org/10.1177%2F003804070507800303. [62]

Donaldson, G. (2015), *Successful Futures: Independent Review of Curriculum and Assessment Arrangements in Wales*, Welsh Government, http://gov.wales/docs/dcells/publications/150225-successful-futures-en.pdf. [7]

Earl, L. and S. Katz (2002), "Leading schools in a data-rich workd", in *Second International Handbook of Educational Leadership and Administration*, Springer Dordrecht Heidelberg London New York, http://dx.doi.org/10.1007/978-90-481-2660-6.   [49]

Earl, L. and H. Timperley (2015), "Evaluative thinking for successful educational innovation", *OECD Education Working Papers*, No. 122, OECD Publishing, https://doi.org/10.1787/5jrxtk1jtdwf-en.   [47]

Education Workforce Council (2017), *National Education Workforce Survey, Research Report, April 2017*, Education Workforce Council, Cardiff.   [44]

Epstein, J. (2001), *School, Family, Community Partnerships: Preparing Educators and Improving schools*, Westview Press, Boulder, CO.   [61]

Estyn (2018), *The Annual Report of Her Majesty's Chief Inspector of Education and Training in Wales 2016-2017*, Estyn, Cardiff, https://www.estyn.gov.wales/document/annual-report-2016-2017.   [14]

Estyn (2017), *Effective distribution of staff responsibilities to promote professional learning and shared responsibility*, Estyn, Cardiff, http://www.estyn.gov.wales/effective-practice/effective-distribution-staff-responsibilities-promote-professional-learning-and.   [8]

Estyn (2017), *Reducing Workload: A Guide for Teachers and Headteachers*, Estyn, Cardiff.   [45]

Estyn (2017), *The Annual Report of Her Majesty's Chief Inspector of Education and Training in Wales 2015-2016*, Estyn, Cardiff, http://www.estyn.gov.wales/sites/default/files/documents/ESTYN_Annual%20Report%202016%20FINAL_ENGLISH_Accessible_WEB.pdf.   [11]

Estyn (2016), *Report Following Monitoring, King Henry VIII Comprehensive School*, Estyn, Cardiff, https://www.estyn.gov.wales/sites/default/files/documents/Monitoring%20report%20King%20Henry%20VIII%20Comprehensive%20School.pdf.   [60]

Estyn (2011), *With a Little Help From my Friends*, Estyn, Cardiff, https://www.estyn.gov.wales/effective-practice/little-help-my-friends.   [36]

Fullan, M. (2014), *The Principal: Three Keys to Maximizing Impact*, Jossey-Bass and Ontario Principal's Council, Toronto.   [66]

Fullan, M. (2011), *Change Leader: Learning to Do What Matters Most*, Jossey-Bass, San Francisco.   [73]

Fullan, M. (2006), *Quality Leadership, Quality Learning: Proof Beyond Reasonable Doubt*, Lionra+, Cork.   [16]

Fullan, M. (1999), *Change Forces: The Sequel*, Falmer Press, London.   [5]

Fullan, M., C. Cuttress and A. Kilcher (2005), "Eight Forces for Leaders of Change", *Journal of Staff Development*, Vol. 26/4, pp. 54-64.   [55]

Furlong, J. (2015), *Teaching Tomorrow's Teachers, Options for the Future of Initial Teacher Education in Wales*, Welsh Government, Cardiff. [64]

George, B., S. Desmidt and J. De Moyer (2016), "Strategic decision quality in Flemish municipalities", *Public Money and Management*, Vol. 36/5, pp. 317-324. [22]

Hallinger, P. and R. Heck (2010), "Collaborative leadership and school improvement: Understanding the impact on school capacity and student learning", *School Leadership & Management*, Vol. 30/2, pp. 95-110, https://doi.org/10.1080/13632431003663214. [74]

Hargreaves, A. and M. Fullan (2012), *Professional Capital: Transforming Teaching in Every School*, Teachers College Press, New York. [20]

Harris, M. and F. van Tassell (2005), "The professional development school as a learning organization", *European Journal of Teacher Education*, Vol. 28/2, pp. 179-194. [21]

Hattie, J. (2012), *Visible Learning for Teachers: Maximizing Impact on Learning*, Routledge, London. [58]

Hattie, J. and H. Timperley (2007), "The power of feedback", *Review of Educational Research*, Vol. 77, pp. 88-112. [35]

Hiatt-Michael, D. (2001), "Schools as learning communities: A vision for organic school reform", *School Community Journal*, Vol. 11, pp. 113-127. [4]

Ingersoll, R. and M. Strong (2011), "The impact of induction and mentoring for beginning teachers; A critical review of the research", *Review of Educational Research*, Vol. 81/2, pp. 201-233. [30]

Jerrim, J. and N. Shure (2016), *Achievement of 15-Year- Olds in England: PISA 2015 National Report*, Department for Education, London, https://www.gov.uk/government/uploads/system/uploads/attachment_data/file/574925/PISA-2015_England_Report.pdf (accessed on 17 November 2017). [32]

Kessels, C. (2010), *The Influence of Induction Programs on Beginning Teachers' Well-being and Professional Development*, Doctoral thesis, Leiden University, Leiden, http://www.voion.nl/downloads/4eaec176-5310-40d0-8bb0-e95ca72aaef3 (accessed on 17 November 2017). [29]

Kools, M. and L. Stoll (2016), "What makes a school a learning organisation?", *OECD Education Working Papers*, No. 137, OECD Publishing, Paris, http://dx.doi.org/10.1787/5jlwm62b3bvh-en. [10]

Leithwood, K., D. Jantzi and R. Steinbach (1998), "Leadership and other conditions which foster organizational learning in schools", in *Organizational Learning in Schools*, Swets & Zeitlinger, Lisse. [59]

Marsick, V. and K. Watkins (1999), *Facilitating Learning Organizations: Making Learning Count*, Gower Publishing Limited, Cardiff. [69]

OECD (2018), *TALIS Initial Teacher Preparation Study*, OECD website, http://www.oecd.org/education/school/talis-initial-teacher-preparation-study.htm. [71]

OECD (2017), *PISA 2015 Results (Volume III): Students' Well-Being*, PISA, OECD Publishing, Paris, http://dx.doi.org/10.1787/9789264273856-en. [9]

OECD (2017), *The Welsh Education Reform Journey: A Rapid Policy Assessment*, OECD Publishing, Paris, http://www.oecd.org/edu/The-Welsh-Education-Reform-Journey-FINAL.pdf. [39]

OECD (2016), *Netherlands 2016: Foundations for the Future*, Reviews of National Policies for Education, OECD Publishing, Paris, http://dx.doi.org/10.1787/9789264257658-en. [15]

OECD (2016), *PISA 2015 Results (Volume II): Policies and Practices for Successful Schools*, PISA, OECD Publishing, Paris, https://doi.org/10.1787/9789264267510-en. [40]

OECD (2014), *Improving Schools in Wales: An OECD Perspective*, OECD Publishing, Paris, http://www.oecd.org/edu/Improving-schools-in-Wales.pdf. [48]

OECD (2013), *Innovative Learning Environments*, Educational Research and Innovation, OECD Publishing, Paris, http://dx.doi.org/10.1787/9789264203488-en. [18]

OECD (2013), *Leadership for 21st Century Learning*, Educational Research and Innovation, OECD Publishing, Paris, http://dx.doi.org/10.1787/9789264205406-en. [67]

OECD (2013), *Synergies for Better Learning: An International Perspective on Evaluation and Assessment*, OECD Reviews of Evaluation and Assessment in Education, OECD Publishing, Paris, http://dx.doi.org/10.1787/9789264190658-en. [52]

Pont, B. and R. Viennet (2017), "Education policy implementation: A literature review and proposed framework", *OECD Education Working Papers*, No. 162, OECD Publishing, Paris, http://dx.doi.org/10.1787/fc467a64-en. [17]

Révai, N. (2018), "Teachers' knowledge dynamics and innovation in education - Part II", *Neveléstudomány*, Vol. 21, pp. 6-17, http://dx.doi.org/10.21549/NTNY.21.2018.1.1. [72]

Robinson, V. (2011), *Student-Centered Leadership*, John Wiley & Sons, San Francisco. [70]

Schechter, C. and M. Qadach (2012), "Toward an organizational model of change in elementary schools: The contribution of organizational learning mechanisms", *Educational Administration Quarterly*, Vol. 48/1, pp. 116-153, http://dx.doi.org/10.1177/0013161X11419653. [51]

Schildkamp, K., L. Karbautzki and J. Vanhoof (2014), "Exploring data use practices around Europe: Identifying enablers and barriers", *Studies in Educational Evaluation*, Vol. 42, pp. 15-24. [54]

Schlechty, P. (2009), *Leading for Learning: How to Transform Schools into Learning Organizations*, John Wiley & Sons. [1]

Schleicher, A. (2018), *World Class: How to Build a 21st-Century School System*, OECD Publishing, Paris, http://dx.doi.org/10.1787/4789264300002-en. [28]

Schleicher, A. (2015), *Schools for 21st-Century Learners: Strong Leaders, Confident Teachers, Innovative Approaches, International Summit on the Teaching Profession*, OECD Publishing, Paris, http://dx.doi.org/10.1787/9789264231191-en. [34]

Schleicher, A. (2012), *Preparing Teachers and Developing School Leaders for the 21st Century: Lessons from around the World*, OECD Publishing, Paris, http://dx.doi.org/10.1787/9789264174559-en. [31]

Senge, P. et al. (2012), *Schools That Learn (Updated and Revised): A Fifth Discipline Fieldbook for Educators, Parents, and Everyone Who Cares about Education*, Crown Business, New York. [2]

Senge, P. et al. (2000), *Schools That Learn: A Fifth Discipline Fieldbook for Educators, Parents, and Everyone Who Cares about Education*, Doubleday. [19]

Silins, H., S. Zarins and B. Mulford (2002), "What characteristics and processes define a school as a learning organisation? Is it a useful concept to apply to schools?", *International Education Journal*, Vol. 3/1, pp. 24-32. [42]

Somech, A. and A. Drach-Zahavy (2007), "Strategies for coping with work-family conflict: The distinctive relationships of gender-role ideology", *Journal of Occupational Health Psychology*, Vol. 12, pp. 1-19. [43]

Thompson, M. et al. (2004), *Study of the impact of the California Formative Assessment and Support System for Teachers: Beginning teachers' engagement with BTSA/CFASST*, Educational Testing Service. [33]

Timperley, H. et al. (2007), *Teacher Professional Learning and Development: Best Evidence Synthesis Iteration*, Ministry of Education New Zealand, Wellington. [27]

Vincent-Lancrin, S. and C. González-Sancho (2015), *Innovation Strategy for Education and Training: Progress Report No. 10*, OECD Centre for Educational Research and Innovation Governing Board. [56]

Watkins, K. and V. Marsick (1996), *In Action: Creating the Learning Organization*, American Society for Training and Development, Alexandria. [46]

Welsh Government (2017), *Education in Wales: Our National Mission 2017-21*, Welsh Government, Cardiff, https://gov.wales/docs/dcells/publications/170926-education-in-wales-en.pdf. [3]

Welsh Government (2017), *Professional Standards for Teaching and Leadership*, Welsh Government, Cardiff, http://learning.gov.wales/docs/learningwales/publications/170901-professional-standards-for-teaching-and-leadership-en.pdf. [38]

Welsh Government (2017), *Schools in Wales as Learning Organisations*, Welsh Government website, http://gov.wales/topics/educationandskills/schoolshome/curriculuminwales/curriculum-for-wales-curriculum-for-life/schools-in-wales-as-learning-organisations/?lang=en (accessed on 30 November 2017). [12]

Welsh Government (2016), *Professional learning communities*, Welsh Government website, http://learning.gov.wales/resources/collections/professional-learning-communities?lang=en (accessed on 07 November 2017). [6]

Williams, B., J. Williams and A. Ullman (2002), "Parental involvement in education", *Research Report*, No. 332, Department of Education and Skills , Norwich, http://dera.ioe.ac.uk/4669/1/RR332.pdf. [26]

Yang, B., K. Watkins and V. Marsick (2004), "The construct of the learning organization: Dimensions, measurement, and validation", *Human Resource Development Quarterly*, Vol. 15/1, pp. 31-55. [53]

Part III. System assessment of the conditions for developing schools as learning organisations

Chapter 4. System-level policies for developing schools as learning organisations

This chapter examines the system-level policies that enable (or hinder) the development of schools as learning organisations (SLOs). Our analysis suggests that promoting a shared and inclusive vision calls for reviewing the school funding model and defining student well-being and common ways of monitoring it.

Developing professional capital and a learning culture argues for: 1) basing selection into initial teacher education on a mix of criteria and methods; 2) promoting collaborations between schools and teacher education institutions; 3) prioritising professional learning in certain areas; 4) a coherent leadership strategy; and 5) greater support for secondary school leaders.

Assessment, evaluation and accountability should promote SLOs through: 1) national criteria for school evaluations; 2) a participatory self-evaluation process; 3) Estyn evaluations safeguarding quality, while focusing more on self-evaluation processes; 4) clarifying the transition to a new system of school evaluations; 5) aligning performance measures to the new curriculum, and 6) system monitoring through sample-based student assessments, Estyn reports and research.

Introduction

This chapter takes a close look at the system-level policies that are considered essential for schools to develop as learning organisations in Wales. It uses Wales' schools as learning organisations (SLO) model as a lens to look at the system around schools to identify those policies that might enable or hinder schools in making this transformation (see Figure 4.1). These policies are grouped into three clusters that shape this chapter:

- policies promoting a shared and future-focused vision centred on the learning of all students

- policies promoting the development of professional capital and a thriving learning culture

- assessment, evaluation and accountability promoting schools as learning organisations (SLOs).

Figure 4.1. System-level policies for developing schools as learning organisations

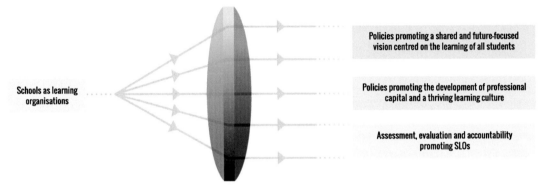

The chapter analyses each cluster separately, discussing the strengths and challenges of the relevant policies. It explores opportunities for greater policy coherence and makes suggestions for the further development of policies, drawing from international research evidence and relevant examples. Figure 4.2 presents the structure and is used at the start of each section to guide the reader throughout the chapter.

Figure 4.2. System-level policies for developing schools as learning organisations

Policies promoting a shared and future-focused vision centred on the learning of all students

The development of an inclusive and shared vision is central to the first dimension of Wales' SLO model (Welsh Government, 2017[1]). The Welsh Government has also put the realisation of the "four purposes" of the new school curriculum at the heart of the model (see Chapter 1, Box 1.1). These refer to developing children and young people into "ambitious capable and lifelong learners, enterprising and creative, informed citizens and healthy and confident individuals" (Welsh Government, 2017[1]; Donaldson, 2015[2]).

Evidence shows that an inclusive and shared vision gives a school a sense of direction and serves as a motivating force for sustained action to achieve individual and school goals (Kools and Stoll, 2016[3]). However, if it is to be truly shared across the system, such a vision must be placed in the context of the national vision, and respond to it, leaving some scope to adapt it to the local context (Greany,(n.d.)[4]; Hargreaves and Shirley, 2009[5]).

The evidence gathered as part of this assessment suggests that this vision is widely shared throughout the school system. However, two issues call for urgent policy attention to enable all schools in Wales to put this vision into practice. The first is the school funding model, which challenges equity. The second is a lack of a common understanding of what student well-being entails which challenges schools' efforts to enhance it. This section will take a closer look at these issues and their policy implications.

Consolidating a compelling and inclusive vision across the national, middle tier and school levels

Having a compelling and inclusive vision at the national level is essential as it can steer a system and draw key people together to work towards it (Hargreaves and Shirley, 2009[5]). When clearly communicated and shared it can help secure reform over the long term, helping to keep changes on track even if they hit initial obstacles (Miles et al., 2002[6]; OECD, 2014[7]; Viennet and Pont, 2017[8]). The vision must be future-focused and should excite new possibilities for action, not least so that it unlocks the energy and passion of key stakeholders who will be key to making it happen. Furthermore, in line with the first dimension of the SLO model for Wales, the vision should define and embody a core set of values, with excellence, equity, inclusion and well-being as central themes (Kools and Stoll, 2016[3]; Welsh Government, 2017[1]).

In addition, it is essential that this vision is shared across all levels of the systems, while providing some freedom of interpretation to take account of local or regional differences. This seems obvious but international research evidence shows that this is not always the case (Burns, Köster and Fuster, 2016[9]; Hargreaves and Shirley, 2009[5]).

One of the key critical points in the OECD 2014 review of the school system was that Wales lacked a long-term vision (OECD, 2014[7]). Informed by this review and several other research reports, Wales developed an education vision and a strategic plan to move towards realising that vision, *Qualified for Life: An Education Improvement Plan* (Welsh Government, 2014[10]). The review of curriculum and assessment arrangements that signalled the start of the curriculum reform has in turn allowed this vision of the Welsh learner to be further refined and given shape through the "four purposes". These four purposes of the new curriculum call for all Welsh learners to develop as "ambitious capable and lifelong learners, enterprising and creative, informed citizens and healthy and confident individuals" (see Chapter 1, Box 1.1). This vision resonates with others developed in recent years by several OECD countries and economies such as Estonia, Japan and Ontario (Canada), and the preliminary findings of the OECD's Education 2030 project which is constructing a framework to help shape what young people should be learning in the year 2030 (OECD, 2018[11]).

Throughout this OECD review, the OECD team have found that this vision seems to be shared throughout the school system in Wales. The OECD team's school visits and interviews with stakeholders resulted in almost unanimous reference to and support for the four purposes of the new curriculum. This is a major achievement and a strength of the curriculum reform that seems to find its roots in the large-scale public consultation process on the curriculum and assessment review arrangements in 2015. Since then, stakeholder engagement – an essential component for effective policy implementation (Viennet and Pont, 2017[8]) – has remained at the heart of Wales' approach to developing and putting the new curriculum into practice in schools across the country.

As discussed in Chapter 1, in 2017, the Welsh Government released its new strategic action plan, *Education in Wales: Our National Mission* (Welsh Government, 2017[12]). The plan builds on both the 2014 Qualified for Life plan (Welsh Government, 2014[10]) and the 2015 review of curriculum and assessment arrangements (Donaldson, 2015[2]). It sets out how the school system will move forward over the period 2017-21 to secure the successful implementation or – as it is often referred to in Wales – the "realisation" of the new curriculum. The Pioneer Schools (see Chapter 1) and the regional consortia play a key role in the Welsh Government's strategy for realising change from the "meso" level (OECD, 2016[13]) – or what some have referred to as "middle-out change" (Fullan and Quinn, 2015[14]; Hargreaves and Ainscow, 2015[15]; Greany,(n.d.)[4]) – that research suggests is essential for creating the collaborative learning cultures and leadership capacity in school systems that will be essential for bringing the new curriculum to life in schools throughout Wales.

It is hard to judge how well the four purposes are really understood by the education profession in terms of what they will actually mean for their daily practice. Their operationalisation will surely stretch people's understanding and the skills needed for teaching and supporting students in their learning, and should not be underestimated, as will be discussed in the cluster of policies below.

A central focus on equity and well-being

Research evidence shows that success in school is possible for all students. Several schools and education systems around the globe have realised a vision of dramatically improving the learning outcomes of the most disadvantaged children (OECD, 2016[13]; Agasisti et al., 2018[16]; Martin and Marsh, 2006[17]). For this to happen, policies must be geared towards creating a fair and inclusive system, whilst also providing additional support for the most disadvantaged schools (OECD, 2012[18]).

The OECD has suggested five systemic approaches to support disadvantaged schools: 1) make funding strategies responsive to students' and schools' needs; 2) manage school choice to avoid segregation and increased inequity; 3) eliminate grade repetition; 4) eliminate early tracking/streaming/ability-grouping and defer student selection to upper secondary level; and 5) design equivalent upper secondary education pathways (e.g. academic and vocational) to ensure completion (OECD, 2012[18]).

What types of policies is Wales implementing to support these? The Welsh education system is based on equity guidelines and Wales has expressed a strong commitment to equity in education and student well-being (OECD, 2017[19]). It has implemented various policies like the Pupil Deprivation Grant and free school meals (FSMs) to target equity challenges in the school system with some noteworthy success in recent years. For example, the 2016 Wales Education Report Card showed that the attainment gap between students who receive FSMs and their peers who do not has narrowed (Welsh Government, 2016[20]). However, two areas call for further policy attention in Wales: the need to make vocational and academic qualifications equal, and the responsiveness of funding strategies to students' and schools' needs. These will be discussed below.

Ensuring equivalent upper secondary education pathways

Upper secondary education is a strategic level of education for individuals and societies, representing a key link between a basic educational foundation and a move into advanced study or employment. Upper secondary should respond to the needs of students and the labour market through the flexible combination of vocational and academic choices

(Sahlberg, 2007[21]). It is important to ensure both equivalence of these diverse pathways, and consistency in quality: all programmes should deliver benefits from both a learning and outcomes perspective and be valued in the same way. Although vocational qualifications in Wales are intended to indeed do this, they are not always valued equally by students, their parents, employers and society at large. Wales is not unique in this challenge as many OECD countries have been trying to raise the prestige of vocational qualifications with varying success (OECD, 2014[22]; OECD, 2016[23]; OECD, 2017[24]).

A few years ago, Wales completed a review of qualifications for 14-19 year-olds (Welsh Government, 2012[25]) that is believed to have contributed to increasing their relevance. Still, the people the OECD team interviewed recognised there is further work to be done to ensure vocational qualifications are equally valued as academic ones. Wales plans to review its qualifications once more when the details of the new school curriculum have become clear. Initial steps were being taken while this report was being finalised. The OECD team agree this is a vital step for ensuring the alignment of curricula and assessment and evaluation arrangements throughout the system, and should be used to promote the relevance of vocational qualifications in Wales.

Challenges arising from the Welsh school funding model

As noted in an earlier OECD assessment, Wales' strong commitment to equity raises the question of whether it is desirable to have differences in local funding models across local authorities. In the current funding model, the Welsh Government provides funding for schools through the local government settlement for the services for which they are responsible, including education. The other main sources of funding for local authority budgets are council tax income and nondomestic rates income. Local authorities decide how much to spend on education, according to their own priorities and local circumstances, and then allocate budgets to individual schools.

Several stakeholders noted that differences in local funding models have caused inequalities for schools, students and school staff across the 22 local authorities. This seems evident when looking at the differences in how much local authorities reallocate the funding provided to them by the Welsh Government for schools. Local authorities have discretion to reallocate up to 30% of the school budget on the basis of a range of factors so that they can take account of individual school circumstances. There is considerable variation in the proportions that are reallocated, ranging from 23.2% in the local authority of Powys to 10.7% in Cardiff in 2017/18. School transportation costs partially explain the differences in reallocation but when these are taken into consideration a 7% difference remains between these two local authorities (Statistics for Wales, 2018[26]). Various stakeholders noted that there are sometimes substantial differences in average expenditure per student between otherwise similar schools simply because they are in different local authorities.

School staff and other stakeholders the OECD team interviewed also mentioned that the lack of stability in funding from one year to the next is particularly challenging. The official data on net revenue expenditure – i.e. the amount of expenditure which is supported by council tax and general support from central government, plus (or minus) any appropriations from (or to) financial reserves – supports this view. In 2017/18, for example, schools in the local authority of Swansea saw a 4.4% increase in education net revenue expenditure compared to the year before, while in the local authority of Conwy there was a decrease of 2.0% (Statistics for Wales, 2018[26]).

The evidence suggests that the differences in school funding between local authorities also affects the working conditions of learning support workers, as well as the professional learning opportunities of school staff. Starting with the former, the OECD rapid policy assessment (2017[19]) noted that the salaries of learning support workers, who in many schools are fulfilling an essential role in supporting students with additional learning needs, vary depending on where they work because the local authority sets their pay. Their experience and responsibilities are not always recognised in the same way in the pay structure (UNISON, 2016[27]).

Furthermore, although the SLO survey data (see Chapter 2) were not analysed at the local authority level, the data suggest schools in Wales are not benefitting equally from professional learning opportunities. Interviews with school staff and other stakeholders support this view and suggest these differences are partially the result of differences in funding allocations to schools by local authorities.

Box 4.1. An example of designing school funding formulas to meet policy objectives – Lithuania

In 2001, **Lithuania** introduced an education finance formula which aimed to increase the efficiency of resource use in education and improve education quality. As well as creating a transparent and fair scheme for resource allocation, the reform aimed to promote the optimisation of local school networks and constant adjustment to the decreasing number of students. Importantly, the funding allocation makes a clear distinction between "teaching costs" (state grant) and "school maintenance costs" (local funds). The major determinant of funding within the central grant is the number of students in the school.

The allocation of a fixed amount per student has promoted greater efficiency. However, this differs from a pure student voucher system in three ways:

- The grant is transferred to the municipality and not directly to the school. The municipality has the right to redistribute a certain proportion of funding across schools. In 2001, this was 15% and it was gradually reduced to 5%, but now stands at 7%. Municipal reallocation may weaken incentives for schools to compete for resources, as municipalities can choose to support "struggling schools".

- The grant takes into account school size. This aims to acknowledge that some smaller schools (with higher costs) have lower enrolment rates due to their rural location. However, school size also depends on municipal decisions to consolidate the network.

- The grant includes some specifications on minimal levels of required expenditure such as on textbooks and in-service teacher education.

The 2001 funding reform has helped to stop the declining efficiency of the school network. The annual adjustments over the exact weighting coefficients used in the funding formula are subject to fierce policy debate, notably over the extent of support to small, rural schools. The use of the formula allows a high degree of transparency on decisions about funding priorities.

Source: Shewbridge, C. et al. (2016[28]), *OECD Reviews of School Resources: Lithuania 2016*, http://dx.doi.org/10.1787/9789264252547-en.

In light of these findings, the Welsh Government should consider reviewing its school funding model as this seems essential for realising Wales' ambitions for equity in education and student well-being (OECD, 2017[19]). It should consider conducting an in-depth analysis of school funding in Wales to explore alternative funding models that promote greater equity and efficiency. It could look to countries and economies like the Flemish Community of Belgium, Latvia, Lithuania and the Netherlands which have established funding formulas for promoting equity (both horizontal equity, i.e. the like treatment of recipients whose needs are similar, and vertical equity, i.e. the application of different funding levels for recipients whose needs differ) while increasing efficiency (OECD, 2017[29]; OECD, 2016[23]; Ross and Levačić, 1999[30]). Increasing equity can be one of the most important functions of a funding formula but other objectives like increasing efficiency often have an influence, as was the case in Lithuania and Latvia (OECD, 2016[23]; OECD, 2017[24]). An action that may be more feasible in the short term is to further limit the funding that local authorities are allowed to reallocate, excluding school transport costs to take into account the differences in population density. For example, Lithuania defined a maximum proportion of funding that municipalities could reallocate. This was adjusted several times to ensure sufficient funding reached the schools (see Box 4.1).

Developing a common understanding of and way(s) of monitoring student well-being in schools across Wales

A sizable proportion of children and young people in Wales face equity challenges, and Wales has a relatively high level of child poverty (OECD, 2017[19]). For example, the Programme for International Student Assessment (PISA) found in 2015 that, although the impact of a student's socio-economic status on performance is lower in Wales than many OECD countries (see Chapter 1, Figure 1.6), there still is large variation in performance within schools in Wales (OECD, 2016[31]). As discussed in Chapter 3, PISA 2015 also pointed to specific areas of improvement concerning students' well-being, including schoolwork-related anxiety and sense of belonging in school (OECD, 2017[32]).

Wales has recognised the importance of student well-being in its strategic action plan where it is part of one of its four "enabling objectives" (see Chapter 2, Figure 2.1). It considers the well-being of children and young people to be central to realising the curriculum and ultimately the vision of the Welsh learner (Welsh Government, 2017[12]).

However, the desk review of policy documents and interviews with school staff, policy makers and other stakeholders by the OECD team revealed there is no common understanding of or ways of monitoring the well-being of children and young people (i.e. adolescents) in Wales. The lack of clarity on and different interpretations of well-being is not unique to Wales: Table 4.1 shows how child and adolescent well-being is given shape differently in international frameworks. In a critical reflection of these frameworks, Choi (2018[33]) points out that while international frameworks include various health behaviours and self-reported health statuses, they lack detailed measures for the elements of emotional well-being.

As mentioned in Chapter 3, the various school visits by the OECD team showed examples of schools monitoring and supporting the well-being of their students, some using different types of survey instruments. The team learned that such survey instruments are commonly used in schools throughout Wales for this purpose, but these vary in their scope.

Table 4.1. Different dimensions and indicators of child and adolescent well-being

	UNICEF	OECD (How's life for children)	OECD (PISA 15-year-old students' well-being)
Material well-being	• Relative income poverty • Households without jobs • Reported deprivation	*Well-being conditions of families where children live* • Income and wealth • Jobs and earnings • Housing conditions • Environmental quality	N/A
Health	• Health at age 0-1 • Preventative health services • Safety	• Infant mortality • Low birthweight • Self-reported heath status • Overweight and obesity • Adolescent suicide rates • Teenage birth-rates	N/A
Behaviours (healthy and unhealthy)	• Health behaviours (eating breakfast, physical activities) • Risky behaviours (alcohol, cannabis use, etc.) • Experience of violence (being bullied, fighting)	N/A	*Physical dimension* • Physical activities in and out of school (# of days) • Eat breakfast or dinner
Education	*Education well-being* • School achievement at age 15 (PISA) • Beyond basics • Tradition to employment	*Education and skills* • PISA mean reading and creative problem-solving score • Youth NEET (neither in employment nor education or training) • Educational deprivation	*Cognitive dimension* • PISA average maths, reading, and science scores
Social	*Relationships* • Family structure • Family relationships • Peer relationships (HBSC)	*Social and family environment* • Teenagers who find it easy to talk to their parents • Students reporting having kind and helpful classmates • Students feeling a lot of pressure from schoolwork • Students liking school • PISA sense of belonging index • Time children spend with their parents	*Social dimension* • Sense of belonging at school • Exposure to bullying • Perception of teachers' unfair treatment
Subjective well-being	• Self-reported health status • School life • Life satisfaction	• Life satisfaction	• Life satisfaction
Personal security	N/A	• Child homicide rates • Bullying	N/A
Civic engagement	N/A	• Intention to vote • Civic participation	N/A
Psychological well-being	N/A	N/A	• Schoolwork-related anxiety • Achievement motivation

Source: Adapted from UNICEF Office of Research (2013[34]), "Child well-being in rich countries: A comparative overview"; OECD (2015[35]), *How's Life? 2015: Measuring Well-being*, http://dx.doi.org/10.1787/how_life-2015-en; OECD (2017[32]), *PISA 2015 Results (Volume III): Students' Well-Being*, http://dx.doi.org/10.1787/9789264273856-en.

These instruments also differ to varying degrees from the student questionnaires Estyn uses to get an insight into student well-being at inspected schools. The new Estyn Framework (Estyn, 2017[36]) also specifically calls for the monitoring of student well-being, in addition to students' attitudes to learning and standards. Arguably students' attitudes to learning are part of the concept of well-being.

The lack of clarity about and measurement of the concept is also recognised in Wales' new strategic education plan. The plan states the intention of the Welsh Government to work with partners, in Wales and beyond, on effective measurements of student well-being (Welsh Government, 2017[12]). Reaching a common understanding of the concept is an essential first step. It should be started as soon as possible, considering the equity and student well-being challenges in Wales, and also if it is to be of use in the development of a national school self-evaluation and development planning toolkit on which work had started while finalising this report.

Policies promoting the development of professional capital and a thriving learning culture

The SLO concept reflects a central focus on the professional learning of school staff – teachers, learning support workers and those in leadership positions – aimed at creating a learning culture in the organisation and other parts of the (learning) system. Although it cuts across all seven dimensions of the SLO model, investment in professional capital – human, social and decisional or leadership capital according to Hargreaves and Fullan (2012[37]) – is particularly evident in four of them: creating and supporting continuous learning opportunities, promoting team learning and collaboration, learning with and from the external environment and larger learning system, and modelling and growing learning leadership.

National or provincial/regional policies and actions can play a significant role in enabling schools and local partners to develop these four dimensions and ultimately establish a sustainable learning culture in their schools. The evidence shows this to be the case for several areas, like the promotion of school-to-school collaboration and the clarification of professional expectations through the teaching and leadership standards.

Several issues deserve further policy attention however. These are:

- the need to establish stronger collaborations between schools and teacher education institutions

- promoting learning throughout the professional lifecycle with three priority areas i.e. investing in the skills and "mindset" for enquiry, exploration and innovation; strengthening induction programmes; and promoting mentoring and coaching, observations and peer review

- developing learning leadership in schools and other parts of the system.

These issues for which policy recommendations are offered will be discussed further in the text below.

Selection into initial teacher education based on a mix of criteria and methods

Policy makers around the world have focused considerable attention on how to attract and retain quality teachers in recent years. This attention follows several studies that have convincingly argued that the quality of a school system cannot exceed the quality of its teachers (Barber and Mourshed, 2007[38]; Hattie, 2012[39]). The criteria for selecting aspiring teachers into initial education programmes are clearly important in this respect. Many countries have raised their entry requirements for teacher education programmes in recent years (Schleicher, 2011[40]; OECD, 2018[41]), and this includes Wales. Entry into initial teacher education now requires a minimum of General Certificate of Secondary Education (GCSE) grade B in English and mathematics to ensure that incoming teachers possess the necessary skills in these subjects. In addition, graduates are assessed on their literacy and numeracy skills during their studies, with failure resulting in exclusion from teacher education (OECD, 2014[7]).

As in many other countries, the raising of entry requirements in Wales has been limited to higher degree requirements and focused on cognitive skills. However, teaching in the 21st century is complex and challenging. It requires a mix of high-level cognitive and socio-emotional skills on a daily basis. In recognition of this reality, teacher education institutions in several OECD countries, such as England, Finland and the Netherlands, have started initiatives around intake procedures and selection options that go beyond formal degree requirements. The evidence shows a wider range of selection criteria can be used effectively (Van der Rijst, Tigelaar and van Driel, 2014[42]; European Commission, 2013[43]). For example, Finland selects secondary graduates based on exam results, a written test on assigned books on pedagogy, observations in school situations and interviews (Sahlberg, 2010[44]).

The Welsh Government should consider following these examples and encourage teacher education institutions to expand and pilot more elaborate, well-rounded selection criteria and intake procedures. This should be part of the ongoing reform efforts that aim to respond to the well-known concerns about the variable quality of initial teacher education programmes and its graduates (Furlong, 2015[45]; Tabberer, 2013[46]). Particular attention should be paid to assessing aspiring teachers' aptitude for teaching the new curriculum and engaging in continuous professional learning.

Furthermore, following the example of OECD countries like Australia and the Netherlands, the Welsh Government is considering diversifying the entry routes into teacher education, for example through work-based routes (OECD, 2018[41]). These routes are currently non-existent in Wales, thereby limiting the inflow of qualified individuals. Despite the capacity challenges involved in developing such alternative teacher education programmes, the OECD team agree that this would be an important step towards ensuring Wales has sufficient numbers of qualified teachers in the coming years. Such alternative routes into teaching also give further impetus to the use of broader selection criteria and methods.

Quality initial teacher education – the need for strong collaborations with schools

Ensuring high-quality initial teacher education is an obvious step to safeguard and/or enhance the quality of the future education workforce. As noted in an earlier OECD assessment (2017[19]) this has long been a problem area for Wales and until recently little progress had been made in improving the situation. Following the release of the report *Teaching Tomorrow's Teachers* (2015[45]) by John Furlong a number of measures have been initiated at the national, institutional and programme levels. Much of the responsibility for putting these changes into practice lies with the universities, both centrally and at the individual programme levels, as well as in the schools, whose practices need to change. The role of government has been to set up the appropriate structures to encourage and support the changes needed to improve initial teacher education in Wales. Furlong made several recommendations to achieve this (see Box 4.2) which have all been adopted by the Welsh Government and are now being implemented.

Box 4.2. Agreed policy measures for improving the quality of initial teacher education in Wales

- That the Welsh Government, as a matter of priority revises the Standards for Newly Qualified Teachers.

- That the Welsh Government establishes a revised accreditation process for providers of initial teacher education.

- That the Welsh Government establishes a Teacher Education Accreditation Board within the Education Workforce Council for Wales.

- That the role of Estyn within initial teacher education be reviewed once a revised accreditation process is fully in place.

- That Estyn's Guidance for Inspection for schools be revised to include specific recognition of the contribution of a school to initial teacher education.

- That the Primary BA (Hons) qualified teaching status (QTS) in its current form be phased out and replaced by a four-year degree with 50% of students' time spent in main subject departments.

- That the Welsh Government monitors closely the impact of financial incentives on recruitment, particularly taking into account different funding levels in comparison with those available in England.

- That WISERD Education be extended to include a pedagogical dimension linked to a network of five centres of pedagogical excellence across Wales.

- That the Welsh Government agrees to resolve future provision of initial teacher education through a process of competitive tendering with the Teacher Education Accreditation Board making the final decision as to how many universities should become accredited providers.

Note: WISERD stands for Wales Institute of Social & Economic Research, Data & Methods. It has been designated by the Welsh Government as a national, interdisciplinary, social science research institute.
Source: Furlong, J. (2015[45]), *Teaching Tomorrow's Teachers: Options for the Future of Initial Teacher Education in Wales*, http://gov.wales/docs/dcells/publications/150309-teaching-tomorrows-teachers-final.pdf.

Several of these recommendations are of particular relevance to supporting schools to develop into learning organisations. This includes the development of new accreditation requirements for higher education institutions offering initial teacher education programmes. An important aspect of the new criteria is their emphasis on partnerships between higher education institutions and schools. This is essential for increasing the quality and relevance of initial teacher education, and for building professional capital within schools to develop themselves into learning organisations and move towards a self-improving school system (Harris and van Tassell, 2005[47]; Kools and Stoll, 2016[3]).

Furthermore, in his report, Furlong called on Estyn's guidance on school inspections to be revised to include specific recognition of schools' contribution to initial teacher education. The OECD team agree this is an important incentive for schools to play their part in establishing sustainable collaboration with teacher education institutions.

This should also be promoted through the school self-evaluation process. Such incentives – or possibly "requirements" would be more accurate – are important as the evidence has shown that few schools in Wales have been willing to make long-term commitments to collaborate with teacher education institutions, often withdrawing, sometimes at the last minute, particularly if they are facing an Estyn inspection (Furlong, 2015[45]). Data from the SLO survey also showed that about two-thirds of school staff (64%) responded positively to the statement that "staff actively collaborate with higher education institutions to deepen staff and student learning". One-third of school staff therefore disagreed with this statement or responded neutrally, which may suggest they did not know (see Chapters 2 and 3).

The team agree with Furlong therefore that the system needs to recognise the contribution of schools to teacher education institutions – and vice versa – more publicly. Making a systematic and sustained contribution to teacher education should be one way for schools to demonstrate that they are good schools, or aspire to be. The same responsibility in turn falls on teacher education institutions and higher education institutions more generally. We will come back to this below when discussing evaluation, assessment and accountability arrangements.

Clarifying expectations for continuous professional learning

The kind of education needed today requires teachers to be high-level knowledge workers who constantly advance their own professional knowledge as well as that of their profession (Schleicher, 2015[48]; Schleicher, 2012[49]; OECD, 2013[50]). There is also a growing body of evidence that shows that teachers' and school leaders' professional development can have a positive impact on student performance and their practice (Timperley et al., 2007[51]). Research evidence shows that effective professional learning should incorporate most if not all of the following elements: it has to be content focused, incorporate active learning, support collaboration, use models of effective practice, coaching and expert support, feedback and reflection, and has to be of sustained duration (Darling-Hammond, Hyler and Gardner, 2017[52]). Taken together, these points have led scholars, education practitioners and policy makers around the world to support the notion of investing in quality career-long professional learning opportunities for teachers.

Depending on the nature of the system in question, national or regional/provincial agencies may need to play a role in securing minimum expectations for professional learning or in providing an architecture that local actions can work within (Greany,(n.d.)[4]). For example, where there is no equivalent of the profession-led General Teaching Council of Scotland which carries out a wide range of statutory functions to promote, support and develop the professional learning of teachers, including the setting the professional standards expected of all teachers, then the government might promote the establishment of a network of education professionals and other stakeholders to establish standards and minimum expectations for professional learning. This latter was done in Wales.

A common understanding of "professional learning"

In its new strategic education plan, the Welsh Government has made a commitment to establishing a national approach to professional learning, building capacity so that all teachers benefit from career-long development based on research and effective collaboration (Welsh Government, 2017[12]). The OECD team found that Wales is clearly moving away from a model of delivering professional learning away from the school setting, towards a more collaborative, practitioner-led experience which is embedded in classroom practice. This is important; although professional learning opportunities outside the school premises, for example formal education courses at universities or participation in workshops, can play an important role in the professional learning of staff, research evidence clearly points to the importance of ensuring professional learning opportunities are sustainable, embedded into the workplace and are primarily collaborative in nature (Fullan, Rincon-Gallardo and Hargreaves, 2015[53]; Kools and Stoll, 2016[3]).

The Welsh Government is in the process of developing its professional learning model, together with stakeholders at various levels of the system. The OECD team agree that this is an important way to jointly define a common understanding of what professional learning entails in the Welsh context. Such a common understanding could not only inform the developmental journeys of school staff. It could also inform the professional learning offered by regional consortia, and the teacher education and continuing professional learning programmes provided by higher education institutions and other parties which will be needed to help put the new curriculum into practice and establish a thriving learning culture in schools across Wales.

Professional standards and a career structure to guide continuous professional learning and growth

As noted in Chapter 1, Wales recently concluded its review of the professional standards for teachers and leaders (Welsh Government, 2017[54]). The new standards reflect a contemporary, research-informed understanding of what good teaching entails and they align with the government's ambitions for the new school curriculum (Donaldson, 2015[2]; OECD, 2017[19]). Importantly, the standards have also been developed by the education profession and other key stakeholders as part of the Pioneer Schools Network. Almost all of the stakeholders the OECD team interviewed appreciated the relevance and usefulness of the standards for guiding teachers' and school leaders' professional learning. Their integration into the Professional Learning Passport is intended to facilitate this learning process. This digital tool is designed to help teachers plan and record their professional learning (Education Workforce Council, 2017[55]). This level of self-guided learning and development is an important element of the professionalisation of the education workforce (Kools and Stoll, 2016[3]).

The standards are aimed at promoting and guiding the professional learning of staff – something this assessment suggests is indeed much needed. For example, in the SLO survey, just over one in five school staff (21%) did not agree that professional learning of staff was considered a high priority in their school, with significant differences between staff categories and levels of education. Teachers and learning support workers were more critical in their views than school leaders, for example. Furthermore, close to three out of ten school staff (28%) responded neutrally or negatively to the statement that "staff receive regular feedback to support reflection and improvement" in their school (see Chapter 3). These findings suggest there is indeed much to gain from the continued promotion of the new teaching and leadership standards in schools throughout Wales.

The revised standards are also intended to guide the development of initial teacher education. Higher education institutions will have to show how their teacher education programmes are relevant to the revised standards as part of the accreditation process – this will be an important step towards raising the quality and relevance of initial teacher education in Wales (OECD, 2017[19]). It will also help to bring teacher education programmes and schools closer together – a condition for schools to function as learning organisations (Harris and van Tassell, 2005[47]) and to realise Wales' objective of a self-improving school system.

As in some other OECD countries, learning support workers make up a significant proportion of the school workforce in Wales (Masdeu Navarro, 2015[56]; OECD, 2017[19]). Over recent years, the role of support staff in schools in Wales has been developed and extended, largely due to implementation of the provisions contained within the *Raising Standards and Tackling Workload – a National Agreement* document, but also as a result of initiatives to improve provision for early years education. The deployment of support staff in new and enhanced roles has been instrumental in securing significant cultural change in the way that the school workforce is deployed and has been a key factor in the drive to raise standards through the provision of high-quality teaching. Recognising that not support staff were not benefitting equally from appropriate support and training, and progression routes the *Action plan to promote the role and development of support staff in schools in Wales* (Welsh Government, 2013[57]) was developed. This plan includes of actions to better the situation.

At the time of drafting, and as part of this plan work was underway to develop new professional standards for support staff. As mentioned in Chapter 1, these new standards are intended to enable them to improve their skills, make a commitment to professional learning and facilitate clearer pathways to the role of Higher Level Teaching Assistant. As such, they form an important step forward in the professionalisation of learning support workers in Wales. This is particularly relevant considering their large share of the education workforce and the important roles they fulfil in enhancing the teaching and learning in schools throughout Wales on a daily basis.

The Welsh Government, alongside key stakeholders like the Education Workforce Council and the regional consortia, aims to establish a coherent career structure that gives learning support workers the opportunity to advance into teaching roles, as is the case in several OECD countries like Estonia, the Netherlands and Sweden (Santiago et al., 2016[58]; Swedish Ministry of Education and Research, 2016[59]; OECD, 2016[60]), although their approaches vary.

All this suggests that, in line with expectations for a system that enables its schools to develop into inclusive and effective learning organisations (Greany,(n.d.)[4]; European Commission, 2017[61]), Wales is making good progress in (re-)defining expectations for the education profession in Wales.

Promoting learning throughout the professional lifecycle – priority areas

To be effective, professional learning must be seen as a long-term continuous enquiry process spanning education staffs' professional careers and focused on school goals and student learning (Silins, Zarins and Mulford, 2002[62]; Timperley et al., 2007[51]).

Quality induction programmes

Well-structured and well-resourced induction programmes should form the starting point for the continuous professional learning of new teachers and learning support workers. Such programmes can support new staff in their transition to full responsibilities (Schleicher, 2011[40]). In some countries, once teachers have completed their initial education, they begin one or two years of heavily supervised teaching. During this period, the beginning teacher typically experiences a reduced workload, mentoring by master teachers and continued formal education. Wales has long had a mandatory one-year induction period for all newly qualified teachers, but not for learning support workers who, as mentioned above, make up a large proportion of the school workforce.

The evidence from this assessment suggests there are also challenges in terms of the quantity and quality of such programmes in some schools and parts of Wales. For example, the SLO survey data showed that about 30% of respondents did not agree that in their school all new staff received sufficient support to help them in their new roles. The data also suggest that fewer new staff in secondary schools benefitted from sufficient induction support than their peers in primary schools. Another challenge is that little is known about the quality of induction programmes in Wales (OECD, 2017[19]).

This is therefore an issue the Welsh Government and the regional consortia should look into further in order to safeguard and enhance the quality of its future education workforce. For example, they might look at the pilot project in the Netherlands, "Coaching Starting Teachers" (*Begeleiding Startende Docenten*). This provides beginning secondary teachers with a 3-year induction programme that has been shaped by collaboration between initial teacher education institutions and schools (Box 4.3). Although the primary beneficiaries of the project are intended to be the new teachers and their schools, the collaboration in turn informs teacher education institutions about the quality of their initial education programmes and effective ways to support teachers' continuous professional learning and development.

Box 4.3. An example of an induction programme – Piloting coaching starting teachers in the Netherlands

In 2014 the Dutch Ministry of Education started a pilot project "Coaching Starting Teachers" (*Begeleiding Startende Docenten*) that targets beginning teachers and aims to increase their professionalism, shorten the transition period from a beginning teacher to an experienced teacher and limit the proportion of beginning teachers who leave the profession. The project covers about one-third of secondary schools and 1 000 starting teachers. It stimulates collaboration between initial teacher education institutions and schools through regional collaborations and provides starting teachers with a strong induction programme that lasts three years.

The advantages for schools participating in the project include:

- novice teachers are more likely to achieve a higher level of effective practice in the classroom

- the school has an appraisal system that fits in well with the appraisal framework of the education inspectorate

- teachers receive free training in observing and guiding colleagues in their "zone of proximal development"

- the school can exchange knowledge and experiences with other participating schools, including academic training schools.

The pilot includes a research component to evaluate and enhance the effectiveness of the project and determine its potential for national implementation. Initial results show greater improvement in teaching skills among participants than among those who did not participate in the project.

Source: MoECS (2015[63]), "Kamerbrief over de voortgang verbeterpunten voor het leraarschap" [Parliamentary letter about the improvement points for the teaching profession], www.rijksoverheid.nl/binaries/rijksoverheid/documenten/kamerstukken/2015/11/04/kamerbrief-over-de-voortgang-verbeterpuntenvoor-het-leraarschap/kamerbrief-over-de-voortgang-verbeterpunten-voorhet-leraarschap.pdf; Helms-Lorenz, van de Grift and Maulana (2016[64]), "Longitudinal effects of induction on teaching skills and attrition rates of beginning teachers", http://dx.doi.org/10.1080/09243453.2015.1035731.

Promoting mentoring and coaching, observations and peer review

In an SLO, colleagues learn about their learning together. They take time to consider what each person understands about the learning and knowledge they have created collectively, the conditions that support this learning and knowledge, and what all of this means for the way they collaborate (Giles and Hargreaves, 2006[65]; Stoll et al., 2006[66]). Wales finds itself in the middle of a curriculum reform that will likely require teachers and learning support workers to engage in trial and error learning and tackle problems together. They can benefit from close relationships with colleagues who have had prior training and experience in the new curriculum (Thompson et al., 2004[67]).

The evidence suggests that on average collaborative working and learning are well embedded in schools throughout Wales. However, several areas of improvement remain. The evidence shows that schools could do more to ensure that staff learn to work together as a team, observe each other more regularly and tackle problems together. The SLO survey data for example showed that some 13% of respondents indicated that mentoring and coaching support was not available for all staff in their school, with a further 22% responding neutrally which may suggest they did not know.

Furthermore, a general conclusion from the assessment is that collaborative working and learning is less well established in secondary schools than in primary schools. This clearly is an issue deserving further attention from secondary school leaders, but also from local authorities, regional consortia and the Welsh Government, to ensure secondary schools have the capacity and create the conditions for staff to engage in collaborative learning and working.

Strong school leadership obviously is a condition for making this happen – for both school types. The new leadership standards call for "leadership to actively promote and facilitate collaborative opportunities for all staff, both in routine aspects of learning organisation and through innovative approaches, including embracing new technologies" (Welsh Government, 2017[54]). School leaders are to be held to account by local authorities for their efforts in establishing such a collaborative learning culture in schools – something that the OECD team learned has been lacking in some local authorities, partially as a result of the assessment, evaluation and accountability arrangements which do not do enough to promote such collaborative practice.

School leaders will also need the necessary support and capacity development to take on this role. In addition to the ongoing investments in leadership development programmes (see below), regional consortia have an important role in promoting collaborative learning and working in and across schools in Wales, and supporting school leaders in putting this into practice. The evidence points to the conclusion they need to more strongly focus their efforts on secondary schools; a finding that was well recognised by the representatives of the regional consortia the OECD team interviewed.

Furthermore, although systems for collecting and analysing data on average seem well established in schools, there is too much emphasis on looking at quantitative data with far less attention being paid to qualitative sources, like classroom observations or peer review. This can partially be explained by the fact that assessment, evaluation and accountability arrangements have devoted relatively little attention to promoting coaching, mentoring, lesson observations and other forms of collaborative practice. The self-evaluation stage ("Step 2") of the national categorisation system (see below) for example devotes little attention to such collaborative practice that is at the heart of a learning organisation (Welsh Government, 2016[68]). Arguably the same can be said about Estyn's self-evaluation guidance document (Estyn, 2017[69]).

The review of assessment, evaluation and accountability arrangements and school evaluation processes in particular should take these findings into consideration. The integration of Wales' SLO model into the national school self-evaluation and development planning toolkit currently under development will be an important means to promote mentoring and coaching, observations and peer review and other forms of collaborative practice (see below).

Developing the skills and mindset for enquiry, exploration and innovation to thrive

The analysis in Chapters 2 and 3 found that developing the skills and mindset for engaging in enquiry, exploration and innovation is an area for improvement for many schools in Wales and the staff working in them. Less than six out of ten schools from the sample (59%) would seem to have established a culture of enquiry, exploration and innovation – just 26% of secondary schools and 63% of primary schools.

The assessment, evaluation and accountability arrangements are perceived by many to be high stakes (Donaldson, 2015[2]; OECD, 2014[7]). The OECD team's interviews with various stakeholders suggested that these arrangements have tempered people's willingness and confidence to do things differently, innovate and engage in enquiry-based practices. The implications of this for the ongoing review of assessment, evaluation and accountability arrangements are discussed below, but when discussing these findings with various stakeholders in Wales, there was a widely shared recognition that this is also an area for further skills development for school staff, the challenge advisors in the regional consortia who are responsible for building capacity in schools and ensuring schools are equipped to drive and sustain improvements, and higher education institutions in Wales. The latter two can play a key role in supporting schools to work and learn together in applying enquiry-based approaches to bring the new curriculum to life.

Enquiry-based approaches are believed to be of great importance for putting in practice the new curriculum that is being shaped around "big ideas" (Sinnema, 2017[70]) or, as it is often referred to in Wales, "what matters". Enquiry-based approaches to learning are challenging to implement, however. They are highly dependent on the knowledge and skills of teachers and other school staff trying to implement them. Teachers and learning support workers will need time and a community to support their capacity to organise sustained project work. It takes significant pedagogical sophistication to manage extended enquiry-based projects in classrooms so as to maintain a focus on "doing with understanding" rather than "doing for the sake of doing" (Barron and Darling-Hammond, 2010[71]).

The OECD team learned about some small-scale projects that aim to enhance schools' capacity to use enquiry-based approaches, which are positive developments that should be further promoted. However, recognising that these approaches are challenging to implement and that there are concerns about teachers' skills for doing quality assessments, it would seem that Wales needs to make a concerted effort to develop teachers' skills in enquiry-based teaching if all schools in Wales are to be able to develop as learning organisations and put the curriculum into practice. The national approach to professional learning that is under development to support the curriculum reform should therefore also focus on developing teachers' and learning support workers' skills in enquiry-based approaches. Higher education institutions are well placed to contribute to this effort. Wales could look to the example of British Columbia in Canada, which established three school-to-school networks – the Network of Performance Based Schools (NPBS), the Aboriginal Enhancement Schools Network (AESN), and the Healthy Schools Network (HSN) (see Box 4.4). These networks operate in tandem with a graduate programme to promote learning leadership and innovation (Certificate in Innovative Educational Leadership), are deeply rooted in enquiry-based teaching and learning, and prominently use the OECD's Innovative Learning Environments Learning Principles (OECD, 2010[72]).

Box 4.4. An example of innovating teaching and learning through collaborative engagement in the "spirals of enquiry" – British Columbia, Canada

A synthesis of extensive research reviews on different aspects of learning by prominent experts led to seven transversal "principles" to guide the development of learning environments, or learning organisations in a school context, for the 21st century (OECD, 2010[72]). These state that to be effective schools should:

- recognise the learners as its core participants, encourage their active engagement, and develop in them an understanding of their own activity as learners (self-regulation)

- be founded on the social nature of learning and actively encourage group work and well-organised co-operative learning

- have learning professionals who are highly attuned to the learners' motivations and the key role of emotions in achievement

- be acutely sensitive to the individual differences among the learners in it, including their prior knowledge

- devise programmes that demand hard work and challenge from all without excessive overload

- operate with clarity of expectations and deploy assessment strategies consistent with these expectations; there should be strong emphasis on formative feedback to support learning

- strongly promote "horizontal connectedness" across areas of knowledge and subjects as well as to the community and the wider world.

Using these principles of learning – which are well aligned with Wales' ambition for the new curriculum – British Columbia's "meso-level" strategies combine:

1) **Spirals of Enquiry:** The disciplined approach to enquiry is informing and shaping the transformative work in schools and districts across the province. Participating schools engage in a year-long period to focus on enquiry learning using the Spiral of Enquiry as a framework with six key stages: scanning, focusing, developing a hunch, new professional learning, taking action and checking that a big enough difference has been made. At each stage, three key questions are asked: What is going on with our learners? How do we know this? How does this matter? Thirty-six school districts (60% of the total) are involved directly in specific leadership development based on the Spiral of Enquiry.

2) **Certificate in Innovative Educational Leadership** (CIEL): This one year leadership programme at Vancouver Island University brings together educational leaders in formal and non-formal positions. The programme has an emphasis on: 1) understanding and applying the Spiral of Enquiry; 2) exploring, analysing and applying ideas from innovative cases gathered by the OECD/Innovative Learning Environments (ILE) project; and 3) becoming knowledgeable about the seven transversal learning principles mentioned above. To date, 3 cohorts totalling over 100 people have graduated, with 30 more enrolled in 2014-15. CIEL graduates are working as formal or informal leaders in 26 school districts.

3) **Networks of Enquiry and Innovation** (NOII) and the **Aboriginal Enhancement Schools Network** (AESN): These networks connect professional learning through principals, teachers and support staff, and accelerate the transformative work across the province. To date, 156 individual schools in 44 districts in British Columbia are active members of NOII and AESN. A grant from the Federal Government funded a research study on the impact of teacher involvement in AESN and examined more than 50 enquiry projects around the province. The focus on enquiry learning has proved to be beneficial to Aboriginal and non-Aboriginal students and teachers. The AESN is considered to be an effective mechanism for sustainable teaching and learning change.

British Columbia is in the midst of redesigning the curriculum and assessment framework, in which several graduates from the CIEL leadership programme are involved. These three strategies create a "third space" that is not dominated by provincial or local politics, even if financial support from the government is involved. It is a grass-roots professional initiative, regulated by meso-level leadership and looking to bring sustainable change to the entire province.

Source: OECD (2015[73]), *Schooling Redesigned: Towards Innovative Learning Systems*, http://dx.doi.org/10.1787/9789264245914-en.

School-to-school collaboration and networking

The potential of school-to-school collaboration and networking lies in two areas. The first comes from tapping the large reservoir of resources, expertise and knowledge that remain dormant or underused in classrooms, schools, educational systems and society at large (Ainscow, 2014[74]). The second lies in testing and further developing the good ideas that do exist are but which remain in isolated pockets, while ground-breaking inventions and innovations come from people who work together to solve complex problems. School-to-school collaboration provides the means of circulating knowledge and strategies around the system, offers an alternative to top-down intervention as a way of supporting struggling schools, and develops collective responsibility among all schools for all students' success (OECD, 2014[7]).

A clearly positive development in recent years in Wales is the progress made in advancing school-to-school collaboration and networking, as was also highlighted in Estyn's annual report for 2016/17 (Estyn, 2018[75]). The regional consortia have played a key role in this, but the government has also continued to promote school-to-school collaboration. One such example is the establishment of the Pioneer Schools Network in 2015. There are several sub-networks of Pioneer Schools, but these schools also meet regularly through national conferences, within schools and on line (for example using the Hwb platform) to challenge and learn from one another in developing the new curriculum and supporting professional learning offers (OECD, 2017[19]).

The findings from this assessment suggest that staff in secondary schools benefit slightly less from engaging in collaborative learning and working with their peers in other schools. While some 80% of primary school staff indicated on the SLO survey that they engaged in such practice, only 73% of their peers in secondary schools responded in a similar vein. Although primary responsibility for changing this situation lies with school leaders, regional consortia have proved themselves able to fulfil an important facilitating role in establishing effective school-to-school collaboration.

The regional consortia should continue these efforts. According to Estyn, in particular they should help schools to improve collaboration between primary and secondary schools, for example in terms of student referral, enhancing collaboration between different language-medium schools and with joint planning of the curriculum (Estyn, 2018[75]) which is of particular relevance due to the ongoing curriculum reform. Both Estyn and an earlier OECD assessment (2017[19]) have highlighted the limited evidence available to date on whether school-to-school collaborations have been effective. We will elaborate more on this below.

Several interviewees noted that it is important for the Welsh Government and the regional consortia to pay particular attention to bringing on board and supporting the schools that, for various reasons, are less likely to participate in networks and other forms of collaborative learning and working, yet which need it most. Chapter 3 noted some regional differences in how far staff and schools engaged in school-to-school collaboration, suggesting this issue requires a strategic response. The OECD team's view is that the development of such a strategic response should include consideration of how the new assessment and evaluation arrangements can further encourage and recognise such collaborations between schools, for example through school self-evaluations and Estyn inspections. This view was almost unanimously supported by the various stakeholders that were interviewed. This issue will be discussed further below.

Promoting partnerships with external partners

Schools as learning organisations function as part of a larger social system, including, in many jurisdictions, their own local community and, frequently, their school district (Rumberger, 2004[76]; OECD, 2015[73]). Schools that engage in organisational learning enable staff at all levels to learn collaboratively and continuously and put what they have learned to use in response to social needs and the demands of their environment (Silins, Zarins and Mulford, 2002[62]; Ho Park, 2008[77]). This means engaging with parents, communities, business partners, social agencies, higher education institutions and other potential partners. National, provincial and local governments each play important roles in promoting this interface between schools and the larger system in which they operate. The evidence from our the assessment suggests that some of these partnerships are not well established in Wales and as such require further action from schools, but also from the policy level.

The first area for further improvement is to promote partnerships with higher education institutions, for the reasons discussed above. These strengthened collaborations may also help increase the use of research evidence and enquiry-based approaches by school staff, which is particularly an issue for secondary schools. In addition to encouraging such collaborations through the higher education programmes accreditation process, the likely integration of Wales' SLO model in the new school self-evaluation and development planning process under development could encourage such collaborations, as should Wales' continued investment in the sort of projects described in Box 3.17 (Chapter 3).

Second, parents or guardians are key partners for schools in strengthening the educational process (Silins, Zarins and Mulford, 2002[62]; Bowen, Rose and Ware, 2006[78]). Students are unlikely to meet the high expectations set by a demanding society without co-operation between families and schools. The evidence from our assessment suggests that secondary schools in Wales find it more challenging to engage parents in the school organisation and educational process – a finding that is common to other OECD countries (Borgonovi and Montt, 2012[79]; Byrne and Smyth, 2010[80]; Desforges and Abouchaar,

2003[81]; Williams, Williams and Ullman, 2002[82]). However, the evidence shows that it is entirely possible to increase parents' engagement in their school organisation and educational process, but it needs to be further promoted (see Chapter 3, Box 3.5 for an example). Such examples could be systematically collected and shared throughout the system. Also on this issue, the ongoing review of the school self-evaluation and development process provides another opportunity to further promote and recognise collaboration between schools and parents (see below).

Learning leadership for developing schools and other parts of the system into learning organisations

Developing school leaders' capacity to establish a thriving learning culture

There is increasing empirical and international evidence that the role of school leadership is second only to that of teachers in establishing the conditions for creating a learning culture in and across schools and enhancing teaching and learning (Leithwood and Seashore Louis, 2012[83]; Robinson, Hohepa and Lloyd, 2009[84]; Silins, Zarins and Mulford, 2002[62]). While committed school leaders are key to the success of SLOs, the support of policy makers, administrators and other system leaders such as superintendents, inspectors and other local leaders is crucial. They can encourage professional learning and development, promote innovations and school-to-school collaboration, and help disseminate good practice (European Commission, 2017[61]; Schleicher, 2018[85]).

However, leadership capacity doesn't just emerge: it needs to be developed and requires modelling by leaders at all levels of the system (OECD, 2014[7]; Schleicher, 2018[85]). The OECD assessment (2017[19]) concluded that, although leadership capacity has been a prominent feature of the Welsh Government's strategic education plans since 2012, in practice many national-level efforts to foster leadership had stalled or were still in the planning and design phase despite several reports pointing to challenges, including:

- a lack of succession planning

- limited number of well-tailored professional development opportunities for senior and middle-level leaders, and teachers

- school leadership is not considered an attractive profession due to the heavy administrative burden

- Estyn inspections identified only a limited number of schools as having excellent practice in leadership and planning for improvement (Estyn, 2018[75]; OECD, 2017[19]; OECD, 2014[7]).

These are worrying findings, especially considering the pivotal role school leaders will play in leading and shaping the realisation of the new curriculum. As discussed in Chapter 2, the new curriculum is bound to stretch people's skills and take them out of their comfort zones – including leaders themselves. These changes may bring with it resistance to change if this process is not carefully managed and facilitated (Hargreaves and Fink, 2006[86]; James et al., 2006[87]).

Many OECD countries have faced similar challenges and investment in the school leadership profession appears to have moved slowly (Pont, Nusche and Moorman, 2008[88]; Pont and Gouedard, forthcoming[89]). Policy reforms targeting this situation have not appeared to be a priority until recently. Several countries have recognised the importance of school leaders – and leaders working at other levels of the system – as a key driver of their change strategies and have established dedicated leadership centres to steer this work, such as such the National College for School Leadership in England, the Australian Institute for Teaching and School Leadership and the National Institute of Education in Singapore.

Wales has recently established a similar agency, the National Academy for Educational Leadership, which aims to oversee the roll-out of support and development for a wider group of education leaders (Welsh Government, 2017[90]). The academy focuses on leadership across education, including senior and middle-level leaders of schools, local authority education staff, and Welsh Government education officials. It will initially focus on the needs of the next generation of head teachers, including:

- ensuring head teachers are well prepared for their role

- considering the structure of qualifications of head teachers, including the National Professional Qualification for Headship

- developing career routes for those who want to be head teachers and supporting new heads in their early years in that role

- working with well-established and successful head teachers to help create a group of leaders who can help promote best practice across schools.

The academy is a welcome development; the success of the ambitious curriculum reform and other reforms that Wales has embarked on depend on having sufficient numbers of capable leaders in schools and other levels of the system.

As discussed above, several other policy measures have been taken recently in response to these challenges. These include the release of the new teaching and leadership standards, setting the expectations for teachers and those in formal leadership positions. As these are aligned with the SLO model, they should support schools putting the dimensions of a learning organisation into practice.

In response to the reported challenges of school leaders' workloads, 11 local authorities are piloting the use of skilled business managers for schools or groups of schools (Welsh Government, 2017[91]). These business managers are likely to help reduce the administrative burden on school leaders so they can focus on educational leadership and developing their schools into learning organisations, and thus help ensure the readiness of staff to take on the new curriculum (OECD, 2017[19]).

Recently, the Welsh Government also decided to integrate Wales' SLO model into all leadership development programmes (e.g. through the Academy for Educational Leadership endorsement process). The OECD team agree this is an essential way to introduce the model to all present and future school leaders in Wales, embedding a mindset geared towards continuous professional learning. It will also develop their capacity to serve as "change agents" in their schools and contribute to the change and innovation efforts of other schools and other parts of the system. The action-oriented dimensions and underlying elements of the SLO model for Wales will provide practical guidance for doing so (Welsh Government, 2017[1]). Other examples are the commitments made by the Welsh Government's Education Directorate (and possibly other directorates) and several middle-tier organisations to develop themselves into learning organisations.

One finding of this assessment that deserves immediate policy attention is that many secondary schools are finding it more challenging to develop into learning organisations than primary schools. The factors behind this are believed to include the more compartmentalised structure of secondary schools, which makes it harder to collaborate across departments and the organisation as a whole. Several interviewees also noted the attitudes of secondary teachers, who tend to be less open to collaboration beyond their subject areas or departments.

Furthermore, as Estyn (2018[75]) also noted, leaders in less successful schools often provide insufficient strategic direction and do not conduct effective self-evaluations. This assessment suggests they are also not doing enough to promote collaborative working and learning and the exchange of information and knowledge across the whole organisation. This would seem to justify prioritising capacity building among secondary school leaders, and providing them with other support. As such, the recently established National Academy for Educational Leadership should pay particular attention to secondary school leaders. Regional consortia also need to focus their efforts more strongly on the secondary sector and review their support services accordingly, and promote school-to-school collaboration not only across secondary schools but also with primary schools. The latter would seem relevant as significantly more primary schools appear to have developed as learning organisations, and it may also facilitate the transitions of students between one level of education to the next.

Leadership capacity of the middle tier for promoting organisational learning within schools and across the school system

As noted, while committed school leaders are key to the success of SLOs, the support of local policy makers, administrators and other system leaders such as superintendents, inspectors and other local leaders is crucial (European Commission, 2017[61]; Kools and Stoll, 2016[3]; Schleicher, 2018[85]). They encourage professional learning and development, promote innovations and school-to-school collaboration, and help disseminate good practice. Without their support for collaboration and collective learning, SLOs will continue to operate in isolation (if at all). The 22 local authorities, the governing boards of education institutions and the 4 regional consortia form the "Tier 2" of the education system of Wales, also referred to as the middle tier. These middle-tier agencies play a pivotal role in enabling schools to develop into learning organisations and promoting collaborative working and learning across the system ("middle-out change"). It is therefore essential to consider their strengths and areas for further improvement. This section focuses on school governing boards and local authorities, while Chapter 5 will elaborate on the regional consortia as part of a discussion about Wales' system infrastructure for school improvement.

Governing boards

Research evidence shows us that effective school boards can contribute greatly to the success of their schools (Land, 2002[92]; OECD, 2016[13]; Pont, Nusche and Moorman, 2008[88]). By contributing to a well-run school, boards can improve the environment of learning and teaching and lead to better student outcomes. Decentralisation and school autonomy have devolved important powers to school boards, including in Wales. In some OECD countries, however, boards – which are often voluntary bodies – have not received the support they need to do the work. Some countries have made a deliberate effort to invest in the capacity of school governing boards, however, and this includes Wales.

According to Estyn, school governance has improved over the course of the 2010-17 inspection cycle (Estyn, 2018[75]), including the work of school governors. School governors as mentioned (in Chapter 2) are elected members of a school governing board consisting of teaching staff, parents, councillors and community representatives. They have a central role in decisions about budgets, development planning and recruitment of a school. At the start of the cycle, governors knew about the relative performance of their school in some three-quarters of schools. By the end of the cycle, this had increased to four-fifths of schools. Estyn found that nearly all primary school governors have now had at least a basic level of training that helps them to undertake their duties with growing confidence. Most have a suitable understanding of their school's strengths and priorities for improvement which – as reflected in Wales' SLO model – should start with their involvement in the shaping of the school's vision. The analysis of the SLO survey showed that in the vast majority of schools this is indeed the case. Only 4% of school staff reported that governors were not involved in shaping their school's vision – 7% in secondary schools and 1% in primary schools.

However, Estyn also found that few schools have governors who fulfil their role as a critical friend well enough, and that they often do not exert enough influence on self-evaluation or improvement planning (Estyn, 2018[75]). The OECD team's interviews with various stakeholders corroborate this finding. The ongoing review of the school self-evaluation and development planning process (see below) should therefore be used to revisit their roles and responsibility in this process. The scheduled pilot of the national school self-evaluation and development planning toolkit, which is likely to integrate the SLO model, provides an opportunity to assess the training needs of all parties involved, including governors.

Local authorities

The research evidence is clear that without the proactive involvement of the local education authority, school capacity will unlikely develop and last (Fullan, 2004[93]; Dimmock, 2012[94]; Leithwood, 2013[95]). Although the regional consortia have been responsible for school improvement services since 2012, local authorities in Wales still are responsible for public schools. It is therefore worrying that Estyn (2018[75]) found that many local authorities in Wales have new education directors, nearly all appointed in the last three or four years. The limited opportunities for professional learning for middle-level and senior leaders in local government education services have limited the development of leaders across the education system in Wales and affected the capacity of the system to support national priorities (Estyn, 2018[75]). The interviews with various stakeholders pointed to the same conclusion.

As will be elaborated in the following chapter, there is a need for further investment in the capacity of middle-level leaders within regional consortia which can be expanded to include the challenge advisors who serve as "change agents" and provide practical guidance and support to schools. This suggests that further action is needed to develop leadership capacity across all levels of the system – not just school leaders, who are currently being prioritised by the Welsh Government and the National Academy for Educational Leadership.

An earlier OECD assessment (2017[19]) called for Wales to make leadership a driver of the reform effort. The Welsh Government responded by making the development of inspiring leadership an enabling objective of its strategic action plan (Welsh Government, 2017[12]). Though recognising that some progress has been made recently, leadership development does not yet seem to be a driving force for the reform. The Welsh Government, the National Academy for Educational Leadership and other stakeholders could look to education systems like Ontario and British Columbia in Canada and Scotland that have developed the capacity of school and system-level leaders, including those of middle-tier agencies. Box 4.5 provides an insight in Ontario's Leadership Strategy, one of the best-known schemes and regarded by many as a successful case in point.

Box 4.5. An example of strategic investment in school and system-level leaders – The Ontario Leadership Strategy

In 2008, the Canadian province launched the Ontario Leadership Strategy. The strategy is a comprehensive plan of action designed to support student achievement and well-being by attracting and developing skilled and passionate school and system leaders.

- Within the strategy, a leadership framework has been defined to provide five key domains that can be adapted to the context: 1) setting direction; 2) building relationships and developing people; 3) developing the organisation; 4) leading the instructional programme; and 5) securing accountability. These are well understood by all actors, adapted to local contexts as needed, used in a new principal appraisal system, and used for training and development. There are many examples of school boards and schools that have adapted the framework to their needs.

- The requirements to become a principal are high, demonstrating the high calibre they are looking for. Potential candidates need to have an undergraduate degree, five years of teaching experience, certification by school level (primary, junior, intermediate, senior), two additional specialist or honour specialist qualifications (areas of teaching expertise) or a master's degree, and have completed of the Principal's Qualification Programme. This is offered by Ontario universities, teachers' federations (unions) and principals' associations, and consists of a 125-hour programme with a practicum.

- There is an overt effort towards leadership succession planning in school boards, in order to get the right people prepared and into the system. Therefore, the process starts before there is a vacancy to be filled.

- Mentoring is available during the first two years of practice for principals, vice-principals, supervisory officers and directors.

- A new results-focused performance appraisal model has been introduced. In the Principal/Vice-Principal Performance Appraisal model, principals set goals focused on student achievement and well-being in a five-year cycle. They are also required to maintain an annual growth plan which is reviewed in collaboration with the supervisor annually.

Source: OECD (2010[96]), "OECD-Harvard Seminar for Leaders in Education Reform in Mexico: School Management and Education Reform in Ontario" (Seminario OCDE-Harvard para líderes en reformas educativas en México: gestión escolar y reforma escolar en Ontario), www.oecd.org/fr/education/scolaire/calidadeducativaqualityeducation-eventsandmeetings.htm.

Learning leadership capacity and the role of central government

Many effective strategies depend on government leadership. Ministries and education agencies provide the legitimacy and the system-wide perspective to push for and facilitate educational change and innovation (OECD, 2015[73]; OECD, 2016[97]). In the case of Wales, this means schools developing into learning organisations and ultimately putting the new school curriculum into practice. For this to happen, leadership at the local level, from networks and partnerships, and from education authorities at central, regional and local levels all need to work together to create responsive 21st century school systems (OECD, 2015[73]; European Commission, 2017[61]; Schleicher, 2018[85]).

The Welsh Government's approach to policy design and implementation responds to this need. It centres around a process of co-construction of policies and puts a great deal of emphasis on realising change from the "meso" level (OECD, 2016[13]) or "middle-out change" (Fullan and Quinn, 2015[14]; Hargreaves and Ainscow, 2015[15]; Greany,(n.d.)[4]), by promoting networking, school-to-school collaborations and partnerships. This network governance leadership role (Tummers and Knies, 2016[98]), in which the senior leadership of the Education Directorate of the Welsh Government encourages its employees to actively connect with relevant stakeholders, represents a significant change compared to several years ago. Then, senior Education Directorate officials mostly led the design of reforms and policies with limited consultation. Not surprisingly these were perceived by many as "top-down" (OECD, 2014[7]). The OECD team's interviews found that this change in approach by the Education Directorate has been welcomed by school staff and middle-tier agencies.

However, it has also been a learning journey for officials in the Education Directorate, as several admitted in interviews with the OECD team. The team also witnessed a number of staff changes within the directorate while this report was being prepared. Senior officials noted these internal transfers were essential for ensuring the best job fit for these people and the organisation, and maintaining the momentum of ongoing reform initiatives.

In all, the OECD team have witnessed a clear change in how the Education Directorate sees and gives shape to its leadership role. The directorate has, as a result of this change, been investing in its capacity to facilitate these changes, which it considers an ongoing effort. While recognising the progress made, several senior officials also noted that the directorate has yet to establish a sustainable learning culture across the whole organisation. The OECD team also found some examples where there seems to be scope for further collaboration and collaboration among officials to ensure greater policy coherence. One such example is the ongoing work on the curriculum and assessment, evaluation and accountability arrangements as will be discussed in Chapter 5. It is therefore a positive development that the Education Directorate has itself committed to developing into a learning organisation.

While the Education Directorate increasingly depends on local and meso-level action – exemplified by its commitment to promoting the development of SLOs as part of the larger learning, or self-improving school, system – this also has implications for other areas of policy including the assessment, evaluation and accountability arrangements in education. These are discussed in the next section.

Assessment, evaluation and accountability should promote schools developing as learning organisations

Although these policies affect the realisation of all dimensions of the learning organisation, this section relates to two dimensions in particular:

- establishing a culture of enquiry, innovation and exploration

- embedding systems for collecting and exchanging knowledge and learning.

SLOs develop processes, strategies and structures that allow them to learn and react effectively in uncertain and dynamic environments. They institutionalise learning mechanisms in order to revise existing knowledge (Watkins and Marsick, 1996[99]; Silins, Zarins and Mulford, 2002[62]; Schechter and Qadach, 2013[100]). Major improvements can be achieved when schools and school systems increase their collective capacity to engage in ongoing "assessment for learning", and regularly evaluate how their interventions are intended to work, and whether they actually do (OECD, 2013[50]).

For a school to become a learning organisation, it is essential that people dare to engage in enquiry, experiment and innovate in their daily practice. Therefore, a system that strives to develop its schools into learning organisations should encourage, support and protect those who initiate and take risks, and reward them for it. If accountability demands dominate over people's ability to use data and information for the purpose of learning, sharing knowledge to inspire and support change and innovation, and take collective responsibility for enhancing students' learning and well-being, then schools are unlikely to blossom into learning organisations. Assessment, evaluation and accountability arrangements therefore play a pivotal role in empowering people to do things differently and innovate their practice (Greany,(n.d.)[4]; OECD, 2013[50]).

This section takes an in-depth look at Wales' assessment, evaluation and accountability arrangements, which are currently undergoing review. This review is essential, as the analysis has found that the current arrangements lack clarity, lead to duplication of effort and are driven by accountability demands, rather than serving the purpose of learning and improvement. As such, they do not do enough to encourage schools to engage in enquiry, innovation and exploration and promote them in developing in learning organisations more generally – a particular area for improvement for many schools in Wales (see Chapters 2 and 3).

A new, coherent assessment, evaluation and accountability framework geared towards learning

Governments and education policy makers in OECD countries are increasingly focused on the assessment and evaluation of students, teachers, school leaders, schools and education systems (OECD, 2013[50]). Wales is no exception. In the last decade its assessment, evaluation and accountability arrangements have undergone considerable change. These have become heavily influenced by accountability demands, rather than serving the purpose of learning and improvement (Donaldson, 2015[2]). Furthermore, assessment, evaluation and accountability arrangements lack in synergy and coherence, with duplications and inconsistencies, for example in school evaluations, as discussed below (OECD, 2014[7]; OECD, 2017[19]).

Accountability plays an important role in safeguarding the quality of schools and the system at large, so the new assessment, evaluation and accountabilities should be implemented in a careful way to prevent unintended effects and encourage schools to engage in enquiry, innovation and exploration – a particular area for improvement for many schools in Wales.

In response to these and other challenges – and above all to support the realisation of the new curriculum – the Welsh Government has embarked on a reform of its assessment, evaluation and accountability arrangements. This is one of the "enabling objectives" of its strategic education action plan, *Education in Wales: Our National Mission* (Welsh Government, 2017[12]). At the time of drafting this report, the early parameters of this new assessment, evaluation and accountability framework were being clarified. Importantly, the Welsh Government is doing this with the education profession and other key stakeholders in a process of co-construction to ensure the new arrangements will indeed be fit for purpose i.e. they place learning at the centre – not just of students, but also that of staff, the school and the wider system.

An OECD review (2013[50]) of assessment and evaluation in education in 28 countries provides Wales (and other countries) with some policy pointers to consider in the further development and finalisation of its new assessment, evaluation and assessment framework (see Box 4.6). Building on these policy pointers, this section aims to provide further guidance and advice on the most important aspects of assessment, evaluation and accountability that can enable schools in Wales develop into learning organisations – and ultimately realise the new school curriculum.

In parallel to the development of these new arrangements, Graham Donaldson conducted an independent review into the role of Estyn in supporting education reform in Wales (Donaldson, 2018[101]). That review report was released in June 2018, i.e. at the time this report was being finalised. Welsh Government and Her Majesty's Chief Inspector of Education and Training had not responded to the report's recommendations at the time of finalising this report. Members of the OECD team were able to discuss and explore some of the early ideas of how Estyn envisaged external school evaluations and its role in the larger assessment, evaluation and accountability framework in light of this report. The analysis presented below draws on discussions with various representatives from Estyn.

Box 4.6. Policy pointers for developing assessment and evaluation arrangements in education

Synergies for Better Learning reviewed the evaluation and assessment of education in 28 OECD countries, analysed the strengths and weaknesses of different approaches, and offered policy advice on using evaluation and assessment to improve the quality, equity and efficiency of education. It found that countries have different traditions in evaluation and assessment and take different approaches. Nevertheless, there are some clear policy priorities:

Take a holistic approach. To achieve its full potential, the various components of assessment and evaluation should form a coherent whole. This can generate synergies between components, avoid duplication and prevent inconsistent objectives.

Align evaluation and assessment with educational goals. Evaluation and assessment should serve and advance educational goals and student learning objectives. This involves aspects such as alignment with the principles embedded in educational goals, designing fit-for-purpose evaluations and assessments, and ensuring school agents have a clear understanding of educational goals.

Focus on improving classroom practices. The point of evaluation and assessment is to improve classroom practice and student learning. With this in mind, all types of evaluation and assessment should have educational value and should have practical benefits for those who participate in them, especially students and teachers.

Avoid distortions. Because of their role in providing accountability, evaluation and assessment systems can distort how and what students are taught. For example, if teachers are judged largely on results from standardised student tests, they may "teach to the test", focusing solely on the skills that are tested. It is important to minimise these unwanted side effects.

Put students at the centre. Students should be fully engaged with their learning and empowered to assess their own progress. It is important, too, to monitor broader learning outcomes, including the development of critical thinking, social competencies, engagement with learning and overall well-being. Thus, performance measures should be broad, drawing on both quantitative and qualitative data as well as high-quality analysis.

Build capacity at all levels. Creating an effective evaluation and assessment framework requires capacity development at all levels of the education system. In addition, a centralised effort may be needed to develop a knowledge base, tools and guidelines to assist evaluation and assessment activities.

Manage local needs. Evaluation and assessment frameworks need to find the right balance between consistently implementing central education goals and adapting to the particular needs of regions, districts and schools.

Design successfully, build consensus. To be designed successfully, evaluation and assessment frameworks should draw on informed policy diagnosis and best practice, which may require the use of pilots and experimentation. A substantial effort should also be made to build consensus among all stakeholders, who are more likely to accept change if they understand its rationale and potential usefulness.

Source: OECD (2013[50]), *Synergies for Better Learning: An International Perspective on Evaluation and Assessment*, http://dx.doi.org/10.1787/9789264190658-en.

As with the previous sections, this section is informed by the analysis of previous chapters, a desk study of policy documents, and studies and interviews with a wide range of stakeholders. In addition, members of the OECD team participated in several policy meetings on the emerging assessment, evaluation and accountability framework during the course of this review, with particular reference to the Secondary Head Teachers' Conference on 7-8 March 2018. During this conference, entitled "Developing a robust evaluation system and accountability arrangements to support a self-improving school system", the participants – over 300 school leaders, teachers, representatives of the Welsh Government's Education Directorate, Estyn, regional consortia, local authorities and many others – were asked to share their views on what was working well, what wasn't and what needed to be included in the new assessment, evaluation and accountability framework in order to deliver the new curriculum. Furthermore, the OECD's contributions to the development of the school self-evaluation and development toolkit, which was just started as this report was being finalised, have enriched the analysis presented below.

Student assessments – putting student learning at the centre

In Wales' SLO model, teaching and learning is focused on a broad range of outcomes – both cognitive and social/emotional, including well-being – for today and the future. The ultimate aims are to ensure students are equipped to seize learning opportunities throughout life; to broaden their knowledge, skills and attitudes; and to adapt to a changing, complex and interdependent world (Kools and Stoll, 2016[3]; Welsh Government, 2017[1]). In the Welsh context, teaching and learning are directed towards the four purposes of the new school curriculum, operationalised in its six Areas of Learning and Experiences (see Chapter 1, Box 1.1).

The curriculum reform in Wales is part of a larger trend across OECD countries to place increasing emphasis within curricula on students acquiring key 21st century competencies (OECD, 2018[11]). Education systems need to adapt their assessment and evaluation approaches so that they promote and capture this broader type of learning. To this end, teachers need to be supported in translating competency goals into concrete lesson plans, teaching units and assessment approaches (OECD, 2013[50]).

The Welsh Government's education strategic plan, *Education in Wales: Our National Mission*, contains a number of actions up to 2021 that aim to do just this (Welsh Government, 2017[12]). The Curriculum and Assessment Pioneer Schools discussed in Chapter 1 (see Box 1.3) play a pivotal role in this through their work on the development of assessment methods and instruments, and professional learning opportunities that aim to support teachers in the assessment of students' learning against the new curriculum. The work of the Pioneer Schools and other measures proposed in the action plan are important considering long-standing concerns in Wales about the capacity of teachers to conduct quality assessments (Estyn, 2014[102]; OECD, 2014[7]). In particular, formative assessments – "assessments for learning" – are reported not to be well embedded in teaching practices. The new curriculum places great emphasis on formative assessments so the work of the Pioneer Schools and planned investments in professional learning in the coming years will be essential for putting the curriculum into practice.

Furthermore, the perceived high-stakes nature of the assessment, evaluation and accountability arrangements in Wales seems to have negatively affected the quality of student assessments (OECD, 2014[7]). This is due to their dual purpose: they are used for accountability as well as their intended primary purpose of informing student learning and staff learning and school improvement more generally.

In 2008, teacher assessments of students were introduced at the end of the Foundation Phase and Key Stages 2 and 3 (see Chapter 1). These assessments have since become part of the annual national data collection cycle that monitors the education system, and is used in school evaluations i.e. as part of the national categorisation system and Estyn inspections that are made public. The results of the teacher assessments are furthermore posted on the My Local School website[1]. There as mentioned for have been concerns about the capacity of teachers to conduct quality assessments (Estyn, 2014[102]; OECD, 2014[7]). Many people the OECD team met noted that the decision to use these data to publicly hold schools to account made them high stakes and it is widely believed to have (further) reduced their reliability.

In recognition of these challenges, annual Statutory National Reading and Numeracy Tests for students were introduced for Year 2 through to Year 9 students in 2013. While these tests were designed as diagnostic tools, they are not always perceived this way at the school level and some teachers still struggle to make adequate use of these formative assessments.

An important step forward in this regard is the ongoing development of a system of adaptive online personalised assessments to replace paper-based reading and numeracy tests (Welsh Government, 2017[12]). With these adaptive student assessments scheduled to be phased in from autumn 2018, Wales finds itself at the forefront of innovative practice in student assessment internationally. Only a few OECD countries, including Denmark and the Netherlands, are using such computer-based adaptive technology, which presents students with test items sequentially according to their performance on previous test items. This makes testing more efficient as more fine-grained information can be obtained in less time (OECD, 2013[50]; Scheerens, 2013[103]). The Welsh Government aims to extend these adaptive tests to other areas of the new curriculum in the coming years. This may prove to be an important means to support teachers in the assessment of student learning across the full width of the new curriculum. These efforts are part of the ongoing development of the new curriculum and associated assessments. The aim is to pay particular attention to developing teachers' capacity for formative assessments (Welsh Government, 2017[12]).

Another important planned step is the review of qualifications, which will be essential for aligning assessment and evaluation arrangements with the new curriculum. Without such alignment there is a real risk that teaching and learning in Key Stage 4 (students aged 14 to 16) will be skewed towards the content of qualifications rather than helping students realise the ambitions of the new curriculum i.e. the four purposes that are at the heart of Wales' SLO model. At the time of finalising this report initials steps were taking to start the review of qualifications – though few school staff and other stakeholders the OECD team spoke seemed to be aware of this positive development.

Monitoring students' socio-emotional skills and well-being

Alongside many other OECD countries, Wales recognises well-being as playing a critical role in the development of its children and young people, as also evidenced by the establishment of "Health and Well-being" as one of the six Areas of Learning and Experience in the curriculum (Welsh Government, 2017[12]). The Welsh Government has indicated its plans for measuring well-being which, as discussed above, should start with reaching a common understanding on the concept.

Many OECD countries and local jurisdictions have also produced guidelines and developed instruments for schools to use to assess students' social and emotional skills, including their well-being. Assessments tend to be administered in a formative manner to help teachers and students identify students' strengths and weaknesses in social and emotional skills and well-being (OECD, 2015[104]). The Welsh Government should consider developing similar guidelines and instruments, based on a national definition of the concept, to support schools in monitoring their students' well-being. It could look to the example of Flemish Community of Belgium, which made tools available to measure primary school students' involvement and well-being in the classroom. The most commonly known and used tool is the instrument developed by the Centre for Experience-based Education. Schools can use this scale to assess the behaviour of primary school students, such as acting spontaneously, having an open mind to whatever comes their way and feeling self-confident (OECD, 2015[104]).

Another example is provided by the US state of Illinois, which provides detailed benchmarks and performance descriptions for each of the predefined standards for its social and emotional learning goals. The performance descriptions help teachers design their curriculum and assess students' social and emotional skills. Since the standards are consistent with the Illinois Early Learning Standards from kindergarten to 12th grade, the system ensures continuity in social and emotional learning from early childhood to adolescence (OECD, 2015[104]).

School evaluations should serve the primary purpose of learning and improvement

During recent decades there has been a clear worldwide trend in education towards greater school autonomy, often due to decentralisation efforts and the adoption of new public management practices. The shift towards decentralisation and increasing school autonomy have often been accompanied by a strengthened role for central governments in setting broad national expectations through the curriculum and reinforcing performance monitoring through various forms of assessment and evaluation (OECD, 2014[105]).

The strong emphasis on performance measurement has resulted in an abundance of information about public service performance, often publicly available. Such publicly available information has several benefits. Apart from informing education planning and policy development – at various levels of the systems, it offers opportunities to engage stakeholders in supporting improvements across the school system (OECD, 2013[50]).

On the other hand there is a risk of unintended consequences. Some studies have found evidence that such performance information, instead of leading to actual organisational learning, has resulted in blame avoidance behaviour among politicians and managers and the naming and shaming of public organisations (George et al., 2017[106]; Hood, 2013[107]; Nielsen and Baekgaard, 2015[108]). Furthermore, it is well documented that in high-stakes systems where performance objectives lack credibility, leaders expend a lot of energy on gaming the system in order to produce the required results (Daly, 2009[109]). As earlier OECD reviews have found (OECD, 2014[105]; OECD, 2017[19]), this has also been the case for Wales, particularly in relation to school evaluations.

Recent paradigmatic shifts in public administration, often labelled the New Public Governance movement, have called for more attention to be paid to such things as learning, trust, and system thinking and networks (Osborne, 2006[110]; Osborne, 2013[111]). In the area of strategic monitoring and evaluation, New Public Governance emphasises a greater focus on processes, stressing service effectiveness and outcomes that rely upon the interaction of public service organisations with their environment. It argues that performance information can indeed be helpful, but not if it is used to stimulate blame games among actors or if it exerts excessive control that in turn may constrain creativity and innovation. Rather, strategic monitoring and evaluation and knowledge management should centre on learning within and beyond the organisation in order to ensure that performance information is purposefully used to adapt strategies and processes to a changing environment (Kroll, 2015[112]).

These general trends in public administration across OECD countries resonate strongly with recent developments Wales' school system. Wales finds itself in the middle of a curriculum reform and is redefining its assessment, evaluation and accountability framework to focus not just on outcomes, but also on the processes that are essential for their realisation. This is reflected in the Welsh Government's interest in "quality indicators" – rather than its previous primary focus on a large number of mostly quantitative indicators – and the prominent role school self-evaluation is expected to play in the new framework.

Trust in the profession and the wider system, collaboration and peer learning, consistency and the alignment of assessment and evaluation arrangements, and the need for "accountability to be about learning" were repeatedly mentioned during the secondary head teachers' conference. Attendees considered these to be key principles for the school evaluations currently being defined and the new assessment, evaluation and evaluation framework more generally. Furthermore, discussions during the conference showed the broad support among school leaders and other key stakeholders for school self-evaluation to play a pivotal role in the new assessment, evaluation and accountability framework.

Avoiding duplication and clarifying expectations

International research evidence shows that school evaluation in any system must be seen in the context of its particular cultural traditions as well as the wider policy arena if its precise nature and purpose is to be understood. Given that school systems are dynamic and that student learning objectives may evolve, as is the case in Wales, school evaluation frameworks need to adapt to meet the demand for meaningful feedback against these changing objectives (OECD, 2013[50]; European Commission, 2017[61]).

School evaluation in Wales has been subject to considerable changes in recent years. One of these has been the replacement of the school banding system that was introduced in 2011 and was intended to increase accountability and target resources onto low-performing schools. This system grouped – or banded – schools together according to a range of indicators such as attendance rates, GCSE results, relative improvement and the proportion of students on free school meals. However, it led to a number of unintended consequences, such as the perception of unfairness of the analysis process and the ranking of schools. This led to inter-school competition and tainting of public trust. Collaboration and learning among schools also suffered due to the high level of competition, which was at odds with Wales' ambition to develop a collaborative professional learning culture across a self-improving school system (Welsh Government, 2017[12]).

In 2014 the Welsh Government therefore decided to replace school banding with the national school categorisation system. Developed collectively by the regional consortia and the Welsh Government, the new system identifies schools most in need of support over a three-year period (compared to the one-year period under the school banding system), using a three-step colour coding strategy. Step 1 assesses publicly available school performance data and Step 2 the school's own self-evaluation in respect to leadership, learning and teaching. Challenge advisors from the regional consortia examine how the school's self-evaluation corresponds to the performance data under Step 1. This is intended to ensure the process is robust. Under Step 3, judgements reached in the first two steps lead to an overall judgement and a corresponding categorisation of each school into one of four colours: green, yellow, amber and red. Categorisation then triggers a tailored programme of support, challenge and intervention agreed by the local authority and the regional consortia (Welsh Government, 2016[68]).

Although national school categorisation in general is considered an improvement on school banding, many people the OECD team spoke to pointed to weaknesses in the system. It was obvious to the OECD team that the national categorisation system is still perceived by many as a high-stakes exercise because the colour coding of schools is made public, creating another type of league table. Several stakeholders interviewed by the OECD team criticised the calculation method based on the school performance data (Step 1), in particular the relative weight given to the number of students receiving free school meals in the final judgement. Referring to the lack of quality of teacher assessments of students' learning some of them admitted the colour coding allowed for "gaming" and as such was unfair.

Participants at the head teachers' conference corroborated these interview findings, with several head teachers adding that the public colour coding of schools stigmatised professionals and schools working in the most challenging communities. One head teacher noted that he was struggling to recruit teachers because his school was categorised as "an amber school".

Furthermore, several participants noted that the judgements of the national categorisation system all too often did not align with external evaluations by Estyn and vice versa. This is not surprising considering the different criteria and methods used to define a good school in Wales (OECD, 2017[29]).

The situation is further complicated by the various school self-evaluation and development instruments and tools that are available to schools in Wales, including the Welsh Government's guidance documents on school development plans, national school categorisation, and Schools in Wales as Learning Organisations (unreleased), Estyn's supplementary guidance document, and similar documents developed by the regional consortia. The challenge for schools is that these documents fail to give them a clear picture of what is expected from them in terms of self-evaluation and development planning. These documents also do not appear fully aligned with each other, while some are in need of updating, and may not do enough to encourage schools to establish a learning culture and change and innovate their practice which will be essential for putting the curriculum into practice.

Against this backdrop the Welsh Government asked Estyn and the OECD to facilitate the work of a stakeholders' group, tasked with formulating a common understanding of what good school self-evaluation and development planning entails in Wales. This is to result in the development of a "national school self-evaluation and development toolkit" (its working title) that is to guide all schools in Wales in their self-evaluation and development planning. This work is given shape through a series of workshops. This chapter could be used to inform the work of the working group, which started in May 2018 just as this report neared its finalisation.

Developing nationally agreed criteria for school quality to guide evaluations

Many OECD countries have aimed to answer the question "what is a good school?" for the development of their school evaluations (OECD, 2013[50]). The evidence suggests that the coherence of school evaluation is considerably enhanced when based on a nationally agreed model of school quality. On the other hand, a lack of clarity about what matters – as is currently the case in Wales – is likely to relegate self-evaluation to something which serves external school evaluation rather than creating a platform for an exchange based on reliable and comparable evidence (OECD, 2013[50]; SICI, 2003[113]). It was evident to the OECD team that this is happening in Wales. Many school leaders the OECD team spoke to admitted doing self-evaluations "for Estyn" – producing a specific report that, as the OECD team were surprised to learn, was not always linked to the school's development plan.

Common criteria for school self-evaluations and external evaluations

There are a growing number of international examples where the criteria used in self-evaluation and external evaluation are similar enough to create a common language about priorities and about the key factors which influence high-quality teaching and learning. The evidence shows that the combination of self-evaluation and external evaluation can play a strong and constructive role in school improvement (Ehren, 2013[114]). This relationship can take a variety of forms, but the trend is towards developing a more synergistic relationship.

For example, both New Zealand and Scotland attach great importance to ensuring that school self-evaluation and external school evaluations use "the same language". The intention is that internal and external school evaluation should be complementary, with self-evaluation forming the core of a holistic evaluation approach. Schools are provided with guidance on self-evaluation that is not prescriptive but stresses the need for rigour and respect for evidence in making evaluative judgements and the need to act on the evidence collected (OECD, 2015[73]).

In terms of criteria or quality indicators, Wales' national model of "a good school" should draw on both international and national research into the factors generally associated with high-quality learning and teaching. Criteria for school evaluations are often presented in an analytical framework comprising context, input, process and outcomes or results. Most countries focus on a mixture of processes and outcomes. It is logical to use evidence of improved practices and processes in a system that aims to improve school quality (OECD, 2013[50]). Although it is for the working group to decide on the actual criteria, the ambition to develop SLOs and putting the new school curriculum into practice argues for the working group to consider what follows in the next sections.

Using data and information on student learning and well-being in school self-evaluations

As discussed above, an SLO in Wales focuses its teaching and learning on a broad range of outcomes – cognitive and social-emotional, including well-being – for now and the future (Welsh Government, 2017[1]). This broad understanding of what teaching and learning entails in the 21st century is captured by the four purposes of Wales' new school curriculum that are also at the heart of its SLO model (Welsh Government, 2017[1]).

Bringing the curriculum to life in schools throughout Wales will depend on school evaluations looking at student learning and well-being across the full breadth of the curriculum. International evidence – and also past experience in Wales – show the risk of the curriculum being narrowed (OECD, 2013[50]; OECD, 2014[7]) when only some parts of it are prioritised in school evaluations and system-level monitoring. Often the more easily measured skills like literacy, mathematics and numeracy, and science end up being prioritised.

The Welsh Government recognises the need for a transition period to the new assessment, evaluation and accountability arrangements as the methods and instruments for parts of the curriculum are still to be developed. Not all the assessment methods and instruments for all six Areas of Learning and Experience are going to be ready for schools to use by the start of the academic year 2018/19, and nor should this work be rushed. The new curriculum and assessment arrangements will be fully available in January 2020 and allow for a broader measurement of the curriculum, thereby further informing school self-evaluations.

The challenge therefore for the Welsh Government lies in managing the transition period and showing the education profession and other key stakeholders that things are indeed changing and moving forward: taking people along on this change process and – as the Welsh Government has indeed been doing – asking them to help shape the journey. During the head teachers' conference discussed above, for example, the Welsh Government presented its suggestions for this transition period. These included giving schools greater autonomy to determine key performance indicators based on local needs but, for the immediate future, retaining national indicators for the key subjects of English/Welsh, mathematics and science (Welsh Government, 2018[115]).

It will be further developed below but given the Welsh Government's commitment to equity and well-being, which is also key to Wales' SLO model (Welsh Government, 2017[1]), it could possibly also consider requiring schools to have processes in place to monitor and support students' health and well-being. Such a process indicator could give an important signal to schools and others about the intention to move towards an assessment, evaluation and accountability system that goes beyond the more easily measured skills but instead aims to cover all skills, values and attitudes included in the new curriculum. The proposed development of guidelines and instruments for schools to assess students' social-emotional skills, including their well-being, could (in time) allow these monitoring efforts to be strengthened.

Promoting schools as learning organisations

As mentioned above, international evidence shows that approaches to school evaluation vary considerably across countries (OECD, 2013[50]). Many countries recognise the need to better integrate external school evaluation with school self-evaluations and/or to better target external school evaluation on those schools in most need of improvement. This has led to a new (or more explicit) emphasis in school self-evaluation on the school's leadership, policies and effectiveness of practices. Different approaches are used to achieve this, but the underlying aspect is a school's capacity for improvement and change (OECD, 2013[50]) or "readiness for change". There may be an explicit evaluation of the school's capacity to improve or, as we would prefer to say, an explicit evaluation of a school's capacity to learn and make sustainable improvements.

Several countries and economies, including the Flemish Community of Belgium, New Zealand and Scotland, have made this evaluation of the school's capacity to learn and/or improve an explicit part of their school evaluations. In Scotland, for example, external school evaluation includes a specific evaluation and report on the school's capacity to improve (one of three professional judgements: confident, partially confident and not confident). Scotland has also developed and promoted a self-evaluation model for schools including a set of quality indicators for schools to use called "How good is our school?" (Education Scotland, 2015[116]). One of the six key questions in this self-evaluation model is "What is our capacity for improvement?". This is a core aim of self-evaluation activities: self-evaluation is forward looking. It is about change and improvement, whether gradual or transformational, and is based on professional reflection, challenge and support.

Wales should look to examples like these and place similar emphasis on schools' capacity to learn and improve by integrating its SLO model into its self-evaluations and development planning. Apart from ensuring greater policy coherence, this will be an important signal to schools about the importance placed on developing thriving learning cultures in schools across Wales – i.e. their "readiness for change" for putting the new curriculum into practice. The various people the OECD team interviewed or heard speaking during several policy meetings and events were in favour of this suggestion.

Explicit recognition of the need for staff learning and well-being in development plans

The development of SLOs and the ongoing curriculum reform call for Wales to pay particular attention to the professional learning and development of staff. Therefore, following the examples of countries and economies like Australia, the Flemish Community of Belgium, New Zealand and Scotland, Wales should pay particular attention to issues of staff management and professional learning in school (self-) evaluations (OECD, 2013[50]). Several of these countries have developed professional standards to guide professional learning and development planning – as has Wales.

The OECD team learned that Wales' teaching and school leadership standards have in general been well received by the education profession. They are now integrated into the Professional Learning Passport. This digital tool aims to help teachers plan and record their professional learning in line with the new professional standards and so can serve as an important point of reference to guide staff in their professional learning and development planning. It is the responsibility of school leaders to ensure that these priorities are aligned with those of the school and are included in staff development plans that in turn form an integrated part of the school's development plans (Kools and Stoll, 2016[3]). Here it is important to note that, in line with Wales' understanding of professional learning (see above), priority is given to using the capacity for change and innovation that is already available within schools with an emphasis on collaborative learning and working. Staff development plans – perhaps better called "staff learning plans" – should reflect this. The OECD team learned this is still far from common practice in schools in Wales.

Furthermore, a school cannot truly be a learning organisation without recognising and responding to the learning and other needs of its staff (see Chapter 2). The OECD team believe that staff well-being should therefore be a component of staff and school development plans. The international policy interest in staff well-being in education stems from the growing awareness that in order to meet the needs of increasingly diverse learners, enhancing teacher and school leader professionalism has become essential (Earley and Greany, 2017[117]; OECD, 2017[118]). The demands placed on education professionals have increased markedly in recent decades. Teachers today face more diverse classrooms than in the past and they need to continuously update their practice through professional learning and collaboration with peers in order to keep their pedagogical knowledge up to date. In many countries, however, this transition towards enhanced professionalism is taking place in difficult conditions in terms of workload, accountability requirements, level of autonomy and budget pressures – as is the case for Wales. As a result of these developments, stress and staff well-being has become an issue in a number of education systems (OECD, 2017[118]).

Therefore, although the ultimate aim is to provide students with a challenging and well-rounded 21st century education, SLOs also explicitly set out to create a supportive learning environment for all their staff; one that is characterised by mutual respect and trust, positive working relationships, and the empowerment of all staff (Watkins and Marsick, 1996[99]; Silins, Zarins and Mulford, 2002[62]). While this is an aim in itself, some empirical evidence suggests a positive relationship between staff well-being and the quality of teaching and ultimately student outcomes (Caprara et al., 2006[119]; Klassen and Chiu, 2010[120]; Silins, Zarins and Mulford, 2002[62]). These findings suggest staff well-being in turn is associated with student learning.

The Welsh Government has for years promoted staff well-being in schools, for example, through the local healthy school schemes. Recently, the issue of staff well-being has gained in prominence through the combined efforts of key stakeholders like the regional consortia, the Education Workforce Council, the unions, Estyn and the Welsh Government to reduce workload issues in schools (Estyn, 2017[121]). The proposal to enhance staff well-being is therefore only small progression of these efforts. A first step in this direction would be to define the concept of staff well-being in the Welsh context.

Participatory school self-evaluations involving the wider school community

In SLOs, the school development plan is informed by evidence, based on learning from self-assessment – or "self-evaluation", as it is currently known in Wales – involving multiple sources of data and information, and updated regularly (Schechter and Qadach, 2013[100]; Senge, 2012[122]). In these self-evaluations, staff and students, but also the broader school community including school governors, parents, other schools, higher education institutions and others, are fully engaged in identifying the aims and priorities for their school.

The evidence from previous chapters suggests that students are rarely involved in school self-evaluations and development planning. It furthermore suggests it will take sustained efforts for schools, in particular secondary schools, to engage parents and external partners in such a process. School governors involvement also leaves scope for improvement as discussed. Schools will need guidance and support to help them make self-evaluations into a truly participatory process and draw the most benefit from this.

The same applies to students. Research underlines the important role that students can play in school self-evaluation and development efforts. As several examples presented in Chapter 2 show, students have a critical role to play in determining how schools and classrooms can be improved, even though they need support to learn how to provide powerful feedback (Rudduck, 2007[123]; Smyth, 2007[124]).

Stimulating and supporting peer review among schools

In several OECD countries and economies, including Finland, the Flemish Community of Belgium, Northern Ireland and the Netherlands, peer review among schools has become a common feature in school self-evaluations and development planning (OECD, 2013[50]).

Such approaches need to be introduced carefully and in line with wider policy and practices around school-to-school collaborations and networks. The advantage of these models is that they can support the development of lateral accountability between schools, so that teachers and leaders are focused on improving outcomes for all students, collectively across a network or area. Importantly, and in line with Wales' SLO model, such practices also serve the purpose of learning between schools, by allowing for structured visits and feedback between schools (Matthews and Headon, 2016[125]).

However, this is easier said than done. Trusting relationships are necessary for deep school-to-school collaboration. These can be fostered by prior agreement on a code of ethics to guide the peer evaluation process (Stoll, Halbert and Kaser, 2011[126]). Furthermore, the context in which schools conduct self-evaluations determines to a considerable extent the nature of the support that a critical friend can offer (Swaffield and MacBeath, 2005[127]). If school self-evaluation is voluntary for the purpose of school development, a critical friend's role can be varied and potentially highly creative. However, if a school self-evaluation is mandated, and takes place in a high-stakes or competitive environment, a critical friend's role is more politicised and unlikely to foster true learning and development.

The discussions about the inclusion of peer reviews as part of Wales' new approach to school self-evaluation and development planning during the secondary head teachers' conference showed that people were clearly supportive of this option. In fact, there was almost unanimous support for making self-evaluations and development planning as participatory as possible i.e. by including students, school governors, parents, other schools, higher education institutions and possible other partners. Interviews by the OECD team supported this point of view.

Review of school self-evaluations and development planning by regional consortia

The endorsement or review of school self-evaluations and development planning was discussed extensively during the secondary head teachers' conference. In line with Wales' understanding of a self-improving school system, the option was raised of having the regional consortia review schools' self-evaluations and development plans. This practice is in fact already part of the national school categorisation system (Step 3, see above) in which the challenge advisors of the regional consortia in a sense serve as a critical friend by challenging schools in the findings of the self-evaluation process, and then helping them respond to these by suggesting ways of improvement and professional learning opportunities, including collaborations with other schools. Participants were generally supportive of continuing this practice in the new model for school self-evaluation and development planning.

However, they also noted that the discussions between schools and challenge advisors was too focused on Step 1 of the national categorisation system, i.e. the performance data, with less attention paid to Step 2, which consists of the school's own self-evaluation in respect to leadership, learning and teaching. This is despite well-known concerns about the quality of the student performance data coming from the teacher assessments of student performance in Key Stages 2 and 3. These findings were corroborated by the interviews the OECD team undertook.

Furthermore, as discussed above, the final judgement of the national categorisation system (Step 3) results in a colour coding of the school. Apart from the concerns about the student performance data on which these judgements are largely based, this practice has led to schools being stigmatised and looking for ways to "game the system", and is also believed to have tempered the willingness of schools to do things differently, innovate their practice and engage with other schools in collaborative working and learning. All of this stands at odds with Wales' ambitions for SLOs. Participants at the head teachers' conference were unanimous in their support for discontinuing this colour coding of schools. The OECD team agree this would seem an essential step for developing schools into learning organisations as long as sufficient checks and balances are built into new assessment, evaluation and accountability arrangements as will be discussed below.

Furthermore, the regional consortia have played a vital role in strengthening the connections between primary and secondary schools in recent years. The OECD team saw several examples of this during its visits to Wales. Even so, representatives of the consortia noted that this remains an area for improvement for many schools in Wales. If schools are truly to become learning organisations, and to help realise the natural connection between primary and secondary education envisaged by the new curriculum, there is good reason to further promote the collaboration between primary and secondary schools through the new model for school self-evaluation and development planning.

This may have organisational implications for the regional consortia, where many of the challenge advisors primarily work in one sector. Having at least some of the challenge advisors work with both types of school, or teaming up challenge advisors who work with different types of schools, seems likely to help strengthen the quality of the review/endorsement process by the regional consortia. This is clearly an issue to take into account in the envisaged pilot phase of the new school self-evaluation and development planning toolkit.

External school evaluations for learning – while safeguarding school quality

As discussed above, the establishment of a common set of criteria for what a good school entails in Wales for use in school self-evaluations and external evaluations would be an important step forward in helping schools with their improvement efforts. Such a common framework could allow Estyn to focus more on monitoring the rigour of the process of self-evaluations and development planning in schools that have shown to have the capacity for conducting quality self-evaluations as happens in countries like Ireland, New Zealand and Scotland (OECD, 2013[50]; European Commission/EACEA/Eurydice, 2015[128]).

If this is to happen, there will need to be sufficient checks and balances in place to safeguard the quality of school self-evaluations and development planning, thereby giving the public greater confidence in the system's ability to monitor progress and identify the schools that are not faring well or need additional support. These may mean that the idea of making school self-evaluation into a more participatory process, peer review by colleagues in other schools, the endorsement by consortia, the external evaluation by Estyn based on a common set of criteria or quality indicators, the publicly available data on the My Local School website[2], complemented by a more comprehensive way of system-level monitoring that covers the full width of the new curriculum (see below), may prove sufficient.

The My Local School website would have to be amended to reflect the new assessment, evaluation and development framework. As already mentioned, one suggestion would be to do away with the stigmatising colour coding of schools that has put pressure on them to try to "game the system".

Similarly, some of the people interviewed by the OECD team raised questions about Estyn's grading of schools into four categories (i.e. excellent, good, adequate and needs improvement, and unsatisfactory and needs urgent improvement). This grading system has driven many schools to focus on gathering evidence to show how good they are, i.e. meeting the requirements of the inspection framework, rather than using the self-evaluation process for the purpose of learning. Aligning the criteria or quality indicators used for self-evaluation and for external evaluation by Estyn is one important response to this challenge, while temporary reconsideration of this grading system as recently proposed by Graham Donaldson (2018[101]) may indeed be needed to give people the confidence to change and innovate their practice.

In parallel with the planned piloting and introduction of the new school self-evaluation and development planning toolkit, there will need to be a transition period before moving to the new approach to Estyn inspections. Donaldson for this purpose proposed a phased way for changing Estyn inspections, in line with the wider reforms, ultimately to one which is directed towards validation of schools' self-evaluation (Donaldson, 2018[101]).

A first phase would involve the redirection of cyclical inspection towards direct support for the reform programme. A temporary suspension of the current inspection and reporting cycle should be used to allow inspectors to engage with schools, individually and in clusters, without the requirement to produce graded public reports. The engagement would have as its prime purpose the building of capacity for school-by-school changes to the curriculum, learning and assessment. A temporary redirection of Estyn's resources would therefore allow schools and inspectors to concentrate on reform.

The second phase would re-introduce inspections which would retain many of the features of Estyn's new inspection arrangements. The timing of the introduction of this phase would be decided on the basis of evidence of progress with the reforms during phase 1. There would be some significant differences from the existing inspection model: the focus of the inspections would be tailored to answer key questions about the school's progress with the reforms and the impact on children's experiences and outcomes; the evaluations would no longer be in the form of headline gradings but described clearly in the text. There would also be a stronger role for school self-evaluation in arriving at judgements, in line with guidance emerging from the joint work on self-evaluation involving OECD and Estyn. This phase would initiate the move towards validated self-evaluation while retaining Estyn's vital role in giving assurance.

The third and final phase would be based on a validated self-evaluation model. As schools mature in their capacity to engage openly and constructively in self-evaluation, the role of external individuals and bodies should be to provide perspectives that probe and extend internal judgements. Schools with a proven ability to conduct and act on self-evaluation could move to a validation model of inspection on an 'earned autonomy' basis. Estyn would engage directly with such schools on an agreed cycle in order to report publicly on its confidence in the self-evaluation process and the integrity of reports from schools. That confidence would be expressed in Estyn's validation (or not) of the school's processes and findings, possibly described through a short narrative expressing the inspectors' degree of confidence in the process. A move to a validated self-evaluation model of accountability would reflect the broader aspiration to create a self-improving system based on professional and organisational learning (Donaldson, 2018[101]).

The proposed phased approach is being considered by Estyn and Welsh Government, who intend to seek the views of the education profession and other stakeholders before deciding.

The analysis in previous chapters clearly points to the challenges ahead in giving people the confidence to do things differently. Providing schools and other stakeholders with clarity about this period of transition will be essential to unleash the energy and willingness needed to realise a culture of enquiry, exploration and innovation in schools throughout Wales.

Estyn also recognises it will have to make the necessary investments in developing the skills and attitudes of its inspectors if they are to be able to take on their new roles and responsibilities in the new arrangements. Similarly, international evidence warns for not underestimating the investment needed in the capacity of school leaders and all other parties involved in the proposed participatory process of school self-evaluations and development planning (Ehren, 2013[114]; OECD, 2013[50]; SICI, 2003[113]) as discussed below.

Investing in the capacity to conduct participatory self-evaluations and development planning

As the new assessment, evaluation and accountability arrangements foresee a strengthened role for school self-evaluations, and place a greater emphasis on participatory self-evaluations and development planning, Wales will need to enhance the skills of all those involved in the process. International evidence points to the need to explicitly recognise that school self-evaluation and development planning is hugely dependent on the capacity of the school's leadership to stimulate engagement, mobilise resources, and ensure there is appropriate training and support (OECD, 2013[50]).

Although the SLO survey found that the vast majority of school staff in Wales agreed that development planning in their schools is informed by continuous self-assessments, the OECD team found that the quality of school self-evaluations and development planning is an area for improvement for many schools in Wales (see Chapter 2). The evidence points to school leaders relying too heavily on data analyses – mostly quantitative – at the expense of gathering first-hand evidence. Much time and effort is devoted to analysing and reporting upwards on a large amount of mostly quantitative data, rather than the systematic use of multiple sources of data and information to develop, implement and regularly update the school's development plan.

As is the case for many OECD countries, it would therefore seem of great importance for Wales to ensure it makes adequate professional learning opportunities available for its school leaders – and other school staff with evaluation responsibilities – to stimulate engagement by a wide range of parties, such as staff, students and governors, in self-evaluation and development planning (SICI, 2003[113]; OECD, 2013[50]; European Commission/EACEA/Eurydice, 2015[128]).

One issue here may be that the new (teaching and) leadership standards pay limited attention to school self-evaluations. These will be used to inform appraisals and professional learning, as well as the content of leadership development programmes in Wales (Welsh Government, 2017[12]). A future review of the standards should be used to increase the prominence of this key responsibility of school leaders.

However, any investment in professional learning should not be limited to school staff but should respond to the needs of all parties involved in the proposed participatory process of school self-evaluation and development planning. The planned pilot of the school self-evaluation and development planning toolkit should be used to identify these parties' professional learning needs.

Furthermore, international evidence shows there is a role for systems to offer support and resources to schools (European Commission/EACEA/Eurydice, 2015[128]; OECD, 2013[50]). Table 4.2 provides a range of examples of national initiatives to support schools in their self-evaluation and development planning, including guidelines for self-evaluation and school development plans, tools for evaluation and data analysis, and promoting examples of schools that are working effectively with self-evaluation and development planning tools.

Table 4.2. National initiatives to support school self-evaluation and development planning

National support for school self-evaluation	
Austria	Quality in Schools (QIS) project Internet platform supplies schools with information and tools for both evaluation and data.
Denmark	The Quality and Supervision Agency runs an Evaluation Portal with online tools and resources for school evaluation and, in collaboration with the Danish Evaluation Institute, offers voluntary training sessions for school principals and teachers.
Ireland	Strengthened support in 2012 includes: guidelines for school self-evaluation in primary and secondary schools, a dedicated school self-evaluation website, Inspectorate support for all schools and teachers, and seminars for school principals which are organised by the professional development service for teachers. In 2003 the Inspectorate developed two frameworks for self-evaluation in primary and secondary schools ("Looking at our schools"). Since 1998, professional development for teachers has been offered in the context of school development planning.
Mexico	Self-evaluation guidance has been developed since the early 2000s, including an adaptation of the Scottish evaluation and quality indicator framework (2003) and a publication on key features of top-performing schools (2007). A collection of guides, support materials and instruments for self-evaluation was distributed to all primary and secondary schools in 2007 ("System for school self-evaluation for quality management"). The National Testing Institute also developed a series of applications for use in self-evaluation, e.g. tools for evaluating the overall school, the school environment and school staff.
New Zealand	The Education Review Office provides support tools and training for school self-review and improvement, suggesting a cyclical approach and providing a framework for success indicators which are the same as those used in external reviews.
United Kingdom (Northern Ireland)	The Education and Training Inspectorate has developed a set of quality indicators ("Together towards improvement") in collaboration with schools and practitioners, which it promotes for use in school self-evaluation. Other tools and guidelines have been developed to support both whole-school evaluation and evaluation in specific subjects, e.g. "Evaluating English".
United Kingdom (Scotland)	Framework for school self-evaluation ("How good is our school?") includes quality indicators in five key areas. The Education Scotland website also provides a range of self-evaluation materials and good practice examples. Education Scotland runs good practice conferences on different themes.

Source: OECD (2013[50]), *Synergies for Better Learning: An International Perspective on Evaluation and Assessment*, http://dx.doi.org/10.1787/9789264190658-en.

Many OECD countries use stakeholder surveys, for example of students and parents, as part of the school self-evaluation process to gather evidence about perceptions and levels of satisfaction. The various people the OECD team spoke to would welcome the inclusion of such guidelines and tools in the toolkit, including stakeholder surveys. Various school leaders the OECD team interviewed noted how the lack of common guidelines and supporting tools has confused and hindered effective school self-evaluations and development planning in the past.

System-level evaluation should promote learning – at all levels of the system

System-level evaluation refers to the monitoring and evaluation of the performance of the education system as a whole, but also the performance of subnational education systems such as local authorities. The main aims of system evaluation are to provide accountability information to the public on how the education system is working and to inform policy planning to improve educational processes and outcomes (OECD, 2013[50]; Burns and Köster, 2016[129]).

While recognising the vital role of evaluation in ensuring public accountability, the SLO model calls for greater emphasis to be placed on gathering data and information to inform learning and for evidence-informed policy (European Commission, 2017[61]; Senge, 2012[122]). As mentioned above, recent paradigmatic shifts in public administration, often in the context of New Public Governance, emphasise a greater focus on processes, stressing service effectiveness and outcomes that rely upon the interaction of public service organisations with their environment (Osborne, 2006[110]; Osborne, 2013[111]).

The first indications are that Wales' new assessment, evaluation and accountability arrangements, and its transition towards them, are seen as encouraging by many people the OECD team interviewed, as they are likely to place greater emphasis on school self-evaluations and development planning. They are thereby recognising the international research evidence that shows the vital contribution these can make towards raising the quality of education and achievement (Ehren, 2013[114]; SICI, 2003[113]). It is also a clear sign of the trust placed in schools and the education profession to achieve these aims.

During the course of this assessment the Welsh Government's Education Directorate also revealed some of its initial ideas for system-level evaluation through a number of "quality indicators". Their content was not known as this report was being finalised but the Education Directorate was clear that it intended to work with the education profession and other key stakeholders to establish a set of quality indicators to monitor progress at the system level – rather than through a large number of mostly quantitative indicators as has been the case for several years. This is clearly a positive development.

Having said this, the OECD team were surprised by the presentation of the Welsh Government's initial suggestions for these indicators or performance measures during the secondary head teachers' conference. Although these were primarily discussed in the context of a transition period before the final curriculum and its corresponding assessment, evaluation and accountability arrangements are put in place in January 2020, the performance measures the government presented showed a tendency to "stay close to the old". They focused on a set of student performance measures, paying less attention to process indicators such as whether schools are monitoring student well-being or engaging in collaborative working and learning with other schools. Such indicators have been used in other countries. In the Netherlands, for example, participation in peer reviews is one of several process indicators for monitoring progress against its Teacher's Agenda (OECD, 2016[60]). Another example of a different type is provided by Ontario, Canada, that has "enhancing public confidence" as one of its performance indicators (Ontario Ministry of Education, 2010[130]) – rather than using the term accountability.

Furthermore, although there was an explicit call for performance measures to be inclusive and focus on the needs of the individual student, and for them to drive an inclusive and diverse curriculum benefitting all students (Welsh Government, 2018[115]), the OECD team are concerned that the proposals presented will not achieve these aims. For example, although the intermediate measures proposed giving schools greater autonomy to determine key performance indicators based on local needs, the proposals also suggested retaining national indicators for the key subjects of English/Welsh, mathematics and science. As one participant to the conference noted, these key subjects are then likely to continue to drive behaviour, drawing attention away from the other parts of the new curriculum, and therefore narrowing the curriculum.

It must be noted that these initial suggestions for key performance measures did not come solely from the Welsh Government but rather were the result of an ongoing dialogue with a group of head teachers, in a process of co-construction. The OECD team could therefore not escape the impression that these head teachers, as well as some Education Directorate officials, may need to think more "out of the box" and be more creative and daring in stepping away from what they know well to ensure alignment with the ambitions of the new curriculum. One suggestion might be to include staff well-being as a key performance indicator, which would fit very well with Wales' objective to develop all schools into learning organisations and responds to its growing recognition as an important policy issue in Wales – and internationally.

Recognising that Wales is trying to move away from its high-stakes assessment, evaluation and accountability arrangements, the OECD team cannot avoid sharing the concerns of the conference participant cited above, that further steps seem needed. Supplementing student performance measures with others, such as the proposed indicator for monitoring student well-being in schools, could give an important message that the intent is to move towards a new assessment, evaluation and accountability framework that reflects the full breadth of the curriculum.

On this issue the OECD team would like to refer back to the recommendations of the *Successful Futures* report by Donaldson (2015[2]). The report proposed that national monitoring of student learning by the Welsh Government should be informed by a rolling programme of sample-based assessments in, for example, English and Welsh literacy, numeracy, digital competence, and science. Currently teacher assessments of student performance at the end of Key Stages 2 and 3 are used for the purpose of monitoring the progress of schools and the system – which as discussed has made them high stakes and is believed to have compromised their reliability.

Research evidence shows that sample-based assessments provide similar high-quality information as full cohort tests and have some cost advantages. Over time, they offer other advantages such as avoiding distortions of results derived from "teaching to the test", and may also allow for a broader coverage of the curriculum (Green and Oates, 2009[131]; OECD, 2013[50]). Donaldson (2015[2]) proposed that such sample-based assessments would only need to involve some children and young people. They would not need to take place every year, and there could be a timetable of such assessments over a period of years with a single topic being assessed each year.

The OECD team agree that Wales should consider such a "rolling" system of sample-based assessments as is used in countries and economies like the Flemish Community of Belgium, Finland and New Zealand, covering the whole curriculum for system-level monitoring of progress in student learning and well-being (see Box 4.7). Wales in fact already has several surveys in place that capture elements of student well-being. Adjusting one or more of these surveys around a common definition and means of measuring the concept would therefore seem very feasible in the short term.

Box 4.7. Examples of national surveys including the assessment of social and emotional skills – New Zealand and Norway

New Zealand has conducted school climate surveys as part of its national survey of health and well-being among secondary school students. In 2012, 91 randomly selected schools throughout the country participated in the survey. The school climate survey aimed to describe the school social environment in terms of support for students and staff, relationships between staff and students, and the safety of students and staff. For example, the questionnaire for teachers included such scales as "student sensitivity" (e.g. "Students in my classes generally respect viewpoints different from their own"), "student disruptiveness" (e.g. "Students in my classes generally disrupt what others are doing") and student helpfulness (e.g. "Most students are friendly to staff"). The student questionnaire also included several school climate questions including "How much do you agree or disagree with the following statements about your school? - Students in this school have trouble getting along with each other, etc."

Students in **Norway** at different grades in primary and secondary education participate in the Pupil Survey that includes the assessment of students' social and emotional well-being at school. The Norwegian Directorate for Education and Training conducts user surveys including the Pupil Survey, Teacher Survey and Parent Survey to allow students, teachers and parents to express their opinions about learning and enjoyment on school. The results from the user surveys may be used to analyse and improve the learning environment at schools. The questionnaire for students include items such as "Do you enjoy schools?", "Do you have any classmates to be with during recess?", and "Are you interested in learning at school?".

Source: OECD (2015[104]), *Skills for Social Progress: The Power of Social and Emotional Skills*, http://dx.doi.org/10.1787/9789264226159-en.

Furthermore, in 2015 Donaldson proposed that assessments of progress towards meeting the four purposes of the curriculum should be part of school inspections and reported on by Estyn on a regular basis (Donaldson, 2015[2]). The OECD team agree that this would allow for another layer of evidence ("checks and balances in the system") to monitor progress across the whole curriculum. Estyn's annual and thematic reports would lend themselves well to this purpose but should draw on a wider range of evidence than school evaluations alone. It may look to the example of the Dutch Education Inspectorate whose annual report, *The State of Education in The Netherlands*, draws from various sources, including school inspections, results from national and international student assessments, and research evidence (Inspectorate of Education of The Netherlands, 2017[132]).

International peer review

As mentioned above, the Welsh Government's Education Directorate has committed to developing itself as a learning organisation. In line with this intention it has adopted an approach of co-construction of its policies. However, it has gone further by explicitly seeking the views of national and international experts, for example during peer learning events. It has been engaging with organisations like the Atlantic Rim and OECD to support its critical reflection of its past, present and future actions. Such international peer review and learning will add another layer to the assessment, evaluation and accountability framework under development.

It was apparent to the OECD team that these measures by the Education Directorate, and its commitment to developing as a learning organisation itself, were welcomed by the participants of the secondary head teachers' conference and the people interviewed during the course of this assessment. The Education Directorate should continue to lead by example or – to use the words of the SLO concept – to "model" such learning leadership (Kools and Stoll, 2016[3]). This also reinforces the message that all tiers of the system (see Chapter 1, Figure 1.3) are in it together to make the curriculum reform a success.

Using research for monitoring and promoting knowledge exchange and learning throughout the system

A research component is often needed to understand how a strategy might be optimised and to create the materials to do so through such means as teacher education and leadership. Creating expert knowledge and converting that into accessible forms and formats may call for specialist institutes (OECD, 2016[97]; OECD, 2015[73]). Many countries with high-quality education systems have a strong research and evaluation capacity located in a mix of government-based research institutes and university-based centres.

Wales is less fortunate in this regard as an earlier OECD review noted (OECD, 2014[7]). Since then, it has taken important steps to strengthen the links between evidence, research and policy. These include a more strategic use of research by the Welsh Government to inform its policy decisions, including the monitoring and evaluation of many of its policies and programmes. For example, the developmental work of the Pioneer Schools Network is monitored and supported through action research. This assessment, providing the Welsh Government and other stakeholders with detailed insight into the progress made towards realising its objective of developing schools in Wales as learning organisations, and the work that remains to be done is another case in point.

The regional consortia have also started to study the effectiveness of their school improvement services and promote enquiry-based approaches in schools. They often engage with higher education institutions in Wales or other countries to do this.

However, the research capacity of higher education institutions in Wales in the field of education remains underdeveloped, as the Welsh Government and the higher education institutions themselves recognise. The higher education institutions, Welsh Government, regional consortia and various other stakeholders have taken several measures recently to strengthen research capacity in Wales. These include the recently established "task and finish group" to advise on the strategic priorities for the provision of education research, advise on the levers for building research capacity and recommend a suitable structure for the longer term planning of education research. The OECD team consider the work of this group to be of great importance for building Wales' research and evaluation capacity at all levels of the education system, thereby supporting the development of SLOs.

Recommendations

Policy issue 1: Promoting a shared vision centred on the learning and well-being of all students

The development of an inclusive and shared vision that promotes equity and well-being is central to the first dimension of Wales' SLO model. The realisation of the "four purposes" of the new school curriculum is also at the heart of the model. The evidence suggests that this vision is widely shared throughout the school system. Two issues however call for urgent policy attention to enable all schools to put this vision into practice:

- **Policy issue 1.1:** Wales' school funding model challenges equity.

- **Policy issue 1.2:** Student well-being needs to be defined and measured.

Recommendations

Recommendation 1.1.1: Review the school funding model to realise Wales' commitment to equity and student well-being. The Welsh Government should consider conducting an in-depth analysis of school funding in Wales to explore a funding model that promotes greater equity and efficiency. One option to explore is limiting the funding that local authorities are allowed to reallocate, excluding school transport costs to take into account the differences in population density. It should carefully monitor any such change in policy and adjust this threshold as needed to ensure sufficient funding is allocated to schools.

Recommendation 1.2.1: Develop a national definition of student well-being and provide guidance and instrument(s) for monitoring it. This work should be fast-tracked so that the definition and supporting measurement instruments and guidance could be field tested as part of the piloting of the national school self-evaluation and development planning toolkit that is likely to start in autumn 2018 (see below). The field testing should allow for any necessary revisions to be made and the guidance and measurement instrument(s) to be shared with schools by September 2019 (i.e. the start of the academic year 2019/20).

Policy issue 2: Promoting the development of professional capital and a thriving learning culture

The SLO reflects a central focus on professional learning of all staff, aimed at creating a sustainable learning culture in the organisation and other parts of the (learning) system. Wales has made good progress recently in several areas, like the promotion of school-to-school collaborations and the clarification of professional expectations through the teaching and leadership standards. Several issues deserve further policy attention however. These are:

- **Policy issue 2.1:** The need for establishing stronger collaborations between schools and teacher education institutions.

- **Policy issue 2.2:** Promoting professional learning throughout the professional lifecycle, prioritising the following identified areas 1) investing in the skills and "mindset" for enquiry, exploration and innovation; 2) strengthening induction programmes; and 3) promoting mentoring and coaching, observations and peer review.

- **Policy issue 2.3: Developing** learning leadership in schools and other parts of the system.

The following recommendations are proposed to respond to these challenges.

Recommendations

Recommendation 2.1.1: Base selection into initial teacher education on a mix of criteria and methods. In line with the teaching and leadership standards, teacher education institutions should expand and pilot more elaborate, well-rounded selection criteria and intake procedures that cover a mix of cognitive and socio-emotional skills, values, and attitudes. Attention should be paid to assessing aspiring teachers' aptitude for teaching the new curriculum and engaging in continuous professional learning.

Recommendation 2.1.2: Promote strong collaborations between schools and teacher education institutions. In addition to the new teacher education programmes' accreditation process, the ongoing reviews of school evaluation (i.e. of self-evaluations and Estyn evaluations) should be used to encourage schools to establish sustainable partnerships with teacher education institutions. Schools, higher education institutions, regional consortia and the Welsh Government should continue investing in specific projects to help realise and grow such innovations, for example for strengthening induction programmes and/or promoting enquiry-based teaching and learning.

Recommendation 2.2.1: Prioritise the following areas for professional learning:

- **Investing in the skills and mindset for enquiry, exploration and innovation to thrive and putting the new curriculum into practice**. The national approach to professional learning that is being developed to support schools in putting the curriculum into practice should include developing teachers' and learning support workers' skills in enquiry-based approaches. Higher education/teacher education institutions are well placed to contribute to these efforts. The new assessment, evaluation and accountability arrangements (see below) should also encourage schools to explore new ways of doing things, engage in enquiry and innovate their practice.

- **Strengthening induction programmes.** The Welsh Government and the regional consortia should explore ways to strengthen induction programmes. Partnerships between teacher education institutions and schools should be promoted because of the benefits to both partners. Learning support workers should not be overlooked.

- **Promoting mentoring and coaching, observations and peer review.** School leaders play a pivotal role in promoting such collaborative practices and should be held accountable for this. However, they also need to be adequately supported in taking on this responsibility. Regional consortia should review their support services in light of these findings and prioritise support for secondary schools. The integration of Wales' SLO model into the national school self-evaluation and development planning toolkit will be important for promoting such collaborative practice.

Recommendation 2.3.1: Develop and implement a coherent leadership strategy that promotes the establishment of learning organisations across the system. Under the leadership of the National Academy for Educational Leadership, Wales should consolidate and speed up efforts to strengthen leadership capacity at all levels in the system. It should develop and implement a leadership strategy that promotes school leaders and other system leaders to develop their organisations into learning organisations.

Recommendation 2.3.2: Provide greater support to secondary school leaders and ensure they have the capacity to develop their schools as learning organisations. The National Academy for Educational Leadership should pay particular attention to the capacity development of secondary school leaders, making sure to include middle-level leaders. The regional consortia should also focus on supporting secondary school leaders. Collaborations between primary and secondary school leaders could be promoted. Future reviews of the (teaching and) leadership standards should place greater emphasis on school leaders' role in self-evaluations and development planning.

Policy issue 3: Assessment, evaluation and accountability should promote schools developing into learning organisations

In the last decade, Wales' assessment, evaluation and accountability arrangements have become heavily influenced by accountability demands, rather than serving the purpose of learning and improvement (Donaldson, 2015[2]). They have also been found to lack coherence and include several duplications. In response the Welsh Government embarked on a reform of assessment, evaluation and accountability arrangements.

This assessment aims to contribute to this reform and identified several issues calling for policy attention for schools to develop into learning organisations. These include:

- **Policy issue 3.1:** Student assessments should put student learning at the centre. Student progress should be monitored across the full breath of the curriculum, rather than focusing on a small number of subjects, thereby narrowing the curriculum.

- **Policy issue 3.2**: School evaluations should serve the primary purpose of learning and improvement rather than accountability. There is currently no common understanding of what good school self-evaluation means in Wales, partially resulting from the lack of synergies between the national categorisation system and Estyn inspections.

- **Policy issue 3.3:** System-level monitoring and evaluation should promote learning – at all levels of the system.

Recommendations

Recommendation 3.2.1: Develop national criteria for school quality to guide self-evaluations and Estyn evaluations. These criteria or quality indicators should promote Wales' SLO model, monitor student learning and well-being across the full breadth of the curriculum, recognise staff learning needs and their well-being in staff development plans that in turn inform school development plans, and give students and parents a voice in organisational and educational matters. These and potentially other criteria or quality indicators should encourage schools to give an account of their own strengths and priorities for improvement – and as such should be about learning and improvement, rather than primarily serving the purpose of accountability.

Recommendation 3.2.2: School self-evaluations should be shaped through a participatory process involving the wider school community. Self-evaluations should involve staff, students, school governors, parents, other schools, higher education institutions and possibly others to identify priorities. Peer reviews among schools should complement this process. Regional consortia should furthermore continue to review school self-evaluations and development planning but this process should no longer result in the public colour coding of schools. A condition for doing so is that sufficient checks and balances are built into new assessment, evaluation and accountability arrangements.

These changes also call for substantial investment in the capacity of all those involved in self-evaluations and development planning. The pilot of the school self-evaluation and development planning toolkit should be used to identify the professional learning needs of all parties involved. Guidelines and tools should be part of the toolkit.

Recommendation 3.2.3: Estyn evaluations should safeguard the quality of schools, while focusing on the rigour of schools' self-evaluation processes and development planning. Estyn should promote schools' development of their own capacity for self-evaluation (i.e. be about learning) and focus on identifying strengths and priorities for improvement. It could focus more on monitoring the rigour of the process of self-evaluations and development planning in those schools that have shown to have the capacity for conducting quality self-evaluations. Sufficient checks and balances – as proposed in this report – would need to be in place, however, to monitor progress and identify those schools that are not faring well and/or are in need of additional support. These changes call for sustained investment in developing the skills and attitudes of Estyn inspectors.

Recommendation 3.2.4: Provide clarity to schools and other stakeholders on the transition to the new system of school self-evaluation and Estyn evaluations. Schools should be provided with clarity on the transition period as soon as possible to unleash the energy and willingness of people to engage in enquiry, exploration and innovation.

Recommendation 3.3.1: Performance measures should go beyond the key subjects of English/Welsh, mathematics and science – also in the transition period. The Welsh Government should consider performance measures (indicators) on student well-being and staff well-being – initially in the form of a process indicator until measurement instruments have been developed. This will be essential to align assessment, evaluation and accountability with the ambitions of the new curriculum and Wales' SLO model.

Recommendation 3.3.2: National monitoring of student learning and well-being should be informed by a rolling programme of sample-based assessments and Estyn reports, as well as research. These assessments should replace the use of teacher assessments of student performance at the end of Key Stages 2 and 3. There could be a timetable over a period of years with a single topic of the curriculum being assessed each year. Furthermore, Estyn's annual and thematic reports should be used to monitor progress in realising the four purposes of the curriculum. These reports should draw on a wider range of evidence, including the proposed sample based assessments, PISA and relevant research.

Notes

[1] See the My Local School website on http://mylocalschool.wales.gov.uk/?lang=en.

[2] Idem.

References

Agasisti, T. et al. (2018), "Academic resilience: What schools and countries do to help disadvantaged students succeed in PISA", *OECD Education Working Papers*, No. 167, OECD Publishing, Paris, http://dx.doi.org/10.1787/e22490ac-en. [16]

Ainscow, M. (2014), *Towards Self-Improving School Systems: Lessons from a City Challenge*, Routledge, New York. [74]

Barber, M. and M. Mourshed (2007), *How the World's Best Performing Schools Come Out on Top*, McKinsey and Company, London. [38]

Barron, B. and L. Darling-Hammond (2010), "Prospects and challenges for inquiry-based approaches to learning", in Dumont, H., D. Istance and F. Benavides (eds.), *The Nature of Learning: Using Research to Inspire Practice*, OECD Publishing, Paris, http://dx.doi.org/10.1787/9789264086487-11-en. [71]

Borgonovi, F. and G. Montt (2012), "Parental involvement in selected PISA countries and economies", *OECD Education Working Papers*, No. 73, OECD Publishing, Paris, http://dx.doi.org/10.1787/5k990rk0jsjj-en. [79]

Bowen, G., R. Rose and W. Ware (2006), "The reliability and validity of the school success profile learning organization measure", *Evaluation and Program Planning*, Vol. 29/1, pp. 97-104. [78]

Burns, T. and F. Köster (2016), *Governing Education in a Complex World*, OECD Publishing, Paris, http://dx.doi.org/10.1787/20769679. [129]

Burns, T., F. Köster and M. Fuster (2016), *Education Governance in Action: Lessons from Case Studies*, Educational Research and Innovation, OECD Publishing, Paris, http://dx.doi.org/10.1787/9789264262829-en. [9]

Byrne, D. and E. Smyth (2010), *Behind the Scenes? A Study of Parental Involvement in Post-Primary Education*, Liffey Press, Dublin. [80]

Caprara, G. et al. (2006), "Teachers' self-efficacy beliefs as determinants of job satisfaction and students' academic achievement: A study at the school level", *Journal of School Psychology*, Vol. 44/6, pp. 473-490. [119]

Choi, A. (2018), "Emotional well-being of children and adolescents: Recent trends and relevant factors", *OECD Education Working Papers*, No. 169, OECD Publishing, Paris, http://dx.doi.org/10.1787/41576fb2-en. [33]

Daly, A. (2009), "Rigid response in an age of accountability: The potential of leadership and trust", *Educational Administration Quarterly*, Vol. 45/2, pp. 168-216, https://doi.org/10.1177%2F0013161X08330499. [109]

Darling-Hammond, L., M. Hyler and M. Gardner (2017), *Effective Teacher Professional Development*, Learning Policy Institute, Palo Alto.. [52]

Desforges, C. and A. Abouchaar (2003), "The impact of parental involvement, parental support and family education on pupil achievements and adjustment: A literature review", *Research Report*, No. 433, Department for Education and Skills Publications, Nottingham. [81]

Dimmock, C. (2012), *Leadership, Capacity Building and School Improvement: Concepts, Themes and Impact*, Routledge, London. [94]

Donaldson, G. (2018), *A Learning Inspectorate*, https://www.estyn.gov.wales/sites/default/files/documents/A%20Learning%20Inspectorate%20-%20en%20-%20June%202018.pdf. [101]

Donaldson, G. (2015), *Successful Futures: Independent Review of Curriculum and Assessment Arrangements in Wales*, Welsh Government, http://gov.wales/docs/dcells/publications/150225-successful-futures-en.pdf. [2]

Earley, P. and T. Greany (2017), *School Leadership and Education System Reform*, Bloomsbury Academic, https://www.bloomsbury.com/uk/school-leadership-and-education-system-reform-9781474273954/. [117]

Education Scotland (2015), *How Good Is Our School?*, Education Scotland, https://education.gov.scot/improvement/Documents/Frameworks_SelfEvaluation/FRWK2_NIHeditHGIOS/FRWK2_HGIOS4.pdf. [116]

Education Workforce Council (2017), *National Education Workforce Survey, Research Report, April 2017*, Education Workforce Council, Cardiff. [55]

Ehren, M. (2013), "Impact of school inspections on improvement of schools—describing assumptions on causal mechanisms in six European countries", *Educational Assessment, Evaluation and Accountability*, Vol. 25/1, pp. 3-43, http://dx.doi.org/10.1007/s11092-012-9156-4. [114]

Estyn (2018), *The Annual Report of Her Majesty's Chief Inspector of Education and Training in Wales 2016-2017*, Estyn, Cardiff, https://www.estyn.gov.wales/document/annual-report-2016-2017. [75]

Estyn (2017), *Common Inspection Framework from September 2017*, Estyn website, https://www.estyn.gov.wales/sites/default/files/documents/2017%20-final%20CIF.pdf. [36]

Estyn (2017), *Reducing Workload Issues. A Guide for Teachers and Head Teachers*, Estyn website, https://www.estyn.gov.wales/sites/default/files/documents/Reducing%20workload%20-%20English%20poster.pdf. [121]

Estyn (2017), *Supplementary Guidance: Self-evaluation*, Estyn, Cardiff, https://www.estyn.gov.wales/sites/default/files/documents/NIA%20Supplementary%20guidance%20-%20self-evaluation_0.pdf. [69]

Estyn (2014), *The Annual Report of Her Majesty's Chief Inspector of Education and Training in Wales*, Estyn, Cardiff. [102]

European Commission (2017), *Teachers and School Leaders in Schools as Learning Organisations: Guiding Principles for Policy Development in School Education*, European Commission, Brussels, https://ec.europa.eu/education/sites/education/files/teachers-school-leaders-wg-0917_en.pdf. [61]

European Commission (2013), *Supporting Teacher Educators for Better Learning Outcomes, Education and Training*, European Commission, Brussels, http://ec.europa.eu/dgs/education_culture/repository/education/policy/school/doc/support-teacher-educators_en.pdf. [43]

European Commission/EACEA/Eurydice (2015), *Assuring Quality in Education: Policies and Approaches to School Evaluation in Europe*, Publications Office of the European Union, Luxembourg. [128]

Fullan, M. (2004), "Leadership across the system", *Insight*, Vol. Winter, http://http//www.michaelfullan.ca/media/13396061760.pdf (accessed on 05 March 2017). [93]

Fullan, M. and J. Quinn (2015), *Coherence: The Right Drivers in Action for Schools, Districts, and Systems*, Corwin Press. [14]

Fullan, M., S. Rincon-Gallardo and A. Hargreaves (2015), "Professional capital as accountability", *Education Policy Analysis Archives*, Vol. 23, p. 14, http://dx.doi.org/10.14507/epaa.v23.1998. [53]

Furlong, J. (2015), *Teaching Tomorrow's Teachers, Options for the Future of Initial Teacher Education in Wales*, Welsh Government, Cardiff, http://gov.wales/docs/dcells/publications/150309-teaching-tomorrows-teachers-final.pdf. [45]

George, B. et al. (2017), "Rational planning and politicians' preferences for spending and reform: Replication and extension of a survey experiment", *Public Management Review*, Vol. 19/9, pp. 1251-1271. [106]

Giles, C. and A. Hargreaves (2006), "The sustainability of innovative schools as learning organizations and professional learning communities during standardized reform", *Educational Administration Quarterly*, Vol. 42/1, pp. 124-156. [65]

Greany, T.((n.d.)), *System-level Policies, Processes and Structures for Enabling Schools to Develop in Learning Organisations*, Background paper for the Developing Schools as Learning Organisations in Wales report (unpublished). [4]

Green, S. and T. Oates (2009), "Considering alternatives to national assessment arrangement in England: Possibilities and opportunities", *Educational Research*, Vol. 51/2, pp. 229-245. [131]

Hargreaves, A. and M. Ainscow (2015), "The top and bottom of leadership and change", *Phi Delta Kappan*, Vol. 97/3, pp. 42-48, http://dx.doi.org/10.1177/0031721715614828. [15]

Hargreaves, A. and D. Fink (2006), *Sustainable Leadership*, Jossey-Bass, San Francisco. [86]

Hargreaves, A. and M. Fullan (2012), *Professional Capital: Transforming Teaching in Every School*, Teachers College Press, New York. [37]

Hargreaves, A. and D. Shirley (2009), *The Fourth Way: The Inspiring Future for Educational Change*, Corwin Press. [5]

Harris, M. and F. van Tassell (2005), "The professional development school as a learning organization", *European Journal of Teacher Education*, Vol. 28/2, pp. 179-194. [47]

Hattie, J. (2012), *Visible Learning for Teachers: Maximizing Impact on Learning*, Routledge, London. [39]

Helms-Lorenz, M., W. van de Grift and R. Maulana (2016), "Longitudinal effects of induction on teaching skills and attrition rates of beginning teachers", *School Effectiveness and School Improvement*, Vol. 27/2, pp. 178-204, http://dx.doi.org/10.1080/09243453.2015.1035731. [64]

Ho Park, J. (2008), "Validation of Senge's learning organization model with teachers of vocational high schools at the Seoul megalopolis", *Asia Pacific Education Review*, Vol. 9/3, pp. 270-284. [77]

Hood, C. (2013), *The Blame Game: Spin, Bureaucracy, and Self-Preservation in Government*, Princeton University Press. [107]

Inspectorate of Education of The Netherlands (2017), *The State of Education in The Netherlands 2015/2016 [De Staat van het Onderwijs in Nederland 2015/16]*, Inspectorate of Education of The Netherlands, Utrecht, https://english.onderwijsinspectie.nl/binaries/onderwijsinspectie_eng/documents/annual-reports/2017/04/12/the-state-of-education-in-the-netherlands-2015-2016/state+of+education+2015+2016+web.pdf. [132]

James, C. et al. (2006), *How Very Effective Primary Schools Work*, Sage, London. [87]

Klassen, R. and M. Chiu (2010), "Effect on teachers' self-efficacy and job satisfaction: Teacher gender, years of experience, and job stress", *Journal of Educational Psychology*, Vol. 102/3, pp. 741-756. [120]

Kools, M. and L. Stoll (2016), "What makes a school a learning organisation?", *OECD Education Working Papers*, No. 137, OECD Publishing, Paris, http://dx.doi.org/10.1787/5jlwm62b3bvh-en. [3]

Kroll, A. (2015), "Drivers of performance information use: Systematic literature review and directions for future research.", *Public Performance & Management Review*, Vol. 38/3, pp. 459-486. [112]

Land, D. (2002), "Local school boards under review: Their role and effectiveness in relation to students' academic achievement", *Review of Educational Research Summer*, Vol. 72/2, pp. 229-278, http://dx.doi.org/10.3102/00346543072002229. [92]

Leithwood, K. (2013), *Strong Districts and Their Leadership*, The Council of Ontario Directors of Education and The Institute for Education Leadership, Ontario, http://www.ontariodirectors.ca/downloads/Strong%20Districts-2.pdf. [95]

Leithwood, K. and K. Seashore Louis (2012), *Linking Leadership to Student Learning*, Jossey-Bass, https://eric.ed.gov/?id=ED527262. [83]

Martin, A. and H. Marsh (2006), "Academic resilience and its psychological and educational correlates: A construct validity approach", *Psychology in the Schools*, Vol. 43/3, pp. 267-281, https://doi.org/10.1002/pits.20149. [17]

Masdeu Navarro, F. (2015), "Learning support staff: A literature review", *OECD Education Working Papers*, No. 125, OECD Publishing, Paris, http://dx.doi.org/10.1787/5jrnzm39w45l-en. [56]

Matthews, P. and M. Headon (2016), *Multiple Gains: An Independent Evaluation of Challenge Partners' Peer Reviews of Schools*, UCL Institute of Education Press, https://www.challengepartners.org/sites/default/files/files/Multiple%20Gains.pdf. [125]

Miles, D. et al. (2002), "Building an integrative model of extra role work behaviors: A comparison of counterproductive work behavior with organizational citizenship behavior", *International Journal of Selection and Assessment*, Vol. 10/1&2, pp. 51-57, http://dx.doi.org/10.1111/1468-2389.00193. [6]

MoECS (2015), *"Kamerbrief over de Voortgang Verbeterpunten voor het Leraarschap" (Parliamentary Letter about the Improvement Points for the Teaching Profession)*, Ministry of Education, Culture and Science, the Netherlands, http://www.begeleidingstartendeleraren.nl/. [63]

Nielsen, P. and M. Baekgaard (2015), "Performance information, blame avoidance, and politicians' attitudes to spending and reform: Evidence from an experiment", *Journal of Public Administration Research and Theory*, Vol. 25/2, pp. 545-569. [108]

OECD (2018), *TALIS Initial Teacher Preparation Study*, OECD website, http://www.oecd.org/education/school/talis-initial-teacher-preparation-study.htm. [41]

OECD (2018), *The Future We Want: The Future of Education and Skills, Education 2030*, OECD Publishing, Paris, http://www.oecd.org/education/2030/oecd-education-2030-position-paper.pdf. [11]

OECD (2017), *Education in Lithuania*, Reviews of National Policies for Education, OECD Publishing, Paris, http://dx.doi.org/10.1787/9789264281486-en. [24]

OECD (2017), *PISA 2015 Results (Volume III): Students' Well-Being*, PISA, OECD Publishing, Paris, http://dx.doi.org/10.1787/9789264273856-en. [32]

OECD (2017), *PISA and TALIS Synergies*, 44th meeting of the PISA Governing Board, 6-8 November 2017, EDU/PISA/GB(2017)21, OECD, Paris. [118]

OECD (2017), *The Funding of School Education: Connecting Resources and Learning*, OECD Publishing, Paris, http://dx.doi.org/10.1787/9789264266490-en. [29]

OECD (2017), *The Welsh Education Reform Journey: A Rapid Policy Assessment*, OECD Publishing, Paris, http://www.oecd.org/edu/The-Welsh-Education-Reform-Journey-FINAL.pdf. [19]

OECD (2016), *Education in Latvia*, Reviews of National Policies for Education, OECD Publishing, Paris, http://dx.doi.org/10.1787/9789264250628-en. [23]

Burns, T. and F. Köster (eds.) (2016), *Governing Education in a Complex World*, OECD Publishing, Paris, http://dx.doi.org/10.1787/9789264255364-en. [97]

OECD (2016), *Netherlands 2016: Foundations for the Future*, Reviews of National Policies for Education, OECD Publishing, Paris, http://dx.doi.org/10.1787/9789264257658-en. [60]

OECD (2016), *PISA 2015 Results (Volume I): Excellence and Equity in Education*, PISA, OECD Publishing, Paris, http://dx.doi.org/10.1787/9789264266490-en. [31]

OECD (2016), *PISA 2015 Results (Volume II): Policies and Practices for Successful Schools*, PISA, OECD Publishing, Paris, http://dx.doi.org/10.1787/9789264267510-en. [13]

OECD (2015), *How's Life? 2015: Measuring Well-being*, OECD Publishing, Paris, http://dx.doi.org/10.1787/how_life-2015-en. [35]

OECD (2015), *Schooling Redesigned: Towards Innovative Learning Systems*, Educational Research and Innovation, OECD Publishing, Paris, http://dx.doi.org/10.1787/9789264245914-en. [73]

OECD (2015), *Skills for Social Progress: The Power of Social and Emotional Skills*, OECD Skills Studies, OECD Publishing, Paris, http://dx.doi.org/10.1787/9789264226159-en. [104]

OECD (2014), *Improving Schools in Sweden: An OECD Perspective*, OECD, Paris, http://www.oecd.org/edu/school/Improving-Schools-in-Sweden.pdf. [105]

OECD (2014), *Improving Schools in Wales: An OECD Perspective*, OECD, Paris, http://www.oecd.org/edu/Improving-schools-in-Wales.pdf. [7]

OECD (2014), *Skills beyond School: Synthesis Report*, OECD Reviews of Vocational Education and Training, OECD Publishing, Paris, http://dx.doi.org/10.1787/9789264214682-en. [22]

OECD (2013), *Synergies for Better Learning: An International Perspective on Evaluation and Assessment*, OECD Reviews of Evaluation and Assessment in Education, OECD Publishing, Paris, http://dx.doi.org/10.1787/9789264190658-en. [50]

OECD (2012), *Equity and Quality in Education: Supporting Disadvantaged Students and Schools*, OECD Publishing, Paris, http://dx.doi.org/10.1787/9789264130852-en. [18]

OECD (2010), *"OECD-Harvard Seminar for Leaders in Education Reform in Mexico: School Management and Education Reform in Ontario" (Seminario OCDE-Harvard para Líderes en Reformas Educativas en México: Gestión Escolar y Reforma Escolar en Ontario)*, http://www.oecd.org/fr/education/scolaire/calidadeducativaqualityeducation-eventsandmeetings.htm. [96]

Dumont, H., D. Istance and F. Benavides (eds.) (2010), *The Nature of Learning: Using Research to Inspire Practice*, OECD Publishing, Paris, http://dx.doi.org/10.1787/9789264086487-en. [72]

Ontario Ministry of Education (2010), *System on the Move: Story of the Ontario Education Strategy*, Ontario Ministry of Education, http://www.edu.gov.on.ca/bb4e/Ontario_CaseStudy2010.pdf.. [130]

Osborne, S. (ed.) (2013), *The New Public Governance?: Emerging Perspectives on the Theory and Practice of Public Governance*, Routledge, London.   [111]

Osborne, S. (2006), "The New Public Governance?", *Public Management Review*, Vol. 8/3, pp. 377-386.   [110]

Pont, B. and P. Gouedard (forthcoming), "School leaders", *OECD Education Working Papers*.   [89]

Pont, B., D. Nusche and H. Moorman (2008), *Improving School Leadership, Volume 1: Policy and Practice*, OECD Publishing, Paris, http://www.oecd.org/education/school/44374889.pdf.   [88]

Robinson, V., M. Hohepa and C. Lloyd (2009), *School Leadership and Student Outcomes: Identifying What Works and Why*, Ministry of Education, Auckland.   [84]

Ross, K. and R. Levačić (1999), *Needs-based resource allocation in education : via formula funding of schools*, UNESCO, International Institute for Educational Planning, https://eric.ed.gov/?id=ED445410.   [30]

Rudduck, J. (2007), "Student voice, student engagement, and school reform", in Thiessen, D. and A. Cook-Sather (eds.), *International Handbook of Student Experience in Elementary and Secondary School*, Springer, Dordrecht.   [123]

Rumberger, R. (2004), "Why students drop out of school", in Orfield, G. (ed.), *Dropouts in America: Confronting the Graduation Rate Crisis*, Harvard Education Press, Cambridge, MA.   [76]

Sahlberg, P. (2010), "Educational change in Finland", in *Second International Handbook of Educational Change*, Springer Netherlands, Dordrecht, http://dx.doi.org/10.1007/978-90-481-2660-6_19.   [44]

Sahlberg, P. (2007), *Secondary Education in OECD Countries: Common Challenges, Differing Solutions*, European Training Foundation, Turin.   [21]

Santiago, P. et al. (2016), *OECD Reviews of School Resources: Estonia 2016*, OECD Reviews of School Resources, OECD Publishing, Paris, http://dx.doi.org/10.1787/9789264251731-en.   [58]

Schechter, C. and M. Qadach (2013), "From illusion to reality: Schools as learning organizations", *International Journal of Educational Management*, Vol. 27/5, pp. 505-516.   [100]

Scheerens, J. (2013), "The use of theory in school effectiveness research revisited", *School Effectiveness and School Improvement*, Vol. 24/1, pp. 1-38.   [103]

Schleicher, A. (2018), *World Class: How to Build a 21st-Century School System*, OECD Publishing, Paris, http://dx.doi.org/10.1787/4789264300002-en.   [85]

Schleicher, A. (2015), *Schools for 21st-Century Learners: Strong Leaders, Confident Teachers, Innovative Approaches*, OECD Publishing, Paris, http://dx.doi.org/10.1787/9789264231191-en.   [48]

Schleicher, A. (2012), *Preparing Teachers and Developing School Leaders for the 21st Century: Lessons from Around the World*, OECD Publishing, Paris, http://dx.doi.org/10.1787/9789264174559-en.   [49]

Schleicher, A. (2011), *Building a High-Quality Teaching Profession: Lessons from around the World*, International Summit on the Teaching Profession, OECD Publishing, Paris, http://dx.doi.org/10.1787/9789264113046-en. [40]

Senge, P. (2012), *Schools That Learn (Updated and Revised): A Fifth Discipline Fieldbook for Educators, Parents, and Everyone who Cares About Educaton*, Crown Business, New York. [122]

Shewbridge, C. et al. (2016), *OECD Reviews of School Resources: Lithuania 2016*, OECD Reviews of School Resources, OECD Publishing, Paris, http://dx.doi.org/10.1787/9789264252547-en. [28]

SICI (2003), *Effective School Self-Evaluation (ESSE)*, Standing International Conference of Inspectorates, Belfast. [113]

Silins, H., S. Zarins and B. Mulford (2002), "What characteristics and processes define a school as a learning organisation? Is it a useful concept to apply to schools?", *International Education Journal*, Vol. 3/1, pp. 24-32. [62]

Sinnema, C. (2017), *Designing a National Curriculum with Enactment in Mind: A Discussion Paper*. [70]

Smyth, J. (2007), "Toward the pedagogically engaged school: Listening to student voice as a positive response to disengagement and 'dropping out'?", in Thiessen, D. and A. Cook-Sather (eds.), *International Handbook of Student Experience in Elementary and Secondary School*, Springer, Dordrecht. [124]

Statistics for Wales (2018), "Local authority budgeted expenditure on schools: 2017-18", *Statistical Bulletin*, No. SB 32/2017, Welsh Government, https://gov.wales/docs/statistics/2017/170706-local-authority-budgeted-expenditure-schools-2017-18-en.pdf. [26]

Stoll, L. et al. (2006), "Professional learning communities: A review of the literature", *Journal of Educational Change*, Vol. 7/4, pp. 221-258, http://dx.doi.org/10.1007/s10833-006-0001-8. [66]

Stoll, L., J. Halbert and L. Kaser (2011), "Deepening learning in school-to-school networks", in Day, C. (ed.), *International Handbook on Teacher and School Development*, Routledge, London.. [126]

Swaffield, S. and J. MacBeath (2005), "School self-evaluation and the role of the critical friend", *Cambridge Journal of Education*, Vol. 35/2, pp. 239-252. [127]

Swedish Ministry of Education and Research (2016), *Country Background Report: Sweden*, OECD website, http://www.oecd.org/education/school/CBR_OECD_SRR_SE-FINAL.pdf. [59]

Tabberer, R. (2013), *A Review of Initial Teacher Training in Wales*, Welsh Government. [46]

Thompson, M. et al. (2004), "Study of the impact of the California Formative Assessment and Support System for Teachers, Report 1: Beginning teachers' engagement with BTSA/CFASST", *ETS Research Report Series*, No. RR-04-30, Educational Testing Service. [67]

Timperley, H. et al. (2007), *Teacher Professional Learning and Development: Best Evidence Synthesis Iteration*, Ministry of Education New Zealand, Wellington. [51]

Tummers, L. and E. Knies (2016), "Measuring public leadership: Developing scales for four key public leadership roles", *Public Administration*, Vol. 94/2, pp. 433-451, http://dx.doi.org/10.1111/padm.12224. [98]

UNICEF Office of Research (2013), "Child well-being in rich countries: A comparative overview", No. 11, UNICEF Office of Research, Florence. [34]

UNISON (2016), *New Era for School Support Staff in Wales*, UNISON website, http://www.unison.org.uk/news/article/2016/04/new-era-for-school-support-staff-in-wales/. [27]

Van der Rijst, R., D. Tigelaar and J. van Driel (2014), *"Effecten van Selectie Ten Behoeve van de Lerarenopleidingen. Een Literatuurreview in Opdracht van NRO" (Effects of Selection on Teacher Education Programmes: A Literature Review Commissioned by the National Research Organisation)*, ICLON, Universiteit Leiden, http://www.nro.nl/wp-content/uploads/2015/06/Effecten-van-selectie-ten-behoeve-van-de-lerarenopleidingen_VanderRijst.pdf. [42]

Viennet, R. and B. Pont (2017), "Education policy implementation: A literature review and proposed framework", *OECD Education Working Papers*, No. 162, OECD Publishing, Paris, http://dx.doi.org/10.1787/fc467a64-en. [8]

Watkins, K. and V. Marsick (eds.) (1996), *In Action: Creating the Learning Organization*, American Society for Training and Development, Alexandria. [99]

Welsh Government (2018), *Developing Robust Evaluation and Accountability Arrangements to Support a Self-improving System*, Welsh Government website, http://learning.gov.wales/docs/learningwales/publications/180312-conference-presentation-en-v2.pdf (accessed on 24 March 2018). [115]

Welsh Government (2017), *Education in Wales: Our National Mission. Action Plan 2017-21*, Welsh Government, Cardiff, http://gov.wales/topics/educationandskills/allsectorpolicies/education-in-wales/?lang=en (accessed on 28 November 2017). [12]

Welsh Government (2017), *National Academy for Educational Leadership*, Learning Wales website, http://learning.gov.wales/resources/collections/national-academy-for-educational-leadership?lang=en. [90]

Welsh Government (2017), *Professional Standards for Teaching and Leadership*, Welsh Government, Cardiff, http://learning.gov.wales/docs/learningwales/publications/170901-professional-standards-for-teaching-and-leadership-en.pdf. [54]

Welsh Government (2017), *Schools in Wales as Learning Organisations*, http://gov.wales/topics/educationandskills/schoolshome/curriculuminwales/curriculum-for-wales-curriculum-for-life/schools-in-wales-as-learning-organisations/?lang=en (accessed on 30 November 2017). [1]

Welsh Government (2017), *Written Statement: School Business Manager Pilots*, Welsh Government website, http://gov.wales/about/cabinet/cabinetstatements/2017/schoolbusinessmanagerpilots/?lang=en (accessed on 05 March 2018). [91]

Welsh Government (2016), *National School Categorisation System Guidance Document for Schools, Local Authorities and Regional Consortia*, Welsh Government, Cardiff, http://gov.wales/docs/dcells/publications/150121-guidance-en-v3.pdf. [68]

Welsh Government (2016), *Wales Education Report Card*, Welsh Government website, http://gov.wales/docs/dcells/publications/160314-qualified-for-life-report-card-en.pdf. [20]

Welsh Government (2014), *Qualified for Life: An Education Improvement Plan for 3 to 19-year-olds in Wales*, Welsh Government, Cardiff. [10]

Welsh Government (2013), *Action plan to promote the role and development of support staff in schools in Wales*, Welsh Government, Cardiff, http://learning.gov.wales/docs/learningwales/publications/131010-action-plan-promoting-the-role-and-development-of-support-staff-en.pdf. [57]

Welsh Government (2012), *Review of Qualifications for 14 to 19-year-olds in Wales*, Welsh Government, Cardiff. [25]

Williams, B., J. Williams and A. Ullman (2002), *Parental Involvement in Education*, Department of Education and Skills, Norwich, http://dera.ioe.ac.uk/4669/1/RR332.pdf. [82]

Chapter 5. Realising schools as learning organisations in Wales

This chapter explores the question of how Wales can ensure the effective implementation – or "realisation" – of its schools as learning organisations (SLO) policy. Our main findings are that Wales should: 1) develop an easy-to-understand narrative explaining how Wales' SLO model is part of the curriculum reform; 2) continue strengthening the capacity of regional consortia; 3) Estyn to continue monitoring the progress of consortia in enhancing their services; 4) enhance the collaboration and alignment between the development of assessment, evaluation and accountability arrangements, and the curriculum; 5) continue the SLO Implementation Group, while striving for greater policy coherence; and 6) expand the public dialogue generated by PISA results to align it to the ambitions of the new curriculum.

The findings and recommendations of this report aim to inform the development of a national SLO implementation plan. This action plan should form an integrated part of the larger curriculum reform effort.

The statistical data for Israel are supplied by and under the responsibility of the relevant Israeli authorities. The use of such data by the OECD is without prejudice to the status of the Golan Heights, East Jerusalem and Israeli settlements in the West Bank under the terms of international law.

Introduction

This chapter completes the analysis of the system-level conditions that could enable or hinder schools in Wales as they develop into learning organisations by looking at issues of implementation (see Figure 5.1). While recognising this is a relatively new policy, it explores the question of how Wales can ensure its effective implementation, or "realisation" (the preferred term in Wales), and concludes with a number of recommendations for consideration by the Welsh Government and other stakeholders at various levels of the system.

Figure 5.1. Realising schools as learning organisations

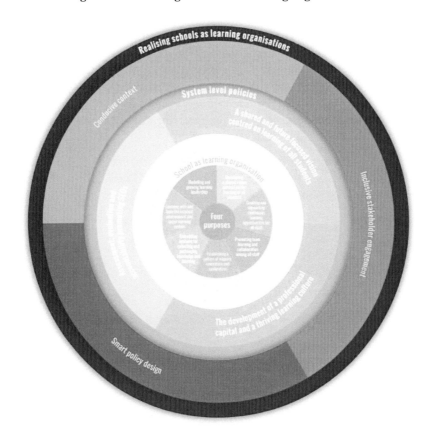

Schools as learning organisations in Wales: Moving from policy design to realisation

As part of Wales' broad education reform agenda, the action plan *Education in Wales: Our National Mission 2017-2021* states that all schools in Wales should develop into effective learning organisations (Welsh Government, 2017[1]). The development of schools as learning organisations (SLOs) has therefore become an explicit policy (see Chapter 2, Box 2.1) that is considered vital for realising the four enabling objectives of the strategic plan and the "realisation" of the new curriculum (see Chapter 2).

The policy has followed a specific process with strong stakeholder engagement. In autumn 2016 the Welsh Government established an SLO Pilot Group to develop a schools as learning organisations model for Wales. The group also supported this study by commenting on the draft SLO survey (see Chapters 2 and 3) and contributing to its field trial. This developmental work was given shape through a series of workshops and meetings between November 2016 and July 2017, facilitated by the OECD. The SLO Pilot Group (later renamed the SLO Implementation Group) consisted of representatives of 28 Pioneer Schools the regional consortia, Estyn, the National Academy for Educational Leadership, the Education Directorate of the Welsh Government and the OECD (see Chapter 1, Box 1.2).

In November 2017, Wales' SLO model was launched (Welsh Government, 2017[2]) and has contributed to the clarification of what an SLO looks like in Wales. The Welsh Government launched a website presenting the model and describing its benefits to schools, its use and the next steps for putting it into practice, which has contributed to raising awareness of the policy (Welsh Government, 2017[2]). This has been complemented by the presentation of the model in various national and regional events attended by school staff and other stakeholders.

As the policy has effectively been launched since the end of 2017, it is important to understand the determinants that may hinder or facilitate its effective implementation. In general, education policies fail to be effectively implemented due to a range of factors such as the lack of a clear vision of the policy itself and how it fits in with the other policies that surround it, potential reactions against the reform by those who are supposed to implement it, or a lack of staff capacity or investment in their training (Viennet and Pont, 2017[3]). More directly, the lack of a clear implementation strategy may leave those in schools without guidance or information and support to make it happen. Policy makers need to consider these issues if they want education policies reach the classrooms. Recent research has grouped a set of determinants for successful implementation into a framework with four dimensions:

- smart policy design
- inclusive stakeholder engagement
- a conducive institutional policy and societal context
- a coherent implementation strategy or plan (Viennet and Pont, 2017[3]).

This chapter looks at how these four determinants can facilitate or hinder the realisation of Wales' SLO policy.

Smart policy design

Research evidence shows that whether a policy is well justified, and offers a logical and feasible solution to the issue at hand will determine to a great extent whether it can be put into practice and how. The nature of a policy solution, and the way it is formulated, influence its "enactment" (Bell and Stevenson, 2015[4]). The core attributes of a policy, the underlying issues which may not have been acknowledged or explored during its formulation phase, carry over to the implementation phase and may alter it (Fullan and Quinn, 2015[5]). Therefore, to understand a policy's potential to be realised, it is important to consider the underlying factors that underpin it: the policy justification, its logic and its feasibility (Viennet and Pont, 2017[3]).

Policy justification and logic

A policy responds to a need, or to the perception of a need, and this need should be outlined clearly to facilitate the formulation, legitimacy and implementation of a solution. Clarifying the reasoning behind a policy, the characteristics of the issue it is supposed to address and the way policy makers analyse these, help make sense of how to put it in practice and can contribute to getting stakeholders on board with the policy reform. In addition, it is important that the justification presents a clear idea of the expected results if it is to move actors and supporters forward (Viennet and Pont, 2017[3]).

In Wales, the SLO policy has had a clear trajectory. In September 2017 the Welsh Government launched its new strategic education action plan, *Education in Wales: Our National Mission*. It formulated its objective to develop schools in Wales into learning organisations and outlined the rationale for this policy: that such schools are vital for realising the four enabling objectives and ultimately for putting the new curriculum in practice (Welsh Government, 2017[1]).

As covered in Chapter 2, research evidence shows that schools that operate as learning organisations can react more quickly to changing external environments and embrace changes and innovations in their internal organisation. The evidence also shows a positive association between the SLO and a range of staff outcomes like job satisfaction, self-efficacy, readiness for change and experimentation (Schechter, 2008[6]; Silins, Mulford and Zarins, 2002[7]; Schechter and Qadach, 2012[8]; Erdem, İlğan and Uçar, 2014[9]; Razali, Amira and Shobri, 2013[10]).

The Welsh Government and many of the key stakeholders like Estyn, the regional consortia, local authorities and many of the school staff the OECD team interviewed all understand that it will take concerted efforts and collaborative working and learning within and across schools to realise the new curriculum. There is recognition that in many cases the teachers, learning support workers, school leaders and many others involved will need to expand their skills (Donaldson, 2015[11]; Welsh Government, 2017[1]).

Previous OECD reviews and other reports have pointed to several challenges, including the capacity of teaching staff to conduct quality assessments and differentiate their teaching approaches to adapt to students' learning needs. There are also concerns about the quality of some school and system leaders who will play a pivotal role in creating the conditions for the curriculum to be put into practice (OECD, 2014[12]; OECD, 2017[13]; Estyn, 2018[14]).

The development of a thriving learning culture in schools and other parts of the education system is expected to play a pivotal role in responding to these challenges and ultimately for putting the curriculum into practice in schools throughout Wales. The development of SLOs – and other parts of the system – has consequently become part of the Welsh Government's strategy to establish strong, mutually supportive connections between schools, aimed at moving towards a self-improving school system.

The OECD has been able to assess progress in the understanding of this policy among stakeholders since September 2016, when it undertook a rapid policy assessment that formed the starting point of a longer-term collaboration with various strands of OECD Education Policy Implementation Support provided to the Welsh Government (see Chapter 1).

Initially the majority of stakeholders the OECD team met were not clear about what the concept of a school as a learning organisation actually entailed in the Welsh context and how it related to the curriculum reform and other policies such as school self-evaluation and development planning. Throughout 2017, the OECD team have gathered information and interviewed a range of stakeholders at various levels of the system and has seen a growing understanding of the rationale or logic behind developing schools as learning organisations. Still, there is clearly more work to be done on this.

The interviews and the OECD team's participation in several policy meetings revealed that the regional consortia have not made equal progress in promoting Wales' SLO model in their regions. The regional consortia are expected to continue to play an important role in helping schools understand how the model can help them in their daily work and supporting them in developing as learning organisations. There would appear to be a need to reduce the variability in the support schools receive from their consortia to develop as learning organisations. However, the OECD team see some challenges here, as the consortia vary in their capacity to take on this role, as will be discussed further below.

The OECD team also believe that further communication and capacity building are needed to ensure school staff, local authorities and other stakeholders are familiar with the model and understand "why" it was developed, and "how" it can be used to support the development of their schools and relates to the larger curriculum reform effort and other policies.

On the latter, the Welsh Government has been striving for greater policy coherence and has been increasingly successful in this, as noted in an earlier OECD assessment (2017[13]). However, it has not always been as successful in communicating its efforts and achievements in this area. An easily understood narrative that explains the logic of developing SLOs and how this fits the curriculum reform effort should form a key component of Welsh Government's communication strategy on the curriculum reform (see below).

The feasibility of developing all schools in Wales into learning organisations

The feasibility of a policy means thinking carefully about the resources and technology involved in putting it into practice (Viennet and Pont, 2017[3]). The Welsh Government has invested in making Wales' SLO model a long-term commitment, with resources to develop and support the realisation of the policy. In addition to the establishment of the SLO Pilot Group, it has commissioned this OECD study primarily to take stock of how far schools in Wales have developed into learning organisations, and identify strengths and challenges as well as areas for further improvement at both school and system level.

Responding to identified challenges and areas of improvement

Chapters 2 and 3 of this study suggest that many schools in Wales are on their way towards developing into learning organisations. However, the data show that a considerable share of schools are still far from realising this objective, with particular challenges at the secondary level. The SLO dimensions "developing and sharing a vision centred on the learning of all students" and "establishing a culture of enquiry, innovation and exploration" would repay particular attention.

Triangulation of various sources of data and information has pointed to the conclusion that there is a need for more critical reflections among school staff for deep learning to take place and to make sustainable progress towards developing as learning organisations. When the OECD team presented the preliminary findings of this study to key stakeholders, they recognised this finding, which some attributed to the high-stakes assessment, evaluation and accountability arrangements that they believed have negatively affected people's confidence, or for some even their skills, to critically reflect on their own behaviour, that of peers and the wider school organisation.

Responding to these and other identified challenges and areas for further action will have resource implications and improvements will take time. Many schools are likely to need additional support to develop into learning organisations.

System infrastructure for supporting schools developing as learning organisations

Developing SLOs calls for consideration of what kind of structures schools need to support them in their developmental journeys. This sounds obvious but international evidence shows that in many cases, reforms and change initiatives pay too little attention to the actual implementation effort, in particular by failing to make sufficient investment in developing the system infrastructure to support the realisation of the policy (Viennet and Pont, 2017[3]; OECD, 2015[15]; Schleicher, 2018[16]).

There are examples of successful reforms and change initiatives that have invested in developing specific infrastructures to deliver a policy. One of the better known examples is Ontario's (Canada) education strategy, launched in 2003. It set out to 1) improve students' acquisition of literacy and numeracy skills; 2) improve the high school graduation rate; and 3) build public confidence (Ontario Ministry of Education, 2010[17]). As part of the implementation strategy, Ontario paid particular attention to developing the leadership capacity at all levels of the system. It also created a new 100-person secretariat responsible for building the capacity and expertise to do the work. Teams were created in each district and each school in order to lead the work on literacy and numeracy. The strategy paired external expertise with sustained internal leadership and promoted the sharing of knowledge and collaborations across the system to push the initiative.

The Welsh Government has also taken several measures to strengthen its system infrastructure, in particular the establishment of the regional consortia.

The four regional consortia

Four regional consortia were established in 2012 to strengthen the infrastructure for improvement and the delivery of school support services (see Chapter 1). These consortia were intended to help the 22 local authorities streamline their school improvement services and to reshape local school improvement functions. The Welsh Government established its National Model for Regional Working in 2014 (Welsh Government, 2015[18]), further clarifying the consortia's core responsibilities and services. These included challenge and support strategies to improve teaching and learning in classrooms, collating data from local authorities and schools on school and student performance and progress and using that data for improvements, and delivery of the national system for categorising schools (Welsh Government, 2016[19]). The national model also introduced the role of challenge advisors to act as agents of change, supporting and challenging school leaders to improve performance and brokering support that has a positive impact on students. The model has helped promote improvements in the quality of services provided to schools by the regional consortia and signalled a deeper commitment to regional working. It emphasised a model of school improvement based on mutual support that was largely new across most of Wales (OECD, 2017[13]).

The OECD team found that much progress has indeed been made in strengthening the regional consortia's school improvement services since their inception; a finding that was corroborated by recent Estyn monitoring reports on the consortia (Estyn, 2017[20]; Estyn, 2017[21]; Estyn, 2017[22]; Estyn, 2017[23]). However, several challenges and areas of improvement remain, a number of which are particularly relevant to the development of schools across Wales into learning organisations.

First, a major challenge not only for developing SLOs, but for supporting schools in their development more generally, concerns the capacity challenges of the regional consortia, which need to be resolved. Estyn's follow-up inspections of the consortia noted Ein Rhanbarth ar Waith (South West and Mid Wales regional consortium; ERW) as failing to make progress in developing its own capacity and improvement services in recent years (Estyn, 2017[20]). The report showed that part of the challenge lies in a lack of clarity over the respective roles and accountabilities of the local authorities and the regional consortium in relation to all school improvement functions and services. The organisation also has a relatively small core team compared to the other consortia, which is believed to have hindered it from building up its own capacity. As Wales is in the middle of a curriculum reform, which will likely increase demands for support by schools, this places further emphasis on ensuring all consortia are fully operational.

Second, this assessment suggests that a considerable proportion of schools in Wales are not yet functioning as learning organisations. Representatives of the four regional consortia and other stakeholders recognised these findings and acknowledged the need to devote particular attention to the secondary sector, and therefore more of their resources.

Third, in all consortia, the emphasis is still too much on accountability and on challenging schools (Estyn, 2018[14]), rather than on providing support and promoting a learning culture in schools and in the hearts and minds of the people working in them. The interviews with consortium representatives showed they were aware of this challenge and have recently started changing their operations to provide more support to schools. They have set up structures to encourage and support schools to work in partnership (Estyn,

2018[14]). The consortia's different governance structures, organisational cultures and ways of working mean they are all at different stages in this process, however.

Recognising that change is a complex, multifaceted process (Viennet and Pont, 2017[3]; Walker, 2006[24]) it is important to recognise the pivotal role the senior management of consortia will have to play in the months to come to change their organisational cultures (which have long been geared towards a primary challenge function with too little attention to providing support), adjusting their operations and developing the capacity of staff to support schools in developing as learning organisations and changing and innovating teaching and learning, with particular reference to the new curriculum.

On the last point, the school staff and various other stakeholders interviewed by the OECD team expressed the need for challenge advisors to receive training to enhance their ability to support schools in putting the new curriculum and assessment and evaluation arrangements into practice. One positive development is the strong involvement of the regional consortia in the curriculum reform, including through their participation in the Pioneer Schools Network. This will be important to help the consortia identify what the new professional learning needs will be within schools and consider what these entail for the capacity of their own organisations.

Furthermore, various stakeholders also raised their concerns that many of the challenge advisors are not yet familiar with Wales' SLO model. The planned workshops for challenge advisors in the summer term will be a much-needed first step towards ensuring they are able to explain the logic of this policy to school staff and support them in their efforts to develop their schools as learning organisations. However, the approaches taken by the different consortia to enhance their own capacity vary. It is too early to assess fully the strengths, weaknesses and impact of the individual consortia's different strategies (Estyn, 2018[14]). It is therefore essential that Wales continues to monitor the progress they are making and that they are collectively looking for ways to enhance their services to schools.

Fourth, despite recent improvements, there is scope to deepen collaboration and co-ordination between consortia. The consortia are positive about the improvement in collaboration and co-ordination so far. They noted it has opened up opportunities for peer learning between them, as well as opportunities to improve the quality of and/or rationalise services, and collaborate over new services they provide to schools (OECD, 2017[13]). This is an important development as it would be a waste of human and financial resources for a small country like Wales, with a tight public budget, to continue doing otherwise.

However, although this assessment has identified several examples of good collaboration between the consortia, such as the development of Wales' SLO model and in the area of leadership development, interviews with various stakeholders and observations by the OECD team also revealed that in some other areas or activities collaboration and co-ordination could be deepened – and that the consortia have room to grow trust and reduce the competition between them.

Fifth is the need for better monitoring and evaluation of the effectiveness of school improvement services (OECD, 2017[13]). According to Estyn, three of the four consortia are progressing well in their efforts to improve their monitoring and evaluation of the effectiveness of school-to-school collaborations and other school improvement services. The OECD team learned of several examples of collaborations between the consortia and higher education institutions (see Chapter 3, Box 3.17 for example) with the latter supporting consortia in the monitoring and evaluation of their improvement services. These collaborations can benefit both sides and help realise the Welsh Government's ambition to establish a self-improving school system (Welsh Government, 2017[1]). Schools in turn are also likely to benefit from the application of research to improve their teaching and learning (Ainscow et al., 2016[25]; OECD, 2013[26]); a clear issue for further improvement for many schools in Wales as was discussed in Chapters 2 and 3.

The need for better monitoring and evaluation of the effectiveness of school improvement services, as noted by consortia representatives, continues to be an area where further progress can and needs to be made in the years to come.

Higher education institutions

Partnerships with higher education institutions can offer schools clear advantages by drawing on their expertise and capacity (Ainscow et al., 2016[25]; Harris and van Tassell, 2005[27]; OECD, 2013[26]). Examples from OECD countries and beyond show that the benefits can work both ways, as innovative ideas and practices can in turn influence the higher education/university level, and the teacher education and service missions of higher education institutions may be very well served by such partnerships (OECD, 2013[26]; Harris and van Tassell, 2005[27]) (see Box 5.1).

Based on the OECD team's interviews with various stakeholders and participation in several policy meetings and events, higher education institutions have also recently started engaging more in collaborations with schools, thereby enriching Wales' system-level infrastructure to bring about change and innovation in education. This development is partly the result of the reform of initial teacher education that was started in 2015, as discussed in Chapter 4. This reform has also promoted collaborations with higher education institutions abroad to complement and enrich the initial teacher education and research capacity currently available in Wales. This increased engagement of higher education institutions with the school system is without a doubt a positive development but, as several stakeholders noted, it is still in its infancy.

Box 5.1. Partnerships between higher education institutions and schools – examples from the United States and the Netherlands

University of Michigan, United States

Teacher preparation programmes at the University of Michigan are run in close partnership with schools in the city of Ann Arbor, and there are close links between research and practice. For example, the secondary programmes use an approach called Learning and Teaching the Disciplines through Clinical Rounds to integrate the content knowledge and practices that teachers need to teach specific subjects. Candidates present a video of their teaching practice and deeply analyse it with peers, school-based mentor teachers, and university faculty course and field instructors. The approach began in 2005 and has grown to cover five content areas: social studies, mathematics, science, English language arts and world languages.

The Elementary Master of Arts with Certification programmes involve full-year internships in an elementary school classroom and focus on high-leverage content and teaching practices that are critical for teaching the school curriculum, such as place value in mathematics and leading a group discussion in class.

The University of Michigan has a clinical professorship track that promotes faculty based on their ability to train teachers and conduct research on how students learn, which helps them prioritise teacher education and applied research. Clinical professors often stay in touch with their graduates and involve them in school-based research projects, such as how to improve elementary school social studies instruction, which contributes to their ongoing professional development.

Schools and teacher education institutions co-creating primary initial teacher education programmes in the Netherlands

Responding to concerns from schools and school boards about the "classroom readiness" of newly qualified primary teachers, the Netherlands Ministry of Education in 2014 launched a range of initiatives to improve the fitness for purpose of primary initial teacher education (ITE). These initiatives have included facilitating and funding much closer integration of the Universities of Applied Sciences, which provide training in primary education, with school boards at the strategic level and with individual schools at both the strategic and operational level.

The initiatives have had a major impact on the ITE system, and almost half of ITE courses are now working closely with schools on course design and delivery. Clearly, there is some variation in the depth of the partnerships between schools and universities. The partnership between LUCAS school board, Snijderschool (a primary school in the city of Rijswijk), and the Hogeschool Leiden (a University of Applied Sciences in the city of Leiden) is a strong example of the deepest type of partnership. The key characteristics of the partnership are:

- LUCAS employs a teacher educator to oversee the partnership, and provides strategic leadership.

- The school and Hogeschool exchange staff who work in each other's institutions.

- The staff from the school and Hogeschool work closely together to develop and refine the ITE curriculum and delivery.

- The school board and the Hogeschool have jointly constructed a selection programme for students and are jointly involved in selection (the programme has a dispensation to select recruits).

- The Hogeschool employs a link person to provide training for teachers interested in becoming mentors, and to brief mentors on what is happening in the Hogeschool element of the programme to ensure good co-ordination between the theory and practice elements.

- The school grades the student on their teaching practice, and the student must achieve a pass mark to be awarded their teaching certificate as part of their bachelor's degree.

- Students, mentors and school leaders are asked every two years for feedback on the programme.

Source: OECD (2018[28]), "TALIS Initial Teacher Preparation study", www.oecd.org/education/school/talis-initial-teacher-preparation-study.htm.

Private companies

In OECD countries such as Austria, the Czech Republic, Israel, Japan, Luxembourg and Spain private companies play a prominent role in providing professional learning activities (OECD, 2014[29]). The evidence from this assessment suggests that a considerable proportion of schools in Wales are also seeking the services of private companies to support them in their development. The eight school visits the OECD team conducted revealed several examples of schools purchasing services from private providers including specific staff training approaches, information and communications technology (ICT) tools to facilitate professional learning and knowledge sharing among staff, and management information systems to monitor school performance data or specific surveys to monitor (aspects of) student well-being.

Although still relatively small players at present, private companies are part of the system infrastructure in Wales. They could be strategically deployed by the Welsh Government, regional consortia and others to advance the ongoing reforms in Wales in the years to come, including the development of SLOs.

Ensuring adequate funding

The inputs needed to implement education policies consist mainly of the funding, technology and knowledge available to the actors, as well as their capacity to use them. The amount, quality and distribution of resources allocated to implementation determine to a great extent whether and how a policy is realised (OECD, 2010[30]; Viennet and Pont, 2017[3]; Schleicher, 2018[16]). Research evidence shows that one of the key factors for schools to develop as learning organisations is the extent to which financial and other resources are perceived as sufficient for learning to occur (Silins, Zarins and Mulford, 2002[31]).

School staff and various other stakeholders the OECD team interviewed expressed their concerns about the recent budget cuts coming just as Wales is in the midst of a curriculum reform which will undoubtedly require additional effort and further professional learning and collaborative working for many. Also, only 40% of schools have been invited to participate in the SLO survey as part of this study. Wider roll-out of an online self-assessment version of the SLO survey scheduled during the 2018 autumn term and other efforts to promote Wales' SLO model will likely significantly increase national engagement. It is obvious that some of the OECD findings and recommendations have resource implications. Future resource requirements will have to be carefully estimated to inform for the development of the proposed SLO implementation plan.

The Welsh Government recognises the challenges to schools and among other things has increased the Pupil Development Grant and allocated an additional GBP 100 million to support the realisation of the new curriculum. Despite these and other investments many schools in parts of Wales seem to be facing budget pressures.

Research evidence shows that while the United Kingdom (UK) has high levels of general public administration efficiency, its health care and education efficiency is weak (Dutu and Sicari, 2016[32]). As covered in Chapter 4, the lack of a level playing field remains a clear challenge for schools in Wales, with the differences in funding allocations between schools across Wales' 22 local authorities. The evidence from this assessment suggests schools in Wales do not have equal access to time and resources to support their staff's professional learning which causes obvious barriers to their ability to establish a learning culture and is likely to affect their ability to put the new curriculum into practice.

The OECD team believe that – especially in light of the fiscal reality the education sector is facing, with possible further budget cuts to come – the Welsh Government should consider reviewing its school funding model as discussed in Chapter 4. The proposed in-depth analysis of school funding in Wales should be used to respond to concerns about unequal treatment of schools in similar circumstances as a result of different local funding models – see Recommendation 1.1.1.

Having said that, it is important to note that many steps to ensure staff have the time and resources to engage in collaborative working and professional learning are within the control of schools. As mentioned earlier (in Chapter 3) several of the examples from Wales presented in this report show that pressures on funding do not need to lead to a reduction in ambition, but rather the opposite. Such good practices could serve to inspire and inform other schools and as such should be systematically collected and shared widely across the system.

Inclusive stakeholder engagement

Whether and how key stakeholders are recognised and included in the design and implementation process is crucial to the success of any policy (Viennet and Pont, 2017[3]; Schleicher, 2018[16]). It is widely acknowledged that stakeholders, whether individual actors or collective entities, formal (e.g. labour unions and implementing agencies) or informal (e.g. parents and political coalitions), should display some agency, which contributes to shaping the policy design and subsequent realisation process (Nakamura and Smallwood, 1980[33]; Spillane, Reiser and Reimer, 2002[34]; Schleicher, 2018[16]).

Co-construction of policies

The interests and capacity of actors determine how they engage or react to a policy. The probability that a policy will be effectively implemented increases significantly when regional or local-level actors, education providers, teachers, principals and parents are on board with it as opposed to protesting against it (Malen, 2006[35]; Viennet and Pont, 2017[3]; Tummers, 2012[36]). Policy makers thus look for ways to get these key actors to agree with the policy and to help implement it. One of the most effective ways to do this is involving them from the start in the design and implementation of the policy (Viennet and Pont, 2017[3]).

As an earlier OECD assessment (2017[13]) concluded, the drive for policy coherence and process of co-construction of policies have become characteristic of the Welsh Government's reform approach. In recent years, many of its policies have been developed together with key stakeholders. This has been done through various means, including the creation of multi-stakeholder working groups for different topics, and the use of stakeholder consultation events to engage schools, local authorities, regional consortia, and other stakeholders in the shaping of policies – from the early stages through to drawing on their active support when putting them into practice.

The evidence collected during the course of this assessment, which included many interviews and discussions with stakeholders at all levels of the education system, suggests that stakeholders welcome this relatively new process of co-construction of policies in support of the curriculum reform effort. For example, several of the school leaders and teachers the OECD team spoke to noted they much appreciated "being asked" to share their views on policies, rather than being informed of what to do – as had often been the case in the past.

The teachers' unions also seem supportive of this new approach and the curriculum reform more generally (of which the SLO policy is a part) although they have raised concerns about the pressures on the school budgets and called on the UK Government to raise the salaries of teachers and school leaders in Wales and England (WalesOnline, 2018[37]); although discussions are ongoing to devolve this responsibility to Wales, the UK Government is currently still responsible for the setting of teachers' and school leaders' salaries. However, these concerns and demands have been raised as issues needing to be resolved to support the ongoing reforms, rather than opposing them. The concerns about the school budget have also been raised by the Association of School and College Leaders (ASCL) Wales, which has also in general been supportive of the curriculum reform and related policy thrusts. ASCL representatives and members are actively contributing to various working groups and participating in consultation events, for example.

Furthermore, Estyn (the inspectorate of education and training in Wales) has also been actively supporting the curriculum reform effort. Its staff are also participating in consultation events and taking part in various working groups, in particular the SLO Pilot/Implementation Group and the development of a national school self-evaluation and development planning toolkit.

As discussed above, Wales' SLO model was developed as part of a process of co-construction. This has played an important role in developing ownership of the model and building support among various stakeholders for putting it into practice. For instance, as discussed above, the SLO Pilot Group's main role when it was founded was initially to make the Welsh Government's SLO policy more concrete by defining the SLO model which was launched in November 2017. Since then this stakeholders' group has been renamed the SLO Implementation Group as the policy moves into the implementation phase. Its membership at the time of finalising this report consisted of representatives of the Welsh Government, the regional consortia, Estyn and the National Academy for Educational Leadership, and it is supported by OECD.

This move into the implementation phase also means the role and responsibilities of the group need to be reviewed. Several stakeholders the OECD team interviewed agreed this multi-stakeholder group should take the lead in developing an SLO implementation plan (see below), monitoring progress and ensuring collective learning among the various stakeholders involved about the most effective ways to support schools in their innovation journeys.

In addition, the group should take on a more explicit role of supporting the Welsh Government's efforts towards greater policy coherence, most immediately in the areas of professional learning and school self-evaluation and development planning. Additional stakeholders may also be engaged in the process. For example, the Education Workforce Council could be invited to join this working group given its mandate as the national regulator and promoter of professionalism and high standards within the education workforce.

In recognition of the fact that the implementation group is well established and the integration of Wales' SLO model in other policies and programmes has gained the necessary momentum, the OECD should scale back its contributions to the implementation group and its work on SLOs in Wales more generally.

A conducive institutional, policy and societal context

An effective policy implementation process recognises the influence of the existing policy environment, the educational governance and institutional settings, and the external context. Acknowledging the institutional, policy and societal context in which the policy is to be put into practice makes success more likely (Viennet and Pont, 2017[3]).

PISA 2009: Recognition of the need for change

Wales' disappointing 2009 PISA results served as a catalyst for a public dialogue on the future of its education. This "PISA shock" had a positive influence in that it resulted in a broad conviction within Welsh society that things needed to change. In 2011 Wales embarked on a large-scale school improvement reform that sought to improve the quality and equity of the Welsh school system (OECD, 2014[12]). This reform effort has evolved and become increasingly comprehensive and guided by a vision of the Welsh learner (OECD, 2017[13]). The curriculum reform, starting with a public consultation process, has further clarified this vision which, as discussed above, is broadly shared by the education profession, key stakeholders and other sections of Welsh society.

PISA 2018 results

One issue raised by several people the OECD team interviewed was their concern that if PISA 2018 results did not show sufficient improvements in student performance, some may use this as evidence against the curriculum reform – of which the SLO policy forms a key part. However, the curriculum reform was only started in 2015, and although the Digital Competence Framework (i.e. the first part of the new curriculum) became available in September 2016, the whole curriculum will only be made available in April 2019 – after the PISA 2018 tests will be conducted. It will therefore be too soon to make any judgements on the curriculum based on PISA 2018 results.

Furthermore, a meta-analysis of effect studies of comprehensive school reforms showed the existence of an "implementation dip" (Borman et al., 2002[38]; Fullan, 2011[39]; Fullan and Miles, 1992[40]). It may take a few years before changes are consolidated and then results keep improving for five to eight years after the initial implementation (Borman et al., 2002[38]; Fullan and Miles, 1992[40]). The results of PISA 2021 and following cycles may therefore be more useful for monitoring progress of the curriculum reform.

In addition, attention should be paid to expanding the public discussion of student performance to align it with the concepts included in the new curriculum. International comparisons of literacy, numeracy and science could be complemented with more in-depth analysis of the data in areas such as the factors influencing student performance, collaborative problem-solving skills and student well-being. These are at the heart of Wales' ambitions for the new curriculum but are often overlooked in public dialogue on PISA results in Wales. A more explicit recognition of the wider PISA results in the system-level monitoring by the Welsh Government and Estyn may support a broader discussion about the learning and well-being of students in Wales.

The (possible) influence of Brexit

An obvious change in the societal context in recent years is the decision of the UK to withdraw from the European Union, often referred to as "Brexit". Although it is impossible to foresee the full impact of these changes for the education sector in Wales, some have warned of possible changes in demand for public services, and in education and housing in particular (Bevan Foundation, 2017[41]; Husbands, 2016[42]; Kierzenkowski et al., 2016[43]). Much will depend on the outcome of ongoing discussions between the UK Government and the European Union.

As mentioned earlier, there are concerns that in the short-to-medium term the education budget is likely to continue to be under pressure (Bevan Foundation, 2017[41]; Kierzenkowski et al., 2016[43]). Whether the funding provided will be enough to support all schools in Wales to develop as learning organisations is impossible to tell at this stage. It is essential that the Welsh Government, local authorities and others to carefully monitor the impact of this fiscal reality on schools throughout Wales.

The findings of this assessment are encouraging however; as discussed above, the OECD team learned of several examples of schools that have not lowered their ambitions due to budget pressures but rather have found other, sometimes creative ways of using the skills and resources available within their school and elsewhere to promote professional learning and improvements in teaching and learning.

Changes in the governance structure

Possible restructuring of local government

The institutional structure of the decision-making and implementation levels influence the way education policies may be put into practice (Fullan and Quinn, 2015[5]). Changes in the institutional context change the rules of the game, leaving the implementers to adapt their practices. The OECD team learned of an ongoing discussion about the possible restructuring of the governance structure, i.e. a possible reduction in the number of local authorities, the bodies responsible for the delivery of school education in Wales.

In 2014 the Commission on Public Service Governance and Delivery had concluded that Welsh public services needed comprehensive reform, including a reduction in the number of local authorities to ensure the provision of integrated and high-quality health and social services across Wales (Commission on Public Service Governance and Delivery, 2014[44]). The OECD team understand this potential restructuring has again become an issue under discussion in Wales, especially considering the challenging fiscal situation.

If the decision is indeed made to reduce the number of local authorities and restructure public services accordingly., the Welsh Government may want to consider delaying action for a few years to help ensure the efforts of all those involved remain focused on working together on establishing a learning culture and bringing the new curriculum to life in schools across Wales.

The need to enhance the support for students with additional learning needs

As covered in Chapter 4, equity, inclusion and well-being are central to the Welsh Government's policy agenda (Welsh Government, 2017[1]) and are as such also explicitly recognised in the first dimension of the SLO model for Wales (Welsh Government, 2017[2]).

Recognising that the system for supporting children and young people with special education needs was no longer fit for purpose, Wales recently decided to introduce new legislation to create a unified system for supporting all learners with "additional learning needs" (Welsh Government, 2016[45]). As noted in the 2017 OECD assessment report, this would seem an important step towards realising Wales' ambitions for equity in educational opportunities and its well-being agenda (OECD, 2017[13]). The OECD assessment also noted that Wales' current governance model offers challenges to the provision of services for students with additional learning needs. Interviews with various stakeholders corroborated these earlier findings and suggested that several of the 22 local authorities, especially the smaller ones, lacked the capacity, both human and financial, to respond to the growing need for support for this group of students.

An additional challenge is what one stakeholder called the "awkward" separation of responsibilities. Local authorities manage the services for students with special education needs (i.e. health and social services), while the regional consortia are responsible for school improvement services.

The new system for additional learning needs aims to respond to this challenge. It will transform the separate systems for special educational needs in schools and learning difficulties and/or disabilities in further education, to create a unified system for supporting students from 0 to 25 with additional learning needs (ALN) (Welsh Government, 2018[46]). The transformed system aims to:

* ensure that all students with ALN are supported to overcome barriers to learning and can achieve their full potential

* improve the planning and delivery of support for students from 0 to 25 with ALN, placing students' needs, views, wishes and feelings at the heart of the process

* focus on the importance of identifying needs early and putting in place timely and effective interventions which are monitored and adapted to ensure they deliver the desired outcomes.

The Additional Learning Needs and Education Tribunal (Wales) Act is expected to come into force from September 2020 and the implementation period will last until 2023. The Welsh Government recognises that the successful transformation to the new system depends on helping services to prepare for the changes ahead and to develop closer multi-agency and cross-sector working practices. It therefore established an ALN Transformation Programme for the skills development of the education workforce, to deliver effective support to students with ALN in the classroom, as well as easier access to specialist support, information and advice. This includes the establishment of a small team of "ALN transformation leads" who will support local authorities, schools, early years settings, further education institutions and other delivery partners to prepare for and manage transition to the new ALN system. Four of the five ALN transformation leads are operating at the regional level and are responsible for supporting local authorities, schools, early years settings and local health boards prepare for and implement the new system. The fifth is responsible for providing the same support to the further education sector (Welsh Government, 2018[47]).

The various stakeholders the OECD team spoke to were all in favour of the new system. Several of them however questioned whether the current local government structure would enable it to be realised across all parts of Wales, with particular reference to some of the smaller local authorities that are believed to lack in capacity. The representatives of the regional consortia the OECD team interviewed recognised they also had to do their part to make this reform into a success.

The Welsh Government should – as it intends to do – carefully monitor the progress made in putting the new ALN system into practice. If progress is lacking and/or there are inconsistencies across parts of Wales, it could consider making regional consortia also responsible for services for students with ALN. Consideration of this option should be done in light of the possible restructuring of public services discussed above.

Moving towards greater policy coherence

The need for continuing efforts towards greater policy coherence

The number and variety of policies can make education a crowded policy field, with the possibility of two policies contradicting or misaligning with each other. This misalignment can arise from a contradiction in the educational practices the policies advocate (Viennet and Pont, 2017[3]; Porter, 1994[48]; Schleicher, 2018[16]). As noted in an earlier OECD assessment (2017[13]) Wales has made considerable progress in recent years in ensuring greater policy coherence. However, the assessment also concluded that there was still scope for further improvement and recommended clarifying the connections between the various reform initiatives.

The Welsh Government has responded positively to this recommendation and used the development of the strategic education action plan, *Education in Wales: Our National Mission* (Welsh Government, 2017[1]) as an opportunity to bring about greater policy coherence. As it progresses from plans to action, the government's reform approach, centred on a process of co-construction, continues to move towards greater policy coherence. The various working groups the government has established for the development and realisation of policies and the established Change Board are important ways to maintain this momentum.

The OECD team have identified several examples where there is scope for greater policy coherence, however. One example is the ongoing development of the assessment, evaluation and accountability framework which, as some stakeholders have pointed out to the OECD team, seems insufficiently connected to the ongoing work on the development of the curriculum and assessment arrangements by the Pioneer Schools (see Chapter 4). There is also a need for better co-ordination of the ongoing work on the development of system-level key performance indicators with the development of the school self-evaluation and development planning toolkit. International evidence shows that failing to co-ordinate and align these strands of work may result in a lack of coherence between the curriculum and the assessment, evaluation and accountability arrangements (OECD, 2013[49]) which in turn puts the whole curriculum reform effort at risk.

Wales' SLO model has been developed to support the curriculum reform but initially was not fully integrated into the current reform efforts. It was not directly linked to related policy areas such as professional learning and school self-evaluations and development planning. However, the Welsh Government and other stakeholders have recognised the need for greater coherence with other policies. The OECD team have been witness to – and asked to contribute to – several attempts to bring about greater policy coherence. One example of this is the recently started development of a national school self-evaluation and development planning toolkit, as mentioned in Chapter 4. This is of particular relevance to realising the SLO model in schools throughout Wales, as the model is likely to be integrated into it. This toolkit is also likely to ensure greater coherence between school self-evaluation and external evaluations. As Chapter 4 covered, another example is the decision to integrate the SLO model into all future leadership development programmes. The OECD team agree this is an important step towards ensuring that present and future leaders develop into "change agents" and work to create the conditions for a learning culture to thrive in schools across Wales.

These efforts towards greater policy coherence and the integration of Wales' SLO model into the larger curriculum reform effort should be continued. One area for further policy coherence – or, more accurately, communication on policy coherence – is the need raised above to better explain to stakeholders how Wales' SLO model is aligned with and supports the realisation of the new curriculum, the teaching and leadership standards, the national approach to professional learning, and Wales' ambitions for a self-improving school system.

Enhancing coherence in policy and practice across the four regional consortia

The regional consortia as discussed play a crucial role in the school improvement system infrastructure of Wales. The earlier OECD assessment made note of the recent progress made in co-ordination and collaboration between the regional consortia (OECD, 2017[13]). As discussed above, this positive trend in collective thinking and working and developing trusting relationships has continued. These collaborative efforts should continue and, where possible, be deepened as they bring many benefits, including more consistency in the quality of school improvement services. Enhanced insight into duplications and best practice may lead to consolidation and jointly offered school improvement services.

These services include helping schools develop into learning organisations. It is essential that schools throughout Wales are equally supported in this. However, although the four consortia have all contributed to the development of Wales' SLO model through the SLO Pilot Group, the OECD team as mentioned found considerable differences in how they are engaging with schools in their region to disseminate this model and support them in putting it in practice.

Therefore, the work of the SLO Implementation Group (previously the SLO Pilot Group) would need to continue to ensure co-ordination and collaboration among consortia and other stakeholders, and collectively look for the best ways to support schools in developing into learning organisations. The joint formulation of a national SLO implementation plan, which is partially made up of regional action plans, will be an important step forward in this area, while still leaving room for regional variation.

The next step: Developing a coherent implementation plan

As this report was being finalised, work was started on the development of an SLO implementation plan that is intended to form an integrated part of a larger reform effort. Several activities are planned or have already been started as part of the plan. These include:

- the establishment of the SLO Pilot Group (September 2016)

- the inclusion of the objective to develop all schools and other parts of the system into learning organisations in the education strategic action plan *Education in Wales: Our National Mission* (September 2017)

- the co-construction and release of Wales' SLO model (November 2017)

- the integration of the SLO model into leadership development programmes (autumn 2018)

- the development of the school self-evaluation and development planning toolkit in which the model is likely to be integrated (started in May 2018)

- ongoing development of an animation aimed at children and young people that explains Wales' SLO model and its relation to the curriculum reform

- scheduled workshops for the regional consortia's challenge advisors (July 2018)

- ongoing development of an online SLO self-assessment survey that can be freely used by school staff (scheduled to be launched November 2018)

- ongoing efforts by the Welsh Government's Education Directorate and several middle-tier organisations to develop into learning organisations.

The OECD team agree these are all important activities to support schools in their development efforts. However, this assessment has identified several other issues and policy areas that call for further action by the Welsh Government, regional consortia, local authorities, Estyn and other stakeholders at various levels of the system that are aim to inform the development of the implementation plan.

Furthermore, recognising the equity challenges and different starting points of schools across Wales, the plan should pay particular attention to bringing on board and supporting those schools that for various reasons are less likely to participate in networks and other forms of collaborative learning and working, but which need it most.

Research evidence calls for the development of an implementation plan or strategy to cover the objectives to be achieved, task allocation (i.e. who does what), the resources and timing involved, communication and engagement with stakeholders, and monitoring of the policy (Viennet and Pont, 2017[3]). The OECD team however would like to urge caution in defining objectives and the monitoring of progress. It is essential that the development of SLOs is not seen as a high-stakes exercise by schools: one that primarily serves the purpose of accountability, rather than serving the purpose of informing professional learning and their developmental journeys.

For example, the Welsh Government could make selective use of research to inform itself and other stakeholders on the progress schools are making in putting the learning organisation dimensions into practice, ideally through a mixed-methods design as this allows for the triangulation and deepening of findings. Data from the planned online SLO self-assessment survey could possibly be used in a limited way for this purpose, as long as individual schools are not identified, as that would raise the stakes. Case study research could provide an insight in the change and innovation journeys schools have undergone, thereby potentially serving as an example to others.

However, these are suggestions; the key issue is to be aware of unintended consequences that could stand at odds with the ambition of developing schools into learning organisations.

Recommendations

Implementation issue 1: Policy design: Enhance the policy justification, its logic and its feasibility

To enhance a policy's implementation potential – in this case the policy to develop all schools in Wales as learning organisations – it is important for it to be well justified, that is, to be built on evidence and respond clearly to a need; to complement other policies; and to be feasible (Viennet and Pont, 2017[3]). The evidence suggests Wales' SLO policy has been well received and is increasingly well understood by the education profession and other stakeholders in Wales. Progress has also been made in strengthening the system infrastructure that is to support schools in developing as learning organisations.

Three issues call for further attention to ensure all schools are able to develop as learning organisation:

> **Implementation issue 1.1:** Improving the communication of the justification and logic of Wales' SLO policy and how it forms an integrated part of the curriculum reform and relates to other policies.

> **Implementation issue 1.2:** Ensuring the education budget and school funding model support schools developing as learning organisations and putting the curriculum into practice.

> **Implementation issue 1.3:** Continuing to strengthen the system infrastructure for supporting schools in their change and innovation efforts.

Recommendations

Recommendation 1.1.1: Develop an easy-to-understand narrative that explains how Wales' SLO model can guide schools in their development, forms an integrated part of the curriculum reform and relates to other policies like the teaching and leadership standards, and contributes to realising the objective of a self-improving school system. This narrative should be shared widely through various means, including policy documents, blogs and presentations by policy makers.

Recommendation 1.3.1: Continue strengthening the capacity of the regional consortia to support schools developing as learning organisations. The Regional consortia should:

- **Continue their efforts to provide greater support to schools and promote a learning culture,** with less emphasis on challenging schools and greater attention to the secondary sector. Regional consortia should optimise their structures and services to be able to meet the demands for support by schools that are likely to grow because of the curriculum reform. Consortia should pay particular attention to enhancing challenge advisors' skills to support schools in establishing a learning culture and putting the new curriculum into practice.

- **Continue expanding and deepening collaborations and co-ordination between consortia.** The senior management of the consortia have a vital role to play in this, including by encouraging and facilitating their staff to work together on projects and activities, and explore ways to reduce duplications and streamline services.

- **Continue improving the monitoring and evaluating the effectiveness of their services provided to schools.**

Recommendation 1.2.2: Estyn should continue to monitor the progress the consortia are making in enhancing and streamlining of their services to schools. Local authorities should continue to also be monitored by Estyn.

Implementation issue 2: Continuing the process of co-construction for the realisation of SLOs across Wales, while supporting greater policy coherence

Whether and how key stakeholders are recognised and included in the design and implementation process is crucial to the success of any policy (Nakamura and Smallwood, 1980[33]; Spillane, Reiser and Reimer, 2002[34]; Viennet and Pont, 2017[3]; Tummers, 2012[36]). The process of co-construction which characterises the reform approach in Wales has played a pivotal role in ensuring a strong ownership of Wales' SLO model among key stakeholders and their active support for its implementation. Further work is needed however to enable and support all schools in Wales to develop as learning organisations and continue the drive for greater policy coherence.

Recommendations

Recommendation 2.1: Enhance the collaboration and alignment between the various work strands on the development of assessment, evaluation and the curriculum. The ongoing development of the assessment, evaluation and accountability arrangements and the work by the Pioneer Schools on the curriculum and assessment arrangements call for better co-ordination. Similarly, is there a need to better co-ordinate and align the ongoing work on the system-level key performance indicators and the school self-evaluation and development planning toolkit. Failing to co-ordinate and align these work strands may lead to a lack of coherence and put the whole curriculum reform at risk.

Recommendation 2.2: The SLO Implementation Group should continue to support the realisation of Wales' SLO policy, while striving for greater policy coherence. The group should lead the development of an SLO implementation plan (see below), monitor progress in realising Wales' SLO policy and ensure further action is taken when necessary. The group should continue to support greater policy coherence, including through collective working and learning about how best to support schools in their innovation journeys. It should furthermore co-ordinate with and collaborate with other working groups, most immediately in the areas of professional learning and school self-evaluation and development planning, and agencies such as the Education Workforce Council.

Implementation issue 3: Continue shaping, monitoring and responding to the changing institutional, policy and societal context

The successful implementation, or realisation, of a policy is more likely when it takes into account the institutional, policy and societal context in which the policy is to be put into practice (Viennet and Pont, 2017[3]). In Wales, the institutional, policy and societal context has been conducive to large-scale curriculum reform and this includes Wales' SLO policy.

There however are two contextual issues to take into particular consideration to ensure that the SLO policy is sustainable:

> **Implementation issue 3.1**: The need to broaden the public dialogue generated by Wales' PISA results.

> **Implementation issue 3.2**: The need to optimise governance arrangements to enable all schools in Wales to develop as learning organisations.

Recommendations

Recommendation 3.1: Expand the public dialogue generated by PISA results to align it to the ambitions of the new curriculum. Skills such as collaborative problem solving, and student motivation for learning and their well-being are central to the four purposes of the new curriculum but are often overlooked in public discussions about PISA in Wales. More explicit recognition of such skills in the system-level monitoring of PISA results by the Welsh Government and Estyn could help support a constructive and broader discussion about how PISA can inform the learning and well-being of students in Wales.

Recommendation 3.2: Continue monitoring the effectiveness of recent and possible further changes to governance structures to ensure all schools in Wales are able to developing as learning organisations and realise the ambitions of the new curriculum for all students.

Implementation issue 4: The need for a coherent implementation plan

While this report was being finalised, work had started on the development of an SLO implementation plan intended to form an integrated part of the larger reform effort. Several activities have been taken already, are planned or ongoing that should be part of this plan. The OECD team agree these are all important activities to support schools in their development efforts. This assessment however has identified several other issues and policy areas that call for further action by the Welsh Government, regional consortia, local authorities, Estyn and other stakeholders at various levels of the system and as such should inform the development of the implementation plan.

Recommendation

Recommendation 4.1: Develop and put in practice a national SLO implementation plan to empower schools across Wales in developing as learning organisations. The SLO Implementation Group should lead the development of an SLO implementation plan, monitor progress in realising Wales' SLO policy, and ensure further action is taken when necessary.

The findings and recommendations of this report are aimed to inform the development of the implementation plan, not as a separate action plan but rather as an integrated part of the larger curriculum reform effort. The national action plan – to be partially made up of four regional action plans – should ensure *all* schools have the opportunity to develop as learning organisations and ultimately put the new curriculum into practice. Particular attention should be paid to bringing on board and supporting those schools that for various reasons are less likely to seek support, participate in school-to-school collaboration and other forms of collaborative learning and working, while needing it most. Furthermore, attention should be paid to:

- **The setting of objectives and the monitoring of progress should not become a high-stakes exercise for schools.** One option could be to regularly mine the anonymised data that will be collected through the online SLO survey. Qualitative research could complement the analysis, aimed at exploring progress, including identifying good practices that should be widely shared, challenges and areas for further improvement.

- **Task allocation.** The regional consortia play a pivotal role in supporting schools in their change and innovation journeys. However as highlighted through this report, higher education institutions and other parties could do their part and complement the system infrastructure.

- **The timing and sequencing of actions will require prioritisation.** Phasing in actions allows efforts to be focused, bearing in mind schools' capacity to develop as learning organisations and bring the new curriculum to life. One action that requires immediate attention is the need to clarify the transition period to the new approaches to school self-evaluations and Estyn evaluations.

- **Communication and engagement strategy with education stakeholders.** An important first step will be, as recommended above, to develop and widely share an easily understood narrative that explains how Wales' SLO model can guide schools in their development, forms an integrated part of the curriculum reform and relates to other policies. The systematic collection and sharing of good practice is another area to consider.

References

Ainscow, M. et al. (2016), "Using collaborative inquiry to foster equity within school systems: Opportunities and barriers", *School Effectiveness and School Improvement*, Vol. 27/1, pp. 7-23. [25]

Bell, L. and H. Stevenson (2015), "Towards an analysis of the policies that shape public education: setting the context for school leadership", *Management in Education*, Vol. 29/4, pp. 146-150. [4]

Bevan Foundation (2017), *After Brexit: An Agenda for Public Services in Wales*, Bevan Foundation, Merthyr Tydfil, http://www.walespublicservices2025.org.uk/files/2017/12/After-Brexit.pdf. [41]

Borman, G. et al. (2002), "Comprehensive school reform and student achievement: A meta-analysis", *Report*, No. 59, CRESPAR (Center for Research on the Education of Students Placed At Risk), Baltimore, http://www.jhucsos.com/wp-content/uploads/2016/04/Report59.pdf. [38]

Commission on Public Service Governance and Delivery (2014), *Commission on Public Governance and Delivery – Full Report*, Commission on Public Governance and Delivery, https://gov.wales/docs/dpsp/publications/psgd/140120-psgd-full-report-env2.pdf. [44]

Donaldson, G. (2015), *Successful Futures: Independent Review of Curriculum and Assessment Arrangements in Wales*, Welsh Government, Cardiff, http://gov.wales/docs/dcells/publications/150225-successful-futures-en.pdf. [11]

Dutu, R. and P. Sicari (2016), "Public spending efficiency in the OECD: Benchmarking health care, education and general administration", *OECD Economics Department Working Papers*, No. 1278, OECD Publishing, Paris, http://dx.doi.org/10.1787/5jm3st732jnq-en. [32]

Erdem, M., A. İlğan and H. Uçar (2014), "Relationship between learning organization and job satisfaction of primary school teachers", *International Online Journal of Educational Sciences*, Vol. 6/1, pp. 8-20, http://dx.doi.org/10.15345/iojes.2014.01.002. [9]

Estyn (2018), *The Annual Report of Her Majesty's Chief Inspector of Education and Training in Wales 2016-2017*, Estyn, Cardiff, https://www.estyn.gov.wales/document/annual-report-2016-2017. [14]

Estyn (2017), *Report Following the Monitoring of ERW Consortium*, Estyn, Cardiff. [20]

Estyn (2017), *Report Following the Monitoring of GwE Consortium*, Estyn, Cardiff. [21]

Estyn (2017), *Report Following the Monitoring Visit to the Central South Consortium*, Estyn, Cardiff. [22]

Estyn (2017), *Report Following the Monitoring Visit to the EAS Consortium*, Estyn, Cardiff. [23]

Fullan, M. (2011), *Change Leader: Learning to Do What Matters Most*, Jossey-Bass, San Francisco. [39]

Fullan, M. and M. Miles (1992), "Getting reform right: What works and what doesn't", *Phi Delta Kappan*, Vol. 73/10, pp. 745-752. [40]

Fullan, M. and J. Quinn (2015), *Coherence: The Right Drivers in Action for Schools, Districts, and Systems*, Corwin Press. [5]

Harris, M. and F. van Tassell (2005), "The professional development school as a learning organization", *European Journal of Teacher Education*, Vol. 28/2, pp. 179-194. [27]

Husbands, C. (2016), *Yesterdays and Tomorrows: What the Referendum Says about Education*, British Educational Association blog, http://www.bera.ac.uk/blog/yesterdays-and-tomorrows-what-the-referendum-says-about-education. [42]

Kierzenkowski, R. et al. (2016), "The Economic Consequences of Brexit: A Taxing Decision", *OECD Economic Policy Papers*, No. 16, OECD Publishing, Paris, http://dx.doi.org/10.1787/5jm0lsvdkf6k-en. [43]

Malen, B. (2006), "Revisiting policy implementation as a political phenomenon: The case of reconstitution policies", in Honig, M. (ed.), *New Directions in Education Policy Implementation: Confronting Complexity*, State University of New York Press, Albany. [35]

Nakamura, R. and F. Smallwood (1980), *The Politics of Policy Implementation*, St. Martin's Press, New York. [33]

OECD (2018), *TALIS Initial Teacher Preparation Study*, OECD website, http://www.oecd.org/education/school/talis-initial-teacher-preparation-study.htm. [28]

OECD (2017), *The Welsh Education Reform Journey: A Rapid Policy Assessment*, OECD, Paris, http://www.oecd.org/edu/The-Welsh-Education-Reform-Journey-FINAL.pdf. [13]

OECD (2015), *Education Policy Outlook 2015: Making Reforms Happen*, OECD Publishing, Paris, http://dx.doi.org/10.1787/9789264225442-en. [15]

OECD (2014), *Education at a Glance 2014: OECD Indicators*, OECD Publishing, Paris, http://dx.doi.org/10.1787/eag-2014-en. [29]

OECD (2014), *Improving Schools in Wales: An OECD Perspective*, OECD, Paris, http://www.oecd.org/edu/Improving-schools-in-Wales.pdf. [12]

OECD (2013), *Innovative Learning Environments*, Educational Research and Innovation, OECD Publishing, Paris, http://dx.doi.org/10.1787/9789264203488-en. [26]

OECD (2013), *Synergies for Better Learning: An International Perspective on Evaluation and Assessment*, OECD Reviews of Evaluation and Assessment in Education, OECD Publishing, Paris, http://dx.doi.org/10.1787/9789264190658-en. [49]

OECD (2010), "Making reform happen in education", in *Making Reform Happen: Lessons from OECD Countries*, OECD Publishing, Paris, http://dx.doi.org/10.1787/9789264086296-7-en. [30]

Ontario Ministry of Education (2010), *System on the Move: Story of the Ontario Education Strategy*, Ontario Ministry of Education, Toronto, http://www.edu.gov.on.ca/bb4e/Ontario_CaseStudy2010.pdf. [17]

Porter, A. (1994), "National standards and school improvement in the 1990s: Issues and promise", *American Journal of Education*, Vol. 102/4, https://doi.org/10.1086/444081. [48]

Razali, M., N. Amira and N. Shobri (2013), "Learning organization practices and job satisfaction among academicians at public niversity", *International Journal of Social Science and Humanity*, Vol. 3/6, pp. 518-521, http://dx.doi.org/10.7763/IJSSH.2013.V3.295. [10]

Schechter, C. (2008), "Organizational learning mechanisms: The meaning, measure, and implications for school improvement", *Educational Administration Quarterly*, Vol. 44/2, pp. 155-186. [6]

Schechter, C. and M. Qadach (2012), "Toward an organizational model of change in elementary schools: The contribution of organizational learning mechanisms", *Educational Administration Quarterly*, Vol. 48/1, pp. 116-153, http://dx.doi.org/10.1177/0013161X11419653. [8]

Schleicher, A. (2018), *World Class: How to Build a 21st-Century School System*, OECD Publishing, Paris, http://dx.doi.org/10.1787/4789264300002-en. [16]

Silins, H., B. Mulford and S. Zarins (2002), "Organizational learning and school change", *Educational Administration Quarterly*, Vol. 38/5, pp. 613-642. [7]

Silins, H., S. Zarins and W. Mulford (2002), "What characteristics and processes define a school as a learning organisation? Is it a useful concept to apply to schools?", *International Education Journal*, Vol. 3/1, pp. 24-32. [31]

Spillane, J., B. Reiser and T. Reimer (2002), "Policy implementation and cognition: Reframing and refocusing implementation research", *Review of Educational Research*, Vol. 72/3, pp. 387-431, http://dx.doi.org/10.3102/00346543072003387. [34]

Tummers, L. (2012), "Policy Alienation of Public Professionals: The Construct and its Measurement", *Public Administration Review*, Vol. 72/4, pp. 516–525. [36]

Viennet, R. and B. Pont (2017), "Education policy implementation: A literature review and proposed framework", *OECD Education Working Papers*, No. 162, OECD Publishing, Paris, http://dx.doi.org/10.1787/fc467a64-en. [3]

WalesOnline (2018), "Teachers in Wales have demanded a "significant" pay rise", *Wales Online*, https://www.walesonline.co.uk/news/education/teachers-wales-demanded-significant-pay-14168088. [37]

Walker, R. (2006), "Innovation type and diffusion: An empirical analysis of local government", *Public Administration*, Vol. 84/2, pp. 311-335. [24]

Welsh Government (2018), *Additional Learning Needs Transformation Leads*, Welsh Government website, https://gov.wales/topics/educationandskills/schoolshome/additional-learning-special-educational-needs/transformation-programme/implementation-transition-support/aln-transformation-leads/?lang=en. [47]

Welsh Government (2018), *Additional Learning Needs Transformation Programme*, Welsh Government website, https://gov.wales/topics/educationandskills/schoolshome/additional-learning-special-educational-needs/transformation-programme/?lang=en. [46]

Welsh Government (2017), *Education in Wales: Our National Mission. Action Plan 2017-21*, Welsh Government, Cardiff, http://gov.wales/docs/dcells/publications/170926-education-in-wales-en.pdf. [1]

Welsh Government (2017), *Schools in Wales as Learning Organisations*, Welsh Government website, http://gov.wales/topics/educationandskills/schoolshome/curriculuminwales/curriculum-for-wales-curriculum-for-life/schools-in-wales-as-learning-organisations/?lang=en (accessed on 30 November 2017). [2]

Welsh Government (2016), *Consultation: Summary of Response: Draft Additional Learning Needs and Education Tribunal (Wales) Bill,*, Welsh Government, Cardiff, https://beta.gov.wales/sites/default/files/consultations/2018-01/160714-summary-of-responses-en.pdf. [45]

Welsh Government (2016), *National School Categorisation System Guidance Document for Schools, Local Authorities and Regional Consortia*, Welsh Government, Cardiff, http://gov.wales/docs/dcells/publications/150121-guidance-en-v3.pdf. [19]

Welsh Government (2015), *National Model for Regional Working*, Welsh Government, Cardiff, https://gov.wales/docs/dcells/publications/140217-national-model-for-regional-working-en-v2.pdf. [18]

Annex A. Authors

OECD analysts

Marco Kools is an education policy analyst with the OECD Directorate for Education and Skills. He currently manages the Directorate's policy implementation support work on Developing Schools as Learning Organisations. He previously has led and/or contributed to Education Policy Reviews in the Netherlands, Latvia, Sweden and Wales, worked on the Innovative Learning Environments project and led the development of the Education Today 2013 publication. Prior to joining the OECD in 2012, Marco worked with UNICEF in the Solomon Islands, Laos and at the UNICEF Innocenti Research Centre in Italy. Before that he worked for several years in the field of education in the Netherlands, where in 1999 he started his career as a teacher. Marco holds several degrees including an MBA, an MA in History and a BSc in Educational Sciences, and is currently pursuing a PhD in Public Administration.

Pierre Gouëdard is an analyst at the OECD Directorate for Education and Skills. An economist specialised in economics of education, he has researched in areas of teacher careers and positive action in high schools, written on a range of related topics and taught in the field of economics. Formerly a researcher from the Laboratory for Interdisciplinary Evaluation of Public Policies (LIEPP, Sciences Po, Paris), he developed an analytical framework to study aspirations of students when they apply to tertiary education. Pierre holds a PhD from Sciences Po, Paris, a Master's in Analysis of Economic Policy from the Paris School of Economics and a Master's in Economics from the University of Montreal.

Beatriz Pont is a senior education policy analyst at the OECD Directorate for Education and Skills. With extensive experience in education policy reform internationally, she currently leads OECD Education Policy and Implementation Reviews and recently led the comparative series on education reforms, Education Policy Outlook. She has specialised in various areas of education policy and reform, including equity and quality in education, school leadership, adult learning and adult skills and has also worked with individual countries, including Mexico, Norway, Sweden and the United Kingdom (Wales) in their school improvement reform efforts.

Previously, Beatriz was researcher on education and social policies in the Economic and Social Council of the Government of Spain and also worked for Andersen Consulting (Accenture). She has a PhD in Political Science from Complutense University, Madrid, a Masters in International Relations from Columbia University and a Bachelor of Arts from Pitzer College, Claremont, California. She has been research fellow at the Institute of Social Sciences (Tokyo University) and at the Laboratory for Interdisciplinary Evaluation of Public Policies (LIEPP, Sciences Po, Paris). She holds an honorary doctorate from Sheffield Hallam University.

Thiffanie Rodriguez is a junior consultant in the OECD Directorate for Education and Skills. She has been working with the Policy Advice and Implementation team on schools as learning organisations and school self-evaluation. She is an International Public

Management Masters' candidate at the Sciences Po Paris School of International Affairs (July 2019). Thiffanie holds a B.A. in political science and economics from Sciences Po Paris. Her research interests include education in emergency and crisis situations, schools as learning organisations and identity and inequalities.

External experts

Louise Stoll is a part-time Professor of Professional Learning at the London Centre for Leadership in Learning at University College London's Institute of Education and an international consultant. Her research and development activity focuses on how schools, local and national systems create capacity for learning in a changing world, with particular emphasis on professional learning communities and learning networks, creative leadership, leadership development, and practitioners' use of evidence. Among other work, she has carried out projects for England's Department for Education, National College for Teaching and Leadership and the European Commission. Louise is a former President of the International Congress for School Effectiveness and Improvement (ICSEI), Fellow of the Academy of the Social Sciences, and expert to the OECD, contributing to projects on Innovative Learning Environments, Developing Schools as Learning Organisations, Improving School Leadership, and Evaluation and Assessment initiatives.

Bert Georges is an Assistant Professor of Public Management at Erasmus University Rotterdam. He holds a PhD in Business Economics, a Master of Science in strategic management and a bachelor of science in business administration from Ghent University. His research focuses on the strategic management-performance relation in government, behavioural public administration and research methods in public management. Bert is Programme Director of the Master in Public Management at Erasmus University Rotterdam and a senior member of the Netherlands Institute of Government. He co-chairs the European Group for Public Administration's Permanent Study Group on Strategic Management in Government. He was awarded the European Group for Public Administration 2013 Best Paper Award of the PhD Symposium (Edinburgh), the European Academy of Management 2016 Best Paper Award of the Public Management SIG (Paris) and the Academy of Management 2017 Top Reviewer Award of the Public and Non-profit Division (Atlanta).

Annex B. Schools as Learning Organisations Pilot Group members

Names of schools	Other stakeholder organisations
Bishop Hedley High School	Central South Consortium (CSC), Central South Wales
Blaenavon Heritage VC Primary	Education Achievement Service (EAS), South East Wales
Caldicot School	Ein Rhanbarth ar Waith (ERW), South West and Mid Wales
Cardiff High School	Estyn, The Inspectorate for Education and Training in Wales
Christchurch Primary School	Gwasanaeth Effeithiolrwydd (GwE), North Wales
Connah's Quay High School	National Academy for Educational Leadership
Craig yr Hesg/Cefn (Fernderation)	OECD
Crickhowell High School	Welsh Government Education Directorate
Eirias High School	
George Street Primary	
Glan Usk Primary	
Heronsbridge school	
Oldcastle Primary School	
Pembroke Dock Community School	
Pontarddulais Comprehensive School	
Romilly Primary school/Rhws primary school	
St. Christopher's School	
Tredegar Comprehensive	
Ysgol Dyffryn Ogwen	
Ysgol Gwynedd	
Ysgol Gyfun Cwm Rhymni	
Ysgol Gyfun Gwyr	
Ysgol Gynradd Aberteifi	
Ysgol Llandrillo yn Rhos	

ORGANISATION FOR ECONOMIC CO-OPERATION AND DEVELOPMENT

The OECD is a unique forum where governments work together to address the economic, social and environmental challenges of globalisation. The OECD is also at the forefront of efforts to understand and to help governments respond to new developments and concerns, such as corporate governance, the information economy and the challenges of an ageing population. The Organisation provides a setting where governments can compare policy experiences, seek answers to common problems, identify good practice and work to co-ordinate domestic and international policies.

The OECD member countries are: Australia, Austria, Belgium, Canada, Chile, the Czech Republic, Denmark, Estonia, Finland, France, Germany, Greece, Hungary, Iceland, Ireland, Israel, Italy, Japan, Korea, Latvia, Lithuania, Luxembourg, Mexico, the Netherlands, New Zealand, Norway, Poland, Portugal, the Slovak Republic, Slovenia, Spain, Sweden, Switzerland, Turkey, the United Kingdom and the United States. The European Union takes part in the work of the OECD.

OECD Publishing disseminates widely the results of the Organisation's statistics gathering and research on economic, social and environmental issues, as well as the conventions, guidelines and standards agreed by its members.

OECD PUBLISHING, 2, rue André-Pascal, 75775 PARIS CEDEX 16
(91 2018 16 1 P) ISBN 978-92-64-30718-6 – 2018